INDIANS AND COLONISTS AT

THE CROSSROADS OF EMPIRE

Indians and Colonists at the Crossroads of Empire

The Albany Congress of 1754

TIMOTHY J. SHANNON

CORNELL UNIVERSITY PRESS

ITHACA AND LONDON

NEW YORK STATE HISTORICAL ASSOCIATION

COOPERSTOWN, NEW YORK

First published 2000 by Cornell University Press
First printing, Cornell Paperbacks, 2002

Printed in the United States of America

Library of Congress Cataloging-in-Publication Data

Shannon, Timothy J. (Timothy John), 1964–
Indians and colonists at the crossroads of empire : the Albany Congress of 1754/
Timothy J. Shannon.
    p.   cm.
Includes bibliographical references and index.
ISBN 0-8014-3657-5 (cloth : alk. paper)
ISBN 0-8014-8818-4 (pbk. : alk. paper)
1. Albany Congress (1754 : Albany, N.Y.) 2. United States—Politics and government—
To 1775. 3. Iroquois Indians—Politics and government. 4. Indians of North America—
Government relations—To 1789. 5. Great Britain—Colonies—North America—
History—18th century. I. Title.
E195.S43   1999
323.1'19755'009033—dc21   99-16951

Cornell University Press strives to use environmentally responsible suppliers and materials to the fullest extent possible in the publishing of its books. Such materials include vegetable-based, low-VOC inks and acid-free papers that are recycled, totally chlorine-free, or partly composed of nonwood fibers. For further information, visit our website at www.cornellpress.cornell.edu.

Cloth printing 10 9 8 7 6 5 4 3 2 1

Paperback printing 10 9 8 7 6 5 4 3 2 1

for Colleen

Contents

Maps and Illustrations

Acknowledgments

T his book has been the proverbial guest who would not leave, and so it is only fitting that I thank those institutions and people who have helped me finally usher it out the door. The Huntington Library provided a William M. Keck Fellowship to fund research in its collections, and a scholarship from the English-Speaking Union, Chicago Branch, made possible research in British archives. A Dissertation Year Grant from Northwestern University's Office of Research, a Faculty Research Grant from the State University of New York, College at Cortland, and grants from the Society of Colonial Wars in the State of Illinois and the National Society of the Daughters of the American Revolution, Fort Dearborn Chapter, made possible further research and writing. I received expert assistance from the archivists and librarians at the Huntington Library, the William L. Clements Library, the New York State Library and Archives, the Albany Institute of History and Art, the Historical Society of Pennsylvania, the Library Company of Philadelphia, the New York Public Library, the New-York Historical Society, the Museum of the City of New York, the British Library, the Public Records Office, the Newberry Library, and the libraries of Northwestern University, the State University of New York, College at Cortland, and Gettysburg College. I owe a special debt to Stefan Bielinski, director of the Colonial Albany Social History Project at the New York State Museum, who generously shared resources and ideas and spent an afternoon walking me through the city to give me a sense of its eighteenth-century dimensions. A Research and Professional Development Grant from Gettysburg College assisted in preparing the manuscript for publication.

A portion of Chapter 1 first appeared in "Dressing for Success on the Mohawk Frontier: Hendrick, William Johnson, and the Indian Fashion," *William and Mary Quarterly* 3d ser., 53 (1996): 13–42. I presented a portion of Chapter 4 at the New York State History Conference in 1994, where I received helpful commentary from George Hamell and Richard Haan.

Tim Breen provided expert guidance for this project from the start, not in the least by insisting that I always refer to it as "the book" and not "the dissertation." Bob Wiebe and Jim Oakes also read the manuscript in its early stages and offered useful suggestions for revision. I thank Dan Richter and Ian Steele, whose thoughtful commentary and criticism helped me tighten my argument. I am also grateful to Thomas Burke, Dick Fitzgerald, Milton Klein, and Jon Parmenter for assistance in research and writing along the way. Late in the process of completing this book, I discovered the annual Iroquois Research Conference and have since learned much from its participants, particularly Jim Axtell, Joe Brandão, Corinna Dalley-Starna, Nancy Hagedorn, Chris Patrick, Dean Snow, and Bill Starna. Many people have helped make this a better book, but I take sole responsibility for any remaining errors.

Armen Sarrafian lent his talents in drawing the maps, and Cinda Gibbon did likewise for the index. Carolyn Snively and Kim Breighner donated their expertise in photography and computer graphics in preparing the illustrations. I deeply appreciate the faith that Peter Agree of Cornell University Press and Wendell Tripp of the New York State Historical Association have expressed in this project and their assistance in bringing it to completion in this form.

My two families, the Shannons of Connecticut and McCauleys of Illinois, have known intuitively when to inquire about my progress and when to remain silent. Completing the manuscript was joyfully delayed by the arrival first of Caroline and then Daniel, both of whom remind me every day that living in the present, as well as the past, has its own rewards. The book's dedication reflects my greatest debt, to Colleen, who remains my wellspring of inspiration and encouragement.

TIMOTHY J. SHANNON

Gettysburg, Pennsylvania

Abbreviations

ACIA Minutes — Minutes of the Albany Commissioners of Indian Affairs, 3 vols., Public Archives of Canada (microfilm).

BF Papers — *The Papers of Benjamin Franklin*, ed. Leonard W. Labaree, W. B. Willcox, Claude Lopez, and Barbara B. Oberg, 34 vols. (New Haven, 1959–).

BM, Add. Mss. — British Museum, Additional Manuscripts, London.

Dinwiddie Papers — R. A. Brock, ed., "The Official Records of Robert Dinwiddie," in *Collections of the Virginia Historical Society* 3–4 (1883–84).

Farrand, *Franklin's Memoirs* — Max Farrand, ed., *Benjamin Franklin's Memoirs: Parallel Text Edition* (Berkeley and Los Angeles, 1949).

Loudoun Papers — The Loudoun Papers—Americana, Huntington Library, San Marino, California.

Mass. Archives — Massachusetts Archives, Boston, Massachusetts (microfilm).

NYCD — *Documents Relative to the Colonial History of the State of New-York*, ed. E. B. O'Callaghan and Berthold Fernow, 15 vols. (Albany, 1853–87).

NYCM — New York Council Minutes, 1668–1783, 97 vols., New York State Archives, Albany, New York.

NY Col. Mss.	New York Colonial Manuscripts, 103 volumes, New York State Archives, Albany, New York.
Penn. Archives	*Pennsylvania Archives,* 9 series (Philadelphia, 1852–1935).
Penn. Council Minutes	*Minutes of the Provincial Council of Pennsylvania,* 16 vols. (Harrisburg, 1852–53).
PRO, CO	Public Records Office, Colonial Office Papers, Kew, England.
Susquehannah Co. Papers	*The Susquehannah Company Papers,* ed. Julian P. Boyd and R. J. Taylor, 11 vols. (Ithaca, 1962–71).
WJ Papers	*Papers of Sir William Johnson,* ed. James Sullivan, Alexander C. Flick, Milton W. Hamilton, and Albert B. Corey, 14 vols. (Albany, 1921–62).
WMQ	*William and Mary Quarterly,* 3d sers.
WS Correspondence	Charles Henry Lincoln, ed., *Correspondence of William Shirley, Governor of Massachusetts and Military Commander in America, 1731–1760,* 2 vols. (1912; rpt. New York, 1973).

Editorial Note

All quoted material appears as it did in the original text with the following exceptions. I have silently lowered superscripts and spelled out abbreviations commonly found in eighteenth-century sources, and I have occasionally inserted punctuation to add clarity. I have rendered "ye" as "the"; "&" as "and"; and "&ca." as "etc." All dates are as they appear in the original sources with one exception: I have not corrected dates rendered in the Old Style Julian calendar, in use in the British-Atlantic empire until 1752, but have assumed January 1 as the start of the year. Thus a date rendered "February 14, 1750/51" in the original manuscript appears here as "February 14, 1751."

INDIANS AND COLONISTS AT

THE CROSSROADS OF EMPIRE

Introduction:
Narratives of the Albany Congress

There was a prior Congress, held at Albany in 1754 or 1755. . . . Where is any account of that to be found?

—John Adams, 1813

O ne story:

In 1812 John Adams renewed his friendship with Thomas McKean of Philadelphia, another patriot leader of the Revolutionary Era. Twenty-two years earlier Adams and McKean had parted ways in a dispute over the French Revolution, but now both were retired and approaching their eighties. Mellowed by the passage of time and the thought that he might soon "glide away, where there is no pen and paper," Adams offered to mend fences.[1] McKean responded with enthusiasm, and for the next three years they corresponded regularly.

Both men sensed that they were the last remnants of a passing generation. McKean identified himself as the sole surviving member of the Stamp Act Congress of 1765 and noted that he and Adams were two of only four surviving members of the First Continental Congress. Ever meticulous, Adams corrected that last figure, counting six survivors of the First Continental Congress. Together these two aging patriots decried the current generation's ignorance of their accomplishments. In offering his thoughts on the Stamp Act Congress, McKean lamented that he had to resort to a copy of its proceedings published in London in 1767 because he could not find any "done in the United States." An indignant Adams replied, "Can you account for the apathy, the antipathy of this nation to their own history? Is there not a repugnance to the thought of looking back?"[2]

[1] Adams to McKean, June 2, 1812, in C. F. Adams, ed., *The Works of John Adams,* 10 vols. (Boston, 1856), 10:12–13.
[2] McKean to Adams, June 13, 1812; Adams to McKean, June 21, 1812; McKean to Adams, August 20, 1813; Adams to McKean, August 31, 1813, ibid., 14–15, 15–17, 60–62, 62–63.

Despite this mutual despair, Adams and McKean continued to discuss the origins of the American Revolution and soon focused on the question of colonial union before 1776. McKean asserted that during the Stamp Act Crisis, the "great mass of the people were at that time zealous in the cause of America." Adams expressed skepticism about such a generalization, but McKean's discussion of the Stamp Act Congress jogged his memory about another intercolonial meeting. He asked McKean, "There was a prior Congress, held at Albany in 1754 or 1755. . . . Where is any account of that to be found?"[3]

A month later McKean responded. Despite "considerable inquiry," he had been unable to find "some account of the Congress at Albany in 1754." He did have a "faint recollection" that it had been "appointed by the British Ministry for the ostensible purpose of ascertaining the boundaries of the several Colonies to the Eastward of Delaware; but in reality to propose the least offensive plan for raising a revenue in America." He attributed the inspiration for the Albany Congress to Sir William Keith, a former colonial governor, who in 1739 had suggested "such an Assembly to the ministry" along with a proposal for imposing a stamp duty on the American colonies. McKean thought the British ministry had eventually embraced both parts of Keith's plan, "the 1st [an intercolonial congress] in 1754, the 2d [the Stamp Act] in 1764."[4]

Adams and McKean put together a confusing account of the Albany Congress but one that fit well into their broader interpretation of the coming of the Revolution. McKean smelled conspiracy: the Crown had called this meeting in 1754 on the pretense of settling colonial borders, but its ulterior motive was taxation. The Albany Congress had merely been an intermediary step between Keith's proposals for an American stamp duty in 1739 and the notorious Stamp Act of 1765, proving, to McKean at least, the British government's long-standing design against colonial liberties. McKean did not mention the plan of colonial union drafted at the Albany Congress, nor did he recall the treaty negotiations between the Indians and colonists gathered there.

In other correspondence during his retirement, Adams indicated greater familiarity with the Albany Congress and Plan of Union. Five years before his exchange with McKean, Adams had stumbled upon a letter he wrote in 1755, in which he had predicted that the American colonies would one day become the seat of a great empire and that the only way Great Britain could

---

[3] McKean to Adams, August 20, 1813; Adams to McKean, August 31, 1813, ibid., 60–63.
[4] McKean to Adams, September 28, 1813, ibid., 73–75. McKean erred in recollecting the date of the Stamp Act; it was passed by Parliament in 1765, not 1764. The plan for an American stamp duty referred to by McKean can be found in "Proposals for establishing by Act of Parliament the Duties upon Stampt Paper and Parchment in all the British Colonies in America," in [William Keith], *Two Papers on the Subject of Taxing the British Colonies in America* (1739; rpt. London, 1767), 13–22.

prevent them from doing so was "to disunite us. *Divide et impera.*"[5] Writing to his friend Benjamin Rush in 1807, Adams offered this long-lost letter as proof that the colonists had been prepared to "defend ourselves, and even conquer Canada, better without England than with her, if she would but allow us to unite and exert our strength, courage, and skill." Such a colonial union, he explained, "was indeed commenced in a Congress at Albany," but it aroused a fear in the British ministry "which induced England to take the war into their own hands."[6] Adams concluded that the Albany Congress and Seven Years' War had drawn the line on which the empire would split, between colonists confident in their united strength and a mother country determined to keep them separate.

In his correspondence with McKean and Rush, Adams placed the Albany Congress as an important milepost along the road to the American Revolution. He suspected sinister motives in the British rejection of the Albany Plan but found in colonial union the irrepressible force that would someday culminate in independence. In an oft-quoted remark, Adams observed to McKean, "The revolution was in the minds of the people, and in the union of the colonies, both of which were accomplished before hostilities commenced."[7] Historians have made famous the first condition in that remark, the revolution in the minds of the people. Equally important to Adams was the second condition, "the union of the colonies." His narrative of the coming of the Revolution enshrined the Albany Congress as a harbinger of that union.

Another story:

In September 1763 Sir William Johnson, the British Crown's superintendent of Indian affairs in the northern colonies, convened a meeting with the Six Nations of Iroquois Indians at his home. Johnson had recently built Johnson Hall, a grand Georgian-style mansion, on his estate north of the Mohawk River. Although isolated on the New York frontier, this new home displayed the considerable wealth and influence Johnson had acquired among Indians and colonists alike since his appointment as the Crown's agent in 1755. The king had awarded him a baronetcy and a substantial salary for his service, enabling Johnson to live in the style of a feudal lord on this periphery of the British Empire.[8]

During the Seven Years' War, Johnson had faced the difficult task of convincing Indians to support the British despite early military setbacks

---

[5] Adams to Nathan Webb, October 12, 1755, in Adams, ed., *Works of John Adams*, 1:23–24.
[6] Adams to Benjamin Rush, May 1, 1807, ibid., 9:591–94. Eight years later, Adams made this point again, writing that the conquest of Canada would have been much easier had Britain "permitted that union of the colonies, which we projected, planned, earnestly desired, and humbly petitioned in 1754." See Adams to William Cranch, March 3, 1815, ibid., 10:131–33.
[7] Adams to McKean, November 26, 1815, ibid., 180–82.
[8] See James Thomas Flexner, *Mohawk Baronet: A Biography of Sir William Johnson* (1959; rpt. Syracuse, 1989), 287–311.

and the pro-French sympathies of many western nations. By 1763, however, the British had conquered Canada and occupied French posts along the Great Lakes and the Ohio River. Johnson and the Crown's other officers in North America had gained an upper hand in negotiating with the Indians, who no longer had their potential alliance with the French to play as a trump card. Accordingly, the British commander in chief General Jeffrey Amherst cut off the presents that the British had been supplying to western Indians, and Johnson grew more dictatorial in his diplomacy, telling Indians what he wanted done and threatening reprisals for those who resisted. This change in British policy had caused war to erupt between the Indians and British along the Appalachian frontier.[9]

Of specific concern to Johnson at this September 1763 meeting were Seneca warriors from the westernmost Iroquois nation, who had taken up arms against the British. He promised peace and trade to those Indians willing "to sit Still" while the British subdued these malcontents and severe treatment for those who supported them. Johnson finished by presenting the Indians with "a fine New Belt" of wampum, the traditional object used in such councils to symbolize the alliance known as the Covenant Chain between the Iroquois and the British colonies.[10]

The following day, an Onondaga chief named Teyawarunte delivered a speech on behalf of the Indians in which he gave Johnson "a verry large Covenant Belt."[11] This belt referred to an earlier treaty conference, conducted at Albany in 1754:

> [Upon the belt] was wrought in white Wampum the figures of Six Men towards one End, as representing the Six Nations, [and] towards the other End, the figure of Nine Men to represent the Nine Governments who Assembled at Albany in the Year 1754, the time when Said Belt was delivered to them; between both was a Heart Signifying the Union and friendship then Settled between them.—at the Top, were the letters G R made of White Wampum, and under that the full length of the Belt was a white line which they were told was a long board to Serve as a Pillow, whereon their and our Heads were to rest, and that as the French were a troublesome People, and had now begun to quarrel with the English, they should at a Stamp given to Said board all wake and rise up as one Man, and attack any Nation who disturbed their Rest.

Teyawarunte then "brightened and renewed the Said Covenant" between the Iroquois and British and asked Johnson to deliver the belt to General

[9] See Francis Jennings, *Empire of Fortune: Crown, Colonies, and Tribes in the Seven Years War in America* (New York, 1988), 438–53.
[10] *WJ Papers*, 10:835–38.
[11] According to the minutes for this conference, this speech was delivered on September 8, but it is inserted in the record for September 11. The minutes do not explain why the speech was recorded out of order. See ibid., 845–46.

Amherst, so that he would know "So many Nations were now firm freinds to the English, and determined to continue so, as long as We would use them kind, and let them live in peace." Johnson accepted the belt and told the Indians he was "much pleased at their keeping in Mind so well the Engagements entered into at Said Treaty in 1754." He concluded that day's meeting by delivering to them a present of goods worth £1,007.[12]

This exchange between Johnson and the Iroquois in 1763 opens another perspective on the Albany Congress of 1754. Like Adams's reflections on that meeting, which began with his discovery of a lost letter in 1807, the Indians' recollections were tied to an artifact: a wampum belt of purple and white beads. Whether the belt they presented to Johnson in 1763 actually came from the Albany Congress is open to question. The description of the 1763 belt differs in several important ways from the description of the "Chain Belt" recorded in the Albany Congress minutes nine years earlier. The official minutes from 1754 mention lines, not human figures, used to represent the Indians and colonists, and do not mention a heart or "G R" woven into the belt.[13] Yet the design of the 1763 belt does accurately reflect the circumstances of the Albany Congress: seven colonies sent delegations to treat with the Six Nations there and two others asked to be thought of as present; the "G R" in the 1763 belt in all likelihood referred to King George II, under whose authority the Albany Congress had convened. If the belt presented by the Indians in 1763 was not the "Chain Belt" from the Albany Congress, it was certainly a reasonable facsimile designed to recall that meeting.[14]

[12] Ibid.
[13] The "Chain Belt" given to the Indians at the Albany Congress is described in *NYCD*, 6:862.
[14] In a 1762 conference at Johnson Hall, an Onondaga speaker delivered to Johnson "a Belt of the Covenant Chain which was formerly given Us at *Albany* by One of the Governors." Since the chiefs who had received it were "mostly Dead," the speaker asked Johnson to remind those present "of the particulars of What was Said thereon." Johnson responded that he could not "repeat Each particular to you, but as I was then present, I can Inform you that the purport thereof was a Renewal of the Antient Covenant Chain of Friendship." In this particular episode, the minutes do not describe the belt's design, only that it was "a large Covenant Chain belt." See *WJ Papers*, 3:709, 712. This same belt may have been the one described above, presented a year later by the Indians to Johnson as a record of the Albany Congress of 1754. In a 1774 conference with Johnson's successor, his nephew Guy Johnson, the Indians again presented a "great old *Covenant* Chain" belt, which they explained had been presented to them by William Johnson "in presence of Commissioners from nine Governments." The minutes are vague about its design as well, noting only that it was made of twenty-one rows of wampum. Nevertheless, judging from the Indians' reference to "Commissioners from nine Governments," this 1774 belt could very possibly have been the same one exchanged in 1763. While some uncertainty remains about whether the Albany Congress "Chain Belt" was actually the same one that resurfaced in 1762, 1763, and 1774, these subsequent conferences have two important implications. First, Indians associated the Albany Congress with the start of Johnson's tenure as Indian superintendent, and second, Johnson actively encouraged this association when he interpreted the belt for them in 1762. For Johnson and the Iroquois, the Albany Congress had nothing to do with colonial union and everything to do with his elevation to the Crown's agent in Indian affairs.

The Indians had retained (or invented) their own record of what happened at Albany in 1754, and it did not address issues of colonial taxation or union. Rather, their narrative of the Albany Congress concerned an alliance known as the Covenant Chain, which maintained peace and trade between the British colonies, the Six Iroquois Nations, and other Indians associated with their confederacy. The Indians at Johnson's home used this belt to remind the British of their promises of support and friendship. In particular, if Johnson and Amherst wished to preserve the Covenant Chain, they had to be mindful of the British pledge to "use them [the Iroquois] kind, and let them live in peace." When Johnson grew highhanded and lectured them on the Crown's ability to smite its enemies, the Indians offered this belt as a reminder that the Covenant Chain was built not on Iroquois submission to the British but on the mutual obligations each had undertaken to the other. That friendship had to be periodically "brightened" or renewed by engaging in diplomatic councils and exchanging presents, as Johnson had done at this meeting. To the Indians, the Albany Congress had been one such episode in this continuing process of intercultural mediation; from their side of the council fire, it had nothing to do with hurrying the colonies toward nationhood.

One more story:

In the 1980s, the Albany Congress resurfaced in popular discourse after languishing for many years in the obscurity of history textbooks. As the United States celebrated the bicentennial of the Constitution, a spirit of inclusivity prompted public statements acknowledging the Native American contribution to American federation and democracy. Supporters of such pronouncements invariably cited the Albany Congress as evidence, explaining that it had gathered Iroquois and colonial statesmen to discuss models of federal union. In New York, an advisory panel recommended that the state's public school curriculum introduce students to the Iroquois contributions to American government. In Washington, D.C., the United States Senate passed a resolution acknowledging the Iroquois influence on the Constitution. Even the *New York Times* described the Albany Congress as a "forum to share ideas between the colonists and the Iroquois" at which delegates heard "Benjamin Franklin champion the Iroquois example as he presented his Plan of Union."[15]

The "Iroquois Influence Thesis" has since grown into a cottage industry, resulting in numerous books and articles for scholarly and popular au-

---

[15] See Philip A. Levy, "Exemplars of Taking Liberties: The Iroquois Influence Thesis and the Problem of Evidence," *WMQ* 53 (1996): 589; and "Iroquois Constitution: A Forerunner to Colonists Democratic Principles," *New York Times*, June 28, 1987, 40. This *New York Times* article misquotes Franklin, putting words in his mouth at the Albany Congress that he had written three years earlier.

diences. Its advocates trace a direct line of inspiration from the Iroquois to the federal union of the United States, and they use the Albany Congress as a cornerstone of their argument, noting Franklin's advocacy of colonial union, his occasional remarks on Native American culture, and his presence at the Albany Congress, Second Continental Congress, and Constitutional Convention of 1787. Detractors of the Iroquois Influence Thesis have been equally energetic in questioning the logic and evidence used by its supporters, particularly their manipulation of sources through selective quotations and editing. Critics have also pointed out the great disparity between eighteenth-century Iroquois and Anglo-American models of government and the lack of any documentation suggesting that the Founding Fathers were serious or perceptive students of Iroquois statecraft.[16]

Despite ten years of debunking, the Iroquois Influence Thesis has become a revisionist narrative about the birth of the United States. It accuses Eurocentric historians of turning a blind eye to the Indian imprint on the nation's founding documents and ideals, especially the Iroquois contribution to American federalism. According to the thesis, colonial statesmen such as Benjamin Franklin and James Madison learned about the Iroquois model of government firsthand in treaty conferences like the Albany Congress, where they listened to Indian orators urge the colonies to unite and borrowed from them the principles that informed the Albany Plan of Union, Articles of Confederation, and Constitution. It is a comforting image of the founding: rather than being cast aside as enemies or nonpartici-

[16] The best introduction to the Iroquois Influence Thesis, with comprehensive bibliographic references, is a forum that appeared in the *WMQ* 53 (1996): 587–636. It includes two articles critical of the thesis: Levy, "Exemplars of Taking Liberties," 588–604, and Samuel B. Payne Jr., "The Iroquois League, the Articles of Confederation, and the Constitution," 605–20. The rejoinder is offered by the two most prolific supporters of the thesis: Donald A. Grinde Jr. and Bruce E. Johansen, "Sauce for the Goose: Demand and Definitions for 'Proof' Regarding the Iroquois and Democracy," 621–36. Another important critique of the Iroquois Influence Thesis is Elisabeth Tooker, "The United States Constitution and the Iroquois League," *Ethnohistory* 35 (1988): 305–36. A response to that article, along with a rejoinder by Tooker, is Bruce E. Johansen, "Native American Societies and the Evolution of Democracy in America, 1600–1800," *Ethnohistory* 37 (1990): 279–97. Johansen and Grinde have elaborated together and individually on the Iroquois Influence Thesis in Grinde and Johansen, *Exemplar of Liberty: Native America and the Evolution of Democracy* (Los Angeles, 1991); Johansen, *Forgotten Founders: How the American Indian Helped Shape Democracy* (Boston, 1982); and Grinde, *The Iroquois and the Founding of the American Nation* (San Francisco, 1977). Other arguments in support of the thesis may be found in Jose Barreiro, ed., *Indian Roots of American Democracy* (Ithaca, 1988), and Oren Lyons et al., *Exiled in the Land of the Free: Democracy, the Indian Nations, and the U.S. Constitution* (Santa Fe, 1992). Other critiques of the Iroquois Influence Thesis can be found in Laurence M. Hauptman, *Tribes and Tribulations: Misconceptions about American Indians and Their Histories* (Albuquerque, 1995), 27–38, and William A. Starna and George R. Hamell, "History and the Burden of Proof: The Case of the Iroquois Influence on the U.S. Constitution," *New York History* 77 (1996): 427–52. William N. Fenton dismisses the Iroquois Influence Thesis out of hand in *The Great Law and the Longhouse: A Political History of the Iroquois Confederacy* (Norman, Okla., 1998), 471–76.

pants, Indians take their place alongside the Founding Fathers as tutors sharing lessons in uniquely American ways of government.[17]

Narratives of the Albany Congress have always been tied up, often in misleading ways, with questions of American state-making. Historians from the Revolutionary generation to the present have examined the Albany Congress as a piece to the puzzle of the American Revolution. How they choose to fit that piece into the puzzle depends on their answer to a variety of questions. When did the colonists begin to think of themselves as Americans sharing mutual interests and attachments? Was the union forged during the Revolutionary Era something that grew organically out of the colonial experience, or was it an expedient response to the Anglo-American crisis of 1765–75? When eighteenth-century Americans conceived plans of federal union, from what models did they draw their inspiration?

John Adams took a nationalist approach to those questions, and he presented the Albany Plan as evidence that colonial union was an irrepressible force that overturned British power in North America. Benjamin Franklin, the Albany Congress's most famous participant, had offered a similar interpretation in the late 1780s. In his narrative of the coming of the Revolution, Franklin argued that the enactment of the Albany Plan would have enabled the colonists to defend themselves during the Seven Years' War, making a British army in North America unnecessary. With no American army or war debts to pay after 1763, the British government would never have needed to tax its American subjects, and thus "the different Parts of the Empire might still have remained in Peace and Union." Franklin described the Albany Plan as the empire's great lost hope, "the true Medium" that could have prevented the loss of so much "Blood and Treasure" on both sides. Yet he did not doubt the colonists' ultimate destiny of independence. Had the Albany Plan been adopted, "the subsequent Separation of the Colonies from the Mother Country might not so soon have happened . . . perhaps during another Century." Franklin believed the Albany Plan's greatest triumph had been its failure, for it had fortuitously hastened the creation of the United States.[18]

[17] I have not written this book to disprove the Iroquois Influence Thesis point by point; that job has already been done admirably by the critics cited above. For a brief statement of my specific objections to the thesis as it concerns the Albany Congress, see my Letter to the Editor and Grinde's and Johansen's response in *WMQ* 54 (1997): 467–69, 469–71. In the chapters that follow, I will present additional evidence against the Iroquois Influence Thesis as appropriate. I believe my overall argument about the origins, nature, and outcomes of the Albany Congress proves conclusively that no evidence exists of an Iroquois influence in the drafting of the Albany Plan of Union.

[18] Franklin's comments on the Albany Plan in the late 1780s come from two sources: his memoirs, which he resumed working on in 1788, and a brief commentary he wrote to accompany a magazine piece on the Albany Plan in 1789. See Farrand, *Franklin's Memoirs*, 326–28, and Benjamin Franklin's "Remark" on the Albany Plan, February 9, 1789, *BF Papers*, 5:417.

Subsequent historians followed the lead of Franklin and Adams and traced a path from the Albany Congress of 1754 to the federal union of 1787. George Bancroft, Francis Parkman, and John Fiske turned Franklin into the prophet of American nationhood and the Albany Congress into a dress rehearsal for the Constitutional Convention.[19] The Albany Congress came to play a small but important role in the nineteenth-century mythology of American union. Richard Frothingham's *Rise of the Republic of the United States*, a post–Civil War paean to the Constitution, trumpeted the Albany Plan as the perfection of all previous efforts at colonial federation, a scheme that was finally "original and American . . . comprehensive and grand."[20] Even Frederick Jackson Turner, in his famous frontier thesis, found the Albany Congress a noteworthy example of how the colonial experience had encouraged a spirit of cooperation and self-government among Americans.[21]

The twentieth-century imperial historians corrected the excesses of the nineteenth-century nationalists by questioning the extent of colonial union before 1765. As part of their effort to depict British rule as benign and prosperous for the colonies, they absolved the Crown from blame for the Albany Congress's failure. Charles M. Andrews reminded readers of the Albany Plan's universal rejection by the colonial assemblies, an act that symbolized their lack of any "self-conscious desire for union among themselves."[22] Nevertheless, his fellow imperial historians continued to present the Albany Plan as early evidence of American constitutional genius. Herbert Levi Osgood called it "the first impression of the constitution-making instinct which was to become so active both in Europe and America before the close of the century."[23] Robert C. Newbold, author of the only previous book on the Albany Congress, worked squarely within this tradition and concluded that the Albany Plan was the "greatest contribution by Americans to political confederation up to that time."[24]

Of all the imperial historians, Lawrence Henry Gipson devoted the most study to the Albany Congress, and he arrived at conclusions remarkably

[19] See George Bancroft, *History of the United States of America, from the Discovery of the Continent*, 6 vols. (1885; rpt. Port Washington, 1967), 2:385–88; Francis Parkman, *France and England in North America*, 2 vols. (New York, 1983), 2:962–64; and John Fiske, *A History of the United States for Schools* (Boston, 1894), 184–88.
[20] Richard Frothingham, *The Rise of the Republic of the United States*, 4th ed. (Boston, 1886), 149. For discussions of the mythology of American union, see Paul C. Nagel, *One Nation Indivisible: The Union in American Thought, 1776–1861* (New York, 1964), and Kenneth M. Stampp, "The Concept of a Perpetual Union," *Journal of American History* 65 (1978): 5–33.
[21] Frederick Jackson Turner, *The Frontier in American History* (New York, 1920), 15.
[22] Charles M. Andrews, *The Colonial Background of the American Revolution* (New Haven, 1924), 27. Also see Andrews, *The Colonial Period in American History*, 4 vols. (New Haven, 1938), 4:417–19, and George Louis Beer, *British Colonial Policy, 1754–1765* (New York, 1907), 18–24.
[23] Herbert Levi Osgood, *The American Colonies in the Eighteenth Century*, 4 vols. (New York, 1924–25), 4:317.
[24] Robert C. Newbold, *The Albany Congress and Plan of Union of 1754* (New York, 1955), 87.

similar to Franklin's. Gipson described the Albany Plan of Union as an inspired piece of statecraft that, if enacted, would have helped preserve the first British Empire.[25] In a thesis that lent scholarly credentials to the ruminations of Franklin and Adams, Gipson traced the causes of the American Revolution to British victory in the Seven Years' War, which created problems the Albany Plan would have solved if implemented back in 1754.[26] Once again, the Albany Congress might have saved the empire, but like the retrospective Franklin, Gipson believed that nothing could have prevented the independence of thirteen colonies that "now embodied a mature and powerful English-speaking community with a mind of its own and a future it considered peculiarly its own."[27]

After two centuries of interpretation, what is so startling about our view of the Albany Congress is how little it has changed. Franklin retains his revered status as an architect of American union. Britain's colonial administrators, while treated sympathetically by the imperial historians, remain myopic and decidedly unimperial in their thinking, too dense to grasp the Albany Plan's significance to the empire's future. Most important, colonial union, rebellion, and independence remain tied tightly together, one leading naturally to the other and culminating in the Constitution of 1787. Even the supporters of the Iroquois Influence Thesis, who have worked the hardest in recent years to alter our understanding of the Albany Congress, have at heart the same agenda as Adams and Franklin: assigning the crafters of the Albany Plan of Union—in this case Iroquois Indians as well as colonial statesmen—the status of Founding Fathers.

This book removes the Albany Congress from that context of state-making and examines it anew within the context of British empire building. The Albany Congress of 1754 was a product of a collision of cultures in colonial America, a convergence of identities rather than the

---

[25] Lawrence Henry Gipson, *The British Empire before the American Revolution*, 15 vols. (Caldwell, Iowa, and New York, 1936–70), 5:138. Besides the two chapters he devoted to the Albany Congress in volume 5 of *The British Empire before the American Revolution*, Gipson also wrote several articles on the congress and the Plan of Union. See "Thomas Hutchinson and the Framing of the Albany Plan of Union, 1754," *Pennsylvania Magazine of History and Biography* 74 (1950): 5–35; "The Drafting of the Albany Plan of Union: A Problem of Semantics," *Pennsylvania History* 26 (1959): 291–316; and "Massachusetts Bay and American Colonial Union, 1754," *Proceedings of the American Antiquarian Society* 71 (1961): 63–92.

[26] For Gipson's thesis on the causes of the American Revolution, see Lawrence H. Gipson, "The American Revolution as an Aftermath of the Great War for Empire, 1754–1765," in *The American Revolution: Two Centuries of Interpretation*, ed. Edmund S. Morgan (Englewood Cliffs, N.J., 1965), 86–104, and Gipson, *The Coming of the Revolution, 1763–1775* (New York, 1954). For a critical review of this thesis, see John M. Murrin, "The French and Indian War, the American Revolution, and the Counterfactual Hypothesis: Reflections on Lawrence Henry Gipson and John Shy," *Reviews in American History* 1 (1973): 307–17. Also see Jack P. Greene, "The Seven Years' War and the American Revolution: The Causal Relationship Reconsidered," *Journal of Imperial and Commonwealth History* 8 (1980): 85–105.

[27] Gipson, *Coming of the Revolution*, 232.

emergence of a single national one. For an event that supposedly presaged the more famous intercolonial congresses of the Revolutionary Era, it occurred in a surprisingly different setting: an Anglo-Iroquois treaty conference, convened by order of the British Crown, and held in a Dutch city on an Anglo-French–Native American frontier. Its story belongs within a larger narrative about eighteenth-century Britain's imperial expansion and its ramifications for the inhabitants of North America.

In recent years, historians writing what might be called the "new imperial history" have begun constructing that narrative from imperial, colonial, and native perspectives. Unlike the work of the earlier imperial historians, which focused on policymaking and administration, this approach examines the cultural as well as political dimensions of Britain's emergence as an imperial power, including its effect on the formation of national and colonial identities and encounters between colonizers and natives.[28] The Albany Congress is ripe for reexamination in light of these questions because it laid bare colonial and Indian reactions to the expansion of British power in North America. In 1754, Britain's grip on its North American colonies appeared to have broken down. French troops had occupied the Ohio Valley, cutting off British access to the continent's interior. Indians in New York had declared the Covenant Chain alliance broken, threatening a full-scale collapse of Indian trade and diplomacy in the northern colonies. Colonial governments, long accustomed to managing their affairs independently, resisted cooperation with each other or the Crown in responding to these events, while colonial administrators predicted disaster if the mother country did not assert much greater authority

---

[28] For recent works that address the connections between empire building and the emergence of the modern British state, see Lawrence Stone, ed., *An Imperial State at War: Britain from 1689–1815* (London, 1994); Kathleen Wilson, *The Sense of the People: Politics, Culture, and Imperialism in England, 1715–1785* (Cambridge, Eng., 1995); David Hancock, *Citizens of the World: London Merchants and the Integration of the British Atlantic Community, 1735–1785* (Cambridge, Eng., 1995); Linda Colley, *Britons: Forging the Nation, 1707–1837* (New Haven, 1992); and John Brewer, *The Sinews of Power: War, Money, and the English State, 1688–1783* (New York, 1989). For works focusing on provincial and colonial identities in imperial contexts, see Bernard Bailyn and Philip D. Morgan, eds., *Strangers within the Realm: Cultural Margins of the First British Empire* (Chapel Hill, 1991); Nicholas P. Canny and Anthony Pagden, eds., *Colonial Identity in the Atlantic World, 1500–1800* (Princeton, 1987); Jack P. Greene, *Pursuits of Happiness: The Social Development of Early Modern British Colonies and the Formation of American Culture* (Chapel Hill, 1988); and T. H. Breen, "Ideology and Nationalism on the Eve of the American Revolution: Revisions *Once More* in Need of Revising," *Journal of American History* 84 (1997): 13–39. Works that address cultural encounters between natives and colonizers in empire building include Eric Hinderaker, *Elusive Empires: Constructing Colonialism in the Ohio Valley, 1673–1800* (Cambridge, Eng., 1997); J. Russell Snapp, *John Stuart and the Struggle for Empire on the Southern Frontier* (Baton Rouge, 1996); and Ian K. Steele, *Betrayals: Fort William Henry and the "Massacre"* (Oxford, 1990). Steele discusses the new imperial history in "Exploding Colonial American History: Amerindian, Atlantic, and Global Perspectives," *Reviews in American History* 26 (1998): 70–95.

over its American dominions. This crisis of empire produced the unique setting and circumstances of the Albany Congress.

Beginning with Benjamin Franklin and John Adams, nationalist historians removed the Albany Congress from its context as an Anglo-Iroquois treaty conference so that it might better resemble the famous congresses of the Revolutionary Era. But contemporaries were well aware that it had as its raison d'être the Covenant Chain alliance. The protocol of Anglo-Iroquois diplomacy provided the format in which its participants met and conducted their business. The Albany Congress was an example of what Richard White has defined as the "middle ground" forged by Europeans and Indians in colonial America who used diplomatic rituals and material goods to negotiate their vast cultural differences.[29] Only by recovering that dimension of the Albany Congress can we recast its Indian participants from romanticized teachers of democracy into eighteenth-century North Americans who, like the Indians who gathered at Johnson's home in 1763, were struggling to adapt to British imperial power on their own terms.

Rethinking the Albany Congress in the context of Britain's imperial expansion also gives us a clearer understanding of the significance of the Albany Plan of Union. The idea of colonial union expressed in the Albany Plan had its origin not in any native or colonial American penchant for political federation but in the long eighteenth-century struggle to define the limits of local and centralized power in the British-Atlantic empire.[30] As Parliament gradually assumed sovereignty over the Crown's dominions, a host of questions arose about the constitutional status of the inhabitants of British North America. Did the colonists enjoy liberties and privileges distinct from those of subjects elsewhere in the empire, or did their colonial status imply a degree of dependency more strict than that of other Britons? How was the Crown to regard the Indian nations over which it claimed sovereignty in North America? Was it possible for the Iroquois to be, as the British often described them, both subjects and allies?[31] Such questions arose from the novel circumstances in which the British Empire found itself in the mid-eighteenth century, trying to maintain control over populous and multiracial colonies an ocean away. The Albany Plan, drafted in response to those circumstances, is best understood as a plan of Anglo-American union that attempted

[29] See Richard White, *The Middle Ground: Indians, Empires, and Republics in the Great Lakes Region, 1650–1815* (Cambridge, Eng., 1991).

[30] Jack P. Greene, *Peripheries and Center: Constitutional Development in the Extended Polities of the British Empire and United States, 1607–1788* (Athens, Ga., 1986), and Samuel Beer, *To Make a Nation: The Rediscovery of American Federalism* (Cambridge, Mass., 1993), 133–214.

[31] See Francis Jennings, *The Ambiguous Iroquois Empire: The Covenant Chain Confederation of Indian Tribes with English Colonies from Its Beginnings to the Lancaster Treaty of 1744* (New York, 1984), 38–39, 191–94.

to define more precisely North America's place in an expanding British Empire.

The Albany Congress represented a crossroads for British North America. It marked a passage from a pattern of imperial and intercultural relations that was predominantly autonomous and commercial in nature to one that was decidedly more "imperial" in the modern sense of the word: hierarchical and bureaucratic and dominated by a distant authority. For colonists and Indians, a world of villages in which power had always been locally held and administered came face-to-face with a world of empires in which power became increasingly centralized. The Albany Congress also marked a divergence in metropolitan and provincial attitudes about the nature of the empire. In promoting the cause of colonial union, Franklin claimed membership for his fellow colonists in a British national people that potentially knew no territorial borders; he assigned an equality of subjecthood to all Britons, regardless of which side of the Atlantic they inhabited, but also excluded from this national empire the non-British racial and cultural groups of North America. From the Crown's colonial administrators another perspective emerged, one that defined empire in terms of conquered territories and foreign peoples fundamentally different from and inferior to the British. Both of these views contributed to the sentiment for colonial union that made the Albany Congress possible, but their differences also guaranteed the failure of the Albany Plan before its American and British audiences.

When John Adams asked Thomas McKean for an account of the Albany Congress, he received one that placed it within a larger story about the coming of the Revolution. But no direct path existed between Albany in 1754 and Philadelphia in 1776. The problem with nationalist narratives of the Albany Congress is that they leave no room for alternative visions of the empire that did not advocate or even address American independence. They merely reduce the Albany Congress, in the words of one historian, to a "magnificent failure" and place it as "a landmark on the rough road of union that leads through the first Continental Congress and the Articles of Confederation to the Constitution of 1787."[32] This book recovers those lost voices and reincorporates them into the history of the eighteenth-century British Empire, revealing how ideas on colonial federation and imperial union grew out of questions about the place of North America in the British-Atlantic world. It is a story about the colonists' and Indians' experiences in a fluid yet expansive empire and their reactions to it.

[32] Clinton Rossiter, *Seedtime of the Republic: The Origins of the American Tradition of Political Liberty* (New York, 1953), 306, 308.

P A R T   I

PATHS WITHIN
THE EMPIRE

$\mathbf{I}$n Anglo-Iroquois diplomacy, the word "path" had dual significance. In its literal sense a path was a route of travel for people and goods between Indian villages and European settlements. These paths crisscrossed northeastern America, following major waterways and linking isolated communities over vast distances. As a diplomatic metaphor, a path also signified communication and exchange. The Covenant Chain alliance, for example, preserved an open path between the Iroquois Confederacy and the northern British colonies. Conversely, a closed or obstructed path signified a dissatisfaction between neighbors that, if not cleared, could lead to hostilities. Such paths, real and metaphorical, connected the colonial and Indian peoples of North America. Other paths linked the inhabitants of the British-Atlantic empire through shared markets, language, and culture. Some followed regular channels of communication such as the post roads and shipping routes carrying newspapers, private correspondence, and the official business of government. Others were more ephemeral, emerging out of the personal alliances and patronage networks that shaped imperial and colonial politics.

Three such paths brought colonists and Indians to the Albany Congress of 1754. First, a breakdown in intercultural relations along a local path on the New York frontier caused a group of Mohawk Indians to declare the Covenant Chain broken in June 1753. This news spread along a second imperial path connecting colonial administrators in London and America, who interpreted the breaking of the Covenant Chain as symptomatic of a much larger crisis threatening Britain's imperial ambitions in North America. They in turn ordered an intercolonial treaty conference to restore the Covenant Chain. As word of this conference spread along a third provincial path linking the northern colonial capitals, Benjamin Franklin seized upon it as an opportunity to promote a colonial union that would permanently alter the colonists' constitutional relationship with each other and the mother country. And so the discontents of a small group of Indians on a distant frontier resonated throughout the British-Atlantic empire.

[1]

A Local Path to Albany:
The Mohawk Valley

Brother:
. . . as soon as we come home we will send up a Belt of Wampum to our
Brothers the 5 Nations to acquaint them the Covenant Chain is broken
between you and us. So brother you are not to expect to hear of me any
more, and Brother we desire to hear no more of you. And we shall no longer
acquaint you with any News or affairs as we used to do.
    —Mohawk chief Hendrick to New York governor George Clinton,
    June 16, 1753

The story of the Albany Congress begins not in the council chambers and assembly halls of colonial capitals but on the fringe of British North America, along a frontier populated by Indians, colonial farmers, traders, and soldiers. In the mid-eighteenth century, the Mohawk Valley was an axis of empire, a borderland between the continent's British, French, and Native American inhabitants. At its eastern end, the Mohawk River flowed into the Hudson, the major interior waterway of New York. Moving west along the Mohawk took the traveler beyond the pale of European settlement into the homelands of the Six Iroquois Nations: from east to west, the Mohawks, Oneidas, Tuscaroras, Onondagas, Cayugas, and Senecas (see map 1.1).[1] North of Albany, the Lake Champlain corridor led to the St. Lawrence River, Montreal, and Quebec.

[1] It is important here to distinguish between the Iroquois League and the Iroquois Confederacy. The League, which originally included five nations (Mohawks, Oneidas, Onondagas, Cayugas, and Senecas) and expanded in the early eighteenth century to six (Tuscaroras), predated European contact. The League's orientation was intramural, focused on maintaining peace and cooperation among the member nations through councils and rituals held in Onondaga. The Confederacy took shape during the seventeenth and eighteenth centuries, as the Iroquois gained influence among neighboring colonists and Indians. Its orientation was extramural, focused on extending Iroquois trade and diplomacy to outsiders, be they other Indians or colonists. Albany was the most common site of Iroquois-European diplomacy conducted under the aegis of the Covenant Chain. See Daniel K. Richter, "Ordeal of the

From London or Paris, the Mohawk Valley divided North America into discrete units: British to the east, Iroquois to the west, French to the north. Such well-defined borders disintegrated when examined more closely, just as increasing magnification will break down an apparently solid object into smaller, less stable pieces. From the perspective of Albany, the Mohawk Valley melted into scattered Indian villages, European settlements, and military and commercial outposts whose inhabitants exhibited remarkable ethnic diversity (see map 1.2). Near the Mohawk River's confluence with the Hudson, Albany's population of Dutch merchants ferried goods between the interior and New York City. Moving west brought a traveler to the Dutch farming community of Schenectady and the Mohawks' country. In the mid-eighteenth century, the Mohawks occupied two villages: Tiononderoge, which Europeans often called the "lower castle," and Canajoharie, or the "upper castle." German, Irish, and Scots-Irish colonists lived near Tiononderoge along the Schoharie River, many of them tenants of wealthy Dutch and British landlords. Fort Hunter, a British post in this area, housed a small military garrison and a series of Anglican missionaries. Farther upstream a traveler arrived in a fertile bottomland known as German Flatts, named after the farmers who settled there in the 1720s. More Germans and some Scots-Irish lived south of this region in Cherry Valley, near the headwaters of the Susquehanna River. The Mohawk River tailed off in the country of the Oneidas, another Iroquois nation, but still no clear line divided Europeans and Indians. Farther west, on the southeastern shore of Lake Ontario, a handful of British soldiers manned a fort at Oswego, the site of a summer market for Indians and colonial traders.[2]

The Mohawk Valley was one of the most important paths of trade and communication between Indians and Europeans in northeastern America. Traders from Albany trekked to Oswego in the spring and returned in the fall with their furs.[3] In addition to serving as a highway for goods, the Mohawk Valley was a conduit of diplomacy. It connected Iroquoia to

---

Longhouse: The Five Nations in Early American History," in *Beyond the Covenant Chain: The Iroquois and Their Neighbors in Indian North America, 1600–1800*, ed. Daniel K. Richter and James H. Merrell (Syracuse, 1987), 1–27.

[2] For descriptions of the Mohawk Valley in the mid-eighteenth century, see William Smith [Jr.], *The History of the Province of New-York*, ed. Michael Kammen, 2 vols. (Cambridge, Mass., 1972), 1:212–15, and Thomas Pownall, *A Topographical Description of the Dominions of the United States of America*, ed. Lois Mulkearn (Pittsburgh, 1949), 33–38. Also see Thomas Burke Jr., *Mohawk Frontier: The Dutch Community of Schenectady, New York, 1661–1710* (Ithaca, 1991), and Ruth L. Higgins, *Expansion in New York, with Especial Reference to the Eighteenth Century* (1931; rpt. Philadelphia, 1976), 47–82.

[3] For a description of the traders' route, see Lewis Evans, *An Analysis of a General Map of the Middle British Colonies* (Philadelphia, 1755), 20, reprinted in Lawrence Henry Gipson, ed., *Lewis Evans* (Philadelphia, 1939).

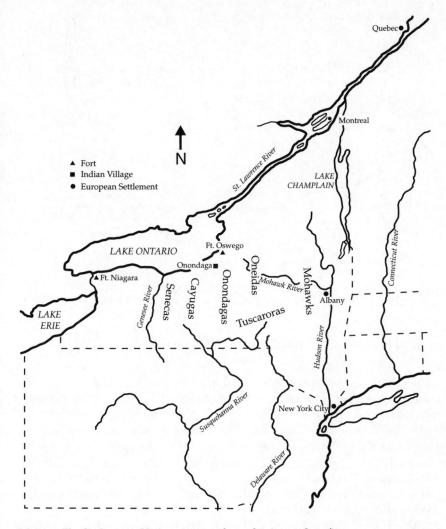

Map 1.1. The Six Iroquois Nations, c. 1750, drawn by Armen Sarrafian.

Albany, which since the late seventeenth century had served as the geographic center of the Covenant Chain, a diplomatic and commercial alliance between the northern colonies and the Iroquois.[4] Europeans participated in the Covenant Chain to preserve the fur trade. Relations with the Iroquois, they believed, were commercial at heart, and therefore, trade

[4] For the origins and nature of the Covenant Chain, see Jennings, *Ambiguous Iroquois Empire*; Daniel K. Richter, *The Ordeal of the Longhouse: The Peoples of the Iroquois League in the Era of European Colonization* (Chapel Hill, 1992); and the essays in Richter and Merrell, *Beyond the Covenant Chain*.

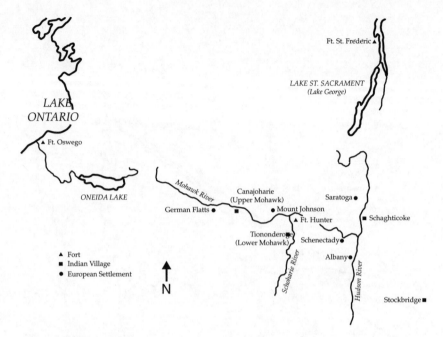

Map 1.2. The Mohawk Valley, c. 1750, drawn by Armen Sarrafian.

offered "the best and surest foundation to secure their Alliance."[5] To ensure the open paths necessary for trade, colonial representatives gathered periodically in Albany to renew or "brighten" the Covenant Chain, by hearing Indian complaints and distributing presents of manufactured goods to them. As New York customs officer Archibald Kennedy explained it, the Covenant Chain served as "the original Contract and Treaty of Commerce" between the colonists and the Iroquois, by which "we have assisted them in their Wars and Wants, and they have assisted us in our Wars, and we have their Furs."[6]

The British also used the Covenant Chain to extend their territorial claims in North America. British officers and diplomats claimed that in a series of Albany conferences between 1684 and 1726, the Iroquois had attached themselves to the British Crown in return for its protection. In the Treaty of Utrecht, completed in 1713, the French recognized the Iroquois as

[5] Peter Wraxall, *An Abridgment of Indian Affairs, Contained in Four Folio Volumes, Transacted in the Colony of New York, from the Year 1678 to the Year 1751*, ed. Charles Howard McIlwain (Cambridge, Mass., 1915), 61. Wraxall, who served as secretary at the Albany Congress, wrote this summary of New York's Indian affairs in 1754 for the Earl of Halifax, president of the Board of Trade.
[6] [Archibald Kennedy], *The Importance of Gaining and Preserving the Friendship of the Indians to the British Interest, Considered* (New York, 1751), 5–6.

British subjects. This treaty, along with land cessions the Iroquois made to the British in this same period, became the cornerstone of Britain's claim to the Great Lakes and the Ohio Valley, regions over which it exercised no military or political control.[7] Since the Iroquois were, as one British writer noted, "as much his majesty's subjects, by their own voluntary act, as we are," French encroachments on their lands "ought to be considered, in the same light, as if they were made on us."[8] This British interpretation of the Covenant Chain is conveyed visually by the colonial seal of New York (Fig. 1.1). On it, two Indian figures kneel before the king, presenting furs to their sovereign, who in return offers security and Christianity.

Like the British, the Iroquois believed the Covenant Chain's principal object was trade, but they did not define it as a lord-vassal relationship. According to Indians who retold the story at treaty conferences, the Covenant Chain began when the first European ship arrived at Albany. Pleased with the goods the ship carried, the Indians tied it to a tree. They later replaced the rope with a chain, which they anchored in Onondaga, so that they would know whenever the ship was endangered. They also planted a Tree of Peace at Albany, its roots and branches spreading to include other colonies and Indian nations in the web of Iroquois diplomacy. The Iroquois often invoked this legend when they renewed the Covenant Chain, using it to remind the English that "a good trade and a good peace always go hand in hand."[9]

The Iroquois regarded the Covenant Chain as one of many "chains" linking them to other native and colonial peoples.[10] They did not treat it as an exclusive relationship, nor did they pay much heed to their supposed British subjecthood. In diplomatic councils, they addressed their British counterparts as "brethren" and protested when the Crown's officers referred to them as "children."[11] They insisted that their land cessions were for protection only and that "We being a Free People, tho' united to the

---

[7] For Great Britain's use of the Covenant Chain to advance its imperial pretensions in North America, see Jennings, *Ambiguous Iroquois Empire*, 10–24, and Dorothy V. Jones, *License for Empire: Colonialism by Treaty in Early America* (Chicago, 1982), 21–35.

[8] [J. Payne], *The French Encroachments Exposed: or, Britain's Original Right to All That Part of the American Continent Claimed by France* (London, 1756), 6.

[9] ACIA Minutes, March 5, 1741, 2:206. For examples of this retelling of the Covenant Chain's origin, see Wraxall, *Abridgment of Indian Affairs*, 24, and ACIA Minutes, July 4, 1730, 1:321a. On the British side, William Johnson provided a very full retelling of this legend at a conference in Onondaga in 1748. See *WJ Papers*, 1:157–59. Archibald Kennedy also included a version of it in *Importance of Gaining and Preserving the Friendship the Indians*, 5–6.

[10] For further explanation of the Iroquois conception of these diplomatic chains, see Mary A. Druke, "Linking Arms: The Structure of Iroquois Intertribal Diplomacy," and Richard L. Haan, "Covenant and Consensus: The Iroquois and the English, 1676–1760," in *Beyond the Covenant Chain*, ed. Richter and Merrell, 29–39, 41–57.

[11] In the late seventeenth century, Governors Thomas Dongan and Edmund Andros of New York tried unsuccessfully to address the Iroquois as "children" in treaty councils. See Richter, *Ordeal of the Longhouse*, 155–56, 160.

Figure 1.1. Great Seal of the Province of New York, c. 1750. Courtesy of the New York State Library.

English, may give our Lands, and be joyn'd to the Sachem we like best."[12] In Iroquois opinion, horizontal links of reciprocity and amity, rather than vertical ones of authority and dependence, held the Covenant Chain together. They expressed this egalitarianism visually in designs they wove into wampum belts presented at treaty conferences, which used various symbols to represent a linking together of equal parts: human figures clasping hands, parallel lines, diamonds joined at their corners (Fig. 1.2).[13] The linear and geometric symmetry of such designs contrasted sharply with the hierarchical representation of the Covenant Chain found on New York's colonial seal. The Indian agent Robert Livingston candidly summarized the Iroquois view of the Covenant Chain when he admitted that "altho' the French Governours are pleas'd to call their Indians, subjects of the French King, and our Governours in like manner call the Indians of the

[12] Cadwallader Colden, *The History of the Five Indian Nations Depending upon the Province of New-York in America* (1727, 1747; rpt. Ithaca, 1958), 42.
[13] My analysis of wampum designs is based on the examples reproduced in the microfilm collection *Iroquois Indians: A Documentary History of the Diplomacy of the Six Nations and Their League,* ed. Francis Jennings et al., 50 reels (Woodbridge, 1985). Reel 50 of this collection contains reproductions and descriptions of approximately 160 Iroquois wampum belts.

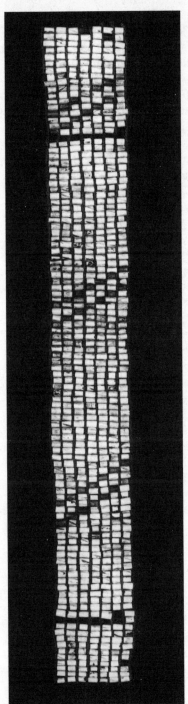

Figure 1.2. The Fort Stanwix Wampum Belt. Courtesy of the New York State Museum, Albany.

Five Nations Subjects of the Crown of England, they [the Indians] do not so understand it, but look upon themselves in the state of freedom."[14]

The Covenant Chain was maintained locally by the inhabitants of the Mohawk Valley. On the European side, Albany's merchants and magistrates administered New York's Indian affairs by distributing presents to the Indians and overseeing the fur trade. On the Indian side, the Mohawks, as the easternmost Iroquois nation, treated with the Albany people and facilitated trade and communication between them and Indians farther west. Both the Albany magistrates and the Mohawks operated with considerable freedom from any higher authority, be it British or Iroquois. Thus the strength or weakness of the Covenant Chain invariably depended on the state of intercultural relations in a forty-five-mile-long corridor between Albany and the upper Mohawk village of Canajoharie.

The Albany Congress convened in 1754 because a year earlier, a small group of Mohawks had traveled to New York City to declare before the royal governor of New York that the Covenant Chain was broken. They placed the blame on the inhabitants of Albany, whom, the Mohawks claimed, had mistreated them since the conclusion of the last Anglo-French war in 1748. This crisis laid bare two important contradictions at the heart of the Covenant Chain. First, the British often referred to the Iroquois as their subjects and allies, but they could not be both.[15] Could the Iroquois in fact ally themselves with whomever they pleased, or were they dependents of the British Crown whose allegiance was no longer volitional? Second, the claims to dominion in North America that Britain made via the Covenant Chain actually rested on Indians and colonists in the Mohawk Valley over whom the Crown exerted little control. The Mohawks aimed their grievances at their colonial neighbors, but their actions had repercussions of imperial dimensions, threatening British pretensions to the continent's interior, exposing colonists to French attack, disrupting the fur trade, and encouraging the wholesale desertion of the Iroquois from the Covenant Chain. To find the roots of the Albany Congress, therefore, we must examine the breakdown in intercultural diplomacy and the flow of goods along this local path between Albany and Canajoharie.

The Mohawks

In the seventeenth century, the Mohawks enjoyed great influence in the colonial fur trade and Indian relations. As neighbors of the

---

[14] NYCD, 4:871.
[15] See Jennings, Ambiguous Iroquois Empire, 38–39, 191–94.

Dutch traders at Fort Orange (later Albany), they acquired guns and other European goods quickly and controlled the access of other Indian nations to those items. The English, after conquering New Netherland and renaming it New York in 1664, continued to curry the Mohawks' favor. During the Iroquois wars of the seventeenth century the Mohawks ironically gained a reputation for martial fierceness among Europeans despite their heavy losses, and they commanded respect in colonial councils throughout Canada and the northern British colonies.[16]

After more than thirty years of warfare along the New York–Canadian frontier, hostilities ceased with the signing of the Anglo-French Treaty of Utrecht in 1713. For most European and Indian inhabitants of northeastern America, this peace meant a resumption of trade and settlement. For the Mohawks, it meant an erosion in diplomatic prestige and economic stability. Despite their reputation as warriors, the Mohawks' power had always rested in their role as diplomatic gatekeepers between Albany and the western Indians. That influence brought trade into the Mohawks' country, as well as material wealth in the form of presents they received at treaty conferences.[17] After 1700, the Mohawks' power waned as the fur trade shifted west and north and colonial settlement encroached on their territory. By mid-century, they were a people in eclipse, barely holding onto their ancestral lands and their influence among colonial and Indian neighbors.[18]

The best glimpse of Mohawk life in the first half of the eighteenth century may be recovered from the correspondence of Anglican missionaries sponsored by the Society for the Propagation of the Gospel (SPG).[19] Fort Hunter, a British post built in 1711 at the confluence of the Schoharie and Mohawk Rivers, included a chapel designated for use by an SPG missionary to the Mohawks. The Reverend William Andrews arrived in 1712 to assume that post and was welcomed by the local Indians.[20] During the

---

[16] For the Iroquois wars, see Richter, *Ordeal of the Longhouse*, 133–89; José António Brandão, *"Your fyre shall burn no more": Iroquois Policy toward New France and Its Native Allies to 1701* (Lincoln, 1997); and George T. Hunt, *The Wars of the Iroquois: A Study in Intertribal Trade Relations* (Madison, 1960). The English exaggerated the Mohawks' reputation for conquest to boost their own pretensions to empire. See Jennings, *Ambiguous Iroquois Empire*, 43–44.

[17] A useful article addressing this diplomatic function for the Iroquois in general is Allen W. Trelease, "The Iroquois and the Western Fur Trade: A Problem of Interpretation," *Mississippi Valley Historical Review* 49 (1962): 32–51.

[18] Richter, *Ordeal of the Longhouse*, 255–80.

[19] This correspondence may be found in the microfilm collection of the SPG Letterbooks.

[20] Andrews to the Secretary of the SPG, September 7, 1713, SPG Letterbooks, Ser. A, 8:184–85. For analysis of the SPG's work among the Mohawks in the early eighteenth century, see Richter, *Ordeal of the Longhouse*, 222–35; Richter, "'Some of Them . . . Would Always Have a Minister with Them': Mohawk Protestantism, 1683–1719," *American Indian Quarterly* 16 (fall 1992): 471–84; and John Wolfe Lydekker, *The Faithful Mohawks* (New York, 1938), 1–60.

next seven years, he observed many aspects of Mohawk life that reflected their adaptation to European contact. Most obvious, of course, was their religion. Upon his arrival, Andrews found that most adult Mohawks were already baptized; they practiced their own version of a Protestant creed, emphasizing baptism and communal prayers and singing. They exhibited less interest in his efforts to catechize their children and in altering their marriage and sexual practices to meet Anglican norms.[21] In their dress, the Mohawks had incorporated European trade cloth with their more traditional use of animal furs, bear's grease, paint, and wampum beads. They had also abandoned their longhouses—multifamily communal dwellings—for smaller huts containing nuclear families.[22]

The negative influences of European contact struck Andrews as he became better acquainted with the Indians near Fort Hunter. He condemned their drunkenness and cursing, both of which he attributed to the examples set by the soldiers and traders who frequented the post.[23] Most notable was the Mohawks' poverty. Andrews could lure children to his school only by providing them with "Victuals and other things . . . Victuals is a great motive wth them for the Indians are very poore and fare hard especially all summer." He reported that some impoverished Mohawks were migrating to Canada, where they resettled in missionary towns established by French Jesuits. Andrews complained of his constant expenses in clothing and feeding the Mohawk elderly, widows, and children who sought relief at Fort Hunter.[24]

Andrews left his post in 1719, lamenting his inability to provide for the beggarly Indians and to keep them on a virtuous path. The SPG did not send a replacement until 1727. Like Andrews, the Reverend John Miln found the Mohawks eager to have their children baptized and often in need of his material support.[25] Miln's successor, the Reverend Henry Barclay, served at Fort Hunter from 1735 until 1746. Barclay spoke Dutch, Mohawk, and English and attracted a large Indian and European congregation. Among the Mohawks living near Fort Hunter he counted only three or four adults unbaptized, forty communicants at his services, and forty young men and children attending his catechisms.[26] Barclay left the mission suddenly in 1746 after receiving an appointment in New York City. By that time, war had returned to the Mohawk frontier, scattering its

[21] See Richter, "'Some of Them,'" 478–80.
[22] Andrews to the Secretary, March 19, 1713, SPG Letterbooks, Ser. A, 143–45. Also see David B. Guldenzopf, "The Colonial Transformation of Mohawk Iroquois Society" (Ph.D. dissertation, SUNY, Albany, 1986), 46–47.
[23] SPG Letterbooks, March 19, 1713, and October 17, 1714, Ser. A, 8:143–45, 10:155–57.
[24] Ibid., July 1715, and October 17, 1715, 10:186–87, 11:269–70.
[25] Miln to the Secretary, November 4, 1730, November 2, 1731, November 15, 1734, and Petition of John Miln, 1735, ibid., 23:85–87, 345–46, 25:43, and 26:1–2.
[26] Barclay to the Secretary, August 31, 1736, ibid., 26:71–72.

Indian and European inhabitants, and Barclay advised not resuming the mission until peace returned.[27]

The experiences of Andrews, Miln, and Barclay indicate some of the challenges that European colonization brought to the Mohawks. Poverty reduced many—especially the elderly and widowed—to begging, while others sought refuge at Jesuit missions in Canada. Rum provided by traders and soldiers moving between Albany and Oswego undermined the stability of Mohawk communities. In the 1730s, Miln counted as many Europeans as Indians at his Fort Hunter services, a testament to the growing settler population west of Schenectady. The Mohawks in this region came to rely on the missionaries for material necessities, expecting food and clothing in return for their attendance at services and catechisms.

The Mohawks' decline can be attributed to two factors: the changing nature of the fur trade and the rising value of Mohawk lands to colonists. The construction of Oswego on the southeastern shore of Lake Ontario in the 1720s broke Albany's monopoly on New York's fur trade. Oswego attracted Indians from throughout the Great Lakes to its summer markets and became the new western terminus of the British fur trade. Albany merchants, who in the seventeenth century had waited for Indians to come to them, now sent agents to Oswego to do business.[28] Since western Indians no longer had to travel to Albany to trade, the Mohawks' importance as brokers between colonists and other Indian nations diminished.

The shift in trade from Albany to Oswego was only part of a larger regional change in the British-Atlantic fur market. During the early eighteenth century, Pennsylvania's share in this trade rose steadily, increasing diplomatic and economic competition between the Quaker colony and New York.[29] Since its founding in the 1680s, Pennsylvania had steered clear of Albany's Indian diplomacy, cultivating its own "Chain of Friendship" with neighboring Indians. In 1722 Pennsylvania governor William Keith opened a path between his colony and Onondaga. Ten years later a delegation of Iroquois chiefs started a council fire in Philadelphia, where they treated with the Pennsylvanians. The Mohawks gained little from this rebalancing in intercolonial Indian relations. They were conspicuously absent from the council fire in Philadelphia and remained so for twenty years, sharing in none of the Pennsylvanians' presents to the Iroquois.[30]

---

[27] Barclay to the Secretary, December 2, 1746, and September 28, 1747, ibid., Ser. B, 14:95–98, 15:97–98.

[28] On the establishment of Oswego and the rise of the western fur trade, see Thomas Elliot Norton, *The Fur Trade in Colonial New York, 1686–1776* (Madison, 1974), 152–73.

[29] See Stephen H. Cutcliffe, "Colonial Indian Policy as a Measure of Rising Imperialism: New York and Pennsylvania, 1700–1755," *Western Pennsylvania Historical Magazine* 64 (1981): 237–68, and Gary B. Nash, "The Quest for the Susquehanna Valley: New York, Pennsylvania, and the Seventeenth-Century Fur Trade," *New York History* 48 (1967): 3–27.

[30] See Francis Jennings, "Pennsylvania Indians and the Iroquois," in *Beyond the Covenant*

During the first half of the eighteenth century, Albany's merchants came to rely much less on the western fur trade, and therefore the Mohawks, for their profits. During the Anglo-French wars of 1689 to 1713, Albany remained neutral and cultivated its own path of trade with the Caughnawagas, Indian refugees and Catholic converts from Iroquoia who had resettled at the invitation of French Jesuits near Montreal. Many of the Caughnawagas were Mohawks, and despite their French alliance, they maintained peaceful relations with their cousins in the Mohawk Valley.[31] This kinship insulated Albany from imperial warfare in the Northeast. Caughnawagas carried furs from Montreal south through the Champlain corridor to Albany, trading them there for cloth, rum, and other goods. The colonial governments of Canada and New York outlawed this trade but found it impossible to stop. During the long Anglo-French peace between 1713 and 1744, such smuggling flourished, and the Caughnawagas attracted much of the diplomatic attention that the Mohawks had once received in Albany. During this period, Albany's merchants also turned their attention to exporting timber and flour.[32] This diversification further eroded the Mohawks' role as cultural brokers and forced them to rely on land sales and the largesse of missionaries to sustain themselves.

The intrusion of European colonists into Mohawk country began in earnest with the construction of Fort Hunter in 1711. This post extended the frontier of European colonization from Schenectady to the Schoharie River, near the lower Mohawk village. Protestant German refugees soon moved into the Schoharie Valley against the wishes of Albany magistrates who claimed the land as their own. In the 1720s, the Germans moved farther west, establishing Stone Arabia and German Flatts. Although some of these colonists participated in the fur trade, most were farmers who exported wheat and peas to Albany and New York City. In the 1730s and 1740s, settlement continued with the arrival of Scots-Irish and Irish tenants working for landlords along the Schoharie, Mohawk, and Susquehanna Rivers. By the outbreak of King George's War in 1744, the Mohawks found themselves literally surrounded by European neighbors.[33] Dutch, German, and British speculators anxious to profit from the flow of colonists

---

Chain, ed. Richter and Merrell, 75–91; Jennings, Ambiguous Iroquois Empire, 214–48, 309–24; and Richard Aquila, The Iroquois Restoration: Iroquois Diplomacy on the Colonial Frontier, 1701–1754 (Detroit, 1983), 156–66.

[31] See John Demos, The Unredeemed Captive: A Family Story from Early America (New York, 1994), 120–24.

[32] For the Albany-Montreal trade, see Norton, Fur Trade in Colonial New York, 121–51; on the diversification of the Albany merchants' interests, see David Arthur Armour, "The Merchants of Albany, New York, 1686–1760" (Ph.D. dissertation, Northwestern University, 1965), 181–217.

[33] On the expansion of colonial settlement in the Mohawk Valley, see Edith M. Fox, Land Speculation in the Mohawk Country (Ithaca, 1949), and Higgins, Expansion in New York, 47–83.

into this region made fraudulent claims to the very land on which the Mohawk villages stood. The Tiononderoge patent, owned by the city of Albany, dated to the late seventeenth century and included thousands of acres near Fort Hunter; the Livingston patent, which dated to the early 1730s, included the lands of Canajoharie. Numerous smaller transactions, in which colonists acquired land in exchange for cash, goods, or provisions given to local Indians, made the Mohawks' territorial integrity even more precarious.[34]

The Albany Commissioners of Indian Affairs, a committee of magistrates and merchants, recorded the rising tensions between Mohawks and colonists in their minutes.[35] Mohawk chiefs complained that the Oswego trade increased rum traffic through their villages, causing drunkenness, violence, and conflicts with colonial neighbors. They petitioned the governor to prohibit the carrying of liquor through their homelands, but to no avail.[36] They also complained about rising prices for goods at Oswego and requested that the governor lower them as a sign of his esteem for the Indians; the governor responded that prices depended on market forces beyond his control.[37] Albany traders en route to Oswego reported that Indians at Canajoharie assaulted and robbed them.[38] During the 1730s, the Mohawks grew more insistent in their objections to colonial land-grabbing. After learning of the Livingston patent to Canajoharie, chiefs from that village threatened to "break the Compass and Chaine" of any

[34] For the Tiononderoge and Livingston patents, see Georgiana C. Nammack, *Fraud, Politics, and the Dispossession of the Indians: The Iroquois Land Frontier in the Colonial Period* (Norman, 1969), 22–28, 47–51, and Fox, *Land Speculation in the Mohawk Country*, 16–27, 34–36.

[35] The Albany Commissioners of Indian Affairs were established in 1696 by the royal governor of New York to regulate the fur trade and conduct Indian diplomacy. Their number fluctuated from as low as five to as high as thirty, but a consistent group of seven to twelve handled the bulk of their business. Robert and Philip Livingston, the father and son who served successively as New York's secretary for Indian affairs between 1675 and 1749, led this group. Most of the commissions passed in a similar manner from one generation to the next in Albany's leading families, including the Bleekers, Schuylers, Cuylers, DePeysters, and Rensselaers. See ACIA Minutes, vols. 1–3, and Lawrence H. Leder, ed., *The Livingston Indian Records, 1666–1723* (Gettysburg, 1956).

[36] For the Mohawks' complaints about the rum traffic caused by the Oswego trade, see ACIA Minutes, October 20, 1725, 1:114a–15; September 7, 1726, 1:167–68a; October 1728, 1:264–68; and July 4, 1730, 1:321. The governors who heard these complaints refused to stop rum sales at Oswego because they considered liquor necessary to draw the trade of western Indians. Governor Montgomerie did order that no rum be sold en route to Oswego, but the persistence of Mohawk complaints suggests that this prohibition was not enforced. See ibid., October 20, 1725, 1:120a–123a, and October 1728, 1:269.

[37] For examples of the Indians' complaints about high prices at Oswego, see ibid., September 7, 1726, 1:167, and March 5, 1741, 2:206. Governor William Burnet gave a typical response in September 1726, when he explained to the Indians, "Sometimes your bever and Skins are worth more money and Sometimes Less on the other Side of the great Lake [Atlantic Ocean]." See ibid., 1:168.

[38] See, for example, ibid., May 23, 1730, 1:317a, and the petition of forty-seven traders submitted to the Albany Commissioners of Indian Affairs, June 1, 1754, in *NYCD*, 6:858.

surveyors who came there and to destroy any settlements made on the disputed land. In the early 1740s, the Albany commissioners heard from colonists in that vicinity about Indians who "destroy their Cattle and Molest them greatly."[39]

The transition of the Mohawk Valley from a fur-trading to an agricultural frontier led to a deterioration in European-Indian relations. Colonists turned their attention away from furs to commodities such as flour and timber, the production of which required little cooperation or assistance from Indians. The Mohawks, finding themselves bypassed by the fur trade and colonial diplomacy, slipped into poverty and dependence. In this new economy, they had little to offer except land, the sale of which undermined their own political and demographic stability.

The Emergence of Hendrick and William Johnson

During King George's War (1744–48), Anglo-French hostilities resumed along the Mohawk frontier, and two figures—one Indian and one European—emerged as the most influential cultural brokers in New York's Indian affairs. Hendrick, a chief from Canajoharie, used the war to revitalize the Mohawks' influence in colonial Indian diplomacy. He traveled with Mohawk delegations to Albany, Montreal, and Boston, treating with colonial governments and acquiring presents for his people at home. Johnson, a Mohawk Valley merchant and landowner, used his access to goods and expertise in Indian diplomacy to gain influence among the Mohawks and political favor with New York's royal governor.

The details of Hendrick's early life have been confused with those of another Mohawk leader who shared his name and flourished between 1690 and 1720.[40] Starting in 1739, his life and leadership among the Mo-

[39] For the Mohawks' complaints about the Livingston Patent, see ACIA Minutes, April 24, 1732, 1:355a–56, and June 26, 1732, 2:3–11. For the colonists' complaints against the Mohawks at Canajoharie, see ibid., October 1741, 2:217, and October 8, 1743, 2:259a.

[40] In a presentation at the 1997 Iroquois Research Conference, Dean Snow postulated that there were two different Mohawk leaders known as Hendrick Peters, whose overlapping lives have been conflated by historians. The first Hendrick Peters was a member of the Wolf Clan and lived from 1660 until 1735. He was a Christian convert baptized by Dutch missionary Godfrey Dellius in 1690 and was one of the four Indians from New York who visited Queen Anne's court in 1710. The second Hendrick Peters was a member of the Bear Clan who lived from 1692 until 1755. He was from the Mohawk village of Canajoharie and attended numerous treaty conferences with colonial officials in the 1740s and 1750s, including the Albany Congress. I would like to thank Professor Snow for sharing his notes from this presentation with me. Two papers presented at the 1998 Iroquois Research Conference, Mary Druke Becker's "Analyzing Data on Iroquois Names" and John Ferguson's "Hendrick Who?" indicated the popularity of the name "Hendrick" among Christian Mohawk Indians in the eighteenth century and the confusion it has caused to scholars. Reference works still refer to a

hawks of Canajoharie become clearer. Often working in conjunction with his brother Abraham, Hendrick presented complaints of land fraud and trading abuses to colonial officials at treaty conferences in Albany and, between 1744 and his death in 1755, extended this diplomacy to include colonial governments in Canada, New England, and Pennsylvania. Of persistent concern to him throughout this period was a fraudulent patent to the lands of Canajoharie owned by the Livingston family of New York.[41]

William Johnson arrived in the Mohawk Valley in 1738 as part of a swelling tide of colonists. Born in County Meath, Ireland, in 1715, he grew up in a family that had converted to Protestantism to circumvent the dispossession of Catholics under the Penal Laws. Because his family's fortunes were unstable in Ireland, Johnson at age twenty-two accepted an invitation from his maternal uncle Peter Warren to emigrate to North America. Warren was a captain in the British Navy, who had married into a wealthy New York family and acquired a substantial estate near Fort Hunter. Johnson came to America to recruit and supervise tenants for these lands.[42] In 1739 he purchased land north of the Mohawk River and about halfway between German Flatts and Albany. There he built "a Store house and Shop" and grew rich intercepting trade headed east to Albany.[43] He named this site Mount Johnson and moved there permanently a few years later, quickly becoming one of the wealthiest fur merchants in New York.

Separated in age by about twenty-five years, Hendrick and Johnson personified the Mohawk Valley's passage from a fur-trading to an agricultural frontier. At first glance, their interests in intercultural diplomacy appear antithetical. Hendrick emerged as a Mohawk spokesman at a time when the fur trade had bypassed his people and European settlers were encroaching on their lands. He did not seem a likely ally for Johnson, the most ambitious merchant and landlord in the Mohawk Valley. Yet both shared a knowledge of the ways in which material goods and diplomatic ritual governed intercultural relations in that region. Their paths crossed and intertwined as each manipulated the Covenant Chain for his own

---

single Hendrick Peters who visited Queen Anne's court in 1710 and attended the Albany Congress in 1754; see, for example, George Brown, ed., *Dictionary of Canadian Biography*, 12 vols. (Toronto, 1966–91), 3:622–23. The most recent scholarship noted above, however, suggests that it is more likely that these were two different people.
[41] The earliest reference I have found to Hendrick's and Abraham's partnership is from a meeting with the Albany Commissioners of Indian Affairs on September 10, 1739. See ACIA Minutes, 2:172a–73a. See also October 5, 1741, 2:217. Hendrick's work in the 1740s and 1750s as an intercultural diplomat is well documented and cited as relevant below.
[42] On Johnson's early life, see Milton W. Hamilton, *Sir William Johnson, Colonial American, 1715–1763* (Port Washington, 1976), 3–14, and Flexner, *Mohawk Baronet*, 13–27.
[43] Johnson to Peter Warren, May 19, 1739, *WJ Papers*, 1:5.

purposes during the 1740s, leading them eventually as partners to the Albany Congress of 1754.

The paths of Hendrick and William Johnson converged when Anglo-French hostilities were renewed in 1744. King George's War ended thirty years of peace in New York and brought new priorities to that colony's Indian affairs. The Oswego fur trade and colonization of the Mohawk Valley created an extended frontier in need of protection. For the Mohawks, the return of war meant an opportunity to recoup some of the diplomatic prestige they had lost since the establishment of Oswego and, with it, access to the material wealth that intercultural diplomacy offered. As the Iroquois Confederacy's "keepers of the eastern door," they remained the most important link in the Covenant Chain between New York and the western Indians. If New Yorkers wanted to protect Oswego and maintain peace and trade along their frontier, they had to preserve the goodwill of the Mohawks.

The Mohawks lost no time in using the war to acquire presents and voice their complaints about Albany's management of Indian affairs. Within a year, they attended treaty conferences in Albany, Boston, and Montreal, reasserting their traditional role as diplomatic intermediaries between Indians and colonists. In June 1744, New York governor George Clinton and commissioners from Massachusetts and Connecticut met in Albany to renew the Covenant Chain and inform the Indians of the war against France. The Indians present explained their inclination to remain neutral in the Anglo-French conflict, a policy that the Six Nations had pursued with success since 1701.[44] They looked askance when Clinton asked them to help protect Oswego and used the occasion to renew their old complaint about the trade there: "The first year or two after that house was built goods were cheap . . . but now goods are sold so dear at that place, that we cannot say we think it advantageous to us upon the Account of trade."[45]

A month later, Hendrick led a Mohawk delegation to Boston to treat with Massachusetts governor William Shirley. New Englanders generally distrusted New York's administration of the Covenant Chain. They described the Albany Dutch as opportunistic neutrals, who steered clear of Anglo-French conflicts so as to continue their illegal trade with Montreal. According to New Englanders, French-allied Indians armed themselves at Albany, raided western Massachusetts and Connecticut, and then returned to sell their loot in Albany.[46] Shirley pressed the Mohawks to take a

[44] On the Iroquois policy of neutrality, see Richter, *Ordeal of the Longhouse*, 206–54; Aquila, *Iroquois Restoration*, 85–128; and Richard Haan, "The Problem of Iroquois Neutrality: Suggestions for Revision," *Ethnohistory* 27 (1980): 317–30.

[45] See Conference between Governor Clinton and the Indians, *NYCD*, 6:262–67.

[46] See, for example, the descriptions of the Albany Dutch in Thomas Hutchinson, *The History*

more bellicose stance against the French. Hendrick resisted, stating that if Canadian Indians attacked the New Englanders, the Mohawks would go to the offending Indians at least three times to negotiate peace before finally taking up the hatchet.[47]

Hendrick and the Mohawks continued this neutralist diplomacy by traveling to Montreal to treat with the governor of Canada, against the objections of the Albany Indian Commissioners. New Yorkers grew nervous whenever the Mohawks conducted diplomacy outside of Albany, and their trips to Canada always aroused fears that they would desert New York and resettle among the Caughnawagas. The Mohawks, however, insisted that they were going to Canada as peacemakers, to warn the French governor not to attack Oswego.[48] In October 1745, Governor Clinton convened another intercolonial treaty conference in Albany. He gave the Indians there "a large Belt with the figure of a Hatchet hung to it," asking them to join the war against Canada. The Indians told him that they would keep the hatchet "in our bosom" until they had sent a delegation to the French "to demand satisfaction for the wrongs they have done to our Brethren."[49]

These treaty conferences in 1744–45 reveal a distinct pattern. The Mohawks wanted to play the role of mediators, not combatants, in this latest Anglo-French war. Invariably, this plan led to more treaty negotiations in Montreal, Albany, and Boston, all of which had material benefits for the Mohawks. At each conference, the host government provisioned its Indian guests and gave them presents. Intercolonial meetings in Albany could be especially lucrative. Many Indians attended these conferences and enjoyed the hospitality of the New York governor for up to several weeks, and the participation of other colonial delegations meant additional presents. An intercolonial Indian conference had not convened in Albany since 1724; during King George's War, four took place within five

---

of the Colony and Province of Massachusetts-Bay, ed. Lawrence Shaw Mayo, 3 vols. (1936; rpt. New York, 1970), 2:104–39, and William Douglass, A Summary, Historical and Political, of the First Planting, Progressive Improvements, and Present State of the British Settlements in North America, 2 vols. (Boston, 1749, 1751), 1:5, 95. At an Albany conference in 1745, the Massachusetts delegation publicly accused the Albany residents of trading with the French Indians and acting "as if they were Subjects to a Neutral Prince." See Mass. Archives, 29:388, and NYCD, 6:302.
[47] See Meeting between Hendrick and the Governor of Massachusetts, [July 1744?], in Mass. Archives, vol. 29. The date of this meeting can be ascertained by cross-referencing it with Dr. Alexander Hamilton's mention of witnessing a meeting between Hendrick, the Mohawks, and the Massachusetts government when he was in that colony in 1744. See Carl Bridenbaugh, ed., Gentleman's Progress: The Itinerarium of Dr. Alexander Hamilton, 1744 (Chapel Hill, 1948), 112–14.
[48] See ACIA Minutes, June 19?, 1745, 3:65–66. For the New Yorkers' fears that the Mohawks would ally with the French, see Clinton to the Board of Trade, July 25, 1745, NYCD, 6:281–82.
[49] Conference between the Commissioners of the Colonies and the Indians, October 1745, NYCD, 6:296–300.

years.[50] The New York Assembly usually provided the governor with £400 for presents when he convened such meetings. This figure meant a sizable donation of goods; the Albany Indian Commissioners received only £170 annually for presents, many of which went to the Caughnawagas.[51] The Mohawks, as the Iroquois nation nearest Albany, attended these conferences in greater numbers than other Indians and departed with the lion's share of presents. For example, 462 Iroquois attended the Albany conference held in 1745. Of these, 163 were Mohawks, almost twice as many as any other nation. At this time, the Mohawks probably numbered between 400 and 500 people; thus between 33 percent and 41 percent of their population benefited directly from colonial treasuries at this meeting, and that does not include the redistribution of presents among villagers once they returned home.[52]

Colonial officials believed that the Mohawks delayed committing to the British so they could extract the largest possible donations of goods. When Mohawk chiefs stated that they were going to Montreal to convince the French governor not to attack Oswego, the Albany Indian Commissioners suspected their primary objective was to gain presents.[53] At Albany in October 1745, Governor Clinton investigated a local rumor that the British were planning to attack the Mohawks; he concluded that it was "a device of their [the Mohawks'] own contrivance in order to induce this as well as the neighbouring Governments to give them presents this year as they did the last."[54] If so, the ruse worked. This meeting attracted delegations from New York, Pennsylvania, Massachusetts, and Connecticut, all bearing presents. Contemporary Europeans often described Hendrick's role in this diplomacy as aimed only at enriching himself. They did not recognize that his leadership had a redistributive function: he gained power at home by giving away rather than hoarding the goods he acquired at treaty conferences.[55]

---

[50] See the Descriptive Treaty Calendar in Francis Jennings et al., eds., *The History and Culture of Iroquois Diplomacy: An Interdisciplinary Guide to the Treaties of the Six Nations and Their League* (Syracuse, 1985), 173–81.

[51] The appropriations provided by the New York Assembly for Indian presents are recorded in New York Council Minutes. See, for example, NYCM, May 11, 1743, 19:240; December 1, 1743, 19:224; September 3, 1745, 21:41; and June 30, 1746, 21:118.

[52] For the attendance figures of Indians at the 1745 Albany conference, see Isaac Norris, Journal and Account Book, 1733–49, HM 3057, Huntington Library, San Marino, California. Norris, a Pennsylvania commissioner at the conference, recorded the figures in his "Journal of the Treaty at Albany, October 1745," contained in this manuscript. In 1750, an SPG missionary, John Ogilvie, estimated the Mohawks' total population at 418, noting that it had been in decline since King George's War because of migration to Canada. See John Ogilvie to the Secretary, SPG Letterbooks, Ser. B, 18:102–3.

[53] ACIA Minutes, June 19?, 1745, 3:65–66.

[54] *NYCD*, 6:290–95.

[55] See, for example, Conrad Weiser's description of Hendrick in "A Journal of the Proceedings of Conrad Weiser in his Journey to Onondago," *Penn. Council Minutes*, 5:471, and

In addition to presents, such diplomacy gave the Mohawks the chance to cultivate new paths with other colonial governments. Throughout the 1730s and early 1740s, their complaints about land frauds and trading abuses to the Albany Indian Commissioners had gone unheeded. The presence of other colonial officials at wartime conferences gave them a wider audience from which to seek redress. When they had access to an outsider's ear, the Mohawks were especially critical of the Albany Dutch. They first expressed this discontent to Conrad Weiser, a Pennsylvanian Indian agent, who traveled through Iroquoia in 1745. Weiser, the son of a German settler, had grown up in the Schoharie Valley and been adopted by the Mohawks at Tiononderoge before he moved south into Pennsylvania's Susquehanna Valley.[56] In June 1745 he visited Canajoharie, where Hendrick told him that the Mohawks believed "the Albany people did intend to Hurt Us and have in a manner ruined us and would . . . destroy us if they could. They have Cheated Us out of Our Land, Bribed our Chiefs to sign Deeds for them, and treat Us as Slaves." He also complained of Albany's trade with the Caughnawagas and reported that the Albany Indian Commissioners "will never suffer us to go to Boston, Philadelphia or any where upon Invitations of our Brethren," nor would they allow other colonial officials "to come to Our Towns nor Speak to Us unless in their presence." Hendrick concluded, "We could see Albany Burned to the Ground or every Soul taken away . . . [and] other people planted there." At Tiononderoge, Weiser heard from Indians who had met with the Albany Indian Commissioners the previous February. They told him that the Mohawks and commissioners had spoken "only by word of Mouth"—that is, not with honesty or amity—and that "the old Cause that we have been Cheated Out of Our Lands Still remains unsettled."[57]

At the intercolonial Albany conference convened the following October, the Mohawks vented their rage against Albany. In a meeting with Governor Clinton, Hendrick repeated many of his complaints to Weiser about land frauds and the Albany commissioners' interference in the Mohawks' diplomacy. The Mohawks feared that they would soon "become the property of the Albany people . . . their dogs. . . . Served at last as our Brethren the River Indians; they [the Albany people] get all their lands and we shall soon become as poor as they."[58] At this same conference, Hendrick met privately with the Massachusetts commissioners, who encouraged the Mohawks' complaints against Albany and told them that "if we have

[T. Pownall], "[Notes on] Indian Affairs," [1753–54], Loudoun Papers, LO 460:9. On the redistributive economics involved in Indian chieftanship, see Richter, *Ordeal of the Longhouse*, 21–22.

[56] On Weiser's early life in the Mohawk Valley, see Paul A.W. Wallace, *Conrad Weiser, 1696– 1760: Friend of Colonist and Mohawk* (Philadelphia, 1945), 3–38.

[57] See Extract from the Journal of Conrad Weiser, July 29, 1745, in NYCM, 21:33.

[58] *NYCD*, 6:294.

occasion to treat with you hereafter it must be in our own Country or yours."[59]

Hendrick's parlays with Clinton and agents from Pennsylvania and Massachusetts made the Mohawks' discontent an intercolonial issue. They laid their problems at the feet of the "Albany people"—traders, speculators, and Indian commissioners—who had ceased to treat the Mohawks as friends by turning their attention to the Caughnawagas and blocking the Mohawks' paths to other colonies. Such neglect threatened to reduce the Mohawks to wards, no better than the dogs or property of Albany. Here Hendrick's comparison to the River Indians is telling. This group of Indians had suffered defeat at the hands of Dutch and English colonists in the seventeenth century. Now, they attended Albany conferences as "children" of the New York government, addressing the governor and the Albany commissioners as "father" rather than "brethren." This status was what the Mohawks dreaded most: poor, dependent, powerless. The Mohawks' diplomacy at the outbreak of King George's War, therefore, was well suited to their needs. By reviving their role as intermediaries, they retained their autonomy, acquired presents, and gained a new forum for their grievances. Walking the fine line of neutrality allowed them to extract the maximum material benefit from their position in the Covenant Chain.

William Johnson as a Cultural Broker

The Mohawks' neutrality shifted in New York's favor in 1746, when William Johnson became the colony's Indian agent. In August of that year Governor Clinton convened another intercolonial conference in Albany, still hoping to convince the Iroquois to join the war against the French. According to the New York councillor Cadwallader Colden, William Johnson made a grand entrance to the city, riding "at the head of the *Mohawks,* dressed and painted after the Manner of an *Indian* War Captain; and the Indians who followed him were likewise dressed and painted, as is usual with them when they set out in War." The Mohawks entered the city's gates with "a running Fire" from their guns, and the governor returned the salute with the fort's cannon.[60] Johnson's leadership of the Mohawk party impressed Governor Clinton, who abandoned the Albany Indian Commissioners and made Johnson his exclusive Indian

---

[59] See Report of the Massachusetts Commmissioners, October 22, 1745, Mass. Archives, 29:391–92, 410–11.

[60] [New York], *A Treaty between his Excellency . . . George Clinton . . . and the Six . . . Nations* (New York, 1746), 7–8. Alice Mapelsden Keys attributed the authorship of this pamphlet to Colden in *Cadwallader Colden: A Representative Eighteenth Century Official* (New York, 1906), 155–57.

agent. Shortly thereafter, the governor appointed Johnson the colonel and commissary for all Indians he recruited to war against the French.[61]

Johnson's emergence as an Indian agent illustrates the interplay of native and colonial cultures in the Mohawk Valley. Contemporaries attributed his influence among the Mohawks to his familiarity with their way of life. Colden, the author of a history of the Iroquois, believed Johnson exhibited a "compliance with their humours in his dress and conversation." Peter Wraxall, who served as Johnson's secretary in the 1750s, noted that the Indians looked upon him "as their Cheif, their Patron and Brother." Red Head, an Onondaga chief, thanked Johnson at a 1753 conference for speaking to the Indians "in our own way, which is more Intelligable to us, because more conformable to the Customs and Manners of our Fore Fathers." Johnson himself wrote, "I am no Stranger to their Customs and Manners."[62]

Johnson spoke to the Indians in their "own way" through the manipulation of diplomatic ritual and material goods. Like Hendrick, his participation in intercultural diplomacy was an extension of his life in the Mohawk Valley. Whereas Hendrick engaged in diplomacy to gain presents and preserve the Mohawks' independence, Johnson did so to increase his mercantile business. As the chief supplier of soldiers, colonists, and Indians in the Mohawk Valley, he had a vested interest in New York's western fur trade.[63] Intercultural diplomacy helped his trade along this path, and Johnson was particularly skillful at using material goods to impress and please the Indians. He appreciated their customs and rituals, and he distributed presents in a way that reflected the values of reciprocity and friendship that Indians associated with the Covenant Chain.

Between December 1746 and November 1747, Johnson kept an expense account detailing the amount and types of goods he distributed as presents to the Indians. According to this account, Johnson spent almost £3,500 on his Indian agency during these twelve months.[64] This is a remarkable figure when compared to the £570 that the New York Assembly allotted annually to the governor and Albany Indian Commissioners for presents

---

[61] See Clinton to William Johnson, August 27 and August 28, 1746, *WJ Papers*, 1:59–61, and Clinton to the Duke of Newcastle, December 9, 1746, *NYCD*, 6:314.

[62] Colden, "The Present State of the Indian Affairs with the British and French Colonies in North America," August 8, 1751, in *Cadwallader Colden Papers, Collections of the New York Historical Society* 53 (1920): 272; Wraxall, *Abridgment of the Indian Affairs*, 248; Minutes of Johnson's Conference at Onondaga, September 8–10, 1753, in NYCM, 23:114; and Johnson to William Shirley, December 17, 1754, *WJ Papers*, 1:433.

[63] In addition to supplying the Indians during King George's War, Johnson served as the commissary for the garrison at Oswego. See Johnson to John Catherwood, April 14, 1746, *WJ Papers*, 1:49. Cadwallader Colden referred to him as "the most considerable trader with the Western Indians and sends more goods to Oswego than any other person does." See Colden, "Present State of the Indian Affairs," 273–74.

[64] For this account, see *WJ Papers*, 9:15–30.

to the Indians. In Johnson, the Mohawks found a new source of goods, one that was much more reliable and generous than they had ever had before.

From this account, Johnson's disbursements can be broken down into nine categories, each involving a different type of good or service that he provided to the Indians (see table 1.1). His largest expense—accounting for 30.3 percent of the total—was for food and drink, which he distributed to Indian men, women, and children depending on the circumstances. War parties and scouts received provisions to sustain themselves during their forays into Canada. Chiefs and warriors who met with Johnson in diplomatic councils received "entertainments" or "treats" that included ceremonial feasting and drinking, such as "for a Warr dance."[65] Johnson also distributed food to the women and children of Indian men who were away fighting.

Johnson's second largest expense, accounting for 26.7 percent of the total, was for clothing. As with food and drink, the clothing he distributed depended on the recipient. Warriors received garments and accoutrements associated with war-making: hunting shirts, laps, ribbon, and paint. Some items were functional, such as snowshoes and hides used in winter raids, while warriors used others, such as ribbons and paint, to decorate their bodies for battle. Chiefs received many of these goods, but their presents always included a ruffled shirt, laced hat, fine coat, or silver medal. For example, on May 11, 1747, ten Indians visited Mount Johnson. To nine, Johnson gave a shirt, paint, and knives. To the tenth, whom he identified as "the Captain," he gave paint and knives, along with "A Shirt very fine with Ruffles and ribon" and "A fine lac'd Hatt . . . with a Cockade."[66] Presents to warriors prepared the body for war; presents to chiefs prepared it for diplomacy (see Figs. 1.3 and 1.4). Johnson also distributed clothing in much larger quantities to Indian villagers, just as he provided them with food. This clothing tended to be utilitarian rather than ceremonial, including strouds (a coarse woolen cloth), blankets, stockings, shirts, and deerskins. He also provided black burial strouds to the relatives of deceased Indians, who considered such items necessary for grieving rituals.[67]

In addition to food, drink, and clothing, Johnson distributed numerous other goods. War supplies, 11.9 percent of the total, included guns, ammunition, hatchets, knives, and the pipes and tobacco that always accompanied war parties. Tools and wares, 1.3 percent of the total, included

[65] See entries made on March 10 and March 19, 1747, for war dances that Johnson sponsored, ibid., 18.
[66] Ibid., 23.
[67] Johnson's distribution of clothing as an Indian present is discussed more fully in Timothy J. Shannon, "Dressing for Success on the Mohawk Frontier: Hendrick, William Johnson, and the Indian Fashion," WMQ 53 (1996): 13–42.

Table 1.1. William Johnson's Expenses as New York's Indian Agent, December 1746–November 1747

Item	Value (£)	Percent of subtotal (%)	Percent of total expense (%)
Food and drink			
provisions for scouts and war parties	602.18.0	57.9	
entertainments and treats for warriors, chiefs, and villagers	324.9.0	31.1	
provisions for women, children, prisoners	114.4.0	11.0	
Subtotal for food and drink:	1,041.11.0	100	30.3
Clothing			
for women, children, prisoners, or unspecified use	629.5.2	68.6	
for warriors	149.8.7	16.3	
for chiefs	114.11.0	12.5	
for the bereaved	24.8.0	2.6	
Subtotal for clothing:	917.12.9	100	26.7
War supplies	408.1.9		11.9
Tools and wares	44.3.11		1.3
Cash	108.6.0		3.1
Other presents (goods not specified)	104.16.0		3.0
Diplomatic expenses			
scalp and prisoner bounties	419.0.0	65.5	
wampum	148.3.6	23.1	
messengers	73.4.6	11.4	
Subtotal for diplomatic expenses:	640.8.0	100	18.6
Transportation	94.14.6		2.8
Miscellaneous services	77.14.6		2.3
Total	3,437.8.5		100

Source: WJ Papers, 9:15–31.

kettles and many cloth-working items used by Indian women. Cash gifts accounted for 3.1 percent of the total, and other presents in which the goods were not specified accounted for 3.0 percent. The remaining three categories of Johnson's disbursements involved services that he either rendered to the Indians or that he paid them to provide to him. Expenses associated with conducting diplomacy, for example, accounted for 18.6 percent of his total disbursements. They included rewarding Indian messengers, purchasing wampum, and paying scalp and prisoner bounties to Indian warriors. The costs of transporting Indians and goods between Albany, Mount Johnson, and Indian villages accounted for 2.8 percent of the total. Miscellaneous services such as mending guns and axes and fortifying Canajoharie accounted for the remaining 2.3 percent of Johnson's expenses.

Although Johnson conducted diplomacy with Indians from all the Iro-

Figure 1.3. "Guerrier Iroquois," hand-colored etching, by J. Laroque, from Jacques Grasset de Saint-Sauveur, *Encyclopedie des voyages* . . . , volume 2: *Amerique* (Paris, 1796). Courtesy of the National Archives of Canada, C-003163.

Figure 1.4. "Grand Chef de Guerriers Iroquois," hand-colored etching, by J. Laroque, from Jacques Grasset de Saint-Sauveur, *Encyclopedie des voyages* . . . , volume 2: *Amerique* (Paris, 1796). Courtesy of the National Archives of Canada, C-003161.

quois nations, his account entries indicate that the Mohawks, particularly those from Canajoharie, benefited the most from his generosity. He served as their agent, employer, and patron to the New York government, and he constantly supplied them with goods ranging from the sacred to the mundane. The Mohawks were his nearest Indian neighbors, and he had to retain their favor if he wished to draw other Indians to the British cause. Of the account's 227 entries, 73 identified Indian nations or villages by name; the Mohawks were mentioned 36 times, 29 more times than any other group. Johnson also mentioned by name 35 Indians with whom he conducted business, of whom 28 were Mohawks. He presented Mohawk chiefs, warriors, and women with gifts individually and collectively, entertaining them in his home and in their villages, feeding, clothing, and arming them and helping them mourn their dead.

It is in these account entries that Johnson's relationship with Hendrick first emerges. Hendrick's name appears thirteen times, eight more than any other Indian's. He received from Johnson a pair of boots, a laced coat, medicine, cash, and an unspecified "private present," as well as provisions, transportation, and entertainments for his warriors, relatives, and dependents.[68] Not surprisingly, most of the warriors Johnson recruited came from Hendrick's village. Three consecutive entries from May 24, 1747, record a typical example of Johnson's expenditures on Canajoharie:

For the Conajohees families Provision £18.6
Cloathing for their Women and Children being naked £49.1
A Treat to the Conajohees Mohawks when they brought in,
   in One Day 15 Prisoners and Scalps and Stayed 3 Days £12.5

These entries indicate the depth of Johnson's commitment to Canajoharie: when sponsoring one war party, he ended up providing several families with food and clothing, as well as bounty payments and an "entertainment" to the warriors. On another occasion, Johnson provided "an Entertainment given to the whole Castle of Conajohee" that included an ox, eight gallons of rum, and a barrel of beer. After a disastrous raid in June 1747 that killed several Mohawks, Johnson's accounts show entries for cash, provisions, and clothing given to eight widows and their children, totaling over £38.[69]

The sheer amount of goods supplied by Johnson could be misleading; quantity was not the only reason for his success with the Mohawks. Indeed, any agent with resources from a colonial or royal treasury could dump goods in the Indians' laps. Critics of the Albany Indian Commis-

---

[68] Other Mohawks named multiple times in this account include Hendrick's brother Abraham (four times) and his son Young Hendrick (twice).
[69] For these entries, see *WJ Papers*, 9:24, 27, 28.

sioners often complained that colonial officials saddled Indians with wagon loads of goods, caring little for how they presented them or how the Indians got them home. Local merchants then traded rum to the Indians for their presents as they left the city, only to sell the goods back to them at "a dear rate" later.[70] Such conduct on the part of colonial officials indicated either a stubborn ignorance or callous disregard for the protocol of Iroquois diplomacy.

Johnson, by contrast, exhibited a keen appreciation for the cultural context of gift giving. His account entries indicate that he selected his presents according to the intended recipient and presented them in culturally sanctioned ways. To Indians, peace and alliance could not be purchased by large, onetime donations of goods. Rather, they needed to be continually renewed by the periodic exchange of presents. As Johnson explained it, in addition to large presents made at treaty conferences, the Indians "expect to be indulged with constant little Presents, this from the Nature of the Indians cannot be avoided and must be complied with."[71]

A large proportion of the goods Johnson distributed fell into this category of "constant little Presents." Besides making grants to entire villages, he presented goods in one-to-one encounters, often noting the recipient by name in his accounts. Consider, for example, Johnson's observance of Indians' condolence rituals. When a treaty conference began, Europeans and Indians usually exchanged speeches to honor each side's recent dead. The Indians also expected and customarily received a present of black burial strouds. When colonial agents did not make these presents, Indians might delay negotiations until the proper ceremony had been observed.[72] Johnson regularly complained that the Albany magistrates ignored this custom in treating with the Indians. "This ceremony is also attended with a great deal of form," he explained to Clinton in 1749, "it was always neglected in the late [Albany Indian] Commissioners time, which gave the French an opportunity of doing it." To Weiser, Johnson wrote that the

[70] See the complaints levied against the Albany Indian Commissioners by New York councillor Archibald Kennedy in *The Importance of Gaining and Preserving the Friendship of the Indians*, 23. Also see Conrad Weiser's criticism of Governor Clinton for leaving a 1751 Albany conference without properly distributing the presents in his "Journal of the proceedings of Conrad Weiser in his Journey to Albany," reproduced in Wallace, *Conrad Weiser*, 329, and [Thomas Pownall to Lord Halifax], July 23, 1754, in Beverly McAnear, ed., "Personal Accounts of the Albany Congress of 1754," *Mississippi Valley Historical Review* 39 (1953): 743. New York governors attending Albany treaty conferences often issued proclamations that forbade trading with the Indians for their presents, but as Pownall observed, local merchants ignored such prohibitions. For one such proclamation, issued by Governor James DeLancey on July 5, 1754, see NYCM, 78:146.

[71] Johnson to William Shirley, May 16, 1755, *WJ Papers*, 1:505.

[72] For a typical example of a condolence exchange, see the minutes to a council held in Albany in 1751, ibid., 340–42. At a treaty conference in Carlisle, Pennsylvania, in 1753, the Indians refused to begin negotiations until the proper condolence presents arrived. See *A Treaty Held with the Ohio Indians at Carlisle in October, 1753* (Philadelphia, 1753), 3.

condolence ceremony was "always expected by the five Nations to be performed by Us, and [is] what they look much upon." His account entries record private condolence presents to Indians as well. An entry from May 7, 1747, lists "1 Black stroud" given to a Mohawk chief "after the Decease of his Son." Another from the same date notes "A Black Stroud for Nickus of Conajohees' Child."[73]

Royal governors believed the presents they gave to Indians in Albany symbolized the recipients' submission to the British Crown. New York governor William Burnet told the Indians attending a 1724 conference that King George II was "your only true and Loving father, who has often fed you and Cloathed you, and is always making you kind presents." In return, the king expected "Obedience, as becomes good Children."[74] The Indians, on the other hand, perceived presents as evidence of mutual respect and equality between friends. By making "constant little Presents" and observing ceremonial detail, Johnson adopted the Indians' perspective. He recognized the important role goods played in intercultural relations, both in providing the Indians with material necessities and in symbolizing friendship and goodwill.

By late 1746, New York's Indian relations had reconfigured around Johnson and the Canajoharie Mohawks. Angered by the governor's use of another agent, the Albany Indian Commissioners resigned.[75] During the following year Johnson sponsored Mohawk raids along the Canadian frontier. His mercantile business expanded dramatically as he supplied warriors and their families, and the governor thanked him with political favors, including a commission as a colonel in the Albany militia and a seat on the governor's council.[76] By trading his influence among the Mohawks for the governor's patronage, Johnson rose rapidly in New York's social and political ranks. Among his Indian neighbors, he acquired the name "Warraghiyagey," which loosely translated to "doer of great things."[77] The Mohawks came to regard him as their indispensable agent to the New York government. As one Indian speaker, probably Hendrick, explained to New York's governor in 1751, "one half of Colonel Johnson belonged to his Excellency, and the other to them [the Mohawks]."[78]

Through Johnson, the Mohawks opened a new path for their diplomacy but did not foreclose others. Despite their participation in Johnson's raid-

---

[73] See Johnson to Clinton, May 26, 1749, *NYCD*, 6:512–13, and Johnson to Weiser, April 2, 1751, *WJ Papers*, 1:326. For the account entries, see *WJ Papers*, 9:17.
[74] ACIA Minutes, September 15, 1724, 1:88a–89.
[75] Ibid., October 27, November 24, 1746, 2:402, 405–6.
[76] See Clinton to Johnson, May 1, 1748, and Johnson to Clinton, December 20, 1750, in *WJ Papers*, 1:166–67, 315–16.
[77] See Hamilton, *Sir William Johnson*, 45.
[78] *WJ Papers*, 1:342. The speaker of this comment is unidentified, but the treaty minutes identify Hendrick in an earlier exchange with Clinton on this topic.

ing parties, they always held out the possibility of defecting to the French to extract what they wanted from the British. At a meeting in July 1747, the Mohawks told Governor Clinton they thought him not earnest in his promises to conquer Canada and warned that if he alienated them, he would find it hard to "satisfye all our Friends and Allies, the far distant Nations (who daily flock to us and offer their services when we call upon them)." A few weeks later Hendrick declared that "unless the English made some attempt against the French this year, they [the Mohawks] would leave the country."[79] In such statements, Hendrick continued to capitalize on the Mohawks' role as intermediaries, threatening to jeopardize New York's relations with other Indians if the colony did not prosecute the war more effectively.

The colonial expedition against Canada never occurred, and the Mohawks suffered heavily in their raids against the French.[80] When Governor Clinton and Massachusetts governor William Shirley met with the Six Nations in Albany in 1748, word of an Anglo-French peace had already arrived in America. The two governors wished to keep this news from the Mohawks, who "were under great Uneasiness and Jealousy from the Disappointments they had with since joining with us." As expected, the Mohawks were angered by the declaration of a truce without their consultation and stated their intention to renew diplomacy with Canada. Only through the intercession of Johnson did Clinton and Shirley convince them to remain at home.[81]

A Broken Chain, a Blocked Path

In addition to the loss of men killed in battle, King George's War disrupted the Mohawks' domestic economy. At a conference with them in 1748, Governor Clinton distributed food to the Mohawks, "as their Crops of Corn and their hunting failed this year, which they said was occasion'd by their being engaged in the War."[82] These conditions worsened rather than improved when peace came. In 1750, a new SPG missionary arrived in Albany, the first in five years. The Reverend John Ogilvie

---

[79] See Clinton's conference with the Indians, July 16, 1747, NYCD, 6:303, and NYCM, August 3, 1747, 21:264. In August 1747 Johnson echoed many of these warnings in his correspondence with Clinton. See NYCD, 6:387–90.

[80] For contemporary reports of the Mohawks' losses in battle, see Johnson to Clinton, March 18, 1747, WJ Papers, 1:81, and Clinton's conference with the Mohawks, July 1747, NYCD, 6:383.

[81] See Clinton and Shirley to the Board of Trade, August 18, 1748, NYCD, 6:437–40, and their proceedings with the Six Nations, July 1748, ibid., 441–52. For William Johnson's efforts to keep the Mohawks at home, see Johnson to Clinton, May 26, August 19, 1749, and February 19, 1750, ibid., 512–13, 525–26, 547. For a good analysis of the Mohawks' role in King George's War, see Steele, Betrayals, 18–27.

[82] NYCD, 6:438.

reported to his superiors that the Mohawks had "universally degenerated Since the War. . . . Many seem to have lost all sense of Religion, and the best are in a state of Indifference." The rum trade continued unabated, and Ogilvie was horrified by the violence it caused in the Mohawks' villages. Their population had dropped as well, which Ogilvie blamed on "the Numbers who have gone over to the french Interest and settled in their Territories" since the war. In another sign of the pressure that colonization was placing on the Mohawks, Ogilvie found that he often baptized and preached to as many Europeans as Indians when visiting Fort Hunter and Canajoharie.[83]

The Mohawks' postwar condition deteriorated in part because Johnson resigned his office as New York's Indian agent in 1750. By his own accounting, Johnson spent £7,177 on Indian presents during his tenure.[84] His liberality caused friction with the New York Assembly, which had protested Johnson's appointment by refusing to reimburse him. Johnson responded by soliciting a royal appointment as Indian agent, which would provide him with a salary and expenses drawn from the Crown. To force the hand of Governor Clinton and his London superiors, Johnson resigned his post before an intercolonial treaty conference scheduled for 1751.[85]

Johnson's resignation cut off the Mohawks' access to presents. They responded by turning to the alternative paths of diplomacy they had opened during the war. Under Hendrick's leadership, they continued to receive presents from the French governor in Canada.[86] During the early 1750s, Hendrick also pursued diplomacy with Pennsylvania through Conrad Weiser. Since opening diplomacy with the Iroquois, Pennsylvania had dealt mostly with the Onondagas and rarely with the Mohawks. Nevertheless, when Weiser tried in 1750 to negotiate peace between the Six Nations and the Catawbas—a southern nation on the Carolina frontier—Hendrick offered his services as an intermediary "if the Governor of Carolina would make him, Henry, a handsome Present, or pay him well for his trouble." The Mohawks at Tiononderoge later told Weiser that their affairs with the New York government "lay neglected and nobody minded them," a subtle offer to join in Pennsylvania's Indian diplomacy.[87] In 1751 Weiser returned

[83] See Ogilvie to the Secretary of the SPG, July 27, 1750, April 14, 1751, and June 29, 1752, in SPG Letterbooks, Ser. B, 18:102–3; 19:71, 20:55.

[84] See Council at Albany, July 2, 1751, *WJ Papers*, 1:343.

[85] For the assembly's objections to Johnson's appointment, see Remonstrance of the New York Assembly to George Clinton, October 9, 1747, *NYCD*, 6:619–20. For Johnson's criticisms of the assembly and his efforts to gain a royal appointment, see Johnson to George Clinton, November 22, 1749, ibid., 541. Also see Johnson to Peter Warren, July 24, 1749, and Johnson to Clinton, December 20, 1750, *WJ Papers*, 1:238–41, 313–16.

[86] For reports of the Mohawks' diplomacy with Canada, see the correspondence between Johnson and Clinton in 1749 and 1750, in *NYCD*, 6:520, 525–26, 546, 589–91.

[87] See Report of Conrad Weiser's Journal on his Journey to Onondaga, August–December 1750, *Penn. Council Minutes*, 5:471. Also see Helga Doblin and William A. Starna, trans. and

to Albany to distribute condolence presents to the Indians on behalf of Pennsylvania and Virginia. He also left his son at Tiononderoge to learn the Mohawks' language. Two years later he visited the Mohawks again.[88] Along the way, he encountered Hendrick en route to Stockbridge, a village of Christian Indians in western Massachusetts. In the early 1750s, Massachusetts officials tried to convince the Mohawks to resettle near Stockbridge to strengthen New England's security. Hendrick apparently took this offer seriously and continued to treat with Massachusetts independently of Albany.[89]

At the heart of the Mohawks' complaints against Albany was their insistence that the New Yorkers had not observed the proper condolence rituals for them since King George's War. Johnson warned Clinton in 1750 that unless he renewed the Covenant Chain with the Mohawks "in a Handsome manner . . . they will certainly think themselves Slighted by us."[90] The governor never granted the appropriate presents. At the only major Albany conference to convene between 1748 and 1754, Clinton left town early, leaving his presents to the Indians undivided and "without taking Some of them [the Indians] by the hand or Saying So Much as farewell." According to Weiser, this neglect left the Indians "very Much exasperated."[91] At a conference in Philadelphia four years later, Hendrick traced the Mohawks' discontent to the aftermath of King George's War, when they received "No Presents . . . No Notice of Peace, No Satisfaction for Blood Spilled." They had "no Countenance nor Respect shewed to Us at Albany," where the Caghnawagas "are extremely caressed . . . supplied with every Thing they want, while no Notice is taken of Us."[92] This failure to observe diplomatic ritual doubly damned the New Yorkers in the Mohawks' eyes, for it denied them necessary goods and signaled an utter disregard for their wartime losses.

Clinton reinstated the Albany Indian Commissioners in November 1752, despite the Mohawks' request to have no one but Johnson as their

---

eds., *The Journals of Christian Daniel Claus and Conrad Weiser: A Journey to Onondaga, 1750* (Philadelphia, 1994).

[88] Weiser's work among the Mohawks at this time suggests that he was trying to wean them away from their affinity for Johnson, whom he considered an untutored upstart in the ways of Anglo-Iroquois diplomacy. See Wallace, *Conrad Weiser*, 247–54, 304–50. Also see the analysis of the Weiser-Johnson rivalry offered by William A. Starna in "Conrad Weiser among the Iroquois," paper presented at 1996 Conference on Iroquois Research, Rensselaerville, New York.

[89] See A Journal of the proceedings of Conrad Weiser in his Journey to Albany, 1751, reproduced in Wallace, *Conrad Weiser*, 329–31, and Journal of Conrad Weiser's Visit to the Mohawks, September 2, 1753, *NYCD*, 6:795–99. On the Massachusetts efforts to win over the Mohawks, see McAnear, ed., "Personal Accounts," 736, n. 43.

[90] Johnson to Clinton, May 4, 1750, *WJ Papers*, 1:278.

[91] See Wallace, *Conrad Weiser*, 329–30.

[92] Hendrick to Pennsylvania governor Robert Hunter Morris, January 17, 1755, *Penn. Council Minutes*, 6:281–83.

agent. Johnson observed that the Albany commissioners paid little heed to the Mohawks anyway and devoted themselves instead to the Caughnawagas. A year passed and the commissioners still had not invited the Mohawks to Albany for a conference.[93] With no treaty conferences or presents to maintain good relations, tensions between the Mohawks and their colonial neighbors returned. Mohawk complaints against the rum traffic through their villages became more insistent. Hendrick, through the intercession of Reverend Ogilvie, petitioned the governor in 1751 to prohibit the liquor trade in the Mohawk Valley; in July 1753 the Indians repeated this request, noting in particular the trade conducted by the inhabitants of German Flatts.[94] As the Mohawks' poverty increased, they placed greater demands on the local colonists for support. In August 1752 Johnson reported that famine pressed the Mohawks "to leave their Castles and come among the Inhabitants there [in the Mohawk Valley] for Relief."[95]

By 1753 the Mohawks considered the Covenant Chain broken. Their grievances against land fraud, the liquor trade, and diplomatic neglect had gone unanswered. During the war they restored some of their prestige by dealing directly with Johnson and other colonial governments. With the war's end and Johnson's resignation, those conferences and the presents evaporated. The disruption of diplomacy had severe material consequences for the Mohawks: no Johnson meant no clothing, provisions, or arms with which to support themselves, which led to social deterioration and out-migration. The Mohawks' lament to Weiser in 1745 had apparently come true. The New Yorkers no longer treated them as brethren but as their dogs and property.

This breakdown prompted Hendrick and sixteen other Mohawks to travel to New York City in June 1753 to see Governor Clinton. Their trip was highly unusual because the governor usually treated with the Indians at Albany on his, not their, initiative. The Indians, however, seemed intent on confronting the governor outside of Albany.[96] In his opening speech to Clinton, Hendrick stated that "the indifference and neglect shewn towards us makes our hearts ake, and if you dont alter your Behaviour to us we fear the Covenant Chain will be broken." Lest Clinton not comprehend the importance of the chain, Hendrick reminded him that it kept "the Roads amongst our Nations open and clear." He warned against evasive an-

---

[93] See Clinton to Johnson, November 5, 1752, and Johnson to Clinton, March 12, 1754, *WJ Papers*, 1:383, 9:123–24; NYCM, November 16, 1752, and November 7, 1753, 23:45, 125; and *NYCD*, 6:720, 725.
[94] NYCM, June 19, 1751, and July 3, 1753, 23:85.
[95] Ibid., August 21, 1752, 23:40.
[96] On the Mohawks' departure for New York, see Johnson to Clinton, May 22, 1753, *WJ Papers*, 9:104–5, and NY Col. Mss., June 5, 1753, 77:96.

swers, telling the governor, "we therefore desire you will do some thing immediately or tell us at once you will do nothing at all for us."[97]

In private councils with Clinton, Hendrick and three other chiefs presented complaints of land frauds perpetrated by Dutch and German residents of Albany County. Pressed by the governor to be specific, they named eight cases involving lands near Canajoharie in which colonial purchasers took up more acreage than the Indians agreed to sell. Clinton found the disputed patents in order and referred the Indians to the Albany Indian Commissioners, who could investigate the alleged frauds further.[98] This answer obviously did not please the Mohawks, who had disavowed working with the commissioners and named three of their number in their accusations.[99]

After hearing Clinton's answer, Hendrick ended the proceedings. He warned that should "any accident happen" to surveyors working near Canajoharie, "we hope you Brother will not expect any satisfaction from us." As for the Albany Indian Commissioners, "we know them so well, we will not trust them, for they are no people but Devils, so we rather desire you'l say, Nothing shall be done for us." Upon returning home, the Mohawks would send a wampum belt among the rest of the Six Nations "to acquaint them the Covenant Chain is broken between you and us. So brother you are not to expect to hear of me any more, and Brother we desire to hear no more from you. And we shall no longer acquaint you with any News or affairs as we used to do." The Indians left abruptly, without any of the customary ceremonies.[100]

Never before had a Covenant Chain treaty conference ended in such a manner, nor had anyone ever declared it broken. A few Mohawks had upset the grand alliance on which New York's Indian relations and Great Britain's pretensions to North American empire rested. The Mohawks did not threaten war; rather, they remained true to their role as diplomatic intermediaries, saying only that they would block any further interaction between the New Yorkers and those Indian nations farther west. The meaning of this "blocked path" became clear once the Mohawks returned home. In Schenectady, they told Arent Stevens, New York's Indian interpreter, that if the governor sent him to Onondaga with any messages for the Iroquois, they would stop him at Canajoharie. In July 1753, Clinton received a message from the Canajoharies informing him that "they will not come down to Albany to speak with him; nor suffer Arent Stevens to pass their Castle to go to the five Nations; and that the Nations shall not

---

[97] Speech of Hendrick to Governor Clinton, June 12, 1753, *NYCD*, 6:781–82.
[98] Ibid., 784–87.
[99] The Mohawks named three current or former Albany Indian Commissioners in their accusations: Philip Livingston Jr., Edward Collins, and Cornelius Cuyler. See ibid., 784–85.
[100] Ibid., 787–88.

come down [to Albany]."[101] The metaphor of a blocked path translated literally into the New Yorkers' inability to communicate with the Six Nations.

Some colonial observers attributed the severing of the Covenant Chain to Hendrick's taste for presents. That was certainly how the members of the New York Assembly perceived it, and they recommended that Clinton deal with the problem by making "a private present of twenty Spanish Dollars" to Hendrick along with an additional £200 worth of presents for his people.[102] Others suspected the hand of William Johnson, guessing that he urged the Mohawks to break the Covenant Chain so he might gain royal favor by mending it. Johnson remained curiously silent during the affair and later reprimanded the Mohawks for their conduct in New York City.[103] Whatever machinations Hendrick and Johnson may have engaged in, the reasons behind the Mohawks' disaffection were compelling enough: fraudulent patents to the land on which their villages stood, a rum trade that was destroying their communities, out-migration of their dwindling numbers to Canada; and the failure of the New Yorkers to acknowledge their wartime losses properly.

When Hendrick declared the Covenant Chain broken, he acted not as some grand Iroquois spokesman but as a Mohawk leader angered by his village's decline. The harsh realities of a changing frontier economy had pushed the Mohawks into a corner, eroding their subsistence and threatening their land. In the wake of Johnson's resignation as Indian agent, the New Yorkers had also defaulted in their diplomacy, failing to observe ceremonies and to provide presents that helped sustain the Mohawks. Hendrick *did not break* the Covenant Chain; he merely recognized it as *being broken* and laid the fault squarely at the feet of the New Yorkers.

In addressing their crisis, the Mohawks created one of imperial dimensions for the royal officials who governed British North America. The British invested tremendous value in the Covenant Chain. It represented Iroquois dependence on the British Crown, which in turn legitimized Brit-

---

[101] Stevens to Johnson, June 21, 1753, NY Col. Mss., 77:108; Canajoharie Mohawks to Clinton, June 1753, ibid., 115; and NYCM, July 28, 1753, 23:88.

[102] See NYCM, June 15, 1753, 23:78.

[103] In a summary of New York Indian affairs written shortly after this event, Thomas Pownall questioned what role Johnson may have played in motivating the Mohawks. See Pownall, [Notes on] Indian Affairs: [Abuses in Trade and Land Jobbing], [1753–54], Loudoun Papers, LO 460:6. William Livingston, a prominent New York attorney, also suspected the hand of Johnson in the Mohawks' behavior. See [William Livingston], *A Review of Military Operations in North-America* (New York, 1757), 76–77. For Johnson's comments on the Mohawks' trip to New York City, see Johnson to Clinton, May 22, 1753, *WJ Papers*, 9:104–5, and the minutes from Johnson's conference with the Mohawks, July 26–27, 1753, NYCM, 23:114. Johnson, as a New York councillor, was in New York at the time of the Mohawks' visit and attended the governor's meetings with them but apparently took no special role in the proceedings. See *NYCD*, 6:781–88.

ish territorial claims in the Great Lakes and the Ohio Valley. Allowing the chain to break would be tantamount to renouncing those claims, admitting Iroquois independence, and capitulating to French expansion in the continent's interior. Thus news of Hendrick's declaration traveled quickly to London and caused a flurry of activity in the ministry. The Board of Trade, which supervised the Crown's correspondence with America, sent word back to the colonial governors, ordering them to convene an intercolonial conference to mend the broken chain.[104]

[104] Lords of Trade to Sir Danvers Osbourne, September 18, 1753, *NYCD*, 6:800–802.

[2]

An Imperial Path to Albany: The British Empire and Britannia's Americans

This Modelling [of] the People into various Orders, and Subordinations of Orders, so as to be capable of receiving and communicating any political Motion, and acting under that Direction as a one Whole, is what the *Romans* called by the peculiar Word *Imperium,* to express which particular Group of Ideas, we have no Word in *English* but by adopting the Word *Empire.* 'Tis by this System only that a People become a political Body; 'tis the Chain, the Bond of Union, by which very vague and independent Particles cohere.

—Thomas Pownall, 1752

I would not thereby be thought to create a Jealousy that the Inhabitants of our Colonies in this Age, are in any ways disposed to throw off their Dependency . . . and so insinuate that they ought to be kept under and governed on Principles of Government more strict and severe than what other Subjects of this Nation are. But, without any such insinuation or false alarm . . . whoever considers seriously must reflect and allow that although they are Subjects, yet they are Subjects under peculiar Circumstances, formed into Separate Societys that in time may feel their new Strength . . . this *difference* is a very material one, whether they are [to] remain Subjects, or to become Confederates.

—James Abercromby, 1752

In October 1753 New York's new royal governor, Sir Danvers Osborne, arrived in the colony, accompanied by his secretary Thomas Pownall. Pownall had most recently worked along with his brother John as a clerk for the Board of Trade, the Crown's advisory council on colonial policy. Thomas was able to secure his appointment to Osborne through his connections there. Young and ambitious, he hoped his sojourn in America would gain him the expertise and patronage necessary for a more prestigious position in colonial administration.[1] Pownall also came to America with a great deal of intellectual curiosity. Many years later, he recalled that upon his arrival, "My imagination was all suspense and every thing made a vivid impression on my mind." His first memory of New York City was the inviting smell of the smoke from the cedar chips colonists used to light their fires, a stark contrast to "the suffocating smell of our Coal Fires" in London.[2] While in America, Pownall collected and recorded such experiences, mentally sizing up this new terrain and trying to fit it into his vision of a British-Atlantic empire.

Pownall's fortunes took an abrupt turn a few days after he landed. Osborne committed suicide, despondent over his prospects in the notoriously factious New York government.[3] The governorship passed to James DeLancey, a member of New York City's mercantile elite, and Pownall found himself with neither patron nor position. He took it upon himself to become a roving observer for the Board of Trade and for the next two years cut his own path through North America. He visited colonies from Virginia to Massachusetts, meeting with governors, attending assembly sessions, and initiating friendships with prominent colonists. He discussed electricity with Benjamin Franklin, Indian relations with William Johnson, and geography with Pennsylvanian mapmaker Lewis Evans. By the time he returned to London in 1756, he had acquired a reputation on both sides of the Atlantic for his knowledge of colonial affairs. The Board of Trade rewarded him with the governorship of Massachusetts, which he assumed in 1757.[4]

Pownall's American apprenticeship included attendance at the Albany Congress of 1754. Although he had no official role in the proceedings, he observed them closely. Treaty-making fascinated him, and he tried to interpret it for his patron the Earl of Halifax, while at the same time relating details about the proceedings not recorded in the official minutes.[5] To make the strange rituals of Iroquois diplomacy comprehensible, Pownall used analogies rooted in the experiences of a British gentleman: the Indians raised their shout of approval, *"Yo-heigh-eigh,"* in the same manner "as the Huntsman sounds the *Hark Forward"*; Indian orators were so

[1] On Pownall's early life and his connections to the Board of Trade, see John A. Schutz, *Thomas Pownall, British Defender of American Liberty: A Study of Anglo-American Relations in the Eighteenth Century* (Glendale, Calif., 1951), 15–30.
[2] Pownall, *Topographical Description*, 41. Pownall originally published this work in 1776 as *A Topographical Description of North America;* it was based on notes, drawings, and computations he made during time spent in the colonies in the 1750s. The edition cited here is based on a revised edition he finished in 1784 but never published.
[3] See Patricia U. Bonomi, *A Factious People: Politics and Society in Colonial New York* (New York, 1971), 140–78.
[4] Schutz, *Thomas Pownall*, 68–84.
[5] [Thomas Pownall to the Earl of Halifax], July 23, [17]54, in McAnear, ed., "Personal Accounts," 740–46.

skilled in the arts of "Political Farce and Compliment" as to "actually exceed the Europeans."[6] At the conclusion of the proceedings, Pownall presented to the colonial delegates his own proposals for intercolonial cooperation in Indian diplomacy and military affairs.[7] In this manner, he managed to get his name inserted into the Albany Congress's official minutes, which further boosted his reputation.

The route Pownall took to Albany was quite different from that of Hendrick or William Johnson. They had followed a local path, one shaped by the changing economy and intercultural relations of the Mohawk Valley. Pownall, in contrast, arrived at the Albany Congress as a stranger to its local participants, a self-described "Stander-by."[8] He might have portrayed himself more truthfully as an unemployed minor official seeking work in British North America. Such a description would have placed him among many other royal officials who came to the colonies by way of the patronage networks that helped govern the empire.[9] Pownall's path was circular, leading out of London into colonial marchlands and eventually back again to the corridors of Whitehall and Parliament.

Yet Pownall was more than a mere placeman. Unlike his erstwhile employer Osborne, he had come to America to start, not end, a life. His position as Osborne's secretary was a toehold in imperial administration, and America offered him a laboratory for his interests in history, politics, and science. In 1752, a year before departing for New York, Pownall published *The Principles of Polity, Being the Grounds and Reasons of Civil Empire*, a long theoretical treatise on the origins of civil government. During his stay in America, he acquired the practical knowledge that informed his most famous work, *The Administration of the Colonies*, which went through five editions between 1764 and 1774. In these books, Pownall used the language of Newtonian physics to explain the natural laws behind political society. He described liberty and commerce as the gravitational forces that caused the different parts of the British Empire to cohere and emphasized the need for it to have a fixed center around which its subordinate polities

---

[6] Ibid., 741.
[7] For Pownall's speech, see "Mr. Pownall's Considerations towards a General Plan of Measures for the Colonies," July 11, 1754, in *NYCD*, 6:893–97. Also see Schutz, *Thomas Pownall*, 37–43.
[8] McAnear, "Personal Accounts," 740.
[9] On the nature of such transatlantic patronage networks, see Stanley N. Katz, *Newcastle's New York: Anglo-American Politics, 1732–1753* (Cambridge, Mass., 1968), and Alison Gilbert Olson and Richard Maxwell Brown, eds., *Anglo-American Political Relations, 1675–1775* (New Brunswick, 1970). Two good studies of transatlantic communications in the first British Empire are Alison Gilbert Olson, *Making the Empire Work: London and American Interest Groups, 1690–1790* (Cambridge, Mass., 1992), and Ian K. Steele, *The English-Atlantic, 1675–1740: An Exploration of Communication and Community* (Oxford, 1986).

would orbit.[10] Pownall's career was motivated as much by his desire to study and implement this theory in colonial administration as by his thirst for preferment.

Pownall did not travel this path alone. He followed the example of several other imperial officials who combined the pursuits of patronage and colonial reform during the early 1750s. Pownall was the only such official to attend the Albany Congress, but he shared many opinions with contemporaries who wrote about the pressing need to rethink colonial administration before the Seven Years' War. Like Pownall, these officials used their American service to gather information about the colonies and then presented their conclusions to the Board of Trade.[11] Although such proposals for reform often differed in content and emphasis, a single thread ran through them: the need for Britain to settle definitively the nature of colonial dependence and imperial authority in its empire.

The reformist impulse exhibited by Pownall and his peers in colonial administration shaped the Crown's reaction to the breaking of the Covenant Chain. Shortly after receiving news of Hendrick's angry speech in New York City, the Board of Trade instructed the colonial governors to convene a "speedy Interview" with the Indians and enter into "one general Treaty" with them.[12] The board saw the broken chain as symptomatic of a more general crisis that had been brewing in America since the end of King George's War in 1748. It included the French military occupation of the Ohio Valley, the colonists' failure to repulse it, and the indifference colonial governments showed to the Crown's authority. This crisis, which threatened Great Britain with the loss of its North American dominions, convinced many imperial officials that the time had come for an extensive reappraisal of the Anglo-American connection.[13]

In their work there is an irony about the Albany Congress that historians have overlooked: the idea of colonial union owed as much to British offi-

[10] See John Shy, "The Spectrum of Imperial Possibilities: Henry Ellis and Thomas Pownall, 1763–1775," in Shy, A People Numerous and Armed: Reflections on the Military Struggle for American Independence, rev. ed. (Ann Arbor, 1990), 43–80; Caroline Robbins, The Eighteenth-Century Commonwealthman: Studies in the Transmission, Development and Circumstances of English Liberal Thought from the Restoration of Charles II until the War with the Thirteen Colonies (Cambridge, Mass., 1961), 311–19; and G. H. Guttridge, "Thomas Pownall's The Administration of the Colonies: The Six Editions," WMQ 26 (1969): 31–46. Shy corrected the error in Guttridge's title by noting that there were in fact only five editions of Pownall's Administration of the Colonies. See Shy, "Spectrum of Imperial Possibilities," 58, n. 19.

[11] Pownall's most important contemporaries in this regard were James Abercromby and Henry McCulloh, both royal revenue collectors who wrote long treatises on colonial reform in the early 1750s, and William Shirley, the royal governor of Massachusetts and a strong advocate of colonial union before the Albany Congress of 1754. The ideas of each are considered in greater detail below.

[12] See Board of Trade to Sir Danvers Osborne, September 18, 1753, NYCD, 6:800–802.

[13] The best brief summary of this crisis is Jack P. Greene, "The Origins of the New Colonial Policy," in The Blackwell Encyclopedia of the American Revolution, ed. Jack P. Greene and J. R. Pole (Oxford, 1991), 95–106.

cials as it did to colonial Americans. By the early 1750s, current or former colonial officials were advocating union as a means of repairing Indian relations, turning back French expansion, and strengthening the royal prerogative in America. Their endorsement of colonial union reflected a fundamental reorientation in the way imperial administrators viewed the colonies. Until 1748, policymakers generally dismissed the idea of colonial union as an unnecessary encouragement of colonial independence.[14] By the mid-eighteenth century, the rapid expansion of the colonial population, its importance as a market for British goods, and the contest with France for North America led to reconsideration of that position. Policymakers increasingly described North America as a continental dominion, rather than a collection of commercial outposts, whose colonial and Indian inhabitants needed closer supervision. The Board of Trade and several of its American officials became advocates of a colonial union that would protect territorial claims, preserve Indian alliances, and reassert royal authority in America. By the time the Albany Congress convened in June 1754, the king's Privy Council had determined on its own to formulate a plan of colonial union that would help secure permanent colonial dependence.

Britannia's Americans

The reformist agenda advocated by some colonial officials after 1748 involved three main issues: defining the constitutional nature of colonial dependence, defending territorial claims in North America from French encroachments, and subordinating Indian affairs to Britain's imperial interests. In grappling with these issues, policymakers and administrators moved away from viewing the colonies in strictly commercial terms to incorporating them into a hierarchical imperial state with political and military, as well as economic, interests in North America.

Seventeenth-century writers commonly described the American colonies as overseas commercial enterprises populated by English settlers and governed by English laws.[15] After 1700, the nature of these colonies

[14] For examples of early eighteenth-century commentaries against colonial union, see William Keith, "Proposal for establishing by Act of Parliament the Duties upon Stampt Paper and Parchment in all the British Colonies in America," in [Keith], *Two Papers on the Subject of Taxing the British Colonies in America*, 13–22; [Joshua Gee], *A Letter to a Member of Parliament Concerning the Naval Store Bill . . .* (London, 1720), 35; and Gee, *The Trade and Navigation of Great-Britain Considered*, 3rd ed. (London, 1731), 71–75, 100–106, 136–37. For British commentators who linked the idea of colonial union with independence, see J. M. Bumsted, "'Things in the Womb of Time': Ideas of American Independence, 1633–1763," *WMQ* 32 (1974): 533–64.
[15] For examples of this seventeenth-century commercial definition of colonies, see Charles D'Avenant's "Discourse on the Public Revenues" (1698), in D'Avenant, *The Political and Com-*

changed considerably. Settlement moved past the seacoast along interior waterways. Non-English immigrant groups poured into North America, including Africans, Germans, and Scots-Irish. Furthermore, non-English colonial populations established in the seventeenth century—such as the Dutch of New York and the French Acadians of Nova Scotia—retained their distinctive cultural identities despite submission to British rule.[16] The Mohawk Valley of Hendrick and William Johnson was a microcosm of this process. Before 1700, it was empty of European settlers west of Schenectady; over the next fifty years it became an imperial marchland, with military posts garrisoned by British troops, new settlements of German, Scots-Irish, and Irish colonists, and older communities of Dutch inhabitants still anchored in Schenectady and Albany. In this entirely different colonial dominion, with a population made up increasingly of non-English settlers and native-born colonists, the "British" quality of British North America was indeed open to question.[17] The American colonists continued to profess allegiance to the British Crown and English laws, but what relation did they bear to the Crown's other subjects in the British Isles? Were they merely Britons living abroad, or did their distance and diversity from those other subjects endow them with a peculiar kind of dependency?

This problem is addressed visually in a print that appeared in London in September 1755. *British Resentment or the French fairly Coopt at Louisbourg* (Fig. 2.1) was published by act of Parliament to commemorate the British naval blockade of Louisbourg, the French fortress on Cape Breton, at the outset of the Seven Years' War.[18] The print is noteworthy because it offers an emblematic representation of North America from the perspective of

mercial Works, 5 vols. (London, 1771), 2:1–76, and Josiah Child, *A New Discourse of Trade . . . A New Edition* (1693; rpt. London, 1775), 166–202. Also see Andrews, *Colonial Background of the American Revolution*, 69–118, and Klaus E. Knorr, *British Colonial Theories, 1570–1850* (Toronto, 1944), 81–105.

[16] For an overview of colonial immigration, settlement, and population after 1700, see Richard Hofstadter, *America at 1750: A Social Portrait* (New York, 1971), 3–32.

[17] It is necessary here to explain my use of the word "British." I have decided to favor it over "English" when describing eighteenth-century colonists and their rulers for two reasons. First, with the rise of Scots-Irish and Irish immigration after 1700, the colonists could no longer be generally described as "English." Second, after the Anglo-Scottish Union of 1707, the ranks of colonial administrators, especially those in the colonies (governors, customs collectors, military officers), became increasingly Scottish in character. Thus the empire that they governed, studied, and wrote about was more "British" than "English" in character. A good analysis of this change can be found in Colley, *Britons*, 117–32. In this chapter and throughout the rest of the book, I use "British" to describe the empire after 1700 and "English" to describe it before then. James Truslow Adams traced the origin of the term "British Empire" to the late seventeenth century and noted that it achieved wide usage during the 1740s and 1750s, at roughly the same time as which the reformers I am discussing in this chapter were writing. See Adams, "On the Term 'British Empire,'" *American Historical Review* 27 (1922): 485–89.

[18] On the blockade, see Gipson, *British Empire*, 6:99–126.

Figure 2.1. *British Resentment or the French fairly Coopt at Louisbourg*, by J. June after L. Boitard, 1755. Courtesy of the John Carter Brown Library at Brown University.

London at a time when royal officials were struggling to govern a growing but vulnerable empire there.

The print's theme is the imperial rivalry between Great Britain and France for North America. In the upper right-hand corner, British sailors rejoice at seeing "the Starving French coopt up" in their fortress. The terrain contested between them extends far beyond Louisbourg. In the lower right-hand corner, a British sailor chokes the "Gallic Cock" and forces it to "disgorge the French usurpations in America," which include Niagara, Ohio, and Crown Point, a fortress on Lake Champlain. Across from the Gallic cock, the British lion guards a map marked "Virginia" and "Nova Scotia," which he has torn away from one marked "Quebec." These images link the print's main action—a naval blockade off Cape Breton—to a much wider struggle along the Great Lakes and Ohio frontiers. In several images, the print also predicts Britain's conquest of North America: an English rose blooms while a French lily wilts in American soil, the British arms eclipse those of the French in the sky above, and in the background, a Frenchman in his canoe drops over Niagara Falls.

Three types of characters—British, French, and American—converge in this scene. The British are soldiers and sailors, uniformed and brandishing weapons, the hard stuff by which empires are won. Also within the British camp are the mythic figures of Britannia, seated on her throne, and Neptune and Mars, twin symbols of Britain's naval and military power, clasping hands under the Union Jack. While these British characters celebrate their victory, the French appear as crestfallen fops surrounded by British arms. Two Indian figures—a man and a woman—represent the third set of characters, identified in the legend as Britannia's "injur'd Americans." Clad only in feathers and blanket, they kneel at Britannia's feet, begging her protection.

British Resentment or the French fairly Coopt at Louisbourg is a remarkably detailed tableau of empire, yet the identity of these two Indian figures at its center remains unclear. Are they meant to represent American colonists or Indians? Their position relative to Britannia implies dependence and inferiority, characteristics which London viewers may very well have associated with the colonists. Or the print's artist may have intended for these Indian figures to represent the Iroquois, whom the British had claimed as subjects since 1713. In their struggle with the French over the North American interior, the British argued that the Iroquois had ceded much of this disputed territory to the Crown, justifying the British aggression depicted in the print. Britannia's "injur'd Americans" may have included colonists, Indians, or both.[19]

---

[19] Lester C. Olson, in *Emblems of American Community in the Revolutionary Era: A Study in Rhetorical Iconology* (Washington, D.C., 1991), 82, argues that the Indian figures in this print are

Nevertheless, this print is an interesting example of how Britons incorporated the American colonies into their mental landscape of the empire. During the eighteenth century, such images became important to the cultural construction of a British identity that placed empire building at the center of a Protestant national mission.[20] *British Resentment or the French fairly Coopt at Louisbourg* was one of the first prints in London to depict the American colonies as part of that imperial state.[21] It employs several images that would have been familiar to any British viewer of the day: Britannia and the British lion represent the British state; soldiers and sailors represent the masculine, expansive power of British arms; effeminate, scheming politicians represent France, Britain's rival for world power. The Indian figures are a new element, which indicates the artist's imaginative effort to include North America in a visual field of the empire. Britannia's Americans are distinguished from the print's other characters by their nakedness, dark skin, and supplicant postures. In other words, they are weak, primitive, foreign subjects, entirely unlike the other Britons who crowd the scene as soldiers and sailors. Whether they are Indians, colonists, or both is unclear, but their exotic, dependent nature is not.

This print captures much of the uncertainty and concern that imperial officials expressed over British North America between 1748 and 1754. These years, sandwiched between two Anglo-French wars, saw a burst of creative energy from colonial officials who agreed that Great Britain could no longer afford to look at the colonies only in commercial terms. Imperial

---

one of the earliest representations of the American colonists in British iconography. Olson provides insightful analysis on the use of the Indian as a symbol for the colonies, but in this case he overlooks a potential alternative explanation: that these Indian figures represent the relationship between the British Crown and the Iroquois. The colonial seal of New York in use at the time *British Resentment or the French fairly Coopt at Louisbourg* was published may have provided that print's artist with inspiration for Britannia's "injur'd Americans." The New York seal (see Fig. 1.1) depicts two Indians, a naked female and a male clad only in a feathered headdress and skirt, kneeling before the British king.

[20] For a discussion of these visual images of empire and eighteenth-century British national identity, see Colley, *Britons*, 55–100; Wilson, *Sense of the People*, 185–205; and Eric Hinderaker, "The 'Four Indian Kings' and the Imaginative Construction of the First British Empire," *WMQ* 53 (1996): 487–526. On the conjunction between empire building and state building in eighteenth-century Britain, see Brewer, *Sinews of Power*, and the essays in *Imperial State at War*, ed. Stone.

[21] *British Resentment or the French fairly Coopt at Louisbourg* was based on another anti-French print published one month earlier in London, *Britain's Rights maintaind; or French Ambition dismantled*. This print was the first in either Britain or America to use an Indian to depict the American colonies, and much of its iconography was incorporated into *British Resentment*, including the figures of Mars, Neptune, Britannia, the foppish Frenchmen, and the British lion reclaiming its territories from the Gallic cock. One notable difference is the Indian, who in *Britain's Rights maintaind* is a diminutive figure, barely half the size of the print's other characters. The major difference between these two prints, then, is that the artist of *British Resentment* chose to make the Indians more prominent by drawing them to scale with the other figures and placing them literally in the center of the action. See Olson, *Emblems of American Community*, 79–102, and Colley, *Britons*, 89.

interests dictated that the colonies had grown too populous and profitable to be left alone. Likewise, the dependence of the Iroquois was as important as that of the colonists themselves because it advanced British claims to the North American interior and provided diplomatic and military advantage against the French. The conflation of colonists and Indians in this print's depiction of Britannia's "injur'd Americans" is indicative of the tendency among reformers to describe both groups as subjects in need of a well-ordered dependency. To that end, the Crown had to achieve a degree of centralization, subordination, and union in colonial government previously unheard-of.

The first issue to concern mid-century reformers was the preservation of colonial dependence. Like the Indian figures in *British Resentment or the French fairly Coopt at Louisbourg,* the American colonists did not have a precisely defined place within the British imperial state. No single constitutional or legal precedent explained the nature of their dependence on the Crown or Parliament. Rather, they governed themselves according to royal charters and instructions granted at the time of their founding. Colonial governments shared the tripartite structure of a governor, council, and popular assembly, but the extent of the Crown's power in them varied considerably. In royal colonies, such as Virginia and New Hampshire, the Crown appointed the governor and council and therefore had a direct voice in their internal affairs. In proprietary colonies, such as Pennsylvania and Maryland, the powers of government were vested in families that received the original land grant from the Crown. In the corporate colonies of Rhode Island and Connecticut, charters granted the powers of government to the inhabitants themselves. In short, no single imperial constitution existed to define the nature of colonial dependence; royal, proprietary, and corporate colonies bore different connections to the mother country and each other.[22]

Between 1660 and 1720, the Crown made several attempts to establish uniform royal authority throughout the colonies. The Latter Stuarts' challenge to corporate colonial charters culminated in the Dominion of New England (1686–89), which replaced the representative assemblies of seven northern colonies with a single governor general. This effort to centralize the Crown's prerogative powers in America was interrupted by the Glorious Revolution of 1688, which ended Stuart-style absolutism in the colonies as well as at home. While some royal officials remained committed to revising colonial charters, transatlantic interest groups opposed to such measures prevented any systematic reorganization of colonial administration. By the 1720s, the Whig ascendancy had settled comfortably into a policy that was precise in commercial regulation but tolerant of diversity

[22] For a summary of the colonial charters and their histories, see Andrews, *Colonial Background of the American Revolution,* 3–25.

and autonomy in local colonial government.[23] Before 1750, therefore, British theorists held no common definition of an imperial constitution and most often described empire in terms of maritime trade and naval power. As long as their outlook remained mercantile, they were more concerned with commerce and profits than with the precise constitutional status of the colonies.[24]

This problem led James Abercromby, a Scottish vice-admiralty officer with fourteen years of experience in America, to write a long treatise on colonial government. Abercromby worked on "An Examination of the Acts of Parliament Relative to the Trade and Government of our American Colonies" between 1748 and 1752, after returning to London from his post in South Carolina. He circulated it among leading ministers in colonial affairs, hoping it would inspire them to establish a uniform constitution for colonial government, a Magna Charta for America.[25] In "An Examination," Abercromby argued that for too long Britain had looked upon the colonies "in a Merchantile view only, and not through the eyes of State," thereby rendering "*Sovereignty* subservient to Commerce" in America. He chided Parliament for not having "hitherto attended to the Interior Government" of the colonies and urged it to exercise its sovereignty over them so that they developed "Consistent with the Policy and Interest of the Mother Country."[26]

Abercromby approached the issue of colonial dependence historically, considering first precedents for colonial rule that British policymakers

[23] Historians disagree as to the success of the Crown's effort in the latter seventeenth century to rein in the diversity and autonomy of colonial governments. In three books, Stephen Saunders Webb has argued that the Crown succeeded in reducing the colonies to a new dependence. See *The Governors-General: The English Army and the Definition of the Empire, 1569–1681* (Chapel Hill, 1979); *1676: The End of American Independence* (New York, 1984); and *Lord Churchill's Coup: The Anglo-American Empire and the Glorious Revolution Reconsidered* (New York, 1995). Webb's chief critic has been Jack M. Sosin, who in three books has argued for the persistence of colonial autonomy. See *English America and the Restoration Monarchy of Charles II: Transatlantic Politics, Commerce, and Kinship* (Lincoln, 1980); *English America and the Revolution of 1688: Royal Administration and the Structure of Provincial Government* (Lincoln, 1982); and *English America and Imperial Inconstancy: The Rise of Provincial Autonomy, 1696–1715* (Lincoln, 1985). For further evidence of the role that transatlantic interest groups played in resisting imperial centralization, see Olson, *Making the Empire Work*, and Richard R. Johnson, *Adjustment to Empire: The New England Colonies, 1675–1715* (New Brunswick, 1981).
[24] See Richard Koebner, *Empire* (Cambridge, Eng., 1961), 61–104, and Knorr, *British Colonial Theories*, 63–125. Jack P. Greene explains the ill-defined nature of the imperial constitution in *Peripheries and Center*, 7–76. Daniel A. Baugh describes the pre-1750 maritime approach to imperial policy in "Maritime Strength and Atlantic Commerce: The Uses of a 'Grand Marine Empire,'" in *Imperial State at War*, ed. Stone, 185–223.
[25] Abercromby's treatise is published in Jack P. Greene, Charles F. Mullet, and Edward Papenfuse Jr., eds., *Magna Charta for America: James Abercromby's "An Examination of the Acts of Parliament Relative to the Trade and Government of Our American Colonies" (1752) and "De Jure et Gubenatione Coloniarum, or an Inquiry into the Nature, and the Rights of Colonies, Ancient, and Modern" (1774)* (Philadelphia, 1986), 43–169.
[26] Ibid., 149, 303.

might imitate. Ancient Greece and Rome offered two models. Greece planted colonies "to be *Confederates*, and more like Municipal Citys," which governed themselves and remained connected to their mother country through trade. The English had likewise colonized distant lands for commercial reasons and granted them self-governing privileges, but Abercromby disliked the political autonomy of Greek colonies. Rome, on the other hand, treated its colonies as perpetual dependents, passing laws and appointing governors to rule them. Abercromby found this model more consistent with the British experience in America, except that Rome colonized by conquering foreign peoples whereas Britain's American colonies were planted by Englishmen who carried the rights and liberties of freeborn subjects with them. Looking elsewhere in the British Empire, Abercromby found few parallels with American colonial government. Ireland was a conquered nation, and its parliament enjoyed far less legislative independence than the colonial assemblies. Several colonies had corporate governments similar to those of English cities, but those colonies by virtue of their distance from England also enjoyed "Some Singular . . . Powers of Government" not vested in municipalities at home. In the past, England had granted self-governing privileges to counties bordering Scotland and Wales, but Parliament abridged those powers in the sixteenth century and had yet to interfere in a similar manner with the American colonial charters.[27]

In brief, Abercromby found the constitutional status of the American colonies unique. Commercial in origin, planted by freeborn Englishmen, and semiautonomous in government, they had no precedents in the ancient or modern world, and therefore, their government "must stand upon its own Principles."[28] Although he did not wish to see Britannia's Americans governed by any principles "more strict and severe, than what other Subjects of this nation are," he did admit that "although they are Subjects, yet they are Subjects under peculiar Circumstances, formed into Separate Societys, that in time may feel their new Strength." Returning to the Greek and Roman models, Abercromby concluded that the time had come to determine whether "they are [to] remain Subjects, or to become Confederates."[29] Like many of his contemporaries in colonial administration, Abercromy preferred the former to the latter: the colonies should be perpetually subject to Great Britain rather than merely commercial partners with it. To achieve that dependence, he urged the Crown to create "a More Consistent Union, Between this Nation, and our American Colonies in General."[30]

[27] Ibid., 68–72. Also see Greene, *Peripheries and Center*, 8–12.
[28] Greene, Mullet, and Papenfuse, eds., *Magna Charta for America*, 72.
[29] Ibid., 172.
[30] Ibid., 48.

Abercromby identified the colonial charters as the chief impediment to that "More Consistent Union." The variety of charters and especially the self-governing privileges they awarded to the proprietary and corporate colonies prevented the Crown from ruling its American possessions with any uniformity. Instead, they worked contrary to that end by limiting the royal prerogative and encouraging the legislative independence of colonial assemblies. Abercromby, therefore, called for Parliament to alter the charters as necessary to "render the said Colonies without Distinction Subservient to the Interest, and Welfare, of this their Mother Country."[31]

A contemporary of Abercromby's in the colonial service, Henry McCulloh, arrived at the same conclusion in a treatise he wrote on colonial administration in 1751. McCulloh returned to London in the late 1740s after serving for several years as a collector of royal revenues in North Carolina. Like Abercromby, he believed that policymakers in London lacked a clear understanding of the American colonies, whose enormous wealth and population were in danger of slipping through Britain's hands.[32] In his long report to the Board of Trade, which he later published in a series of four pamphlets, McCulloh warned that the Crown must act quickly to secure "an immediate dependence" of the colonies or face their loss. He blamed "the unwarrantable Constructions which some Colonies have put on the charters granted to them by the Crown" for the erosion of royal authority in America and recommended "having the Parliament . . . Aid the Prerogative of the Crown" by enacting legislation that would alter the charters and levy taxes to fund royal government there.[33]

Three assumptions, each apparent in Abercromby's and McCulloh's work, shaped an emerging consensus among imperial officials that the colonies needed to be reduced to a uniform dependence. First, colonies by their nature should be perpetually dependent on their mother country. Of the two alternatives outlined by Abercromby, the Roman model of governing colonies as "Subjects" was more appropriate for Britannia's Americans than the Greek model of governing them as "Confederates." Second, colonies were useful only inasmuch as they contributed to the wealth of their mother country. Both Abercromby and McCulloh included detailed information in their treatises on the remarkable expansion of British North

[31] Ibid., 77.
[32] Henry McCulloh, "To the Right Honourable Earl of Halifax," December 10, 1751, BM, Add. Mss., No. 11514. For biographical details on McCulloh, see John Cannon, "Henry McCulloch and Henry McCulloh," WMQ 15 (1958): 71–73. Between 1754 and 1757, McCulloh published anonymously four pamphlets based on this report: General Thoughts on the Construction, Use and Abuse of the Great Offices (London, 1754); A Miscellaneous Essay Concerning the Courses Pursued by Great Britain in the Affairs of Her Colonies (London, 1755); The Wisdom and Policy of the French in the Construction of Their Great Offices (London, 1755); and Proposals for Uniting the English Colonies on the Continent of America, So as to Enable Them to Act with Force and Vigour against Their Enemies (London, 1757).
[33] See McCulloh, "To the Earl of Halifax," ff. 9–13, 58–59, 73–77, 95–101.

America's trade and population since 1700, but each warned that Britain would lose this wealth if it failed to govern the colonies effectively.[34] Third, as parts of the British Empire, the colonies were subject to Parliament's authority as well as the Crown's. This last proposition did not mean that colonists were to be denied the rights of freeborn Englishmen that their charters originally guaranteed them. As another colonial official explained, the question was not whether "*British* Subjects in the Plantations" had a right to all "those Rights and Privileges which are derived to them as natural-born Subjects of *Great-Britain*" but whether they enjoyed "any Sort of Rights or Privileges, that are of a higher or more independent Nature than what their Brethren . . . can claim at Home."[35] If Parliament was the supreme legislative authority in the empire, then certainly the American colonists could not claim that their charters were somehow immune to parliamentary revision.

The fundamental question that Britain had failed to resolve up to 1750 was where the imperial authority of the Crown and Parliament ended and the local authority of the colonial charters began.[36] When Abercromby and McCulloh argued for parliamentary legislation to alter colonial charters, they challenged local colonial government in a way that appeared natural and inevitable considering Britain's eighteenth-century evolution as an imperial state.[37] After all, Parliament had already exerted its sovereignty over Scotland with the Act of Union in 1707 and over Ireland with the Declaratory Act of 1720. A similar act had yet to define the dependence of Britannia's Americans, although since the late seventeenth century, Parliament had been taking a more active role in governing them, including regulating their trade and manufactures and even subsidizing the colonization of Georgia and Nova Scotia.[38] Colonists had offered little resistance to this piecemeal extension of parliamentary authority in America, and Abercromby and McCulloh did not expect them to object to a parliamentary act that settled once and for all the nature of colonial dependence.

The second major issue on the reformists' agenda concerned the French "grand design" to conquer North America. Like other British observers on

[34] Greene, Mullet, and Papenfuse, eds., *Magna Charta for America*, 62–68, and McCulloh, "To the Earl of Halifax," ff. 86–102.
[35] [Keith], *Two Papers on the Subject of Taxing the British Colonies in America*, 17. Keith served as governor of Pennsylvania between 1717 and 1726, before returning to London and writing several pamphlets on colonial administration.
[36] See Greene, *Peripheries and Center*, 55–76.
[37] John Phillip Reid refers to this interpretation of the eighteenth-century British constitution as "the constitution of sovereign command," which vested in Parliament the right to legislate for all parts of the empire as well as Britain. See *Constitutional History of the American Revolution*, abridged ed. (Madison, 1995), 3–25, 49–72.
[38] See Ian K. Steele, "The British Parliament and the Atlantic Colonies to 1760: New Approaches to Enduring Questions," in *Parliament and the Atlantic Empire*, Philip Lawson, ed. (Edinburgh, 1995), 29–46.

American affairs, McCulloh believed that the French planned to link Canada and Louisiana by way of the Ohio and Mississippi Rivers, creating a fortified western barrier beyond which British colonists could not pass. By engrossing the fur trade with western Indians, the French would wean away native allies of the British, such as the Iroquois, and incite them to war against colonists east of the Appalachians. Confined to a thin strip of seacoast, the British colonies would atrophy and become useless to the mother country.[39] In the seventeenth century, British administrators had expressed little concern for establishing dominion over the North American interior. The political economist Charles D'Avenant stated the prevailing opinion when he wrote that the wise nation avoided acquiring colonial possessions so large that their populations became dispersed and too costly to defend and govern.[40] As the eighteenth century progressed, however, the British became more concerned with stopping French expansion in North America. When French troops marched into the Ohio Valley in 1749, the contest over the continent's interior took on new urgency.[41] McCulloh and several other writers decried the underhandedness of the French grand design but usually ended up recommending that the British imitate it in their own colonial policy.

McCulloh's descriptions of the French reflected the strong Galliphobia that shaped British nationalism during the eighteenth century. Popular prints, songs, and literature cast the French as Catholic in religion, absolutist in politics, and effeminate in manners, all of which stood in opposition to British Protestantism, liberty, and masculinity.[42] This stereotyping is evident in the foppish French characters in *British Resentment or the French fairly Coopt at Louisbourg*, whom the print's legend describes as scheming politicians caught in their own game. Such impressions of French intrigue and treachery were at the core of British descriptions of French colonial policy in North America. One anonymous London pamphleteer described

[39] McCulloh describes the French "grand design" in "To the Earl of Halifax," ff. 13–38, and *Wisdom and Policy of the French*, 80–133. For similar descriptions of the French design also see [Otis Little], *The State of Trade in the Northern Colonies Considered* (1748; rpt. Boston, 1749); T. C., *A Scheme to Drive the French Out of All the Continent of North America* (Boston, 1755); and [John Mitchell], *The Contest in America between Great Britain and France, with Its Consequences and Importance* (London, 1757), 85–148. James Abercromby briefly recapitulated the progress of the French design in a letter to William Pitt in November 1756. See Charles F. Mullett, ed., "James Abercromby and French Encroachments in America," *Canadian Historical Review* 26 (1945): 54–55. For a good analysis of French intentions in the Ohio and Mississippi Valleys, see Hinderaker, *Elusive Empires*.

[40] See Charles D'Avenant, "Discourses on the Publick Revenues" (1698), in *Political and Commercial Works*, 2:25–26. Also see Child, *New Discourse of Trade*, 166–98; and Samuel Fortrey, *England's Interest and Improvement. Consisting in the Increase of the Store, and Trade of This Kingdom* (London, 1673), reprinted in J. R. McCulloh, ed., *Early English Tracts on Commerce* (1856; rpt. Cambridge, Eng., 1954), 243–44.

[41] See Jennings, *Empire of Fortune*, 8–70, for a summary of these events.

[42] See Colley, *Britons*, 33–35, 87–98, and Gerald Newman, *The Rise of English Nationalism, 1740–1830* (New York, 1987), 63–84.

New France as an empire built by French priests, soldiers, and traders who deceived Indians into giving up their souls, land, and furs.[43] Another writer portrayed the French in North America "as rats in a good old cheese," who, having gained entrance via the St. Lawrence and Mississippi Rivers, were busy gnawing their way to the center to "claim the whole as their own."[44] Such observers encouraged British military aggression as the only proper response to French encroachments in disputed regions. "Barely making settlements will not do," one pamphleteer warned. "We must *out-fort*, as well as *out-settle* them."[45] Another writer recommended eliminating French place-names from American maps and replacing them with "all *English*, or *Indian* names" to make clear British possession.[46]

In his 1751 treatise and subsequent pamphlets, McCulloh condemned the French empire in North America but found in it a useful model for British colonial reform. His long comparison of French and British colonial administration provided the fullest exposition of the French grand design by a British commentator. French abolutism, he admitted, may have left French subjects miserable at home, but "*France* may be justly said to be happy in the Management of their *American* Colonies, and in the Conduct of War and Negotiations."[47] French colonial governors, soldiers, traders, and priests worked according to "one regular uniform and intire Rule of Action" in establishing frontier posts, converting Indians, and acquiring their trade.[48] The irony was not lost on McCulloh: by relying on absolutist imperial officers and conniving priests, the French had gained the upper hand in America over liberty-loving, Protestant British subjects. As nefarious as it was, the French scheme had an "Order, Coherence, and Union" that he could not help but admire.[49]

Like Abercromby, McCulloh insisted that his purpose was not to attack colonial liberties. But he did believe that to deal with the French in North America, the British would have to curb colonial self-government. In *Proposals for Uniting the English Colonies on the Continent of America* (1757), he wrote that the colonies may be considered "with respect to each other, as so many independent States, yet they ought to be considered as one with respect to their Mother Country; and therefore a Union of the Colonies, for their general Defence . . . can only be made by the Wisdom of our Legislature." He proposed parliamentary legislation to amend colonial charters, create an intercolonial military establishment, and levy a poll tax or stamp

---

[43] *State of the British and French Colonies in North America . . . in Two Letters to a Friend* (London, 1755), 14.
[44] [Payne], *French Encroachments Exposed*, 10–11, 43.
[45] *State of the British and French Colonies*, 37, 105.
[46] [Payne], *French Encroachments Exposed*, 44.
[47] [McCulloh], *Wisdom and Policy of the French*, 36.
[48] McCulloh, "To the Earl of Halifax," f. 28.
[49] Ibid., and [McCulloh], *Wisdom and Policy of the French*, 80.

duty that would raise an American common fund. McCulloh even suggested creating a "Bank of *America*" modeled after the Bank of London, which could serve as a depository of royal revenues and issue a single American currency or "Bills of Union" for paying American taxes, customs, and quitrents.[50] Such a union, McCulloh believed, would increase the colonies' dependence on the mother country and enable the Crown to make better use of them in its struggle against France.

According to McCulloh, the genius of the French system was its efficiency: the absolutist French colonial administration operated like "a piece of Clock work which by its Springs directs the Wheels in Motion."[51] The implications for British colonial policy were obvious. If the British Crown intended to defeat the French design, it should centralize and strengthen the royal prerogative in America, redouble its efforts to win Indian allies, and reduce the colonies to a uniform system of government. Other writers agreed that colonial division had become one of the crown's chief liabilities in North America. The political economist Josiah Tucker believed "England labours under a peculiar Disadvantage in Comparison to *France, as its Colonies are not so much under the Command of their Mother Country, nor so studious of her Welfare.*"[52] Another writer tersely observed of British colonial policy, "the maxim *divide et impera,* appears to have operated more for the interest of the *French* than of *Great Britain.*"[53]

McCulloh's recommendations for meeting the French menace in North America were reinforced by colonial governors corresponding with the Board of Trade. King George's War, which ended with an indecisive armistice in 1748, had offered valuable lessons to those governors. Foremost among them was William Shirley, the royal governor of Massachusetts and the most active prosecutor of the British war effort in North America. After the war, he spent two years in Paris on an Anglo-French commission appointed to settle American boundary disputes.[54] His involvement in the escalating imperial struggle over North America broadened his perspective on the empire. He treated with Indians in Albany and Boston, made plans for governing French colonists in Nova Scotia, and launched intercolonial expeditions against Canada. These experiences taught him to view North America as an extension of Europe and the colonies as stepping-stones for his own career. Like that of Pownall, Abercromby, and McCulloh, Shirley's colonial service combined a quest for patronage with a

---

[50] [McCulloh], *Proposals for Uniting the English Colonies,* 15–17, 22–24, 27–29.
[51] McCulloh, "To the Earl of Halifax," f. 13.
[52] [Josiah Tucker], *A Brief Essay on the Advantages and Disadvantages Which Respectively Attend France and Great Britain, with Regard to Trade,* 2d ed. (London, 1750), 45.
[53] *State of the British and French Colonies,* 58.
[54] For Shirley's early career, see John Schutz, *William Shirley: King's Governor of Massachusetts* (Chapel Hill, 1961), 3–43. On the boundary commission, see ibid., 149–67, and Gipson, *British Empire,* 5:303–22.

reformist impulse. He advocated colonial union because he believed it would restore colonial dependence and assist in the British conquest of New France.

Shirley's greatest success came early in his career. In 1745 he planned an attack by New England colonists on Louisbourg, the French fortress on Cape Breton Island that guarded the mouth of the St. Lawrence River. That victory ignited within him dreams of royal favor as he spearheaded the conquest of New France. A portrait of Shirley from 1747 reflects these aspirations (Fig. 2.2). Appearing in the fine clothes and wig of a royal official, Shirley rests his left hand on his sword and points with his right to the fleet assembled below him in Boston Harbor. The plans of Louisbourg are unfolded on a desk behind him. It is a portrait that anticipates the conquest of New France by a royal governor capable of marshaling colonial resources and manpower in the service of the Crown. In 1746 and 1747 Shirley devoted his energies to such an intercolonial assault on Canada. He organized the recruitment of several thousand provincial troops, but his expedition stalled when naval support from Britain failed to arrive and his colonial army disintegrated from sickness, desertion, and mutiny.[55]

In letters to his superiors, Shirley presented two primary reasons why the Crown should take a more aggressive stance against the French in North America. First, he emphasized the strategic importance of Nova Scotia, which if secured as a British possession would open a gateway to Canada and the French fur trade.[56] Second, Shirley believed that the conquest of Canada would tighten the Crown's grip on the colonies to the south, should they ever "grow Restive and dispos'd to shake off their Dependency upon their Mother Country."[57] Like Abercromby and McCulloh, Shirley noted for his London patrons how rapidly the colonial population was expanding. This British population in America would "lay a foundation for a superiority of British Power upon the Continent of Europe" and provide a market for British trade that would "for ever be in her [Great Britain's] favor."[58] Yet this remarkable increase in the Crown's American subjects would be for naught if Britain failed to maintain their dependence. Shirley's vision of the future approximated Abercromby's commercial Roman-style empire made up of permanently dependent colonies. Britannia's Americans would multiply and eventually account for

---

[55] For Shirley's efforts during King George's War, see Schutz, *William Shirley*, 80–148. For his dissatisfaction at the war's end, see Shirley, *Memoirs of the Principal Transactions of the Last War between the English and French in North-America*, 3d ed. (Boston, 1758), 70–80, and Shirley to Newcastle, October 28, 1748, and January 23, 1750, *WS Correspondence*, 1:457–60, 493–98.
[56] Shirley to the Duke of Newcastle, January 14, 1745, *WS Correspondence*, 1:161–64.
[57] Shirley to the Board of Trade, July 10, 1745, ibid., 244.
[58] Shirley to Newcastle, October 29, 1745, ibid., 284–85.

Figure 2.2. *His Excellency William Shirley,* by Peter Pelham after John Smibert, 1747. Courtesy of the National Portrait Gallery, Smithsonian Institution.

the majority of her subjects, but their role in the empire would always remain subordinate: to supplement Britain's power in Europe and provide ready markets for British goods.

Shirley had little patience for colonial self-government when it interfered with his plans for imperial conquest. He blamed his failure to conquer Canada on the "Disunion of Councils" in the colonies and the stubborn colonial assemblies that refused to fund his efforts.[59] In 1748 he wrote a scathing indictment of the New York Assembly for its outright resistance to the expedition against Canada. That example, Shirley warned, threatened the Crown's prerogative powers in all the colonies "through influence which so bad an example . . . may have among them."[60] To strengthen the Crown's power he recommended several changes in colonial administration, including stricter colonial union. In a joint letter to the Board of Trade, Shirley and New York governor George Clinton blamed colonial division for undermining the Six Nations' attachment to the British. They also complained that colonies insulated from Anglo-French hostilties, such as New Jersey and Rhode Island, refused to assist those with exposed borders. Convinced that the colonies would never voluntarily cooperate, Shirley and Clinton urged that the Crown impose mandatory quotas of men and money for each to contribute to a common fund. Such a policy would free royal governors from their assemblies and allow them to manage military and Indian affairs in greater accordance with Crown interests.[61]

When the renewal of Anglo-French warfare appeared imminent in 1753, Shirley resumed his calls for colonial union. Anticipating another expedition against Canada, he wrote to the ministry urging the "necessity of an union among all the Colonies," which would be impossible to achieve without "a well concerted scheme" enforced by the Crown.[62] Virginia governor Robert Dinwiddie made similar warnings as he tried to organize an intercolonial response to the French invasion of the Ohio Valley. In 1753 he sent to the Board of Trade a plan for dividing the colonies into northern and southern districts to coordinate their military and Indian affairs.[63] When tensions along the Ohio increased in 1754, he warned the board that an "Act of Parliament" was necessary to "compell the Colonies to contribute to the Common Cause, independently of Assemblies."[64] Over the next few months he elaborated on this idea, recommending "a general Poll

[59] Shirley, *Memoirs of the Last War*, 68.
[60] Shirley to Clinton, August 13, 1748, *NYCD*, 6:433–36.
[61] Shirley and Clinton to the Board of Trade, August 18, 1748, ibid., 437–40.
[62] Shirley to Holdernesse, January 7, 1754, *WS Correspondence*, 2:18–23.
[63] Dinwiddie refers to this plan in letters he wrote to James Abercromby and the Earl of Halifax in 1754, after he saw the Albany Plan. See *Dinwiddie Papers*, 3:285, 406.
[64] Dinwiddie to the Board of Trade, June 18, 1754, ibid., 205–7.

Tax" imposed by Parliament on America to circumvent the assemblies' control over colonial treasuries and militias.[65]

Shirley and Dinwiddie, as royal governors of two populous colonies with exposed borders, gave an urgency to calls for colonial reform. Abercromby and McCulloh wrote long, reasoned treatises on the imperial constitution. Shirley and Dinwiddie wrote brief exclamatory letters predicting dire consequences if the Crown did not move quickly to check French encroachments and colonial autonomy. The net result was the same. These officials uniformly favored some kind of Parliament-mandated union that would raise an American revenue independent of the assemblies and place colonial resources squarely under the control of royal officials.

The last major component of this reformist agenda was a recommendation to centralize Indian affairs under the Crown, thereby ending each colony's independent pursuit of Indian diplomacy and trade. This desire to submit Indian affairs to imperial supervision shared much with the reformers' other two goals of securing colonial dependence and turning back French encroachments. Central to it was the idea that Indian diplomacy could no longer be left in the hands of local agents concerned only with their pocketbooks. James Abercromby warned that the Crown had for too long looked at the colonies "in a Merchantile view only, and not through the eyes of State." The same principle underlay the drive to create a Crown office for conducting Indian affairs; only such a position would have the authority necessary to ensure that Indian trade and diplomacy served imperial ends rather than personal profits.

The Iroquois played an important role in the debate over the administration of Indian affairs. Since 1701, the British Crown had described them as subjects, and throughout the first half of the eighteenth century, British officials and writers assiduously constructed the "Iroquois mystique": an image that presented the Six Nations as the conquerors of a vast inland empire stretching from the Great Lakes to the Mississippi River, which they had placed under British protection.[66] By 1750, the Iroquois were no longer simply trading partners but, incongruously, subjects and allies, who needed to be made properly dependent on the British Crown. King George's War had been a disaster in this regard. Of the Six Iroquois Nations, only the Mohawks had declared for the British cause and only because of William Johnson's intercession. With the arrival of peace in 1748, the Mohawks denounced the British for the weakness of the colonial war effort. Relating this news to the Board of Trade, Governors Shirley and Clinton suggested that diplomacy with the Six Nations be removed from

---

[65] Dinwiddie to Halifax, July 24, 1754, and Dinwiddie to Hamilton, July 31, 1754, ibid., 251, 256.

[66] On the "Iroquois mystique," see Jones, *License for Empire*, 21–35.

the hands of the Albany magistrates, whom they accused of having "more regard to their private profitt than to the publick good."[67]

This criticism of the Albany Commissioners of Indian Affairs increased over the next several years. Two New Yorkers, Cadwallader Colden and Archibald Kennedy, were particularly influential in turning opinion against the Albany commissioners and in favor of a royal Indian superintendent. Both were allied with Governor Clinton's faction in New York, which criticized Albany's neutrality with Canada and wished to use the fur trade as a tool for western imperial expansion. Colden, a member of the New York council, warned William Shirley in 1749 that the fur trade was not only "a very considerable branch of the Brittish Commerce in North America but likewise the Security of the Colonies in North America depends upon it."[68] In a 1751 report on Indian affairs, he attacked the Albany commissioners for their localism and neutrality, claiming that they ignored the Six Nations and strengthened the French cause by trading with Montreal. To make the fur trade serve British interests more effectively, Colden suggested that "We may learn from our natural Ennemies the French of Canada, what is proper to be done." He praised the French for their western fur trade and noted, "The great advantage the French have is, that their affairs among the Indians are all directed by one Council, and no expence is thought too great, which is necessary for their purposes." Colden urged the Crown to centralize Indian affairs in a similar manner under a single royal official, funded by "a Duty on all wines and spirits, imported into or made in any of the Colonies of North America."[69]

Archibald Kennedy shared Colden's distaste for Albany's administration of Indian affairs. As a member of Governor Clinton's council, Kennedy had attended treaty councils and witnessed the Mohawks' discontent firsthand. In 1751 he published a pamphlet titled *The Importance of Gaining and Preserving the Friendship of the Indians to the British Interest, Considered*, in which he proposed a Crown-appointed "*Superintendant of Indian Affairs*" to oversee relations with the Six Nations.[70] This Indian superintendent would tour Iroquois villages to make presents and hear complaints. He would supervise an annual "grand Fair" held in the Six Nations' territory, where all prices would be fixed to avoid alienating

---

[67] Shirley and Clinton to the Board of Trade, August 18, 1748, *NYCD*, 6:437–40.

[68] Colden to William Shirley, July 25, 1749, *Colden Papers*, 53 (1920): 119–29. Colden originally published his history of the Iroquois in two volumes in 1727 and 1747; a modern edition is Colden, *History of the Five Indian Nations*.

[69] See Colden, "The present state of the Indian affairs with the British and French Colonies in North America," *Colden Papers*, 53:271–87. Colden completed this report for Governor Clinton, who enclosed it in a letter to the Board of Trade in October 1751. See *NYCD*, 6:738–47.

[70] For Kennedy's biography and the importance of his pamphlet, see Milton M. Klein, "Archibald Kennedy: Imperial Pamphleteer," in *The Colonial Legacy*, Vol. 2, *Some Eighteenth-Century Commentators*, ed. Lawrence H. Leder (New York, 1971), 75–105.

Indian customers. To fund this office, Kennedy suggested a parliamentary duty on all Indian goods imported to and exported from America, to be collected by the royal customs service. Like Colden, he described the Albany Indian Commissioners as Dutch mercenaries who for the sake of profits colluded with the French, "our natural Enemies and Competitors in every Corner of the World."[71]

Kennedy's pamphlet heavily influenced Thomas Pownall, who dissected New York's Indian affairs in dispatches to the Board of Trade in 1753 and 1754.[72] Upon arriving in New York City, Pownall immediately recognized "the violent parties that subsist here about the management of Indian affairs," and in a report that he prepared on the topic, he explained how they contributed to the breaking of the Covenant Chain.[73] According to Pownall, New York's Indian affairs had always been subject to the abuses of two political factions, "One Party alway[s] joined with the Governor the other with the People that opposed him." Unlike Colden and Kennedy, who blamed the Albany Dutch for everything wrong in New York's Indian affairs, Pownall considered all New Yorkers culpable in mistreating the Indians. "The whole Drift of the Party that happened to gett the Transaction of Indian Affairs into their hands," he explained, "has been constantly to amass a hasty Fortune by every means fair and foul." While the party in power fleeced the Indians, the opposition sowed "distrust and dissatisfaction" between the Indians and the colony's government. He placed William Johnson at the head of the governor's party and Albany's magistrates at the head of the opposition. Both participated in New York's frenzied land speculation, "sometime with more Art, keeping themselves out of sight and making the Indians appear Principals." In a note appended to this last comment, Pownall expressed skepticism about "the Real Motive of Hendricks Complaint last summer," insinuating that Johnson might have encouraged the breaking of the Covenant Chain to advance his own interests in this New York rivalry.[74]

From this cynical review of New York's Indian affairs, Pownall concluded that the best way to salvage the Covenant Chain was to take it out of the hands of local political factions whose trading, land-jobbing, and rivalries so irritated the Indians. Like Colden, his primary concern was to stop French expansion into the continent's interior. French posts such as

[71] [Kennedy], *Importance of Gaining and Preserving the Friendship of the Indians*, 6–8, 12–13, 16–18.
[72] See John R. Alden, "The Albany Congress and the Creation of the Indian Superintendencies," *Mississippi Valley Historical Review* 27 (1940): 193–210.
[73] Pownall to the Board of Trade, October 30, 1753, *NYCD*, 6:804–5, and [T. Pownall], "[Notes on] Indian Affairs," [1753–54], Loudoun Papers, LO 460. Pownall wrote this document sometime between Hendrick's breaking of the Covenant Chain in June 1753 and the convening of the Albany Congress a year later.
[74] [Pownall], "[Notes on] Indian Affairs," 2–3, 6.

Niagara drew the Six Nations away from the British and could cause the defection of the Mohawks to Canada. Referring specifically to Kennedy's pamphlet, Pownall endorsed the idea of placing Indian affairs for the northern colonies under the direction of a "disinterested Superintendent," funded by a Crown salary. He also favored prohibiting private land purchases from the Indians and barring fur traders and merchants from Indian diplomacy.[75]

These arguments for centralizing Indian affairs under a royal superintendent underscored the changing role of the fur trade in Britain's North American empire. Since the late seventeenth century, the Albany Commissioners of Indian Affairs had conducted New York's Indian diplomacy according to local interests. They preserved Albany's prosperity and security by striking a neutrality with French-allied Indians in Canada, despite orders from New York's royal governors to the contrary. While this insular diplomacy kept trade flowing into Albany, it angered royal officials who wished to use the fur trade as a tool for expanding British imperial power along the Great Lakes, as well as the New England colonists who bore the brunt of Anglo-French hostilities in the Northeast. Critics of the Albany Indian Commissioners ascribed to them an "Albanian spirit" that was weak, disloyal, and greedy.[76] Modern historians have disputed that portrayal, noting that by the 1730s Albany's merchants had diversified their business to include brewing, tanning, land-leasing, and exporting foodstuffs, and therefore they relied less on the fur trade for their profits. They continued to discharge Indian affairs in their community's interest, which dictated keeping the peace with their Canadian neighbors.[77]

British prejudices against the Dutch account in part for Albany's mercenary reputation, but more important, the issue boiled down to conflicting

---

[75] Ibid., 10–12.

[76] For descriptions of the "Albanian spirit," see Wraxall, *Abridgment of the Indian Affairs*, 59, 66, 111, n. 1, 221, n. 1. Wraxall was New York's secretary of Indian affairs in the early 1750s and later served as William Johnson's secretary. For the contest between the Albany Indian Commissioners and royal officials, see McIlwain's introduction, ibid., xxxv–lxxxv; Arthur H. Buffington, "The Policy of Albany and English Westward Expansion," *Mississippi Valley Historical Review* 8 (1922): 327–66; Allen W. Trelease, *Indian Affairs in Colonial New York: The Seventeenth Century* (Ithaca, 1960), 204–331; and Norton, *Fur Trade in Colonial New York*, 121–51. For a good description of the role of the fur trade in British imperial expansion, see Cutcliffe, "Colonial Indian Policy as a Measure of Rising Imperialism."

[77] See Armour, "Merchants of Albany," 181–258, and Norton, *Fur Trade in Colonial New York*, 100–120, 174–97. For a contemporary defense of the Albany Commissioners of Indian Affairs, see the "Journal and Copybook of Abraham Yates Jr., 1754–1758," Abraham Yates Jr. Papers, New York Public Library. Yates's early entries in this journal note his service to the Albany Indian Commissioners as a secretary for ten months in 1754–55. He defends their reputation and explains their conduct toward the Caughnawagas by noting that "these Gentlemen, Governed themselves According to the following Maxime that An Indian Will Either fite or trade And That the Only Way to keep them from fighting is by tradeing With them." I am indebted to Stefan Bielinski for sharing his typed transcript of Yates's journal with me.

local and imperial perspectives on Indian affairs.[78] The Indian commissioners put Albany's interests first, while royal governors such as Shirley and Clinton wanted Indian affairs to serve Britain's imperial expansion. As Kennedy explained at the outset of his pamphlet, "The Preservation of the Whole Continent depends upon a proper Regulation of the Six Nations," and the British could no longer allow the preferences of Albany to dominate Indian diplomacy.[79] The three ends embraced by the imperial reformers—colonial dependence, territorial expansion, and centralization of Indian affairs—came together in the office of an Indian superintendent who would work free from the interference of local merchants and stingy colonial assemblies to turn Indians into strong allies and good subjects.

The reform proposals submitted to the Board of Trade between 1748 and 1754 came from a variety of sources: governors gearing up for renewed Anglo-French warfare, colonial observers concerned about the break in the Covenant Chain, customs collectors distressed by the wholesale disregard for royal authority in the colonies. Their ideas reflected a variety of experiences in the colonial service but shared opinions on Britannia's Americans. The colonists were undergoing remarkable growth yet were unable to defend themselves against the French. They relied on Indian allies for security yet abused those Indians in trade and diplomacy. Most worrisome of all, Britannia's Americans—colonists and Indians alike—had grown indifferent to royal authority, and the Crown needed to secure their dependence if it wished to preserve its American empire. This reformist spirit emphasized uniformity and centralization. It encouraged a partnership between Parliament and the Crown in which the former would use its legislative power to amend charters, enforce colonial union, and levy taxes to fund royal government. To achieve such change, the reformers needed a sympathetic ear in the ministry. They found their ally in George Montagu Dunk, the Earl of Halifax, who became president of the Board of Trade in November 1748.

[78] The ethnic tensions between the British and Dutch in colonial New York were noted by the Swedish naturalist Peter Kalm, when he toured the region in the late 1740s. See Adolph B. Benson, ed., *Peter Kalm's Travels in North America: The English Version of 1770*, 2 vols. (New York, 1937), 1:343–46. Kennedy, Colden, and Pownall exhibited the prejudices against the Albany Dutch common among British officials at this time, describing them as unprincipled and covetous; see especially Colden's "Present State of Indian Affairs," 273–75, and Wraxall, *Abridgment of Indian Affairs*, passim. The roots of this prejudice can be traced to the differing perspectives that the Dutch and British took to occupying and profiting from colonial New York. See Donna Merwick, *Possessing Albany, 1630–1710: The Dutch and English Experiences* (Cambridge, Eng., 1990), 286–95.

[79] See [Kennedy], *Importance of Gaining and Preserving the Friendship of the Indians*, 7.

The Board of Trade, Britannia's Americans, and Colonial Union

Since its creation in 1696, the Board of Trade had served as a switchboard between colonial reformers and the king's Privy Council. During its first twenty-five years, the board had a reformist agenda, pursuing the resumption of colonial charters and the standardization of colonial governments under the royal model. The board's lack of executive powers, however, hampered its efforts. The secretary of state for the Southern Department monopolized the distribution of royal patronage in America and therefore controlled the implementation of colonial policy. Between 1724 and 1748 Thomas Pelham-Holmes, the Duke of Newcastle, occupied that office and steadily marginalized the Board of Trade in the ministry until it became little more than a secretarial staff for transmitting the Privy Council's orders to the colonies.[80]

The position of the Board of Trade within the ministry began to change with the appointment of the Earl of Halifax as its president in 1748. Since entering the House of Lords in 1739, Halifax had hung about the fringes of ministerial politics, awaiting an opportunity to gain office. His chance came in 1748, when the Duke of Newcastle resigned as secretary of state for the Southern Department to take over the Northern Department. In the ministerial reshuffling that followed, Halifax's patron the Duke of Bedford became secretary of the Southern Department. When Lord Monson, the Board of Trade's longtime president, died later that year, Bedford awarded the post to Halifax. Not prepared to waste his ambitions on the minutiae of colonial correspondence, Halifax broke from the customary channels of authority to make the board of Trade the primary organ of colonial administration.[81]

Under Halifax's leadership, the Board of Trade revived its reformist approach to colonial policy and acquired the political power necessary to influence the ministry. Between 1748 and the renewal of Anglo-French warfare in 1754, the board pursued several objectives in America that historians would later associate with the Seven Years' War and its after-

[80] See Ian K. Steele, *Politics of Colonial Policy: The Board of Trade in Colonial Administration, 1696–1720* (Oxford, 1968); Oliver M. Dickerson, *American Colonial Government, 1696–1765: A Study of the British Board of Trade in Its Relations to the American Colonies, Political, Industrial, Administrative* (1912; rpt. New York, 1962), 133–223; James A. Henretta, *"Salutary Neglect": Colonial Administration under the Duke of Newcastle* (Princeton, 1972), 60–165; and Andrews, *Colonial Background of the American Revolution,* (New Haven, 1938), 4:378–95.

[81] For the background of Halifax's career, see Steven G. Greiert, "The Earl of Halifax and British Colonial Policy, 1748–1756" (Ph.D. dissertation, Duke University, 1976), 36–66. On his commitment to revitalizing the Board of Trade, see Jack P. Greene, "An Uneasy Connection: An Analysis of the Preconditions of the American Revolution," in *Essays on the American Revolution,* ed. Stephen G. Kurtz and James H. Hutson (Chapel Hill, 1973), 65–80, and Arthur Basye, *The Lords Commissioners of Trade and Plantations, 1748–1782* (New Haven, 1925), 32–104.

math: the establishment of frontier military garrisons, the creation of an American revenue independent of the assemblies, the centralization of Indian affairs, and the amendment of charters to achieve a uniform system of colonial government. Thus the new imperial policy pursued by Great Britain after 1763 had deep roots in Halifax's efforts to grapple with the problems of empire during the interwar years of 1748 to 1754.[82] It was in this context of an overall reevaluation of colonial policy that the Board of Trade received the news of the broken Covenant Chain in the late summer of 1753. It responded by endorsing many of the objectives of the reformers discussed above, especially the idea of a parliamentary-enforced colonial union that would reduce Britannia's Americans to a uniform dependence on the Crown.

In transacting the Board of Trade's business, Halifax appeared more inclined toward quick action than studied reflection, but one document hints at the imperial view he brought to his office. Halifax probably wrote a brief essay titled "Some Considerations relating to the Condition of the Plantations; with Proposals for a better Regulation of them," shortly after he took over the Board of Trade.[83] It bears a striking resemblance to the reform proposals that Abercromby and McCulloh were writing at the same time, sharing with them a concern about the growth of the American colonies and their potential for independence.

According to Halifax, two pressing issues faced Britain in its colonial policy. First, taking a skeptical view of the colonists' fecundity, he warned that their daily increase made it "of the utmost Consequence to regulate them, that they may be usefull to and not rival in Power and Trade their Mother Kingdom."[84] Sound policy dictated restricting the development of colonial economies, especially their manufacturing, to ensure that North America remained a captive market for the mother country's goods. Second, Halifax argued that the Crown's North American subjects "are too apt to imbibe Notions of Indepen[den]cy of their Mother Kingdom." He attributed these notions to the self-governing privileges granted in colonial charters. Halifax believed that those charters had given great latitude to the colonies at the time of their settlement to encourage their population and limit their cost to the Crown. Now that the colonies had reached a near self-sufficiency, such indulgences were no longer necessary, and the

---

[82] See Greene, "Origins of the New Colonial Policy, 1748–63," 95–106; Bernhard Knollenberg, *Origin of the American Revolution, 1759–1766,* rev. ed. (New York, 1965) and Alan Rogers, *Empire and Liberty: American Resistance to British Authority, 1755–1763* (Berkeley, 1974).
[83] [Earl of Halifax], "Some Considerations relating to the present Conditions of the Plantations; with some Proposals for a better Regulation of them," [n.d.], PRO, CO 5/5:313–17. This document appears to be in Halifax's hand; even if he is not its author, he followed its agenda so closely during subsequent years that it may still be considered a suitable representation of his opinions on colonial administration.
[84] Ibid., 313.

Crown could amend or revoke the charters as it saw fit. Like Abercromby, Halifax believed that the imperial yoke should tighten rather than loosen over time. Not wishing to see "little Independent Commonwealths" where there had once been dependent colonies, Halifax rejected outright the idea of an empire made up of loosely confederated, self-governed polities.[85]

In this context of heightened concern over colonial independence and security, the Board of Trade received the minutes of the June 1753 conference in which Hendrick had declared the Covenant Chain broken. Reporting on those proceedings to the Privy Council, the board noted that "the Indians went away hastily from this Conference, expressing great resentment, and declaring they considered the Alliance and Friendship between them and the Province of New York to be dissolved."[86] It sent orders to Sir Danvers Osborne, then crossing the Atlantic to assume the New York governorship, expressing grave displeasure with that colony's Indian affairs and ordering him to arrange a meeting to "wipe away all remembrance of that neglect the Indians now complain [of]." Osborne was to decide the meeting's time and place, but the board suggested that Onondaga might be "the most proper place" since Albany, "which has been the usual Place of Meeting is obnoxious to them." In letters to the governors of Massachusetts, New Hampshire, New Jersey, Pennsylvania, Maryland, and Virginia, the board advised those colonies to send commissioners and presents to the conference. If possible, all colonies represented were to enter into a single treaty with the Six Nations, "it appearing to us that the practice of each Province making a separate Treaty for itself in its own name is very improper and may be attended with great inconveniency to His Majesty's service."[87] In this last statement, the board accepted the reformers' argument that leaving Indian diplomacy up to each colony was no longer agreeable with Great Britain's imperial interests.

News of the broken Covenant Chain arrived in London shortly after the ministry had debated responses to French military movements along the Great Lakes and Ohio frontier.[88] The possible loss of the Iroquois alliance made the French actions even more alarming, and in two reports written in April 1754, Halifax formulated a plan for meeting this crisis. The first report, "The Proceedings of the French in America; of which Great Britain has cause of Complaint," laid out the French grand design in North America as British colonial officials had come to recognize it. "The great Object of the French," Halifax wrote, "has for many years been to unite their Settlements upon the River St. Lawrence with those upon the Mississippi

[85] Ibid., 314–16.
[86] Board of Trade to the Earl of Holdernesse, September 18, 1753, BM, Add. Mss., 32732:661–62.
[87] Lords of Trade to Sir Danvers Osborne, September 18, 1753, NYCD, 6:800–802.
[88] See Halifax to Newcastle, August 12, 1753, BM, Add. Mss., 32732:450–51, and the Earl of Holdernesse, circular letter to the colonial governors, August 28, 1753, NYCD, 6:794–95.

. . . whereby they might secure to themselves all the valuable and extensive lands upon those two Rivers." If successful, they would "confine the
English to as narrow Limits as possible" and eventually gain a continental
dominion in the New World. Halifax believed that the French design had
always been thwarted in the past by the Iroquois alliance with the British.
But now that the Mohawks had declared the Covenant Chain broken, the
French stood on the verge of monopolizing the continent's interior.[89]

In a second report, "Proposals for building Forts etc. upon the Ohio and
other Rivers in North America," Halifax explained his plan for preserving
"Our Commerce and Correspondence with the Indians." He recommended that the British build a chain of forts from Nova Scotia to Georgia,
curving along the Great Lakes and the Ohio River, meeting the French
posts point by point. The colonial assemblies would raise the men and
money necessary to build them, and the Crown would provide troops to
garrison them. Once in place, these forts would also serve as "warehouses
for Goods used in the Indian Trade, which might be directed and regulated
by a Commissary to be stationed in each Fort." These commissaries would
license traders and settle disputes between Indians and colonists; they
would be supervised by "two general Commissaries [to] be apppointed in
the Nature of the Surveyors General of the Customs." Each would work
his own district, visiting posts to inspect accounts, renew treaties, and
make presents to the Indians in the king's name. To finance this operation,
Parliament would consolidate all royal revenues collected in America into
"one permanent and fixed Fund." This plan, he assured his superiors,
would enable the colonists to defend themselves and make war against
Canada "in Case of any future Rupture with France."[90]

Halifax's plan, devised in the months between the breaking of the Covenant Chain and the convening of the Albany Congress, distilled in spirit
and specifics many of the reform proposals that had come before the Board
of Trade since 1748. Answering the concerns of royal governors, it promised to contest French encroachments and fortify colonial frontiers with
British troops. Also, it proposed parliamentary legislation to establish a
common American fund beyond control of the individual assemblies. Last,
it presented a detailed plan for placing Indian affairs under the supervision of royal officials charged with regulating trade and conducting
diplomacy. Halifax may have owed the idea of splitting the Indian trade
into two royally supervised districts to Governor Dinwiddie of Virginia,
who had previously administered the southern half of the American cus-

[89] "The Proceedings of the French in America; of which Great Britain has cause of Complaint," April 1754, PRO, CO 5/6:96–100.
[90] "Proposals for building Forts etc. upon the Ohio and other Rivers in North America," April
30, 1754, PRO, CO 5/6:101–5. A similar version of this plan is in the Newcastle Papers, BM,
Add. Mss., 33029:109–12.

toms service and had recommended dividing the colonies into two military districts on a similar model.[91] Overall, Halifax's plan advanced the three major objectives of colonial reformers: it would use parliamentary power to curb colonial autonomy, organize the military occupation of contested regions, and place Indian affairs under imperial administration.

On June 13, 1754, just a few days before the Albany Congress convened, leading ministers gathered to discuss a recent letter from William Shirley, in which the Massachusetts governor wrote of his hopes that the colonial delegates would cement "a general Union between all his Majesty's Colonies upon this Continent" at the upcoming conference in Albany.[92] After reviewing this correspondence, the ministers decided "that immediate Directions shall be given, for promoting the Plan of a General Concert, between His Majesty's Colonies, in order to prevent or remove, any Encroachments upon the Dominions of Great Britain." They charged Halifax's Board of Trade with preparing "such a Plan of Concert." A week later Sir Thomas Robinson, the new secretary of state for the Southern Department, wrote to Shirley assuring him that the Crown had taken up the issue of colonial union.[93]

Robinson's letter belatedly endorsed the efforts of royal governors in America to promote colonial union. In their reports home, Shirley and Dinwiddie had written not only of the necessity of union but of the slim chance that the colonies would pursue it on their own. Although the king's ministers had not included colonial union in their original instructions for the Albany Congress, by the time that meeting convened they were convinced of the need for such reform. Unable to alter its instructions for the Indian conference, the Privy Council delegated the job to the Board of Trade. From an imperial perspective, the breaking of the Covenant Chain became an opportunity to take colonial military and Indian affairs out of local hands and place them in royal ones.

British policymakers considered colonial union a means of cementing the dependence of Britannia's Americans, colonists and Indians alike. Some writers earlier in the eighteenth century saw in colonial union the threat of colonial independence.[94] But the Board of Trade did not inherently oppose the idea because it recognized union's potential utility in governing an empire that was at once commercial and territorial and whose expansive colonial population needed to be placed in a proper

[91] See *Dinwiddie Papers*, 3:285, 406.
[92] For Shirley's letter, see Shirley to Holdernesse, April 19, 1754, *WS Correspondence*, 2:52–60.
[93] "Meeting at Newcastle House," June 13, 1754, BM, Add. Mss., 32995:266–67; and Robinson to Shirley, June 21, 1754, *WS Correspondence*, 2:70–71.
[94] See Bumsted, "Things in the Womb of Time," 541–42. Bumsted notes that this association between union and independence was often made by American writers defending colonial charters from parliamentary revocation or amendment.

dependency on the mother country. At several points before 1754, the Board of Trade had endorsed colonial union as a means of making the American colonies more tractable. In 1721, the board had recommended that the Crown centralize its authority in North America by placing all colonies from Nova Scotia to South Carolina "under the Government of one Lord Lieutenant or Captain General" with a salary independent of the colonial assemblies.[95] In 1739, board member Martin Bladen devised a novel plan for colonial union that called for the creation of a "Plantation Parliament," which, if properly weighted to favor royal colonies, could help overcome the resistance that individual assemblies often presented to royal authority.[96] These earlier proposals, like those advanced by Abercromby, McCulloh, and others after 1748, linked union to the creation of clearer boundaries of authority and dependence between the Crown and the colonies.

Rather than springing entirely from American soil, the idea of colonial union took shape in this wider transatlantic dialogue about colonial policy. The eighteenth century saw the rise of a British imperial state committed to expanding its sovereignty over other peoples. By mid-century, royal officials no longer viewed North America as a collection of semiautonomous plantations founded by English entrepreneurs; rather, they described it as a valuable dominion populated by what James Abercromby called "Subjects under peculiar Circumstances." This transformation in British attitudes was especially evident in the Covenant Chain. Originally a commercial alliance between Indians and colonists in the Mohawk Valley, it had become by 1753 Britain's first line of defense in its imperial struggle against France for North America. Reconstituting the chain demanded a unified colonial response under the Crown's direction. In America, the colonists who responded to that call invoked the same cause of union, but for very different reasons.

[95] "State of the British Plantations in America," September 8, 1721, *NYCD*, 5:629–30. For other instances of the board's efforts to promote colonial union before 1754, see Dickerson, *American Colonial Government*, 209–16.
[96] See Jack P. Greene, ed., "Martin Bladen's Blueprint for a Colonial Union: 'Reasons for Appointing a Captain General for the Continent of North America,'" *WMQ* 17 (1960): 516–30.

[3]

A Provincial Path to Albany:
Benjamin Franklin and
Colonial Union

JOIN, OR DIE.

—*Pennsylvania Gazette*, May 9, 1754

On May 3, 1754, word reached Philadelphia that Virginia militiamen building a fort on the forks of the Ohio River had surrendered to a French army. The May 9 edition of Benjamin Franklin's *Pennsylvania Gazette* reported this news and warned of French plans to "establish themselves, settle their Indians, and build Forts, just on the Back of our Settlements . . . from which . . . they may send out their Parties to kill and scalp the Inhabitants, and ruin the Frontier Counties." This item ended by comparing "the present disunited State of the British Colonies" with that of the French, who were "under one Direction, with one Council, and one Purse." It was immediately followed by a cartoon of a snake divided into eight pieces (Fig. 3.1). Initials placed by each segment of the snake denoted particular colonies or groups of colonies: New England, New York, New Jersey, Pennsylvania, Maryland, Virginia, North Carolina, and South Carolina. A caption beneath the snake read "JOIN, OR DIE."[1]

This cartoon and its accompanying report on the Virginians' surrender to the French circulated rapidly throughout other colonial newspapers. Four days after publication in the *Pennsylvania Gazette*, they appeared with minor variations in the *New-York Mercury* and the *New-York Gazette*. The May 20 edition of the *Boston Evening-Post* reprinted the paragraph on the Virginians' surrender without the snake cartoon. The following day this item also appeared in the *Boston Gazette*, with a differently styled version of

[1] *BF Papers*, 5:273–75.

Figure 3.1. "Join, or Die," *Pennsylvania Gazette,* May 9, 1754. Courtesy of the American Antiquarian Society.

the snake cartoon, featuring a fiercer-looking serpent, out of whose mouth came the motto "Unite and Conquer" (Fig. 3.2). The May 23 edition of the *Boston News-Letter* reproduced the paragraph and snake cartoon, borrowing the "Unite and Conquer" motto from the *Boston Gazette*.[2]

Newspapers in the southern colonies also made use of the snake cartoon. The July 19 edition of the *Virginia Gazette* reported another French victory on the Ohio, this time over a contingent of Virginia militiamen commanded by George Washington. Complaining of the slowness with which other colonies had reacted to the Ohio Valley crisis, the newspaper hoped that this news would *"inforce a late ingenious Emblem well worthy of their Attention and consideration."* In its August 22 edition, the *South Carolina Gazette* explained that the "late ingenious Emblem" referred to by the Virginia newspaper was *"a Figure of a Snake, (exhibited in the* Pennsylvania

[2] For a full listing of the snake cartoon's appearances in colonial newspapers between 1754 and 1775, see Albert Matthews, "The Snake Devices, 1754–1776, and the *Constitutional Courant,* 1765," in *Publications of the Colonial Society of Massachusetts* 11 (1910): 409–53.

Figure 3.2. "Join or Die," *Boston Gazette,* May 21, 1754. Courtesy of the Massachusetts Historical Society, Boston.

Gazette *and other* Northern *News-Papers,) divided into 8 Pieces represented by the lines underneath:*

S C.	V.	P.	N.Y.
N.C.	M.	N J.	N.E."

The "Join, or Die" snake cartoon is the most recognized image associated with the Albany Congress. Although the cartoon did not mention the congress, historians have always equated it with the Plan of Union drafted at Albany a few weeks later and Benjamin Franklin's subsequent career as an American patriot. This interpretation has ironically reversed the meaning of the cartoon, turning it from a dire warning about disunion into a herald of the federal union achieved during the Revolutionary Era. Such a perspective does little to account for the imaginative appeal of this "ingenious Emblem" at the time of its publication; only with the privilege of hindsight can we interpret it as a sign of a nascent American desire for independence. Recapturing the cartoon's meaning in 1754 requires examining it in light of British North America on the eve of the Seven Years' War. The exhortation to "Join, or Die" alerted the colonists to their vulnerability as a new Anglo-French war broke out. The long paragraph that preceded the cartoon summarized the infamous French design to conquer the continent and urged the colonists to imitate French unity or be defeated by it. Far from being a confident expression of emerging nationhood, the cartoon had an alarmist tone and predicted the potential extinction of the British colonies.

The snake cartoon was the first widely published image in British North America to represent the colonies as a single body, albeit a fragmented one. Franklin never explained why he chose a snake as his symbol. In all likelihood, he borrowed the image from a seventeenth-century French emblems book which included a picture of a snake cut in two, but Franklin customized it for his purposes by cutting the snake into several pieces and turning them into a map of the colonies.[3] The popularity of this image may be attributed in part to the fascination that Europeans had for American snakes. Travelers and naturalists from the Carolinas to New England published works during the eighteenth century that carefully described rattlesnakes and blacksnakes, creatures who supposedly practiced a power of hypnosis over their prey.[4] Because indigenous American snakes were a subject of study throughout the colonies, the symbolism of the severed snake in Franklin's cartoon could transcend regional borders in a way that other visual devices associated with the colonies—such as a tobacco leaf, a beaver, or a codfish—could not.

Although Franklin's snake cartoon did have a universal appeal in the colonies, the way it was reproduced by different newspapers reveals the persistence of local identities and prejudices. The message to "Join, or Die" reached audiences through a network of corresponding newspapers that provided colonists with their primary means of exchanging public information over great distances.[5] Rather than transmitting the snake cartoon through a single, centralized medium as the Associated Press might do today, each of these newspapers recreated and tailored it for a different local audience. The New York papers only slightly changed the *Pennsylvania Gazette*'s original, but differences became more pronounced outside of the middle colonies. In Boston, the cartoon became more aggressive. Newspapers added the "Unite and Conquer" motto, befitting Massachu-

---

[3] Olson, *Emblems of American Community*, 21–56, and Karen Severud Cook, "Benjamin Franklin and the Snake That Would Not Die," in *Images and Icons of the New World: Essays on American Cartography*, ed. Cook (Cambridge, Eng., 1996), 88–111.

[4] See, for example, Robert Beverley, *The History of Virginia, in Four Parts*, 2d rev. ed. (Richmond, 1855), 243–49; William Byrd, *Histories of the Dividing Line betwixt Virginia and North Carolina*, ed. William K. Boyd (New York, 1967), 158; J. Hector St. John de Crèvecoeur, *Letters from an American Farmer and Sketches of Eighteenth-Century America*, ed. Albert E. Stone (New York, 1981), 180–86; John Bartram, *Travels in Pensilvania and Canada* (London, 1751) passim; and Kenneth Silverman, *The Life and Times of Cotton Mather* (New York, 1984), 247–48.

[5] On the role of colonial newspapers in developing intercolonial community, see Steele, *English-Atlantic*, 132–67, and Richard L. Merritt, *Symbols of American Community, 1735–1775* (New Haven, 1966), 40–59.

setts's past support for wars against French Canada. In the southern colonies, local interests and preferences also affected the cartoon's reproduction. The *Virginia Gazette* merely referred to it as an *"ingenious Emblem"*; the *South Carolina Gazette* substituted a line drawing in place of the snake. Southern newspapers probably avoided reproducing the snake cartoon because the southern colonies appeared as the snake's tail, implying inferiority to the northern colonies at its head. The *South Carolina Gazette* solved this problem by reducing the cartoon to a more egalitarian broken line. This rendering not only removed South Carolina's embarrassing association with the snake's tail, but by turning the cartoon into a line of text read from left to right, it placed South Carolina at the head of its neighbors to the north.[6]

Like the snake in Franklin's cartoon, the colonies in 1754 could be described as both coming together and splitting apart. Contemporaries portrayed the colonies as a collection of peculiar communities that varied widely in their governments, religions, social orders, and economies. Travelers were struck by the different languages and customs they encountered when they moved beyond their homes, and they uniformly agreed that constitutional and political differences made any colonial union arising from shared sympathies unlikely. "Fire and water are not more heterogeneous than the different colonies in North America," one such observer noted. "Nothing can exceed the jealousy and emulation, which they possess in regard to each other."[7] Historians have endorsed this conclusion. They describe the colonists in the mid-eighteenth century as more different than alike and more inclined to identify with Great Britain than with each other. Any basis for a shared colonial identity existed in the colonists' common attachment to their mother country rather than to each other.[8]

Nevertheless, forces of integration existed alongside forces of division in eighteenth-century America. The most important of these were print communications and intercolonial trade, which expanded dramatically in the first half of the century and made the development of an intercolonial

---

[6] Olson, *Emblems of American Community*, 28.

[7] See Andrew Burnaby, *Travels through the Middle Settlements in North-America, in the Years 1759 and 1760* (London, 1775), 92. For a similar description of the impossibility of colonial union, see Lewis Evans, *Geographical, Historical, Political, Philosophical, and Mechanical Essays. The First, Containing an Analysis of a General Map of the Middle British Colonies in America* (Philadelphia, 1755), reproduced in Gipson, *Lewis Evans*, 176. Two travel narratives from the mid-eighteenth century that describe the local peculiarities in colonial culture are Benson, ed., *Peter Kalm's Travels in North America*, and Bridenbaugh, ed., *Gentleman's Progress*.

[8] See Jack P. Greene, "Search for Identity: An Interpretation of the Meaning of Selected Patterns of Social Response in Eighteenth-Century America," *Journal of Social History* 3 (1970): 189–220; John Murrin, "A Roof without Walls: The Dilemma of American National Identity," in *Beyond Confederation: Origins of the Constitution and American National Identity*, ed. Richard Beeman, Stephen Botein, and Edwin C. Carter II (Chapel Hill, 1987), 333–48; and Michael Zuckerman, "Identity in British America: Unease in Eden," in *Colonial Identity in the Atlantic World, 1500–1800*, ed. Nicholas Canny and Anthony Pagden (Princeton, 1987), 115–57.

community possible. Corresponding newspapers, the North American post office, subscription libraries, stagecoach routes, and improved roads created paths for regular communication between distant communities.[9] Indeed, the very designation "provincial" used by historians to describe the colonies in this period emphasizes the replication of values and institutions from the mother country that gradually lessened local and regional peculiarities.[10]

As a printer, postmaster, and public figure, Benjamin Franklin stood at the center of this intercolonial communication network and acquired a unique perspective on North America's place in the British Empire. The opinions that Franklin expressed about the Anglo-American relationship in the years leading to the Albany Congress shared much in common with those of the imperial reformers discussed in Chapter 2: he worried about French expansion, wished to see Indian affairs under more uniform regulation, and assigned the colonies a central role in Britain's future prosperity. But Franklin's perspective on North America differed from that of imperial reformers in several important ways. Whereas the Board of Trade and its American officials cast wary eyes on colonial population and economic growth, Franklin celebrated British North America's maturation into a stable, self-sustaining society. Rather than an empire held together by bonds of authority and dependence, Franklin envisioned one of equal partners, in which all of the Crown's subjects shared a common membership. He was less concerned with defining the nature of colonial subjection and more interested in identifying the cultural values and achievements that united American Britons with their fellow subjects across the Atlantic. His was an empire held together by consanguinity, filial affection, and material prosperity. It was egalitarian but also exclusive, eliminating from membership those peoples—especially Indians and Africans—who because of racial or ethnic difference did not possess what he considered to be the distinguishing characteristics of Britishness.

Franklin's provincial perspective on the empire played a pivotal role in turning the Board of Trade's intercolonial Indian conference into a forum on colonial union. Before the Albany Congress, Franklin described colonial union as a natural by-product of the development and refinement of colonial society. As the colonists grew more proficient in their emulation of their British cousins, Franklin expected them to develop the cultural bonds that would make their political union feasible and desirable. Franklin believed intercolonial elites such as himself would take the lead in this pro-

---

[9] James Truslow Adams, *Provincial Society, 1690–1763* (New York, 1927), 258–323.
[10] See ibid., 258–92; Clarence Ver Steeg, *The Formative Years, 1607–1763* (New York, 1964), 129–51; and Jack P. Greene, "Political Mimesis: A Consideration of the Historical and Cultural Roots of Legislative Behavior in the British Colonies in the Eighteenth Century," *American Historical Review* 75 (1969): 337–60.

cess by first cultivating their own common interests and then promoting union among their fellow colonists. His plans for achieving colonial union reflected his faith in the progress of colonial society and its readiness for incorporation into a more equal partnership with the rest of the British Empire.

In pursuing these objectives, Franklin met resistance mostly from the colonial assemblies, not imperial officials. The agents of imperial government, such as Governor William Shirley of Massachusetts, joined Franklin in placing colonial union on the agenda for the Albany Congress because it would assist their organization of colonial defenses against the French. The colonial assemblies, in contrast, were skeptical of any efforts to reform imperial relations that involved altering their powers of self-government. Their enthusiasm for the Albany Congress was tempered by their desire to protect local control over Indian affairs, western lands, and colonial treasuries. In the end, a writhing, severed snake proved to be an apt metaphor for the contentious and competing interests that would assemble in Albany to debate Franklin's plan for colonial union.

Benjamin Franklin: A Portrait in Provincial Assertion and Anxiety

During the 1740s, Benjamin Franklin grew rich enough from his printing business to contemplate the life of a gentleman. The success of the *Pennsylvania Gazette* and *Poor Richard's Almanac* allowed him to enter into a partnership and remove himself from the daily operations of his printshop in 1748. This retirement was necessary if Franklin were to assume genteel status, which was defined in part by freedom from manual labor. Franklin's aspirations were evident in his first portrait, completed sometime around 1746 (Fig. 3.3). In pose and costume, Franklin appears not as the rustic American with unkempt hair and beaver cap familiar to us from later portraits but as a parvenu ready to claim membership in the better sort of colonial society.[11] The portrait suggests the confident self-promotion familiar to readers of Franklin's autobiography but also the social uncertainty of a rising tradesman. Having left behind the leather apron of his craft, he dresses the part of a gentleman but is careful not to assume too much: the background is plain, giving no indication of estate or reputation; his wig is brown, not the white that signified great office or wealth; his clothing is understated, displaying none of the bright colors

---

[11] *BF Papers*, 2:xiii, and Charles Sellers, *Benjamin Franklin in Portraiture* (New Haven, 1962), 25–27. For a recent study of Franklin's early career that emphasizes his aspirations to ascend Philadelphia's social ladder, see Jennings, *Benjamin Franklin, Politician*, 59–71. Also see Robert Middlekauff, *Benjamin Franklin and His Enemies* (Berkeley, 1996).

Figure 3.3. *Benjamin Franklin,* by Robert Feke, c. 1746. Courtesy of the Harvard Portrait Collection, President and Fellows of Harvard College, Bequest of Dr. John Collins Warren, 1856.

worn by men of higher rank. The portrait, like its subject, seems unfinished, a work in progress to which more distinguishing elements might be added later.

As he stood on the threshold between tradesman and gentleman, Franklin embodied the aspirations of the provincial society around him. By the mid-eighteenth century, American colonists proudly displayed their achievements and prosperity to the outside world. They wrote about the rapid progress of British North America from an unplanted wilderness to a bustling marketplace, praised its productivity, and erected homes and public buildings to display their wealth. Underlying this confidence, however, was a creeping anxiety that colonial society did not quite measure up, that it was less refined and somehow incomplete when compared to the European standards it emulated.[12] In a famous letter to his London friend William Strahan in 1744, Franklin wrote: "We have seldom any News on our Side the Globe that can be entertaining to you on yours. All our Affairs are *petite*. They have a miniature Resemblance only, of the grand Things of Europe. Our Governments, Parliaments, Wars, Treaties, Expeditions, Factions, etc. tho' matters of great and Serious Consequence to us, can seem but Trifles to you."[13] This admission to the embarrassing smallness of colonial affairs revealed Franklin's insecurity about his position, and that of all colonial Americans, within the larger British-Atlantic world. It is also indicative of the heightened sensitivity Franklin exhibited to perceived slights against colonial character by Europeans.[14]

Franklin's thoughts on colonial union originated during his passage from humble to elevated status, and they are best interpreted as a manifestation of this provincial anxiety. As he cultivated his reputation among other prominent colonists, Franklin described union as an organic product of the colonial experience, the result of men of high reputation realizing their mutual sympathies. Colonial union arising from such circumstances would represent a new stage in provincial America's evolution from primitive origins to cultural achievements on par with those of Europe. Frank-

[12] See Richard Bushman, *The Refinement of America: Persons, Houses, Cities* (New York, 1992), 3–203, and Jack P. Greene, *The Intellectual Construction of America: Exceptionalism and Identity from 1492 to 1800* (Chapel Hill, 1993), 95–129.
[13] Franklin to Strahan, July 4, 1744, *BF Papers*, 2:411.
[14] An excellent example of this sensitivity is Franklin's 1751 editorial "Felons and Rattlesnakes," which protested Britain's policy of transporting convicted felons to the American colonies. See ibid., 4:130–33. It is also exhibited in Franklin's numerous editorials in London newspapers during his career as a colonial agent. See Verner W. Crane, ed., *Benjamin Franklin's Letters to the Press, 1758–1775* (Chapel Hill, 1950). Of related interest are Jack P. Greene's two essays exploring the pyschological dimensions of Franklin's provincial identity: "The Alienation of Benjamin Franklin—British American," *Journal of the Royal Society of Arts* 124 (1976): 52–73, and "Pride, Prejudice, and Jealousy: Benjamin Franklin's Explanation for the American Revolution," in *Reappraising Benjamin Franklin: A Bicentennial Perspective*, ed. J. A. Leo Lemay, (Newark, Del., 1993), 119–42.

lin believed it only natural that the support for union should come first from a cadre of enlightened gentlemen who possessed the learning and refinement necessary to rise above the entrenched localism of colonial life and recognize their common interests. Such was the language he used in 1743, when he proposed the creation of the American Philosophical Society to join "all the Virtuosi or ingenious Men residing in the several Colonies." Franklin modeled this society, the first of its kind in colonial America, after the learned societies of Europe, and he intended it to showcase American advancements in the arts and sciences for the rest of the world. In his own words, it would signal that the "first Drudgery of Settling new Colonies was over" and that Americans like him were now ready to contribute to "the Benefit of Mankind in general."[15]

Franklin's opinions on colonial union were shaped by his inclusion in a circle of learned gentlemen who shared his interests in the natural sciences and intercolonial issues. They included John Bartram, a botantist, and Lewis Evans, a cartographer, both of Pennsylvania; Cadwallader Colden and Archibald Kennedy of New York, both noted for their interests in Indian affairs; John Mitchell, a Virginian physician and cartographer; James Alexander, a New Yorker who studied mathematics and astronomy; and William Douglass, a Boston physician and historian. These men enjoyed the status to which Franklin aspired, and like him, they brought a provincial perspective to questions of imperial and intercolonial relations. All but Bartram had emigrated to North America from elsewhere in the British Empire: Mitchell from England; Evans from Wales; Colden, Kennedy, Douglass, and Alexander from Scotland. They were men well acquainted with the empire's other realms who modeled for colonial society the latest fashions, tastes, and manners from Britain. Several of them were a part of the Crown's officialdom in America and therefore favored the expansion of royal authority there, but because of their provincial status, they defended the colonists' rights and liberties as British subjects.

During the late 1740s and early 1750s, this circle of correspondents engaged in a collective task to reacquaint the rest of the British Empire with colonial North America. They wrote histories of British colonization, published maps of British possessions, explained the nature of colonial politics, and classified North America's plant and animal life. Their inclination to study the colonies derived in part from the backgrounds of so many participants in this network, which was dominated by well-educated Scots. These men migrated to America in the wake of the Anglo-Scottish Union of 1707, seeking the opportunities denied them by an English aristocracy who dismissed them as rude and grasping country cousins. In North America, their education, capital, and connections to

[15] BF Papers, 2:380–82.

other Scots in colonial administration gave them access to patronage and status unavailable in Britain.[16] They shared Franklin's style of self-promotion as well as his provincial anxiety. As transplants from one periphery to another, they did not wish to see their status as British subjects compromised by the move. They worked assiduously to publicize the progress of colonial society, an impulse best expressed in the title of William Douglass's encyclopedic work, *A Summary, Historical and Political, of the First Planting, Progressive Improvements, and Present State of the British Settlements in North-America.*[17]

These provincial observers, taking the whole of British North America as their subject, pondered the same question as the imperial reformers discussed in the previous chapter—how did the colonies and the rest of the empire fit together?—but with important differences in perspective. First, imperial reformers such as Thomas Pownall, James Abercromby, and Henry McCulloh were sojourners in America; they treated the colonies as stepping-stones in their careers, which always led back to London. Provincial commentators, on the other hand, were in North America to stay, and they were much more inclined to be laudatory and defensive about their adopted homeland. Whereas imperial reformers addressed ways of arresting America's economic and political independence, provincial observers emphasized the evolutionary nature of colonial development and the need to keep colonial liberties on par with those of other British subjects. Also, provincial observers were much more likely than imperial ones to make distinctions about the ethnic and racial composition of British North America. To them, Britannia's Americans were not an amalgamation of dependent peoples inhabiting a distant place; on the contrary, they were liberty-loving Britons. They excluded from membership in this definition those groups that could not share in a fundamental Britishness because of racial or ethnic difference.

William Douglass began his history of the colonies by stating, "The people in Europe . . . have a very indistinct notion of these settlements."[18] Likewise, Archibald Kennedy in his 1750 pamphlet *Observations on the*

---

[16] For Scots in America and their influence on provincial culture, see Eric Richards, "Scotland and the Uses of the Atlantic Empire," in *Strangers within the Realm,* ed. Bailyn and Morgan, 67–114; Colley, *Britons,* 117–32; Ned Landsman, "The Provinces and the Empire: Scotland, the American Colonies, and the Development of British Provincial Identity," in *Imperial State at War,* ed. Stone, 258–87; and John Clive and Bernard Bailyn, "England's Cultural Provinces: Scotland and America," *WMQ* 11 (1954): 207–8.

[17] Douglass published his history initially in separate brief pamphlets in the late 1740s. He collected them into two volumes published in 1749 and 1751. Benjamin Franklin sent copies to his London correspondent Peter Collinson and, through a mutual correspondent, helped Douglass collect information on smallpox inoculations in America. See *BF Papers,* 3:461, n. 9 and 4:336–38, 340–41. Also see David Freeman Hawke, "William Douglass's *Summary,*" in *Colonial Legacy,* ed. Leder, 43–74.

[18] Douglass, *Summary,* 1:1.

Importance of the Northern Colonies Under Proper Regulations suggested that the Crown send agents over to America to reacquaint London ministers with the land and its people, as "They have generally but a very vague Idea of these Colonies."[19] This desire to reeducate Britain about North America animated much of the writing by these transplanted provincials, who wished to impress upon their readers the "considerable Maturity" of the colonies and to challenge policies aimed at arresting colonial development.[20] Kennedy wrote *Observations on the Importance of the Northern Colonies under Proper Regulations* to recommend that instead of merely restricting colonial trade, the mother country channel it in directions more beneficial to the empire. He found that the Navigation Acts placed unnecessary restrictions on the colonists' productivity and prevented them from addressing their trade imbalance with the mother country. Instead, he wanted to see regulations that governed colonial industries "by a proper Encouragement, not by coercive or restraining Laws." Any policy that sought to secure the colonists' dependence by keeping them poor and low, Kennedy warned, would face resistance in America because they were contrary to "the Conceptions we have of *English Liberty*."[21]

Douglass saw a similar threat in current colonial policy. In what he called a "*Utopian Amusement*," he offered a grand plan for reforming British rule in North America by revising colonial charters on the royal model, redrawing colonial borders, and establishing a colonial aristocracy. All of these measures would have appealed to imperial reformers, who also sought to standardize colonial government, but equally important to Douglass was the protection of colonial liberties. His "MAGNA CHARTA OF THE BRITISH COLONIES IN AMERICA" would guarantee religious toleration for all Protestants, freedom from impressment for military service, colonial control over American courts and judges, and an easing of the Navigation Acts to allow for colonial trade with foreign countries.[22]

Neither Douglass, Kennedy, nor any other provincial writer in their circle doubted Parliament's power to effect such changes in colonial government. They did not feel it necessary to defend colonial charters or the varied local powers they granted to colonial assemblies. On the contrary, they were generally critical of the "Inconveniences of the *Politia* or *Polity* of the several Colonies" and encouraged their reduction to "some general

---

[19] Archibald Kennedy, *Observations on the Importance of the Northern Colonies under Proper Regulations* (New York, 1750), 21. A good summary of Kennedy's life and approach to imperial policy is Milton M. Klein, "Archibald Kennedy: Imperial Pamphleteer," in *The Colonial Legacy*, ed. Leder, 75–105.

[20] Douglass, *Summary*, 1:241. See also [Mitchell], *Contest in America*, iii–xlix.

[21] Kennedy, *Observations*,10–20, 31. For a similar view of the Navigation Acts by another Scottish transplant, see Cadwallader Colden, "Of the Trade of New York," June 25, 1723, *NYCD*, 5:689.

[22] Douglass, *Summary*,1:233–63.

Uniformity."[23] The more pressing issue was making sure that colonial policy encouraged rather than retarded British North America's growth. Again, the Scottish background of these writers is important. Before the Act of Union in 1707, the English Navigation Acts had prevented the Scots from sharing in the profits of empire. The union lifted those restrictions and opened new opportunities for Scots. Those who resettled in America did not wish to see their ambitions denied by discriminatory policy still in place against another of the empire's provinces.

Closely related to this concern for colonial liberties was a preoccupation with asserting the "British" character of British North America. One reason Kennedy and Douglass devoted so much energy to applauding North America's progress was to revise their adopted homeland's reputation elsewhere in the empire. The inhabitants of Britain generally looked down on North America as the poorer cousin of the sugar colonies of the West Indies, a refuge for religious fanatics, criminals, and ne'er-do-wells who left home to escape persecution, debt, or the noose.[24] Well-heeled Scottish emigrants such as Douglass and Kennedy did not wish to be identified with such unflattering depictions of America, and they did their best to present the colonies as loyal, prosperous, and populated by what Douglass called "good, industrious, frugal, pious, and moral Gentlemen."[25]

Provincial writers were also disturbed by the growing number of non-British people in the colonial population. These colonists fell into three categories. The first included non-British Europeans who retained their distinctive customs, religions, and languages by living apart from the larger British colonial population. The Dutch of Albany were notorious for their insular and peculiar ways. Kennedy and Colden blasted them for disloyalty, and Douglass dismissed the Dutch in general as "an amphibious Man-Animal."[26] Also of concern were the French Acadians of Nova Scotia and the Germans of Pennsylvania and New York. Douglass believed that "Foreigners imported, should not be allowed to settle in large separate Districts, as is the present bad Practice; because for many Generations they may continue, as it were, a separate People in Language, Modes of Religion, Customs and Manners." He urged that they be "intermixed with the *British* Settlers" and gradually anglicized by placing English schoolmasters, ministers, and churches among them. Archibald Kennedy rec-

---

[23] Ibid., 242. Kennedy also criticizes the localism and short sightedness of colonial assemblies in *Observations*,7.

[24] For comments on this reputation, see Kennedy, *Observations*,20–21, and [Mitchell], *Contest in America*, xix.

[25] Douglass, *Summary*,1:223. See also Kennedy's description of hardworking, productive, and loyal colonists in *Observations*, 4–10.

[26] [Kennedy], *Importance of Gaining and Preserving the Friendship of the Indians*,12–13; Cadwallader Colden, "The present state of the Indian affairs with the British & French Colonies in North America," *Colden Papers*, 53:271–87; and Douglass, *Summary*,1:5.

ommended the same for the large number of Germans flowing into Pennsylvania.[27]

Foreign Europeans at least had the potential to be anglicized. Two other groups presented a more persistent challenge to the British character of the colonial population: Indians and Africans. African slavery increased rapidly in North America after 1710, and by 1760 slaves accounted for 60 percent of South Carolina's population and 40 percent of Virginia's.[28] This expansion in the slave population did not escape writers in the northern colonies, who lamented the changing complexion of colonial society.[29] Indians presented another problem. After a century and a half of colonization, the English had failed in their self-appointed task to "reduce the Indians to civility": Indian converts were few and stubbornly retained their native ways. Eighteenth-century writers worried about the cultural degeneracy of colonial society, especially along the frontier, where "Indianization" rather than "anglicanization" seemed to be the norm.[30] Douglass condemned Indians as "Men-Brutes of the Forest" lacking all the hallmarks of civilization: "no Civil Government, no Religion, no Letters." Throughout his long analysis of Indian culture and government, Douglass found a place for them in colonial society only once, when he observed, "Many of our intermixed *Indians* are of good Use as Servants."[31] In his eyes, they most certainly did not deserve inclusion among Britannia's Americans.

Anxious provincials feared that British North America's changing racial and ethnic character would cause Britons across the Atlantic to view the colonists as a foreign, conquered people rather than kin. Again, Douglass summarized the problem best: "All our *American* Settlements are properly *Colonies*, not Provinces as they are generally called. *Province* respects a conquered *People* . . . under a Jurisdiction imposed upon them by a Conqueror; *Colonies* are formed of national People, *v.g.* British in the *British* Colonies, transported to form a Settlement in a foreign or remote Country."[32] For Douglass, the process of colonization involved the transplantation of a national people in new soil, where they replicated in miniature the

[27] Douglass, *Summary*,1:209, and [Kennedy], *Importance of Gaining and Preserving the Friendship of the Indians*, 9–10.
[28] See Greene, *Pursuits of Happiness*,178–79.
[29] See, for example, Hutchinson, *History of the Colony and Province of Massachusetts-Bay*, 2:340, and Benjamin Franklin, "Observations Concerning the Increase of Mankind," 1751, *BF Papers*, 4:229.
[30] See James Axtell, *The European and the Indian: Essays in the Ethnohistory of Colonial America* (Oxford, 1981), 39–86, 168–206, and Greene, *Intellectual Construction of America*, 66–67. For contemporary fears of "Indianization" on the colonial frontier, see, for example, Crèvecoeur, *Letters from an American Farmer*, 76–79; and Charles Woodmason, *The Carolina Backcountry on the Eve of the Revolution: The Journal and Other Writings of Charles Woodmason, Anglican Itinerant*, ed. Richard J. Hooker (Chapel Hill, 1953), passim.
[31] Douglass, *Summary*,1:154–56.
[32] Ibid., 206.

institutions and values of the mother country. This view of empire implied a greater parity between the colonists and the rest of the Crown's subjects, but it also drew a clear line between those people who could claim membership in this British identity and those who could not.

Benjamin Franklin's perspective on the British Empire was sympathetic with that of such Scottish transplants as Douglass, Colden, and Kennedy for several reasons. First, he shared with them an intellectual kinship and corresponded with them on such topics as medicine and the natural sciences. Second, these men were the models of learned gentility and public-spiritedness to which Franklin aspired. They held degrees from universities, belonged to clubs and voluntary associations, and had traveled throughout Europe, the West Indies, and North America. When he began writing about imperial relations and colonial union in the early 1750s, Franklin joined in their celebration of America's prosperity, their defense of colonial character and liberties, and their criticism of restrictive policies that relegated British North America to a second-class status in the empire. He also shared their concern about the racial and ethnic diversity of the colonies. Most indicative of Franklin's indentification with these men was his plan for colonial union. Any such union, he wrote, would not be initiated by the colonial governments, which he considered too parochial to realize its utility. Rather, union would be achieved through the efforts of a "Half a dozen Men of Good Understanding and Address," who possessed the foresight and reputations necessary to act as ambassadors for such a plan: in other words, his cadre of provincial elites.[33]

Franklin expressed his provincial perspective on the empire in two essays—one on colonial demography and the other on colonial union—which he wrote in 1751. Both embodied Douglass's notion that the colonies were an extension of a "national people" and that their most important bond to each other and the mother country was a shared British identity. Read together, they present Franklin as the anxious and assertive colonist of his portrait, quick to celebrate the maturation of colonial society and equally quick to defend it from discriminatory policies or attitudes originating across the Atlantic.

Central to Franklin's perception of the empire was his faith in British North America's progress from a collection of rude, isolated settlements into a prosperous, cultivated society. Colonies, like childen, matured and gradually became capable of greater autonomy. In human families, the bonds of filial affection and duty remained, but nature dictated that children ultimately assume a parity with their parents. So too did Franklin expect colonial development to transform the old imperial relationship into a new partnership between British North America and Britain. This

[33] *BF Papers*, 4:118. This plan will be discussed at length below.

partnership, valued and preserved by Britons living on both sides of the Atlantic, would have no need of laws and regulations that proscribed colonial trade and liberties. Franklin most clearly articulated this vision of the empire in "Observations Concerning the Increase of Mankind," a treatise on colonial population growth in which he used familial imagery to assert the transatlantic consanguinity of British peoples.

"Observations Concerning the Increase of Mankind" originated as a critique of what Franklin considered to be a misguided piece of parliamentary legislation. The Iron Act of 1750 prohibited the construction of additional mills, forges, and furnaces for iron production in America.[34] Mercantilist theory dictated that colonial industries had to be proscribed to preserve export markets for the mother country's manufactured goods. Franklin turned that belief on its head by arguing that colonial economic development posed no threat to Britain because the abundance of land in America drew colonists away from manufacturing and into agriculture. Even without manufacturing of their own, the colonists were reproducing so fast that they would soon surpass Britain's ability to supply them. Prohibiting the development of colonial industries, therefore, would only hurt the mother country by unnecessarily slowing the colonial economy and reducing American demand for British goods. To preserve its American markets, Franklin concluded, Britain had to adopt a policy that encouraged rather than inhibited colonial population and economic growth.[35]

Franklin's analysis found in the prolific colonial family a model for the British Empire. Since the seventeenth century, writers had used the family metaphor to explain the relationship between colonies and mother country. The Crown ruled as a nurturing parent, while colonies acted as obedient children, returning allegiance and adding to the wealth of the mother country.[36] British writers usually invoked the family metaphor to illustrate Britain's parental authority over the colonies.[37] Franklin used it differently. To him, the family was an apt metaphor because the purpose of empire was regenerative: to extend a national people across time and space. Any policy that discouraged colonial population growth was bad, while "the Prince that acquires new Territory, if he finds it vacant, or removes the Natives to give his own People Room . . . and the Man that invents new Trades, Arts, or Manufactures . . . may be properly called *Fathers* of their Nation, as they are the Cause of the Generation of Multitudes." Mercan-

---

[34] For an explanation of the Iron Act's influence on "Observations Concerning the Increase of Mankind," see *BF Papers*, 4:225–26.

[35] For the text of "Observations," see ibid., 225–34.

[36] On the family metaphor for empire, see Greene, "Uneasy Connection," 34–65.

[37] For examples, see [John Bennet], *The National Merchant: or, a Discourse on Commerce and Colonies* (London, 1736), 116–18, 125, and [John Trenchard and Thomas Gordon], *Cato's Letters: or Essays on Liberty, Civil and Religious, and Other Important Subjects,* 4 vols. (London, 1783), 4:7–12.

tilist policy such as the Iron Act was of no value because it slowed colonial expansion and, by "weakening the Children, weakens the whole Family."[38]

In "Observations Concerning the Increase of Mankind," Franklin sympathized with Douglass's definition of a colony as a society "formed of national People" transplanted to a new realm.[39] He speculated in terms reminiscent of Douglass that if the world were empty, "it might in a few Ages be replenish'd from one Nation only; as, for Instance, with Englishmen" by colonizing themselves abroad. Of course, the world was not empty, but in Franklin's eyes North America was. Contemplating the reproductive potential of the million British subjects already there, he waxed eloquently about a continental British dominion: "This Million doubling, suppose but once in 25 Years, will in another Century be more than the People of England. . . . What an Accession of Power to the British Empire by Sea as well as Land! What Increase of Trade and Navigation! What Numbers of Ships and Seamen!" Within a few generations, Franklin wrote confidently, "the greatest Number of Englishmen will be on this Side the Water." Once that population shift occurred, little more than distance would be left to distinguish between Britons in the British Isles and those in America: the empire would be a transatlantic dominion inhabited by a single national people.[40]

To strengthen his claim for the colonists' inclusion in that collective British identity, Franklin specifically excluded from it such non-British inhabitants of North America as slaves, Indians, and Germans. In a list of policies that "must diminish a nation," he included the "Introduction of Slaves" because whites who owned slaves became "enfeebled" by their idleness "and therefore not so prolific."[41] He regarded Indians as a primitive people destined to melt away in the face of the more numerous and civilized colonists. At the beginning of "Observations Concerning the Increase of Mankind," Franklin explained that Indians "subsist mostly by hunting," which kept their populations low and dispersed. Colonists easily prevailed upon them to sell land in return for trade goods and, by this process, displaced Indians wherever they settled.[42] Like many eighteenth-century writers, Franklin misinterpreted the Indians' use of land and ignored their horticulture, but such oversight was necessary to sustain his vision of a British North America devoid of its native inhabitants. In a famous passage from his autobiography, he recalled witnessing a drunken Indian feast at a 1753 treaty conference and observed, "if it be

[38] *BF Papers*, 4:229, 231, 233.
[39] Whether Franklin read Douglass's work is not clear, but he did send copies of it to his London correspondent Peter Collinson. Ibid., 3:461; 4:414, 456, 5:191, 454.
[40] Ibid., 4:233.
[41] Ibid., 230–33.
[42] Ibid., 228, 231.

the Design of Providence to extirpate these Savages in order to make room for Cultivators of the Earth, its seems not improbable that Rum may be the appointed Means."[43] No less a force than Providence had doomed the Indians to extinction and provided the British with the goods necessary to do so. As he did with slaves, Franklin placed Indians well beyond the borders of the British community he imagined arising in North America.[44]

Franklin's concern for protecting the British character of North America also surfaced in his denunciation of Pennsylvania's German population. In "Observations Concerning the Increase of Mankind" he wondered why "the Palatine Boors [should] be suffered to swarm into our Settlements, and by herding together establish their Language and Manners to the Exclusion of ours? Why should Pennsylvania, founded by the English, become a Colony of *Aliens*[?]" The bestial imagery used to describe the Germans is unmistakable: they "swarmed" and "herded" together, threatening "to Germanize us instead of our Anglifying them." They showed no inclination to "adopt our Language any more than they can acquire our Complexion," and Franklin doubted the ability of such a large body of foreigners to become good British subjects.[45] "This will in a few Years become a German Colony," he wrote to a New York correspondent in 1751. "Instead of their Learning our Language, we must learn their's, or live as in a foreign Country."[46] Like Douglass, he believed that foreign Protestants could be assimilated into the British colonial population, so long as they were not allowed to perpetuate their cultural differences: "all that seems necessary is, to distribute them more equally, mix them with the English, [and] establish English Schools where they are now too thick settled."[47]

Franklin flatly stated the racial exclusivity underlying his notion of empire in the closing paragraph of "Observations Concerning the Increase of Mankind." He wrote, "the Number of purely white People in the World is proportionately very small. All Africa is black or tawney. Asia chiefly tawney. America (exclusive of the new Comers) wholly so." The Saxons and the English made up "the principal Body of white People on the Face of the Earth," and Franklin wished to see their numbers increased. "And while we are, as I may call it, *Scouring* our Planet by clearing America of Woods . . . why should we . . . darken its People? Why increase the Sons of Africa by Planting them in America, where we have so fair an Oppor-

[43] Farrand, *Franklin's Memoirs,* 306.
[44] Franklin, as a colonist immersed in print culture and frustrated by a sense of provincial inadequacy, fits Benedict Anderson's model for the type of creole inclined to imagine and claim membership in an expansive national identity. See Anderson, *Imagined Communities: Reflections on the Origin and Spread of Nationalism* (London, 1983).
[45] *BF Papers,* 4:234.
[46] Franklin to James Parker, March 20, 1751, ibid., 120. Also see Franklin to Peter Collinson, May 9, 1753, ibid., 484–85.
[47] Ibid., 485.

tunity, by excluding all Blacks and Tawneys, of increasing the lovely White and Red?" Franklin, of course, did not expect "the lovely Red" to increase, for the reasons outlined above. But he did admit his partiality to "the Complexion of my Country" and lamented that "100 Years of Exportation of Slaves" had already "blacken'd half America."[48] North America was to be in complexion and character an extension of Britain, not an amalgation of Europe, Africa, and the Americas.

Ostensibly a treatise on population growth, "Observations Concerning the Increase of Mankind" contained the fullest expression of a provincial American view of the British Empire up to that time. Franklin sought colonial respectability by breaking down the distinctions between colonist and Briton and challenging traditional mercantilist assumptions about colonial dependence. In a statement with bold implications for the British Empire, he predicted a day when the majority of Britons would live in North America. And in closing, he made clear that the colonists' inclusion in this empire depended on the exclusion of non-British others. He defined his empire by racial and cultural borders rather than territorial ones, including within it all those peoples sharing "the English Laws, Manners, Liberties and Religion."[49] Not surprisingly, when Franklin published this essay, it appeared as an appendix to William Clarke's *Observations on the Present Conduct of the French* (1755), a pamphlet advocating the conquest of Canada so that the British colonial population might continue to expand unhindered by the French.

In the same year that Franklin wrote "Observations Concerning the Increase of Mankind," he published for the first time a plan for colonial union. His interest in imperial affairs drew him naturally into intercolonial relations, and the context in which Franklin's plan appeared indicated his concern with the most pressing intercolonial issue of that time, Indian policy. Yet what is most notable about Franklin's 1751 plan is its promotion of a union formed by the colonists themselves, rather than by Parliament or the Crown. Franklin believed that if the proper gentlemen promoted the plan, they would be able to circumvent the normal channels of colonial government and form a union premised on the colonists' mutual sentiments and interests. Such a union would decrease the jealousies that had separated the colonies and bring British North Americans into a new partnership with each other and the empire.

Franklin's proposals for colonial union originated in his correspondence with Archibald Kennedy and Cadwallader Colden about Indian affairs. In early 1751 the New York printer James Parker sent Franklin a manuscript copy of Kennedy's *The Importance of Gaining and Preserving the Friendship of the Indians to the British Interest, Considered,* asking for his comments. Frank-

---

48 Ibid., 233–34.
49 Ibid., 485–86.

lin endorsed Kennedy's scheme for a Crown-appointed Indian superintendent and added his own recommendations for a comprehensive colonial union. Parker sent Franklin's comments to Kennedy, who shared them with Colden. When Parker published Kennedy's essay in May 1751, Franklin agreed to have his letter attached as an appendix.[50]

Franklin believed that the chief obstacle to implementing a union was the resistance offered by the individual colonial governments. In the past, the sentiment for colonial union had always fallen prey to antagonisms between popular and prerogative powers, as represented by the assemblies and royal governors, respectively. A governor who saw "the Necessity of such an Union" would write to his fellow governors and ask them to present the idea to their assemblies. But governors were often at odds with their assemblies and held little influence among their members. Some governors, Franklin suspected, "may privately throw cold Water" on such plans, fearing that a union would create new expenses that would reduce their salaries. Without the genuine support of the assemblies or the governors, the scheme "'tis easily dropt, and nothing is done." In place of this method Franklin suggested that "Half a Dozen Men of good Understanding and Address" act as ambassadors for a plan of union, visiting other colonies, "where they might apply particularly to all the leading Men, and by proper Management get them to engage in promoting the Scheme." By purposely bypassing the assemblies and governors, Franklin's agents would win support for the plan before local objections could "spread and gather Strength in the Minds of the People."[51]

As for the plan itself, Franklin favored the formation of an intercolonial legislature or "general Council" in which each colony received representation proportional to its contribution to a common treasury. The Crown would appoint a governor general to preside over this body, and together they would would frame laws on "every Thing relating to Indian Affairs and the Defence of the Colonies." To fund the treasury, Franklin proposed "an equal Excise on strong Liquors in all the Colonies" but did not say whether Parliament or the intercolonial legislature would impose it. He also suggested that the General Council convene in a different colony each year so that its members might become "better acquainted with the Circumstances, Interests, Strength or Weakness, etc. of all."[52] Simply by participating in this union, the colonists would cultivate the sympathies necessary to make them more cooperative in the future.

Franklin conceived of his plan as an alternative to the traditional institutions of colonial government. The intercolonial legislature would allow forward-thinking colonists to overcome local interests and factions, and an

[50] See Franklin to James Parker, March 20, 1751, ibid., 117–21.
[51] Ibid., 118.
[52] Ibid., 118–19.

intercolonial liquor tax would free this new government from dependence on the assemblies. He exhibited little concern for the charter privileges of individual colonies. For the "half a Dozen Men of good Understanding and Address" who would serve as the plan's ambassadors, Franklin had in mind men such as himself, Kennedy, and Colden: influential colonists who already shared intercolonial contacts and reputations. They would act as the political equivalent of the American Philosophical Society, communicating on matters of defense and Indian affairs. Franklin placed a great deal of faith in this sort of intercolonial correspondence, and he hoped that Kennedy's pamphlet would spark "a more general Communication of the Sentiments of judicious Men on Subjects so generally interesting." Most important, he wanted this union to be the product of colonial effort. "A voluntary union," he explained, "would be preferable to one impos'd by Parliament; for it would be perhaps not much more difficult to procure and more easy to alter and improve."[53] In short, it would leave the initiative in the hands of the cosmopolitan men who formed the union, whom Franklin expected to be above the factious and insular politics of individual colonies. Moreover, it would prove to Great Britian the colonists' willingness and ability to assume greater responsibility in managing their own affairs.

In his letter outlining this plan, Franklin compared his proposed union to the Iroquois Confederacy: "It would be a very strange Thing, if six Nations of ignorant Savages should be capable of forming a Scheme for such an Union, and be able to execute it in such a Manner, as that it has subsisted Ages, and appears indissoluble; and yet that a like Union should be impracticable for ten or a Dozen English Colonies, to whom it is more necessary, and must be more advantageous; and who cannot be supposed to want an equal Understanding of their Interests."[54] Some scholars have interpreted this passage as evidence that Franklin used the Iroquois as a model for his plan of union.[55] That interpretation is clearly flawed when the passage is analyzed in the wider context of Franklin's remarks about Indians and their place in British North America.

When Franklin referred to "Six Nations of Ignorant Savages," he was using the Iroquois as a negative example to illustrate the colonists' failure to recognize their own common interests. This statement was consistent with Franklin's tendency to assert the civility of colonial society by juxtaposing it with what he perceived as the savagery of the Indians. For example, in the 1744 letter to William Strahan in which Franklin confessed the smallness of American affairs, he also promised to send Strahan copies

[53] Ibid., 118, 121.
[54] Ibid., 118–19.
[55] See the discussion of the Iroquois Influence Thesis in the Introduction for the relevant bibliographic citations.

of the proceedings from an Indian treaty conference, "as the Method of doing Business with those Barbarians may perhaps afford you some Amusement."[56] This statement was entirely consistent with the anxious provincial voice Franklin assumed with his London correspondents. To assert his membership in polite British society, he needed to distance himself from the primitiveness Europeans associated with American society. He turned the Indians into a negative image of the colonial world he inhabited, contrasting their foreign and savage quality with the progress he claimed for British North America. Whether in sending copies of an Indian treaty to London or in invoking the example of "Six Nations of Ignorant Savages" to promote colonial union, Franklin purposely distanced colonial society from the native peoples of America. While he recognized the strength and durability of the Iroquois Confederacy, it could offer no lessons for Franklin in modeling colonial union because of its primitive origins. To imitate it would be to reverse the direction of his aspirations for colonial society, modeling it after "Barbarians" rather than the polite European society to which he desired admission.

Franklin expected colonial union to serve two ends. At one level, it would cultivate among the colonists a recognition of their mutual interests. The intercolonial General Council would be one step toward a truly organic union, in which communication and cooperation replaced isolation and division. It would facilitate an ongoing process of political and cultural integration, bringing the colonists into closer contact with each other and the rest of the British Empire. Second, Franklin considered colonial union a necessary passage in the continuing evolution of the imperial relationship. The cooperation between a royal governor general and an intercolonial legislature would signal a new Anglo-American partnership in which imperial authority in British North America loosened and the colonists assumed greater responsibility in governing intercolonial affairs.

Indeed, the breaking down of intercolonial barriers complemented Franklin's desire to eradicate the distinctions between "colonist" and "Briton." As an American, he wished to see the colonists included among the British people without any special liabilities or qualifications attached to their colonial status. In "Observations Concerning the Increase of Mankind," he expanded the meaning of "British" to include "British-American" while taking pains to exclude non-Britons—Indians, slaves, unassimilated Germans—from that group. Imperial officials such as Lord Halifax or William Shirley would have considered the operative word in "colonial British America" to be "colonial" because it implied the dependence they associated with all of North America's inhabitants, be they native or European. In Franklin's case it was "British," for through that

[56] *BF Papers*, 2:411.

cultural designation the colonists could distance themselves from North America's other inhabitants and claim their rightful place in the larger British Empire.

The Paths to Albany

When the Board of Trade's orders to convene an intercolonial Indian conference reached America in late 1753, the colonial governments did not react in the way Franklin would have preferred. Rather than expressing any united resolve, they took off in many different directions, much like the pieces of the snake in his cartoon. Colonial assemblies regarded the board's orders suspiciously and responded in ways that protected their particular interests in Indian affairs, western lands, and frontier defenses. When appointing commissioners to attend this meeting, several assemblies specifically forbade them from discussing any plans to create an intercolonial authority in these matters. Two colonial governors—James DeLancey of New York and William Shirley of Massachusetts—did advocate using the conference to form some kind of union, but even they had contrary purposes in mind. None of this behavior surprised Franklin and his circle of provincial correspondents; they expected the colonial governments to act out of parochial jealousies, even in times of common peril. As the convening of the Albany Congress neared, Franklin remained committed to colonial union but became more skeptical about the colonists' willingness to pursue it. He warmed to the idea of appealing to Parliament to impose a union that would force the colonies to cooperate in meeting Britain's imperial crisis in North America.

A twist of fate altered the colonial reception of the Board of Trade's orders for the conference. The board had addressed its orders to Sir Danvers Osborne, the royal governor of New York, and its letter indicated extreme displeasure with that colony's past management of Indian affairs.[57] When the board's letter reached New York, however, Osborne was dead and his office had passed to Lieutenant Governor James DeLancey, a political and commercial ally of the Albany merchants.[58] In carrying out the board's orders, DeLancey reversed their spirit by attempting to protect his colony's monopolistic management of the Covenant Chain. He set June 14, 1754, as the date for the conference to open, and although the Board of

[57] Board of Trade to Osborne, September 18, 1753, NYCD, 6:800–801.
[58] For a description of DeLancey and his political career before 1754, see Bonomi, Factious People,140–66. On Osborne's suicide, see Smith, History of the Province of New-York, 2:132–35. On DeLancey's leadership of the faction opposed to Governor Clinton during the 1740s and 1750s, see Katz, Newcastle's New York,164–244. On DeLancey's alliance with the Albany merchants, see Milton Klein, "William Livingston's A Review of the Military Operations in North-America," in Colonial Legacy, ed. Leder, 110–12.

Trade had suggested Onondaga as the meeting place, he selected Albany because he believed it "the most proper and the usual place of holding General Conferences with the Indians." He sent word to the governors of Massachusetts, New Hampshire, New Jersey, Pennsylvania, Maryland, and Virginia about the conference and also invited Rhode Island and Connecticut, two colonies not included on the Board of Trade's original list.[59]

In this correspondence with other colonial governors, DeLancey set his agenda for the upcoming conference. He warned that the Covenant Chain would be lost if the colonies did not take joint measures to protect the Six Nations' homelands from French encroachments, and he called on the other governments to assist in fortifying the New York frontier.[60] To William Shirley he noted that such work called for "an Union of Councils and a joint expence of all the Colonies," which might be "accomplished at the interview at Albany or at least a plan for this purpose agreed on."[61] DeLancey defended New York's primacy in the Covenant Chain to Connecticut governor Roger Wolcott, explaining that while other colonies should contribute to building forts in Iroquoia, "yet it might be expected a Scheme for that Purpose should take its rise here [New York]."[62] When Pennsylvania governor James Hamilton asked DeLancey what business the Albany conference would address, he responded that its primary end was to "concert measures for building Forts" that would keep the Six Nations in the British interest.[63]

DeLancey's call for intercolonial cooperation was defensive in nature, designed to protect his colony from attack and preserve its control over the Covenant Chain. He spoke strongly about the union of councils necessary in Albany, but he did not share the expansionist imperialism of William Shirley. Rather, his intentions resembled those of Robert Livingston, another New Yorker, who in 1701 had promoted colonial union chiefly as a means of raising the money necessary to build forts on New York's frontier and protect its fur trade.[64] While DeLancey borrowed substantially from Archibald Kennedy's 1751 pamphlet on Indian affairs in making his plans for the Albany Congress, he remained silent about Kennedy's proposal for an intercolonial Indian superintendent, for such a measure would have ended New York's hold on the Covenant Chain.

---

[59] DeLancey to the Board of Trade, December 24, 1753, *NYCD*, 6:817–19. DeLancey apparently invited Connecticut and Rhode Island after William Shirley encouraged him to do so. See DeLancey to Shirley, March 5, 1754, Mass. Archives, 4:442–44.

[60] See DeLancey to Holdernesse, April 22, 1754, BM, Add. Mss., 32735:154–57, and *Penn. Council Minutes*, 6:34.

[61] DeLancey to Shirley, March 5, 1754, Mass. Archives, 4:444, 450–51.

[62] DeLancey to Wolcott, April 22, 1754, *Collections of the Connecticut Historical Society* 16 (1916): 441–43. Also see DeLancey to Wolcott, March 9, 1754, ibid., 437–38.

[63] DeLancey to Hamilton, April 1, 1754, *Penn. Council Minutes*, 6:13–16.

[64] See Robert Livingston to the Lords of Trade, May 31, 1701, *NYCD*, 4:874–78.

Other colonies reacted with varying degrees of enthusiasm to the call for an Indian conference in Albany. In New England interest was high. Massachusetts governor William Shirley matched DeLancey's vigorous promotion of the treaty conference, and his assembly appointed five treaty commissioners with the power to enter into a union with the other colonies represented. Connecticut also responded favorably, commissioning three representatives to treat with the Six Nations and consult on "proper measures for the general defence and Safety" of the colonies. New Hampshire, although not usually a participant in such conferences, commissioned four representatives to "agree upon, Consult, and Conclude what may be necessary for Establishing a Sincere and lasting Friendship and good Harmony" with the Six Nations. Even Rhode Island, which had never previously participated in Covenant Chain diplomacy, agreed to send two commissioners with powers to consult about preserving the friendship of the Six Nations.[65] The sentiment for colonial union in New England sprang from several sources. First, precedents for intercolonial cooperation in that region dated back to the seventeenth century, when the United Colonies of New England had jointly administered military and Indian affairs.[66] Second, Shirley was a popular governor who had favored the cause of colonial union ever since organizing the victorious Louisbourg expedition in 1745. Third, the New Englanders were already unified by their disgust with New York's management of Indian affairs, and they seized on this chance to place the Covenant Chain under intercolonial authority.

South of New York, results were mixed. Virginia governor Robert Dinwiddie supported colonial union, but he did not expect his colony to participate in the Albany treaty conference. He had already planned a May conference with several southern Indian nations, and since the Virginia Assembly had appropriated funds for that meeting, it was unlikely to send commissioners to another a month later. Besides, Dinwiddie explained to the Board of Trade that "the Southern Indians are more to be courted than the five Nations, being ten times their Number."[67] Pennsylvania and Maryland cooperated but with less enthusiasm than the New England governments. In Pennsylvania, the assembly remained unmoved by DeLancey's and Shirley's plans for colonial union. Finding that past experience offered little reason to expect any "Union of the Colonies in Indian Affairs," the assembly instructed its commissioners to act only on matters relevant to mending the Covenant Chain. Maryland's government appeared equally suspicious of DeLancey's and Shirley's plans and instructed its two com-

[65] The commissions carried by colonial delegations attending the Albany Congress are reprinted in *Penn. Archives*, 1st ser., 2:137–43.
[66] See Harry M. Ward, *The United Colonies of New England, 1643–1690* (New York, 1961).
[67] Dinwiddie to the Board of Trade, March 12, 1754, *Dinwiddie Papers*, 3:98–99.

missioners that "you are not impowered to Stipulate, or engage that this Province will advance any Sum of Money or Number of Men" for any union discussed at Albany.[68]

The most negative response to the Board of Trade's orders came from New Jersey. In a speech on April 25, 1754, Governor Jonathan Belcher related the growing danger from the French and pressed the assembly to send commissioners to Albany. The assembly responded that New Jersey had never been party to trade or diplomacy with the Iroquois in the past and therefore would send neither commissioners nor presents to Albany. Belcher retorted that "hitherto having escaped the Expense of treating with the Indians" was a poor excuse for not participating now. The Board of Trade was equally angry, calling the assembly's response "frivolous and without foundation."[69] Nevertheless, the assembly remained adamant in its refusal to participate.

Seven of the nine colonies invited to join in the treaty accepted. DeLancey and Shirley had been less successful in making colonial union the meeting's priority. Only Massachusetts specifically instructed its commissioners to enter into a union with the other colonies, and only Connecticut came close to granting similar powers to its delegation. DeLancey and Shirley tried to convince other governments that this conference presented an excellent opportunity for advancing intercolonial cooperation, but their overtures had the opposite effect. Assemblies wary of surrendering their pursestrings told their commissioners to stick closely to Indian affairs and discuss nothing else. As the conference neared, the extent of colonial division and insularity in British North America became obvious. Of those colonies participating, most did so grudgingly and sharply limited their delegations' powers. The governments of Pennsylvania, New York, and New England also exhibited contrary intentions concerning Indian affairs that would make cooperation difficult, if not impossible, to achieve.

Intercolonial competition for western lands also affected the colonial response to the Board of Trade's orders. Pennsylvania and Virginia competed with each other as well as the French for the Ohio Valley; the Virginia government's decision not to attend the Albany Congress is attributable in part to the attention it was then devoting to courting the Ohio Indians at the expense of the Iroquois. Further north, Connecticut and Pennsylvania had locked horns over the Wyoming Valley, a region along the northern branch of the Susquehanna River. Land speculators in Connecticut claimed that the Wyoming Valley fell within Connecticut's boundaries, as defined in that colony's seventeenth-century "sea-to-sea" charter. In July 1753 they formed a joint-stock venture known as the Susquehannah Com-

---

[68] Penn. Council Minutes, 6:37–38, 45–46, and Penn. Archives, 1st ser., 2:143, 139–40.
[69] See Archives of the State of New Jersey, 1st ser., 42 vols. (Newark, 1880–1949), 8:190–92, 294–96, 9:361–64, 16:455–58.

pany. Pennsylvania proprietor Thomas Penn, upon hearing that Connecticut agents were scouting land in the Wyoming Valley, ordered his colony's secretary Richard Peters and governor James Hamilton to complete an Indian purchase that would preempt the Connecticut claims.[70]

The race between the Penn family and the Connecticut speculators intensified before the Albany Congress because each side realized an intercolonial treaty conference would present an excellent opportunity for purchasing land from the Indians. The Penn family relied on the colony's Indian interpreter Conrad Weiser, who wrote confidently that he could complete a purchase if he found among the Indians in Albany "some greedy fellows for Money, that will undertake to bring things about to our wishes."[71] Both sides competed fiercely for William Johnson's favor. On March 9, 1754, Pennsylvania governor James Hamilton wrote to Johnson and asked him to have nothing to do with the Connecticut scheme. In return, Hamilton would have Pennsylvania's commissioners to Albany consult with Johnson upon their arrival. Shortly after this overture, a leading Susquehannah Company investor wrote to Johnson with "a Short Sketch of our proceedings . . . which may be depended on for Truth In This Affair" and promised that Johnson's cooperation would prove most beneficial "To you and us."[72] Johnson allied himself with the Penn family. As an owner of Susquehanna lands north of the Pennsylvania–New York border, he had a vested interest in seeing Connecticut's pretensions to that region checked. He may have also expected that in return for his assistance, the Penn family would advance his ambitions for royal favor in London. Thomas Penn recognized as much when he wrote to Richard Peters that "Colonel Johnson's behaviour is that of a Man who expects to be courted."[73]

The speed with which the Penn family and the Susquehannah Company moved, as well as Johnson's calculated response to their dispute, offered further proof of the colonists' fractured response to the call to Albany. The predatory conduct of the Penns and their Connecticut rivals was typical of Indian land purchases. Private speculators and colonial governments operated independently, and no intercolonial authority existed to mediate or curb their scramble for western lands. This cavalier attitude toward buying Indian lands was precisely what the Mohawks had protested in declaring the Covenant Chain broken and what advocates of a royal Indian superintendency wanted to end.

While colonial assemblies and land speculators scrambled to protect

[70] *Susquehannah Co. Papers*, 1:lviii–lxxxix, 28–39, 42, 51–52.
[71] Weiser to Richard Peters, March 15, 1754, ibid., 63–66.
[72] Hamilton to Johnson, March 9, 1754, and John Fitch to Johnson, April 2, 1754, *WJ Papers*, 1:397–98, 398–401.
[73] Thomas Penn to Richard Peters, [n.d.], *Susquehannah Co. Papers*, 1:95–99.

their interests, Benjamin Franklin continued to investigate ways to reorganize Indian affairs and intercolonial relations. Pennsylvania's Indian relations engaged his attention in 1753, when he traveled to the frontier town of Carlisle for a conference with Indians from the Ohio Valley.[74] After hearing Indians complain about abuses in Pennsylvania's fur trade, Franklin tapped his intercolonial correspondents for advice. In October 1753 he wrote to James Bowdoin of Boston, requesting a copy of the Massachusetts law governing that colony's Indian trade. Bowdoin replied a month later, explaining Massachusetts's system of pubic truckhouses, in which colonial officials kept Indians happy by selling goods at a wholesale rate. By these methods, Massachusetts consistently outsold the French and minimized friction between Indians and traders along its frontier. Bowdoin even provided Franklin with a detailed description of a typical truckhouse, which was 150 feet long, armed with two cannon, surrounded by palisades, and large enough to house a small garrison. Franklin was impressed by this system, which made the fur trade serve public as well as private ends, and a few days after receiving Bowdoin's letter, he joined fellow Pennsylvania assemblyman Isaac Norris in proposing a similar plan for their colony.[75]

Franklin also asked Cadwallader Colden for information on New York's management of the Indian trade. Colden's response reinforced Franklin's opinion that unrestrained private trade was working contrary to Britain's imperial interests. Colden, as usual, complained of New York's unwillingness to stop the Albany-Montreal trade, and he noted that the last time he visited Albany, he saw over two hundred Caughnawaga Indians there buying goods for French merchants in Montreal. After printing the Carlisle treaty in Philadelphia, Franklin sent a copy to Colden, confiding that he hoped it would "introduce a Regulation of our Indian Trade . . . as is done by Massachusetts."[76] Thus, by late 1753, Franklin had become convinced that a public regulation of the Indian trade was necessary to limit the negative influence of private commercial interests on Indian relations. The Massachusetts system offered a model for not only Pennsylvania but for the northern colonies as a whole.

The subject of colonial union remained on Franklin's mind as he journeyed to Albany with the other Pennsylvania commissioners. On June 5 they arrived in New York City and spent the next three days purchasing

[74] See *A Treaty Held with the Ohio Indians at Carlisle in October, 1753* (Philadelphia, 1753), in Julian P. Boyd, ed., *Indian Treaties Printed by Benjamin Franklin, 1736–1762* (Philadelphia, 1938), 123–34. Additional documents on Franklin's service at this treaty are in *BF Papers,* 5:62–66. Franklin's own recollections of it are contained in Farrand, *Franklin's Memoirs,* 302–6. Jennings analyzes Franklin's early service in Indian affairs in *Benjamin Franklin, Politician,* 81–93.
[75] Franklin to Bowdoin, October 18, 1753, and Bowdoin to Franklin, November 12, 1753, *BF Papers,* 5:79–80, 110–15. Also see Ronald D. Macfarlane, "The Massachusetts Bay Truck-Houses in Diplomacy with the Indians," *New England Quarterly* 11 (1938): 48–65.
[76] Colden to Franklin, November 29, 1753, Franklin to Colden, December 6, 1753, *BF Papers,* 5:121–26, 144–45.

Indian goods, meeting friends, and preparing for the boat trip to Albany. During this time Franklin drafted new proposals for a colonial union. He completed "Short hints towards a scheme for uniting the Northern Colonies" on June 8 and forwarded it to New Yorkers James Alexander and Cadwallader Colden, instructing them to send their comments to him in Albany.[77]

Franklin's "Short hints" closely resembled his remarks on colonial union published three years earlier in conjunction with Archibald Kennedy's plan for regulating Indian affairs. The basic components of his plan remained the same. A Crown-appointed governor general would preside over an intercolonial council selected by the assemblies. Each colony would receive representation proportional to its contributions to the common treasury, which would be funded by a tax on strong liquors or other luxuries. Franklin preferred such a tax to a quota system because it would naturally adjust itself as the wealth of the colonies increased, without causing disputes over how much each colony should contribute. Meetings of the Grand Council (the "General Council" in his 1751 plan of union) would rotate through the colonial capitals. Its powers would extend to intercolonial military and Indian affairs and include regulating the fur trade, maintaining frontier fortifications, and establishing new western settlements.[78]

In one very important respect, Franklin's "Short hints" differed from his earlier plan for colonial union. In 1751 he had suggested that any plan of union be voluntary because that would allow the colonies greater flexibility in altering it. In 1754 he reversed himself, advising that after the commissioners approved the plan in Albany, it "be sent home, and an Act of Parliament obtain'd for establishing it."[79] Although he did not state his reasons for this reversal, much of Franklin's experience over the preceding months offers clues as to why he now favored parliamentary enactment. The New Jersey Assembly's failure to appoint commissioners to the Albany conference and his own assembly's refusal to empower its commissioners to discuss union gave Franklin living proof of the entrenched insularity of colonial governments.

The most likely source of Franklin's change of heart was Dr. William Clarke of Boston, a close associate of William Shirley, who began corresponding with Franklin in March 1754. In a letter to Franklin dated May 6, 1754, Clarke wrote at length on the need for colonial union. "But this Union is hardly to be expected to be brought about by any confederacy, or

---

[77] Ibid., 335–36. In his autobiography, Franklin states that he showed his plan to Archibald Kennedy, but as the editors of the BF Papers note, there is no evidence of Kennedy's remarks on the plan. See Farrand, Franklin's Memoirs, 326, and BF Papers, 5:336, n. 3.
[78] BF Papers, 4:117–19, 5:337–38.
[79] Ibid., 5:338.

voluntary Agreement, among ourselves," he observed. "The Jealousies the Colonies have of each other, with regard to their real and imaginary different Interests, etc. will effectually hinder any thing of this Kind from taking place." Although the colonies might recognize the need for union, Clarke believed that they would never enter into one until "we are forced to it, by the Supreme Authority of the Nation." He enclosed some notes for a pamphlet he was writing on the current crisis and asked Franklin for his comments, "particularly [on] the nature of the Union, that ought to be established amongst his majesty's Colonies, on this Continent."[80] Clarke may have convinced Franklin of the expediency of parliamentary intervention at this critical juncture to circumvent the assemblies' obvious resistance to union.

Franklin's support for parliamentary enactment marked an important change in his promotion of colonial union. In 1751, he had thought the colonists might achieve union through the agency of "half a Dozen Men of good Understanding and Address." These men, the leading gentlemen of American society, would help the colonists cultivate their mutual interests, affections, and kinship. Three years later, he was less convinced that the colonists were capable of forming such a union on their own. He appealed to a more powerful agency—the British Parliament—to impose union from above. As Franklin traveled to Albany, circulating his "Short hints" among a few correspondents, he no longer believed that a union arising organically from American soil would be strong or timely enough to preserve the British Empire in North America; on the contrary, a union of sentiment between the colonists would have to be the result, rather than the cause, of a political union enforced by Parliament.

Historians have long noted that the most important constitutional issue affecting Anglo-American relations in the eighteenth century concerned the interpretation of colonial charters. Defenders of the charters upheld local control of colonial government and insisted that the colonists enjoyed certain rights and liberties that could not be abrogated by the Crown or Parliament. Critics of the charters described colonial governments as creations of royal power that could be altered as necessary to preserve colonial dependence. This division pitted advocates of centralized imperial government, upholding the sovereign authority of Parliament over the colonies, against advocates of local autonomy, usually represented by the colonial assemblies.[81] Franklin and his provincial circle of correspondents introduced a seldom recognized third element to this debate. They sought

---

[80] Clarke to Franklin, May 6, 1754, ibid., 268–71.
[81] See Reid, *Constitutional History of the American Revolution*, 3–25; Greene, *Peripheries and Center*, 7–76; Andrews, *Colonial Background of the American Revolution*, 3–66; and Charles Howard McIlwain, *The American Revolution: A Constitutional Interpretation* (1923; rpt. Ithaca, 1958), 1–17.

the intercolonial management of Indian relations, military affairs, and western expansion, and they identified the individual assemblies as the chief impediments to this end. Yet they were not apologists for imperial power. They defended the character of colonial society from its critics, discouraged discriminatory policies that restrained colonial development, and claimed for the colonists a political and cultural parity with the Crown's other subjects. In short, they framed the Anglo-American relationship neither in terms of strict dependence nor autonomy but as a partnership between a maturing colonial society and the transatlantic empire to which it belonged. They favored a union that would derive its powers directly from what they recognized as the supreme legislative authority in the empire, Parliament, rather than from the individual assemblies, of which they were often critical.[82] The "Short hints" Franklin carried to Albany were a blueprint for such a union, a truly novel proposal for reforming imperial and intercolonial relations.

Participants followed differing paths to the Albany Congress in June 1754, and few of them had common expectations or purposes for the treaty conference there. Just about the only common ground between them could be found in their shared experiences within an expanding British Empire. For some, such as the Mohawks, this expansion was negative, eroding their subsistence and upsetting traditional methods of mediating intercultural relations. For the colonial assemblies, the expansion of British power threatened charter privileges and local autonomy. For provincial and imperial reformers, the breakdown in administering Indian relations represented an opportunity to reconfigure Anglo-American relations in a way that would serve the expansion of British power more efficiently. As these various interests converged at Albany, their lack of unanimity was apparent to all involved, and their treaty conference became a forum on the future of the British Empire in North America.

[82] See Beer, *To Make a Nation*, 155–56.

PART II

AT THE CROSSROADS

The Albany Congress convened in a setting and context far different from those of the intercolonial congresses of the Revolutionary Era. Albany in 1754 was a colonial crossroads with split Dutch and British identities. Its Dutch population pursued the fur trade and other commercial interests with much of the same insularity as it had during the seventeenth century. But Albany was also a garrison town, an outpost of British power that became a center of imperial and intercolonial politics whenever colonial delegations traveled there to treat with the Indians. These treaty conferences followed the customs and agendas set by Anglo-Iroquois diplomacy, making Albany a crossroads for native and colonial cultures as well.

The treaty conference at Albany in 1754 is of particular significance because it laid bare a crisis in colonial Indian relations that had profound implications for the British Empire in North America. The broken Covenant Chain was part of a much wider problem in an empire that had long valued local autonomy and private commercial initiative over the systematic or centralized administration of power. Different participants in the Albany Congress responded to this breakdown according to their particular advantage. The Mohawks wished to see management of New York's Indian affairs removed from Albany's hands and restored to William Johnson's. Likewise, the colonial commissioners worked to deflate New York's power over the Covenant Chain so that they might put it to their own uses in acquiring Indian land and defending their frontiers. The New Yorkers, besieged on all sides, worked to restore an old order in intercultural relations that preserved their authority over Indian trade and diplomacy.

The specific problem addressed by Indians and colonists at the Albany Congress was who would hold the reins of a reconstituted Covenant Chain. That question was tied up with a host of other imperial and inter-colonial problems brought upon the colonies by their own expansion. Benjamin Franklin and his fellow commissioners conceived of the Albany Plan as a comprehensive solution to this crisis, which would redistribute local and imperial power in British North America, thereby securing a stronger and more permanent Anglo-American union.

[4]

Treaty-Making at Albany:
Setting and Characters

Sunday, 30th June. Went to Church forenoon and afternoon, after which attended at Church w[h]ere the Mohawks were Call[e]d to Prayers and the Service in their Langwage, which was Performed with the utmost Decency. Many of them had books and responded.
—Theodore Atkinson, Albany, 1754

Few firsthand accounts of the Albany Congress exist. Historians have had to rely on the official minutes of the treaty conference with the Indians, reports completed by some of the colonial delegations for their home governments, and occasional recollections by individual participants, some written a few days after the congress and some as much as thirty years later. Singular among these sources is the journal kept by New Hampshire commissioner Theodore Atkinson, which provides an eyewitness account of what transpired in Albany between June 19 and July 11, 1754.[1] Atkinson comes across on these pages as a taciturn, often cranky New Englander alternately irritated and intrigued by his trip to that far-off place, Albany. He resented the difficulty of travel through western Massa-

---

[1] Atkinson's journal is in the Force Papers, Manuscripts Division of the Library of Congress. Beverly McAnear reproduces the entries from Atkinson's arrival in Albany to his departure in "Personal Accounts." A typescript of the journal including the entries for Atkinson's trip to and from Albany is included in Jennings et al., eds., *Iroquois Indians*, reel 16. McAnear also included in "Personal Accounts" the draft of a letter most likely written by Thomas Pownall to the Earl of Halifax, from New York on July 23, 1754. Three other sources provide eyewitness observations on the Albany Congress: the official minutes of the congress, reprinted in *NYCD*, 6:853–92; the report submitted by the Massachusetts commissioners to Massachusetts governor William Shirley on November 1, 1754 in Mass. Archives, 4:459–64; and the report submitted by John Penn and Richard Peters to Pennsylvania governor James Hamilton on August 5, 1754 concerning their land negotiations at the congress, reprinted in *Penn. Archives*, ser. 4, 2:696–724 (hereinafter cited as the Penn and Peters Report). The personal recollections of Benjamin Franklin and Thomas Hutchinson many years later will be discussed in Chapter 6.

chusetts and Connecticut. The weather, a toothache, poor roads, and even worse directions conspired to make him miserable. In Albany, excessive heat, thunderstorms, and flooding added to his discomfort. Atkinson often seemed bored by the proceedings: he dutifully summarized each day's business but expressed little personal interest in the affairs of the congress even though he sat on the committee that drafted the Plan of Union. Like many a business traveler, he took more interest in his food, drink, and companions than in the official matters he had been sent to complete.

Anyone traveling to Albany today might be forgiven for not thinking of it as an exotic locale. With the exception of its monumental state government buildings (which sit on the same hill as the city's eighteenth-century fort), modern Albany looks and feels much like any other American city of middling size. In 1754, Atkinson encountered an entirely different place. He was struck by the diversity of characters that assembled for this treaty conference. Of his twenty-two journal entries while in Albany, the two most revealing in this regard came on the Sundays of June 23 and June 30. On Sundays, the colonial commissioners conducted no official business so Atkinson spent his time going to church. On the morning of the twenty-third he attended a sermon in Albany's Anglican church delivered by Richard Peters, one of the Pennsylvania commissioners and an Anglican clergyman. In the afternoon he returned for one delivered by the church's rector and missionary to the Mohawks, the Reverend John Ogilvie. That evening Atkinson heard Elisha Williams, one of the Connecticut commissioners and a Congregational minister, preach in Albany's Dutch church. The following Sunday, June 30, Atkinson again attended Peters in the morning and Ogilvie in the afternoon, after which he observed the worship of some Christian Mohawks. The Indian converts impressed Atkinson, who wrote that the service "was Performed with the utmost Decency" and that many of the Indians "had books and responded." Ogilvie, who officiated for the Mohawks in their language and baptized two of their children, noted in his journal "the Presence of a great Number of Gentlemen" at the service, no doubt other visitors who shared Atkinson's curiosity about the Indians.[2]

Atkinson's Sunday worship tells us much about the setting and characters for the Albany Congress. The two churches he attended, one Anglican and one Dutch Reformed, testified to the city's split British and Dutch personality. Theodorus Frelinghuysen, the pastor of the Dutch church, usually performed his services in Dutch, but he accepted an invitation from the New England commissioners to preach to them in English. He

[2] McAnear, "Personal Accounts," 733, 736, and Milton W. Hamilton, ed., "The Diary of Reverend John Ogilvie, 1750–1759," *Bulletin of the Fort Ticonderoga Museum* 10 (1961): 344.

delivered what was undoubtedly a pleasing jeremiad for the visiting New Englanders, chastising Albany's inhabitants for their intemperance and avarice and predicting the wrath of God in the form of marauding Frenchmen and Indians unless they reformed.[3] The other local minister Atkinson attended was John Ogilvie, an SPG missionary sent to Albany to minister to the needs of Protestant Mohawks, British soldiers, and a hodgepodge of European colonists. When Atkinson attended these services, he found himself in the presence of colonists from Massachusetts to Maryland as well as Indian men, women, and children, all of whom had crowded among Albany's local merchants and tradesmen. They were a volatile mix of local, regional, and imperial constituencies, an ethnic and cultural cross section of the British Empire in North America.

Historians who have depicted the Albany Congress as a precursor to the colonial congresses of the Revolutionary Era have lost touch with its context as an Indian treaty conference, which accounts for the diversity of peoples encountered by Atkinson. Such intercolonial meetings had convened periodically in Albany since 1677, and five had occurred in the decade before 1754, making the city British North America's leading site of Indian diplomacy.[4] Albany was an intercolonial capital long before Philadelphia or New York City, but with a different purpose: to mediate intercultural relations along a commercial and imperial frontier. The Albany Congress, therefore, is best examined in the context of Britain's empire building during the first half of the eighteenth century, not American state-making in the latter half of the century.

A Covenant Chain treaty conference was a highly ritualized affair that brought together Indians, colonial commissioners, royal officials, and a variety of local and visiting bystanders. The protocol that governed such meetings established roles for everyone involved, and the success of the negotiations hinged on the participants' familiarity with and willingness to follow these roles. Two overarching divisions also influenced the proceedings: the separation of participants into hosts and guests and the demarcation of public and private spaces for treaty negotiations. Within these human and physical dimensions of treaty-making, participants jostled each other with competing interests and opinions. Indians, colonial commissioners, and bystanders exhibited little united resolve, nor did they appear to be making a confident step toward American nationhood. Instead, a picture forms of peoples—many of them strangers—coming together for different reasons and struggling to deal with an empire in crisis.

[3] Theodorus Frelinghuysen, *A Sermon Preached on Occasion of the Late Treaty Held in Albany, by His Honour Our Lieutenant Governor, with the Indian Nations, and the Congress of Commissioners from Several Governments in These British Colonies* (New York, 1754).
[4] Jennings et al., eds., *History and Culture of Iroquois Diplomacy*, 3–36, 85–98, 157–88.

The Setting

Albany in 1754 resembled no other city in British North America. At a time when most colonial population centers still clung to the Atlantic shoreline, it was an inland anomaly, 160 miles north of New York City. Travel to it took four days by boat and sometimes as long as a week.[5] Eighteenth-century visitors noted the city's close adherence to Dutch language, customs, and material culture and complained of feeling like strangers in a strange land. Their discomfort stemmed in part from Albany's split personality, for it was in reality two different cities. Dutch Albany resembled a commercial medieval town whose inhabitants devoted their time to the transport and sale of goods. British Albany was a garrison town on a colonial marchland, defended by a stone fort and professional soldiers in the pay of a distant king.[6] This division of Albany into commercial and military communities shaped public and private spaces at the Albany Congress.

In June 1752, the corporation of Albany adopted a new "common seal." As the beaver on that seal attested, the city owed its existence to the fur trade (Fig. 4.1).[7] Founded as a Dutch trading post in 1624, it marked the furthest point north to which large ships could navigate the Hudson River. When the English secured their possession of New York in 1676, they did little to alter the character of this fur depot, and a municipal charter granted in 1686 recognized Albany as a virtually independent city-state.[8] The escalation of the Anglo-French imperial rivalry in the late seventeenth century, however, made Albany an important strategic spot for the English. It stood in between the Mohawk River, Hudson River, and Lake Champlain, which provided Indians and Europeans with their major commercial and military routes between New York and Canada. That location also made it the center of diplomacy with the Iroquois and a defensive bulwark for the rest of the northern British colonies. These three factors— the fur trade, the Anglo-French rivalry, and Indian affairs—gave Albany its unique and important place in the British Empire.

Dutch Albany in 1754 was a small, self-contained community of distinctive architecture and manners (map 4.1). Its streets lacked the gridiron precision and public squares of other colonial cities, but they reflected in

---

[5] When Peter Kalm traveled to Albany from New York City in 1748, it took him four days. In 1754, it took James DeLancey a week to make the trip. See Benson, ed., *Peter Kalm's Travels in North America*, 1:326–32, and the reports on DeLancey's progress in the *New-York Mercury*, June 10, 24, 1754.

[6] On Dutch and English perceptions of Albany and its landscape, see Merwick, *Possessing Albany*.

[7] See Joel Munsell, ed., *The Annals of Albany*, 10 vols. (Albany, 1850–59), 10:149–50.

[8] On the city charter, see Armour, "Merchants of Albany," 1–8. For Albany's independent role in colonial New York's politics, see Bonomi, *Factious People*, 39–48.

Figure 4.1. Seal of the City of Albany, 1752. From *Albany's Tercentenary* (Albany, 1924).

name and design the community's commercial origins.[9] Jonkheer Straat—modern State Street—ran east to west from the riverside to the fort. Several of the city's leading residents lived here, thus giving the street its name, a Dutch term for a wealthy gentleman. Handlaers Straat—modern-day Broadway—ran from north to south and served as the city's major thoroughfare. As its name indicates ("handlaer" was the Dutch term for a fur trader), it was home to the city's market days, which occurred on Wednesdays and Saturdays and attracted people from the surrounding countryside. Pearl Straat, west of Handlaers and intersecting with Jonkheer, also housed some of the city's mercantile elite. Other unnamed lanes and alleys facilitated the flow of people and goods to the markets, riverside, and city gates.[10]

At the time of the Albany Congress, the city's Dutch residents had two prominent public buildings and approximately three hundred houses.[11]

[9] Richard Bushman describes two styles of colonial cities: medieval, with haphazard streets and open market spaces, and Renaissance, with geometric layouts of streets and public places. Albany, founded in the early seventeenth century and maintaining the same fundamental plan through the colonial era, falls into the former category. See Bushman, *The Refinement of America: Persons, Houses, Cities* (New York, 1992), 140–45.

[10] My description of Albany's physical layout is derived from contemporary sources cited below and my conversations with Stefan Bielinski, director of the Colonial Albany Social History Project at the New York State Museum in Albany. Also important are two articles by Bielinski: "A Middling Sort: Artisans and Tradesmen in Colonial Albany," *New York History* 73 (1992): 261–90; and "The People of Colonial Albany, 1650–1800," in *Authority and Resistance in Early New York* ed. William Pencak and Conrad Edick Wright (New York, 1988), 1–26. Also useful are the maps and accompanying explanatory notes in Charlotte Wilcoxen, *Seventeenth Century Albany: A Dutch Profile*, rev. ed. (Albany, 1984), 10–13.

[11] In 1756, the Earl of Loudoun, commander in chief of the British forces in North America, ordered an inventory of Albany's buildings so that he might know how many troops he could quarter there. The resulting document listed 329 buildings. See "List of Inhabitants of the City

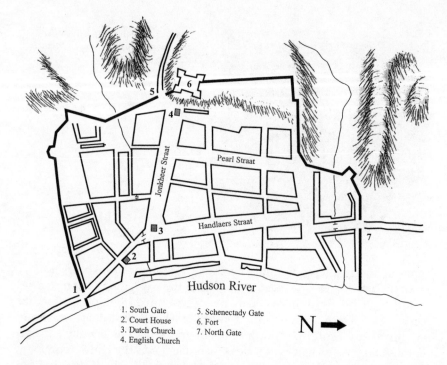

Map 4.1. Albany, c. 1754, drawn by Armen Sarrafian, based on "Plan of the city of Albany . . . in the Year 1756–57," British Museum, Additional Manuscript No. 33231, N.N. 2.

The Stadt Huys, or courthouse, was a three-story building near the city's southern gate and close to the river. The Dutch church, also near the riverside, was an imposing structure at the intersection of Jonkheer and Handlaers Streets that marked the center of the Dutch community. One late eighteenth-century traveler noted that it looked "more like a powder magazine than a place of worship . . . with a monstrous, high, pitched roof, in a pyramidal form, with a cupola and bell."[12] Albany's homes had a distinctive style that reminded visitors of the Old World. The Swedish naturalist Peter Kalm, who visited the city in 1748, described them as built "in the old Frankish way, with the gable end towards the street." They were tall, narrow structures with stepped gables, built on lots only twenty feet wide, which gave the streets a cramped, urban look. Some had roofs

---

of Albany . . . ," November 1756, Loudoun Papers, LO 3515. I am indebted to Stefan Bielinski for sharing his transcription of this document with me.
[12] See "Dr. Belknap's Tour to Oneida, 1796," in Dean R. Snow, Charles T. Gehring, and William A. Starna, eds., *In Mohawk Country: Early Narratives about a Native People* (Syracuse, 1996), 355.

slated with tile imported from Holland.[13] After seeing Albany, Thomas Pownall remarked, "The Whole Town except a Few New Houses, is intirely built after the Dutch mode."[14]

The Dutch appearance of Albany extended to its inhabitants as well. At the time of the Albany Congress, the city's population was approximately two thousand.[15] It had grown during the first half of the eighteenth century and diversified its economy, but residents retained their Dutch language and customs. Kalm wrote, "They speak Dutch, have Dutch preachers, and the divine service is performed in that language; their manners are likewise quite Dutch." Dr. Alexander Hamilton, who visited Albany in 1744, complained of the "Volleys of rough sounding Dutch" that assaulted his ears. Both men found the Albany Dutch clannish and disagreeable. Kalm's hosts charged him two, three, and even four times the rates he paid elsewhere in the colonies for food and lodging. Hamilton noted the Albanians' well-kept homes and fine china but found them "in their persons slovenly and dirty." Kalm thought the same of the city's streets, which he described as "very dirty" because residents allowed their livestock to roam at night.[16] Another traveler upon seeing the place for the first time simply observed: "I arrived at Albany, Where there is a fine River, And but a Nasty dirty Town."[17]

Visitors generally noted the wealth of Albany's inhabitants but lamented their failure to meet genteel standards of cleanliness and hospitality. Hamilton found it incongruous that Albany's residents kept neat houses yet failed to devote the same attention to their personal appearance. Kalm complained that his hosts were stingy and rarely filled the punch bowl for strangers: "I could at once see what kind of blood ran in their veins, for they either fixed exorbitant prices for their services or were very reluctant to assist me." Warren Johnson, a brother of William, criticized the Albanians' manners: they smoked too much, sat down without being invited to do so, and never used forks when eating. In brief, "the People . . . have something Odd about them."[18] Dirty streets, unkempt bodies, and poor manners all indicated an unwholesome pursuit of filthy lucre. According to Kalm, an "immeasurable love of money" defined Albany society. Hamilton thought likewise: "They live here very frugally and

---

[13] Benson, ed., *Peter Kalm's Travels in North America*, 1:341.
[14] Pownall, *Topographical Description*, 38. Pownall completed many of the observations included in this book while traveling in the northern colonies in 1754–55, including his stay in Albany during the Albany Congress.
[15] See Munsell, ed., *Annals of Albany*, 3:203; and Bielinski, "A Middling Sort," 267.
[16] Benson, ed., *Peter Kalm's Travels in North America*, 1:342–47. For Hamilton's descriptions, see Bridenbaugh, ed., *Gentleman's Progress*, 63, 69, 71–74.
[17] See "Journal of Warren Johnson, 1760–61," in Snow, Gehring, and Starna, eds., *In Mohawk Country*, 253.
[18] Ibid., 253, 261–62.

plain, for the chief merit among them seems to be riches, which they spare no pains or trouble to acquire, [they] are a civil and hospitable people in their way, but att best, rustick and unpolished."[19]

Hamilton's and Kalm's opinions were no doubt influenced by stereotypes of Dutch avarice and frugality then current among Anglo-Americans. Hamilton admitted as much when he wrote that the Albanians' mercenary nature was "the common character of the Dutch every where."[20] Despite such prejudice, their comments convey the singularity of this community. After almost a century, Albany remained untouched by its inclusion in the British Empire. At a time when expanding trade and communication were reducing much of the cultural distinctiveness between colonial cities and regions, Albany remained a peculiar place. The colonial commissioners who converged there in June 1754 would find their eyes, ears, and tastes challenged by the most un-British city in British North America.

There was another Albany. British Albany formed a defensive perimeter around Dutch Albany with palisades, blockhouses, and a fort. To a traveler arriving by way of the Hudson, this British presence became apparent only when moving away from the Dutch-defined riverside landings and markets. On a high, steep hill on the west end of the town stood Fort Frederick, a reminder of Albany's place in a larger empire. The fort impressed Hamilton, who noted its four bastions, each with "eight or ten great guns."[21] Inside its walls were two brick buildings: the Governor's House, where New York's royal governor stayed when visiting Albany to treat with the Indians, and a barracks for British troops (Fig. 4.2). About one hundred soldiers usually lived in the fort, rotating their duty with comrades farther west at Fort Hunter and Oswego.[22] Kalm described the fort as the highest building in Albany, yet one poorly positioned to defend the city because higher ground commanded it beyond the palisades.[23]

Nestled in the fort's shadow was Albany's Anglican church, St. Peter's. Built of stone in 1714, it acquired a steeple and bell in 1752 to give it a

[19] Bridenbaugh, ed., *Gentleman's Progress*, 73; Benson, ed., *Peter Kalm's Travels in North America*, 1:344–46.
[20] Bridenbaugh, ed., *Getleman's Progress*, 73. Kalm also invoked general stereotypes of the Dutch as support for his conclusions about Albany. See Benson, ed., *Peter Kalm's Travels in North America*, 1:344–45. For a good overview of the social and cultural character of Dutch colonial communities in North America, see A. G. Roeber, "'The Origin of Whatever Is Not English among Us': The Dutch-Speaking and German-Speaking Peoples of Colonial British America," in *Strangers within the Realm*, ed. Bailyn and Morgan, 220–37.
[21] Bridenbaugh, *Gentleman's Progress*, 71.
[22] On the soldiers garrisoned at Albany, see Stanley Pargellis, "The Four Independent Companies of New York," in *Essays in Colonial History Presented to Charles McLean Andrews by His Students* ed. J. Franklin Jameson (New Haven, 1931), 96–123, and Bielinksi, "A Middling Sort," 277–78.
[23] Benson, ed., *Peter Kalm's Travels in North America*, 1:342. Pownall also noted the fort's exposure to attack. See *Topographical Description*, 38.

degree of respectability with the Dutch church down the hill.[24] A stockade made from pine trees enclosed the city, although it was in constant disrepair. In 1744, Hamilton observed workmen "putting up new palisading or stockadoes to fortify the town." Four years later, they had deteriorated so much that Kalm found "no city gates here but for the most part just open holes through which people pass in and out of the town."[25] A few months after the Albany Congress convened, local magistrates petitioned the governor for money to fortify the city, noting that its rotted stockade was "Ready to tumble Down." The city gates, blockhouses, and batteries were also "all out of Repair."[26]

The protective shell that British Albany cast around Dutch Albany had a hollow ring. St. Peter's and Fort Frederick gave tangible form to the institutions of church and state, but they lacked human filling. Hamilton found St. Peter's "the meanest congregation ever I beheld," an assembly of only fifteen to twenty worshipers besides the soldiers from the fort.[27] Indeed, the soldiers of Fort Frederick made up the bulk of the city's British population. Thomas Pownall described them as a desperate lot who lived under "a kind of Transportation for Life," which rendered them "drunken and besotted with Rum and . . . soon Invalids or worse."[28] Another observer at the Albany Congress recalled that the garrison was so poorly armed that soldiers standing guard at the governor's door arrived at their post without guns.[29] Some soldiers after retiring from the army settled in Albany as craftsmen or keepers of taverns and dramshops. They tended to settle in the city's southwestern corner, not far from the fort.[30]

British Albany was a military and missionary outpost, the end of a tentacle of empire. In 1754, the Dutch inhabited Albany, but the British still only occupied it. This fact shaped the spatial geography of the Albany Congress. When the governor traveled from New York City to Albany for Indian negotiations, persons concerned with the Crown's business followed him. Albany then briefly became an administrative center for the empire. Public negotiations occurred in the fort and the Governor's House, and city magistrates temporarily deferred their powers to the governor, who issued special proclamations regulating the interaction of local resi-

---

[24] Bridenbaugh, ed., *Gentleman's Progress*, 68, n. 169, and Hamilton, ed., "Diary of Ogilvie," 334–35. In his visit of 1748, Kalm had noted the lack of a steeple on St. Peter's when comparing it to the Dutch church. See Benson, ed., *Peter Kalm's Travels in North America*, 1:341.

[25] Bridenbaugh, ed., *Gentleman's Progress*, 66; Benson, ed., *Peter Kalm's Travels in North America*, 1:342.

[26] See Albany Commissioners of Indian Affairs to Governor DeLancey, January 21, 1755, NY Col. Mss., 80:4a.

[27] Bridenbaugh, ed., *Gentleman's Progress*, 68.

[28] McAnear, "Personal Accounts," 745–46.

[29] See Smith, *History of the Province of New-York*, 2:174.

[30] See Bielinski, "A Middling Sort," 277–78.

Figure 4.2. Plan of Fort Frederick at Albany, showing Governor's House and Barracks. From Ann Rocque, *A Set of Plans and Forts in America* (London, 1765).

dents with visiting Indians.[31] But the local Dutch community did not stand by idly. They opened their homes to visiting officials and their private negotiations; traders conducted business with Indian men and women despite the governor's proclamations; and craftsmen repaired Indian guns and tools. During a treaty conference, Albany became two dueling sites of negotiation: one public, official, and charged with the Crown's business,

---

[31] Governor DeLancey issued two such proclamations at the Albany Congress. The first, issued on June 21, prohibited rum sales to the Indians attending the conference. The second, issued on July 5, prohibited local merchants from purchasing presents given to Indians. See NY Col. Mss., 78:130–31, 137, 146. For other examples of this practice at previous Albany treaty conferences, see ACIA Minutes, 1:156, 262, 335.

the other private and often hidden, shaped by local patterns of European-Indian relations.

The Characters

The physical spaces of Dutch and British Albany provided a stage on which treaty participants assembled. According to the protocol of Anglo-Iroquois diplomacy, treaty hosts provided for their guests' lodging, provisions, and entertainment. The conference's official proceedings occurred in public spaces before public audiences, where a secretary recorded them for review by royal officials in London. A successful conference exhibited amity, consensus, and cooperation: hosts and guests came together to renew alliances and exchange presents, and they parted with professions of friendship and peace. Maintaining such a spirit in public demanded that difficult and contentious negotiations transpire in private, or "in the bushes," where treaty participants could iron out differences without disturbing the official proceedings.[32] The number of participants multiplied at an intercolonial treaty conference, making it more difficult to keep the boundaries between host and guest and public and private clear. Questions arose over who hosted the proceedings and who should be regarded as guests. Parallel negotiations between different colonial commissioners and different Indians affected the tenor of public proceedings, and participants debated what should and should not be a part of the official treaty record. These questions were especially important at the Albany Congress of 1754, as will become apparent in the next chapter. First, we must gather the characters on the stage and assign them to their proper places.

The Indians were by far the largest group of participants in the Albany Congress. Eyewitnesses estimated that between 150 and 200 Indians attended the congress, a number which struck these observers as small for a conference so widely publicized. By comparison, more than 450 Indians had attended a conference held at Albany in 1745 and over one thousand attended one held at William Johnson's home in 1755. Contemporaries interpreted the meager number of Indians at the Albany Congress as a sign of the Indians' discontent with the New Yorkers.[33] No one at the Albany

[32] The best overview of Iroquois diplomacy and its adaptation to Albany treaty-making is Jennings et al., eds., *History and Culture of Iroquois Diplomacy*, esp. chaps. 1–2.

[33] Theodore Atkinson estimated that 200 Indians attended the congress. The estimate in the official minutes is 150. This difference may be attributable to the presence of the River and Schaghticoke Indians, nearby groups not included in the Iroquois League. The figure given in the minutes may have been an estimate of only the Iroquois Indians present. See McAnear, "Personal Accounts," 733, and *NYCD*, 6:877. For the figures on the conferences of 1745 and 1755, see *NYCD*, 6:289, 964.

Congress counted the number from each of the six Iroquois nations present, but Indian names listed in a report on the Pennsylvanians' land purchase reveal that each of the six was represented. As was the case with most Albany conferences, the number from each nation tended to reflect its proximity to Albany rather than any special influence or strength within the Iroquois Confederacy. The Pennsylvanians' report listed 103 names. Of these, 49 can be identified as Mohawks and 17 as Oneidas or Tuscaroras, the easternmost nations. The report lists Indians from the confederacy's westernmost nations in much smaller numbers: seven Senecas, five Cayugas, and four Onondagas. While the Pennsylvanians' report accounts for only about half or two-thirds of the Indians present at the Albany Congress, it indicates that the Mohawks attended in numbers far superior to other Iroquois.[34]

Indians other than the Iroquois attended the Albany Congress, but they played very small roles, or none at all, in the official proceedings. The River Indians and the Schaghticokes were refugee peoples from seventeenth-century wars who had resettled north and east of Albany.[35] At Albany treaty conferences they had a junior status. They exchanged speeches with the New York governor, but, unlike the Iroquois, they addressed him as "father" and he called them "children."[36] Caughnawagas from Jesuit missionary villages near Montreal were also in town during the Albany Congress, although it is impossible to determine for how long and in what numbers. Although they often met in councils with the Albany Commissioners of Indian Affairs, these French-allied Indians had no diplomatic relationship with the New York governor and so did not participate in his treaty negotiations in Albany. In fact, visiting colonial officials may have been oblivious to the presence of the Caughnawagas if the Mohawks did not point it out. The only reference to them in the Albany Congress proceedings comes from Hendrick, who in a speech to Governor DeLancey noted that there were some "French Indians in Town" who would most certainly carry news of the conference back to Canada.[37]

Indians attending Albany treaty conferences encamped beyond the

---

[34] See Penn and Peters Report, 722–23. A useful comparison can be made to the Albany conference of 1745, in which Isaac Norris broke down the Iroquois in attendance as follows: 163 Mohawks, 75 Oneidas, 87 Tuscaroras, 81 Onondagas, 56 Cayugas, and no Senecas. See Isaac Norris, "Journal of a Treaty at Albany, October 1745," HM 3057, Huntington Library, San Marino, California. This journal was published as "The Journal of Isaac Norris, during a Trip to Albany in 1745," *Pennsylvania Magazine of History and Biography* 27 (1903): 20–28, but without these figures.

[35] See Neal Salisbury, "Toward the Covenant Chain: Iroquois and Southern New England Algonquians, 1637–1684," in *Beyond the Covenant Chain*, ed. Richter and Merrell, 69–71.

[36] For the usage of "brethren" and "father" at the Albany Congress, see *NYCD*, 6:880–81, 884–85. For the use of kinship terms in Covenant Chain diplomacy, see Jennings et al., eds., *History and Culture of Iroquois Diplomacy*, 119–20.

[37] *NYCD*, 6:882, and *NYCM*, July 8, 1754, 23:205.

city's palisades for the duration of the meeting, often two or more weeks. Albany's local ordinances prohibited Indians from remaining within the city's walls after dark, and in the seventeenth century the city magistrates built huts on a hill west of town for such visitors. The magistrates stopped appropriating money to maintain these huts when the city's western fur trade declined in the early eighteenth century. In 1746, Governor Clinton ordered Albany's mayor to build more Indian huts, perhaps to accommodate participants in treaty conferences convened during King George's War.[38] For the Albany Congress, a small village of about two hundred Indians suddenly appeared on the high ground beyond the city's fort. Theodore Atkinson conveyed a sense of the novelty of this situation in his journal. After dinner on June 22, he walked up the hill "on the Back of the Town to View the Indians."[39] There, next to Fort Frederick, he looked upon a scene that in any other colonial city would have suggested a siege.

Treaty conferences usually corresponded with the Indians' seasonal cycle of production. New York's governors preferred to convene them in the summer, when Indian males would be back from their hunting and fair weather allowed for holding public councils out-of-doors. Summer diplomacy brought Indian men, women, and children to Albany during their regular trading season and stimulated the local economy. Traders busied themselves in streets and homes trying to attract customers; rum sales and the attendant complaints of cheating, drunkenness, and violence tested the patience of magistrates. Local tailors, silversmiths, gunsmiths, and blacksmiths produced goods or provided services for visiting Indians who brought kettles, hoes, knives, and guns to be mended. Indian women found employment making wampum belts for use in councils.[40] And, of course, Indians attending such meetings enjoyed the largesse of their hosts in food, drink, and presents. These gifts made the trip worthwhile for Indians old and young, male and female, regardless of whether the governor had invited them. Small groups such as the River Indians and Schaghticokes found treaty-making an easy way to supplement their precarious subsistence. Hendrick's village of Canajoharie, its economic independence eroded by land sales and a declining fur trade, had come to rely on treaty-making for the same material benefits.

[38] On the Indian huts, see *NYCD*, 5:701. For Clinton's orders to rebuild them, see *NYCM*, August 6, 1746, 21:181.

[39] McAnear, "Personal Accounts," 733.

[40] For descriptions of the Albany trading season, see Merwick, *Possessing Albany*, 77–103, and Norton, *Fur Trade in Colonial New York*, 66–69. For the economic opportunities that Indian trade and diplomacy gave Albany craftsmen, see Bielinski, "A Middling Sort," 269–79. Wampum-making was one of Albany's industries, involving colonial craftsmen skilled in manufacturing beads from marine shells and Indian women skilled in turning them into belts. See Norton, *Fur Trade in Colonial New York*, 89–90; Jennings et al., eds., *History and Culture of Iroquois Diplomacy*, 17. For a contemporary description of wampum manufacturing in Albany, see Bridenbaugh, ed., *Gentleman's Progress*, 73.

Palisades segregated Indians from a treaty conference's other participants, but they formed a porous barrier. The Indians' presence was obvious throughout the city's streets during a conference. At the Albany Congress, Indians assembled as a group within the city's walls whenever they exchanged speeches with Governor DeLancey. These councils took place outside the door to the Governor's House, before an audience of colonial commissioners and curious onlookers. The colonists and Indians held six such meetings between June 29 and July 8. In addition, leading chiefs met with colonists privately to air complaints, recruit support, and negotiate land sales. Thomas Pownall realized the importance of these meetings when he wrote of the chiefs that "they must all be Closetted privately and experience very palpable and solid marks of our friendship for them, or all the Rest we do is doing nothing."[41] Trade and drink also brought Indians into local homes and taverns. A 1756 inventory of Albany's buildings counted five dramshops, four inns, three liquor retailers, two taverns, and one mead house, not to mention the homes of forty-seven merchants and ten Indian traders. All of these businesses presented possible sites for Indians and local residents to interact. The governor tried to regulate such behavior by prohibiting the sale of liquor to the Indians and trading with them for their presents, but such proclamations were not locally enforced. Pownall, in his summary of the Albany Congress, complained of traders who purchased the Indians' provisions out of "their very mouths," in exchange for rum that left the Indians "dead drunk, in the Face of Day, at their [the traders'] Doors."[42]

After the Indians, New Yorkers made up the most important set of participants in a Covenant Chain treaty conference. New York's royal governor traditionally presided over these meetings. As acting governor of New York in 1754, James DeLancey ironically became the king's mouthpiece at the Albany Congress. In the 1740s, DeLancey had achieved considerable influence in New York as a lawyer, judge, and dogged opponent of royal governor George Clinton. He led the faction that allied with the Albany Dutch and resisted Clinton's efforts to enlist the Iroquois in the war against Canada. The unexpected death of Clinton's successor catapulted DeLancey into the governor's office and broadened his political ambitions. He looked upon the Albany Congress as a chance to win royal favor and perhaps gain a permanent appointment to New York's governorship.

[41] [T. Pownall], "[Notes on] Indian Affairs," [1753–54], Loudoun Papers, LO 460:9.
[42] McAnear, "Personal Accounts," 743. For DeLancey's proclamations against liquor sales and trading for presents, see NY Col. Mss., 78:130–31, 137, 146. For the number of traders, merchants, and various liquor makers and sellers in Albany, see the "List of the Inhabitants," Loudoun Papers, LO 3515.

Like other governors before him, DeLancey traveled to Albany with members of his council. These Crown-appointed officials also represented the royal government of New York; they joined the governor in his private meetings with Indian leaders and assisted him by investigating Indian grievances. Four members of the New York council joined DeLancey at the Albany Congress: John Chambers, Joseph Murray, William Smith, and William Johnson. Of these four, only Murray was a faithful political ally of DeLancey. Governor George Clinton had appointed Chambers and Smith to the council late in his administration to counter DeLancey's influence there. Johnson had served as Clinton's Indian agent until 1751, when he resigned the post because the DeLancey-led faction in New York's assembly refused to pay his expenses.[43]

DeLancey and his councillors brought an imperial perspective to the proceedings and concerned themselves with the Crown's business. By contrast, the other New Yorkers present at the Albany Congress had local concerns. Governor Clinton recommissioned the Albany Commissioners of Indian Affairs in November 1752, after Johnson had resigned as his Indian agent. Since that time, the Canajoharie Mohawks had refused to meet with them, but the Albany commissioners retained their important role in Covenant Chain diplomacy as mediators between local colonists and Indians. Their records served as New York's archives on Indian affairs, and the governor relied on their familiarity with Indian diplomacy when he attended treaty conferences. When a governor was at odds with the Albany Indian Commissioners, as George Clinton was in the 1740s, he found it next to impossible to treat successfully with the Iroquois in Albany. DeLancey had better prospects. His past leadership of the anti-Clinton faction and his family's mercantile interests in the fur trade gave him ties to the Albany Dutch that Clinton had not enjoyed.

The New Yorkers attending the Albany Congress shared a wealth of experience in Covenant Chain diplomacy. They took center stage at the public and private councils held within and outside of the governor's quarters. Of the congress's participants, they were the only ones who were truly at home in Albany. Therefore, they played the role of hosts, welcoming and entertaining visiting Indians and colonial delegations but always expecting to direct the proceedings in return. In April 1754, DeLancey wrote the Board of Trade asking for more money to help defray his costs at the upcoming treaty conference. The assembly had appropriated only £150 for his expenses in Albany, a sum that would "prove but a scanty allowance" if he was to "keep a Good Table" for the commissioners from the other colonies.[44] Having attended previous treaty conferences, DeLancey

[43] For a summary of these changes in the New York council, see Stanley N. Katz, *Newcastle's New York*, 189–91.
[44] DeLancey to John Pownall, April 22, 1754, in Jennings et al., eds., *Iroquois Indians*, reel 16.

knew that his role as presiding officer entailed social obligations. Keeping "a Good Table" was expensive, but it was also one of the ways by which he asserted authority over the proceedings.

A sizable third group of participants—commissioners from Massachusetts, New Hampshire, Connecticut, Rhode Island, Pennsylvania, and Maryland—made the Albany Congress an atypical treaty conference. Intercolonial representation at Albany conferences dated back to the late seventeenth century, but never before had so many colonial representatives attended such a meeting at one time. The six delegations from outside of New York were twice as many as had been present at previous intercolonial conferences in 1745 and 1751.[45] In all, these colonial delegations included twenty commissioners, who were councillors and assemblymen chosen by their respective governments. Such a large group easily eclipsed the number of New York councillors present and challenged DeLancey's ability to run the conference as he pleased.

The most important characteristic shared by these commissioners was their experience in Indian diplomacy, especially those in the Pennsylvania, Massachusetts, and Connecticut delegations. Three of the four Pennsylvania commissioners—Richard Peters, Isaac Norris, and Benjamin Franklin—had served in the same capacity less than a year earlier at the Carlisle treaty. Norris had also attended an Albany conference in 1745.[46] Three of the five Massachusetts commissioners had previous experience in Indian diplomacy. Samuel Welles and Oliver Partridge attended Albany conferences in 1745 and 1751 respectively. Thomas Hutchinson, a staunch ally of Governor William Shirley on the Massachusetts council, participated in three Albany conferences in the 1740s.[47] Of the three Connecticut commissioners, William Pitkin had attended an Albany conference in 1751.[48]

The Massachusetts, Connecticut, and Pennsylvania governments had been rivals of the New Yorkers in Covenant Chain diplomacy since the early eighteenth century. New York governors presiding at intercolonial

[45] The previous maximum of colonies represented at an Albany treaty besides New York was three: South Carolina, Massachusetts, and Connecticut sent delegations to a 1751 conference, and Pennsylvania, Massachusetts, and Connecticut sent delegations to one in 1745. See NYCD, 6:289–305, 717–26. In all, thirteen intercolonial treaty conferences convened in Albany before the Albany Congress. Most were prompted by wartime threats to colonial security. See the "Descriptive Treaty Calendar" in Jennings et al., eds., History and Culture of Iroquois Diplomacy, 160–86.

[46] See NYCD, 6:289–305, for the 1745 Albany conference, and A Treaty Held with the Ohio Indians at Carlisle in October, 1753 (Philadelphia, 1753), in Boyd, ed., Indian Treaties Printed by Benjamin Franklin, 123–34.

[47] For Welles and Partridge, see NYCD, 6:289–305, 717–26. Hutchinson noted his service as a Massachusetts Indian commissioner in an autobiographical summary he wrote later in life. See Peter Orlando Hutchinson, ed., The Diary and Letters of Thomas Hutchinson, 2 vols. (1884–86; rpt. New York, 1971) 1:55.

[48] NYCD, 6:717–26.

Albany conferences found themselves stuck between the Charybdis of Pennsylvania Quaker pacifism and the Scylla of New England aggression. Pennsylvania developed its own "Chain of Friendship" with the Iroquois and convened conferences with them in Philadelphia, Lancaster, and Carlisle. When the Pennsylvanians participated in a 1745 Albany conference, they balked at asking the Indians to war against the French and insisted on treating with them independently of the other colonial delegations so as not to compromise their pacifist principles. Isaac Norris, a Quaker, irritated New York governor George Clinton by refusing to remove his hat when attending the governor's audiences.[49] The Massachusetts and Connecticut governments, on the other hand, had long resented Albany's neutrality in the Anglo-French wars, which the New Englanders complained purchased New York's security at the expense of their own. During the Albany conference of 1745, New England commissioners met privately with the Iroquois to convince them to go to war against the French after Governor Clinton had given up on doing so.[50] If the past was any indication, the Pennsylvania, Massachusetts, and Connecticut delegations would arrive at the Albany Congress intent on challenging DeLancey's leadership rather than submitting to it.

Those colonies unaccustomed to Covenant Chain treaty-making selected commissioners from their councils and assemblies. New Hampshire split its delegation between two councillors, Richard Wibbard and Theodore Atkinson, and two assemblymen, Meshech Weare and Henry Sherburne Jr. Both Rhode Island commissioners, Stephen Hopkins and Martin Howard Jr., came from that colony's assembly. The Maryland delegation consisted of Abraham Barnes, an assemblyman linked to the proprietary party, and Benjamin Tasker Jr., a councillor.[51] A speculative desire for Indian lands also connected some of the Albany Congress commissioners. All three members of the Connecticut delegation—William Pitkin, Elisha Williams, and Roger Wolcott Jr.—held shares in the Susquehannah Company. John Penn, the fourth Pennsylvania commissioner, attended the Albany Congress to assist Richard Peters in negotiating a land purchase for the Penn family.

The colonial commissioners met daily in the Stadt Huys, which in their minutes they called the courthouse. The commissioners held thirty-two meetings there between June 19 and July 11, usually assembling for morning and evening sessions.[52] The New York councillors joined them for

[49] See "Journal of Norris," 23–25, and NYCD, 6:289–305.
[50] See Report of the Massachusetts Commissioners, October 22, 1745, Mass. Archives, 29:391–92, 410–11.
[51] A full listing of the commissioners for each colony can be found in the Albany Congress minutes, NYCD, 6:853, and in their commissions, reprinted in Penn. Archives, 1st ser., 2:137–43.
[52] A useful summary of these proceedings may be found in BF Papers, 5:344–53.

these meetings, although the governor rarely did. The commissioners attended DeLancey's public speeches to the Indians, but in keeping with Covenant Chain protocol, they sat impassively while the governor and Indian orators spoke. For private councils, DeLancey met with the Indians in his quarters inside the fort. This division of space became obvious early in the congress, when, after receiving a request from the commissioners to join them in the courthouse, DeLancey replied that "he could not possibly attend, being so Surroinded with the Indians."[53] The courthouse and the Governor's House symbolized separate turf and different duties. DeLancey was in town to settle Indian complaints and mend the Covenant Chain; the commissioners kept their distance from him and carried on their affairs mostly behind the closed doors of the courthouse.[54] This segregation reinforced divisions and suspicions between DeLancey and the visiting commissioners that worsened as the conference proceeded.

Beyond the courthouse doors, visiting commissioners engaged in their own activity "in the bushes," mostly socializing with Albany's residents. From the moment they arrived in Albany, the commissioners shared lodging, meals, teas, and entertainments with the town's leading gentlemen and magistrates in a manner that defied Hamilton's and Kalm's descriptions of a rude, unpolished Albany society. This dimension of treaty-making sheds considerable light on how conference participants interacted outside of official proceedings. The personal journals kept by Isaac Norris in 1745 and Theodore Atkinson in 1754 are particularly helpful in this regard. The parallels between them reveal that colonial participants in treaty conferences followed their own rituals of hospitality designed to make plain the New Yorkers' role as hosts and the commissioners' role as guests.

During their stay in Albany, colonial commissioners found themselves treated as public guests by the governor and the town's magistrates. After Isaac Norris and his fellow Pennsylvanians disembarked from their sloop in 1745, one of the city's most prominent citizens, Philip Livingston Jr., approached them with an invitation to stay in his home.[55] In 1754 the New Hampshire commissioners made arrangements to lodge at the home of "one Lansighs," the name of another of the city's leading families. Also in 1754, the Pennsylvania commissioners stayed with James Stevenson, one

[53] McAnear, "Personal Accounts," 734.
[54] In relation to the Iroquois Influence Thesis, it is important to note here that no Indians attended any of the courthouse sessions in which the colonial commissioners debated the Albany Plan of Union. In other words, all discussion of the Plan of Union contained in the official proceedings of the Albany Congress occurred independently of any Indian participation in the conference. This fact makes it hard to sustain the image of colonial statesmen and Iroquois chiefs discussing how the Iroquois Confederacy might serve as a model for American union and democracy.
[55] See "Journal of Norris," 22.

of Albany's leading merchants.[56] Opening their homes to the visiting commissioners gave the residents of Albany an excellent opportunity to influence their opinions on Indian affairs. It also gave the commissioners the privacy they needed to conduct their own Indian negotiations, such as the land purchases they would pursue at the Albany Congress.

Once in the city, the colonial commissioners dined and socialized frequently with the governor and the gentlemen of Albany. Upon arriving in Albany in 1745, Norris attended "a large and plentiful dinner" at the home of Stephen Van Rensselaer that included Governor George Clinton and "almost all the gentlemen of the place [Albany]."[57] Over the next two weeks he dined separately with the Connecticut and Massachusetts commissioners and the mayor of Albany. Atkinson's 1754 journal records a similar round of invitations and engagements. On his first night in Albany, he and the other New Hampshire commissioners joined Governor DeLancey and twenty other gentlemen for "a Handsom Enter[t]ainment." On subsequent days he dined with leading Albany gentlemen Philip Schuyler and Cornelius Cuyler and enjoyed tea with the mayor, a merchant, Robert Sanders. The high point of this socializing came on the night of July 3, when the magistrates provided "a great Dinner and wine" for the colonial commissioners and numerous other gentlemen. Seventy-one persons attended this dinner, according to the bill submitted to the Albany Common Council by a local tavern keeper. "Were very merry," the laconic, and perhaps a bit inebriated, Atkinson related in his journal. Two days later the visiting commissioners reciprocated by entertaining "the Governor and Council of York, the Mare [Mayor] and the Corporation and Gentlemen of Albany, Strangers, etc." with a dinner at the courthouse.[58]

What explains this sudden change in Albany's social climate when a treaty conference convened? Certainly, local magistrates and gentlemen wished to impress the governor and representatives from other colonies: the maintenance of their authority over Indian affairs depended in a large part on their ability to convince such outsiders that they were doing their job. More important, such hospitality put the visiting commissioners in their place: they were interlopers in New York's Indian affairs. Their status as guests of the Albany magistrates reinforced their peripheral status in the Indian negotiations and thereby strengthened the New Yorkers' role in the proceedings.

[56] For the New Hampshire commissioners, see McAnear, "Personal Accounts," 730. McAnear posits that this "Lansighs" was probably Jacob J. Lansing, a leading Albany resident. See ibid., 730, n. 11. For the Pennsylvania commissioners, see Richard Peters to William Alexander, March 28, April 17, 1754, Susquehannah Co. Papers, 1:78, 85–86.
[57] "Journal of Norris," 22–23.
[58] McAnear, "Personal Accounts," 730, 733, 737–39. Also see Albany Common Council minutes for July 2 and August 13, 1754, in Joel Munsell, ed., Collections on the History of Albany, from Its Discovery to the Present Time, 4 vols. (Albany, 1865–71), 1:90.

The Indians, New Yorkers, and colonial commissioners made up the three primary groups of participants in the Albany Congress, but they were not the only players on the stage. At any Albany treaty conference, an assortment of other characters observed and sometimes participated in the action. The most important of these were the interpreters who served as cultural brokers between the Indians and colonists. Each Covenant Chain conference had an official interpreter who attended the governor. Any number of other men and women conversant in English, Dutch, French, and Indian languages also acted as unofficial interpreters in private councils or for particular colonial delegations.[59]

Despite their considerable influence over treaty proceedings, interpreters did not enjoy a good reputation. Their positions endowed them with a capacity for duplicity and corruption that made other treaty participants, even fellow New Yorkers, suspicious. In his history of the Iroquois, Cadwallader Colden complained that while Indians chose their words carefully so that "they might have their full force on the imagination," interpreters translated their speeches "in as few words as it could be exprest."[60] Furthermore, Albany interpreters usually came from a lower tier of society than other colonial participants in a treaty conference. Often of cross-ethnic parentage, they made their livings on the routes between Albany, Oswego, and Montreal. Their participation in the notoriously fraudulent Indian trade along with their mixed lineages led European contemporaries to associate their multilinguistic fluency with genetic and moral corruption. Thomas Pownall, who wrote primarily from experience gained at the Albany Congress, found that the Albany interpreters were "generally of Dutch Extraction," thereby necessitating that any Indian speech "must first come to us in Dutch from such as know very little of their own or any other Language." He assumed that any interpreter using Dutch as a primary language lacked the intelligence to be proficient in his own and other languages.[61] Such interpreters might not face similar criticism from the Dutch-speaking inhabitants of Albany, but neither did they enjoy the social and political status of the Albany merchants who managed the town's Indian affairs.

The Board of Trade knew of the Albany interpreters' poor reputation, and it instructed the New York governor to make sure that he employed

[59] On the role of interpreters in Covenant Chain diplomacy, see Nancy Hagedorn, "'A Friend to Go between Them': The Interpreter as Cultural Broker during Anglo-Iroquois Councils, 1740–70," *Ethnohistory* 35 (1988): 60–80, and Hagedorn, "Brokers of Understanding: Interpreters as Agents of Cultural Exchange in Colonial New York," *New York History* 76 (1995): 379–408.

[60] Colden, *History of the Five Indian Nations*, xi. Also see Wraxall, *Abridgment of the Indian Affairs*, 154–55.

[61] Thomas Pownall, *Proposals for Securing the Friendship of the Five Nations* (New York, 1756), 4, and McAnear, "Personal Accounts," 742.

only "men of ability and integrity" at the Albany Congress.[62] At this time New York's interpreter was Arent Stevens, an Indian trader. Peter Wraxall, the city's clerk and secretary at the Albany Congress, described him as "the Son of a Negro Woman . . . [who] understands neither Dutch nor English Well." Thomas Pownall shared Wraxall's opinion, calling Stevens's work at the Albany Congress "most extream bad" and the interpreter himself "a most extream stupid, ignorant and illiterate Person." DeLancey tried to recruit Pennsylvanian Conrad Weiser to serve as the official interpreter for the Albany Congress, which suggests that Stevens was not well regarded by either his governor or the Albany Indian Commissioners.[63]

DeLancey did not succeed in enlisting Weiser as his interpreter, but Weiser and several other interpreters did attend. Weiser declined DeLancey's offer because he had already agreed to assist Richard Peters and John Penn in their land purchase. His rivals in this capacity were the Indian missionary Timothy Woodbridge and Albany trader John Henry Lydius, both of whom worked on behalf of the Susquehannah Company.[64] The Albany Congress minutes also identify a "Mr. Killogg" employed by the Massachusetts delegation. This person was either Martin or Joseph Kellogg, brothers and child captives of the Caughnawagas who after their redemptions occasionally served as interpreters for Massachusetts.[65]

During a treaty conference, Albany turned into a sort of colonial Babel. While Stevens served as DeLancey's offical interpreter, any number of individuals stood in the wings ready to offer alternative interpretations of the action. So many private and impromptu interpreters gave the congress a maddening linguistic elasticity: no one could be sure of exactly what another party had said. Rumors developed quickly and gained wide currency. When the Mohawks arrived at the Albany Congress, they told DeLancey that they had heard local colonists exchanging negative reports about them. One of their chiefs explained, "There are some of our People who have large open Ears and talk a little broken English and Dutch, so

[62] *NYCD*, 6:801.
[63] Wraxall, *Abridgment of the Indian Affairs*, 155. For Stevens's appointment as New York's interpreter, see NYCM, December 25, 1747, 21:280; for his service at the time of the Albany Congress, see NY Col. Mss., 78:114. Stevens was actually the son of an English colonist and a woman of mixed Indian-European parentage. See Hagedorn, "Brokers of Understanding," 382. For Pownall's comments, see McAnear, "Personal Accounts," 742. For DeLancey's efforts to recruit Weiser, see *Penn. Council Minutes*, 6:15, 49.
[64] *Susquehannah Co. Papers*, 1:45.
[65] *NYCD*, 6:874. Martin Kellogg had previous experience working with the New York Mohawks and therefore may have been the "Mr. Killogg" present at the Albany Congress. See Martin Kellogg to Hendrick, [December 23, 1751], *WJ Papers*, 1:357–58. "Captain Joseph Kellogg" is identified as an interpreter present at the signing of the Susquehannah Company's land deed at the home of John Henry Lydius on the final day of the Albany Congress. See *Susquehannah Co. Papers*, 1:119–20. For the Kelloggs' captivity, see Demos, *Unredeemed Captive*, 169–70, 183.

that they sometimes hear what is said by the Christian settlers near them." DeLancey, in an effort to stop the rumor mill, replied, "I caution you not to hearken to common reports, neither of us or your Brethren the other Nations."[66] Such "common reports" circulated quickly in the Mohawk Valley, and they could easily upset a treaty's proceedings.[67]

Thomas Pownall summarized the situation perfectly. He admitted that his criticism of Arent Stevens might seem unjustified since Pownall himself did not know the Indians' language. "But," he explained to the Earl of Halifax, "Many of the Indians know English. Many almost all the Albany people speak Indian. I always gott some one, when I cou'd, that cou'd speak it to stand next me, and I am intimately acquainted with a Gentleman who speaks the Language readily."[68] By following Pownall's example, anyone could find a personal interpreter and tap into the treaty negotiations in the same way that a bystander on a busy street corner might become privy to hundreds of passing conversations. The Albany Congress minutes contained the official record of the conference, but the inability to confine the dialogue to a single channel substantially lessened that document's authority. This uncertainty placed an additional burden on nonlinguistic forms of communication. Ceremonial greetings, gift exchanges, and other forms of physical interaction became all the more significant because they compensated for a lack of clarity and trustworthiness in the spoken word. No linguistic transaction took place without some dramaturgical form of communication—a wampum belt passed, a present given, a toast made—to confirm its meaning.

The last group of characters to participate in the Albany Congress were the mostly anonymous bystanders in its audience. Public and private accounts of the congress identify them merely as "many Gentlemen" or "Strangers" who attended public and private councils with the Indians and joined in the colonial commissioners' socializing.[69] An intercolonial treaty conference attracted an audience from beyond Albany, which accounts for the "great Number of private Gentlemen" who accompanied DeLancey when he sailed from New York City for Albany.[70] Some of the colonial commissioners traveling to Albany took along their sons to introduce them to a wider polite society. In 1745, Pennsylvania commissioner

---

[66] NYCD, 6:868.
[67] An example of the problems caused by such rumors is the Albany conference of 1745, in which Governor George Clinton tried to determine who was responsible for rumors of a British plan to attack the Mohawks. See ibid., 294–96. For an interesting study of how rumors affected European-Indian diplomacy, see Gregory Evans Dowd, "The Panic of 1751: The Significance of Rumors on the South Carolina-Cherokee Frontier," WMQ 53 (1996): 527–60.
[68] McAnear, "Personal Accounts," 742.
[69] See for example, ibid., 737–38.
[70] New-York Mercury, June 10, 1754. In his 1744 journal, Alexander Hamilton noted passing three sloops on the Hudson River carrying Governor Clinton's entourage back to New York City after treating with the Indians in Albany. See Bridenbaugh, ed., Gentleman's Progress, 59.

Thomas Lawrence brought his son John with him. In 1754, Benjamin Franklin brought his son William.[71] An Albany treaty conference also attracted settlers from the Mohawk frontier seeking the governor's assistance in patenting Indian lands. Much of DeLancey's time at the Albany Congress was consumed by such business, which he transacted with Mohawks from Canajoharie, their German neighbors, and a Scottish fur trader named Teady Magin.[72]

These peripheral characters played no official role at a treaty conference; they were there to satisfy their curiosity and self-interest. The only trace William Franklin left at the Albany Congress was his signature as a witness on the land deed executed by John Penn and Richard Peters. The audiences that assembled for DeLancey's speeches to the Indians performed a similar act of notarization: their presence legitimated such meetings as public and open and eligible for inclusion in the treaty's official record. Like the interpreters, these anonymous bystanders occupied no fixed position on the stage; they formed a moving chorus, coming and going to observe and reflect on the action. The most prominent person among them was Thomas Pownall, the erstwhile secretary who had become the Board of Trade's correspondent in the field on American affairs. DeLancey invited him to attend the Albany Congress, probably hoping that Pownall would report favorably to the ministry on his management of the conference.[73]

For Albany's local folk, a treaty conference brought public spectacle as well as economic opportunity. Indians and colonial commissioners marched in processions to outdoor councils; the governor ordered the fort's cannon discharged to honor his guests; and Indians danced through the city's streets for the entertainment of their hosts.[74] Processions, dances, and speeches must have attracted local men and women simply for the good theater and welcome diversions they provided. Treaty-making and all of its related business temporarily touched the lives of everyone in Albany, genteel or plebian, with an atmosphere that combined the sober formality of the council fire with the kinetic disorder of streets, markets, and taverns filled with strangers.

Like the actors in a play, participants in the Albany Congress fit into easily identified leading and supporting roles. The Indians, New

[71] For Lawrence, see "Journal of Norris, 1745," 21, 28; for Franklin, see Penn and Peters Report, 713.
[72] See NYCM, July 2 through July 6, 1754, 23:196–204. These transactions will be discussed at greater length in the next chapter.
[73] See McAnear, "Personal Accounts," 729.
[74] Indian processions and war dances were common at Albany treaty conferences. See, for example, "Journal of Norris," 25; [New York], A Treaty between His Excellency, 8; and "The Journal of Tench Tilghman" (1775), in Samuel Harrison, Memoir of Lieut. Col. Tench Tilghman (Albany, 1876), 91–93.

Yorkers, and colonial commissioners remained the focus of the conference's official proceedings, but interpreters, private gentlemen, and other bystanders assumed parts as well. Players distinguished themselves from each other according to the spaces they occupied on the stage, which provided physical and symbolic boundaries to reinforce their roles as hosts and guests. Participants also constantly challenged those well-defined settings and roles. Barriers, both physical and linguistic, were too weak to be maintained; communication traveled through too many channels to be monopolized. The treaty conference at the Albany Congress followed a protocol intended to promote at least the appearance of harmony and friendship. The people who gathered in Albany challenged the smooth operation of that format and laid bare the divisions that had brought the Covenant Chain to its crisis in the first place.

[5]

The Treaty Conference

The fire here is burnt out.

—Mohawk speaker Abraham, July 2, 1754

On Saturday, July 6, an encounter occurred between colonists and Indians at the Albany Congress that was not recorded in the official minutes. While John Worthington and Meshech Weare attended a meeting in the courthouse, their fellow New Hampshire commissioners Theodore Atkinson and Richard Wibbard remained in their lodgings. At about 10:00 A.M. an Indian delegation led by Hendrick and including "2 Sachems of Each Tribe and Some few others" arrived. Atkinson and Wibbard made a speech and gave presents to these Indians in the name of the New Hampshire government. The Indians responded with a speech of their own, in which they "gave us the name of *Sosaquasowane*" and asked for "*a Discription of our Province.*" The New Hampshire commissioners obliged, and Hendrick "*Said he had been there.*" Shortly thereafter, Atkinson and Wibbard gave the Indians some wine and excused themselves to join the other colonial commissioners in the courthouse. But they had not finished their business with the Indians. During the Saturday morning meeting, the chiefs hinted that "*the*[y] *Expected Some thing as a Treat* when they united and gave a Name." In particular, they "Bespoke *a Cow.*" Atkinson and Wibbard purchased one, and on the following Monday morning they sent for Hendrick, who "came and Liked her." Some younger Indians retrieved the cow, which they slaughtered in the Indians' camp.[1]

Although not a part of the Albany Congress's minutes, this meeting offers an important glimpse into the nature of the diplomacy conducted there. Treaty conferences consisted of two parallel sets of negotiations. Unofficial private meetings, such as the encounter described above, began before the formal opening of a treaty conference and continued until its conclusion. In them, Indians and colonists presented grievances, ironed

---

[1] McAnear, "Personal Accounts," 738–39.

out differences, and exchanged favors, all of which made it possible for them to maintain an air of civility and amity in public. Public councils followed a format adapted from Iroquois condolence rituals, in which each side took turns making speeches and presenting gifts. Colonial secretaries recorded the public speeches in treaty minutes, which were forwarded to the Board of Trade and occasionally published for a wider readership in America and Britain. Whether in published or manuscript form, treaty minutes tended to follow a standard narrative of coming together, settling differences, and parting as friends.[2]

Atkinson and Wibbard's private meeting with a small group of chiefs mimicked in miniature the ceremonial acts of exchange that made up a treaty conference. Each side brought something to the table and expected something in return. Atkinson and Wibbard brought goods and acted as hosts, waiting "for the Indians to come and receive our Present." The Indians brought something more abstract but equally important: access to the Covenant Chain, which offered peace and trade with the Iroquois. The New Hampshire government had not previously participated in such treaty-making; Atkinson and his colleagues were unfamiliar with its customs. In return for the New Hampshirites' presents, the Indians extended the Covenant Chain to them, as signified by the granting of the name "Sosaquasowane." All colonies party to the Covenant Chain received such names, usually attached to their governors, by which the Iroquois addressed them.[3] This private exchange took place with the gravity typical of a public council; what little conversation occurred was limited to polite small talk, and Atkinson and Wibbard excused themselves from the Indians' company quickly after completing their duties.

[2] Two useful sources on the protocol of Covenant Chain treaty-making and its foundation in Iroquois condolence rituals are William N. Fenton, "Structure, Continuity, and Change in the Process of Iroquois Treaty Making," in *The History and Culture of Iroquois Diplomacy*, ed. Jennings et al. 3–35, and Michael K. Foster, "On Who Spoke First at Iroquois-White Councils: An Exercise in the Method of Upstreaming," in *Extending the Rafters: Interdisciplinary Approaches to Iroquoian Studies*, ed. Michael K. Foster, Jack Campisi, and Marianne Mithun (Albany, 1984), 183–207. For analysis of published Indian treaties, see Lawrence C. Wroth, "The Indian Treaty as Literature," *Yale Review* n.s., 17 (1927–28): 749–66.

[3] For example, in treaty conferences, the Iroquois referred to New York's governor as "Corlaer" and Pennsylvania's as "Onas." For the derivation of these names, see Jennings et al., eds., *History and Culture of Iroquois Diplomacy*, 235, 246. In his eighteenth-century history of New Hampshire, Jeremy Belknap wrote of his investigation into the meaning of the name granted to his colony at the Albany Congress: "I have inquired of the Reverend Mr. Kirkland the meaning of this name: He informed me that *So* signifies, AGAIN; *saquax*, a DISH; and *owane*, LARGE." See McAnear, "Personal Accounts," 738. n. 50. Another such naming occurred for Maryland in the bushes at the Albany Congress. At an entertainment provided for the Indians by the Pennsylvania and Maryland commissioners, a Cayuga chief made a speech in which he gave the Maryland commissioners the name "Tocarryhogon," by which he told them, "We have admitted you of Our Council, and you are become One of Us." See "Speech of Gatchradodow," July 6, 1754, in Jennings et al., eds., *Iroquois Indians*, reel 16.

In its private and public manifestations, Covenant Chain diplomacy followed this intercultural tit for tat. The colonists had the goods—clothing, provisions, weapons, tools, and liquor—for which the Indians offered alliance, trade, and peace. Diplomatic ceremony structured this exchange, but each party manipulated that ritual to suit its needs. As hosts, colonists set an agenda in the opening speech. Iroquois diplomacy did not allow for the introduction of new issues until previous ones were settled, so this position gave considerable advantage to the party who spoke first.[4] The duration of the conference, however, depended on the Indian guests. By delaying their arrival, taking a long time to prepare answers, or hesitating to renew the Covenant Chain, they could prolong the conference and increase its expense to their hosts. The Indians' hint to Atkinson and Wibbard that they expected an additional present for granting a name is an excellent example of how they used diplomacy to extract goods from the colonists. The chiefs framed their request as an explanation of how to observe the naming ritual properly. Rather than begging as humble clients before a mighty patron, Hendrick and his fellow chiefs used their expertise in treaty-making to negotiate with the New Hampshirites from a position of strength. A treaty conference could easily become a test of wills as each side pursued its objective: colonists might withhold presents to get Indians to agree to their propositions, while Indians could prolong the conference until they received the answers and presents they desired.

Colonists and Indians at the Albany Congress exhibited such hard-nosed, competitive behavior. The romantic image put forth by the Iroquois Influence Thesis of eager colonists and wise Indians sitting around a fire to swap advice on union simply does not stand up in light of this evidence.[5] According to the official minutes, the Indians did receive their presents, renew the Covenant Chain, and go home professing friendship with the British. But several levels of conflict became apparent as parties pursued contesting interests. James DeLancey and the Albany magistrates wanted to monopolize negotiations with the Indians, especially those concerning the Mohawks' grievances. The Mohawks, still angered by the diplomatic neglect of the New Yorkers, wanted to wrestle the Covenant Chain out of their hands and open new paths to other colonial governments. Meanwhile, commissioners from Pennsylvania and New England pulled the

---

[4] See Foster, "On Who Spoke First at Iroquois-White Councils," 192–97.
[5] For example, see Bruce E. Johansen's description of the Albany Congress in *Forgotten Founders: How the American Indian Helped Shaped Democracy* (Boston, 1982), 69–71. Johansen's undocumented claim that Hendrick "received a special invitation from James de Lancey, acting governor of New York, to provide information on the structure of the Iroquois Confederacy to the Colonial delegates" (69) has absolutely no support in the documentary record of the congress and is a deliberate twisting of DeLancey's private councils with Hendrick to address the Mohawks' land complaints. See *NYCD*, 6:866–68.

Covenant Chain in opposite directions, using it to acquire Indian lands and to defend their own frontiers.

At the center of this conflict stood Hendrick and William Johnson. Hendrick acted as the chief spokesman for the Indians in their public and private councils. Johnson attended the Albany Congress as one of De-Lancey's councillors, but he hardly followed the governor's agenda for mending the Covenant Chain. For ten years, he had been butting heads with the Albany magistrates and the New York Assembly over management of that colony's Indian affairs. He arrived at the Albany Congress as a free agent committed to Britain's imperial expansion and his own quest for an appointment as the Crown's Indian agent. A three-way contest developed between DeLancey, the Mohawks, and the visiting colonial delegations at Albany that made it apparent to all concerned that an older method of conducting intercultural diplomacy was breaking down. Johnson and Hendrick positioned themselves to assume leadership of the reconstituted Covenant Chain that emerged from this crisis.

"One General Treaty"

The New York governor customarily acted as the presiding officer at Albany treaty conferences, and he relied on his councillors and the Albany Commissioners of Indian Affairs to help him conduct business. When delegations from other colonies attended, they made their own speeches and granted their own presents to the Indians. Acting in the king's name, the New York governor occasionally renewed the Covenant Chain on behalf of all the British colonies, but the unspoken rule observed by hosts and guests alike was that each colonial delegation treated separately with the Indians.[6]

In its instructions for the Albany Congress, the Board of Trade expressed discontent with this system, "it appearing to us that the practice of each Province making a separate Treaty for itself in its own name is very improper and may be attended with great inconveniency to his Majesty's service." The board told the New York governor "to take care that all the Provinces be (if practicable) comprized in one general Treaty to be made in his Majesty's name."[7] These instructions broke with tradition and presumed to tell the New York governor how to conduct Indian diplomacy, rather than merely outlining objectives for it. It is important to recall that the board wrote these instructions for Sir Danvers Osborne, a novice who owed his appointment to the board's president, the Earl of Halifax. Realiz-

---

[6] For examples of these practices in action, see the conferences described in *NYCD*, 6:289–305, 441–52, and in Wraxall, *Abridgment of the Indian Affairs*, 10–16, 141–43, 226–28.
[7] *NYCD*, 6:801.

ing Osborne's inexperience, Halifax seized this opportunity to change the way colonial governments conducted Indian affairs.

James DeLancey, who assumed Osborne's office after his death, had plenty of experience in New York's Indian affairs and showed no signs of acting in the spirit of the board's orders. Instead, he went about business as usual, convening his councillors and the Albany Indian Commissioners to prepare for the Indians. Almost immediately, he met resistance from the other colonial delegations. At stake was the privilege the New Yorkers claimed to manage the Covenant Chain as they saw fit because of their long-standing commercial and diplomatic ties with the Iroquois at Albany. The colonial commissioners believed New York's mismanagement had caused the breaking of the Covenant Chain, and they wished to see it mended to suit their own purposes. This division between DeLancey and the visiting commissioners made it difficult to present to the Indians the united front that the Board of Trade desired.

After DeLancey arrived in Albany on June 13, one of his first acts was to order the Albany Indian Commissioners to brief him for his "approaching interview, with the Six Nations."[8] The commissioners met twice in a local tavern to prepare their answer. They recommended that the governor include four points in his opening speech to the Indians. First, he should press upon them the need to stop living in a "dispersed and confused" manner and "to unite and dwell together in their respective Castles, and that the Mohawks should live in one Castle only." Second, they endorsed DeLancey's plan to get permission from the Iroquois to build two forts in their country. This permission was necessary if DeLancey wished to proceed with his plan to fortify the New York frontier at intercolonial expense, which he had suggested to other colonial governments at the time he invited them to the Albany Congress.[9] Third, the Albany Indian Commissioners asked DeLancey to order the Indians to expel any Frenchmen currently living or trading among them. Finally, they referred to DeLancey a petition from forty-seven fur traders, complaining that the Canajoharie Mohawks and Oneidas had been stopping traffic en route to Oswego, stealing rum and threatening harm if the traders did not pay "a most exorbitant price" for the Indians' assistance.[10]

As these recommendations indicated, the Albany Indian Commissioners were concerned about New York's frontier security and trade. Of foremost importance to them was stopping the out-migration of Iroquois to French missionary towns along the St. Lawrence, particularly Oswegatchie, a French post near Lake Ontario that had attracted a consider-

---

[8] Ibid., 856.
[9] See the discussion of DeLancey's agenda for the Albany Congress in Chapter 3.
[10] *NYCD*, 6:856–58.

able number of Onondagas and Cayugas. In asking DeLancey to press the Indians to "live together in one Castle according to their ancient and prudent Custom," the Albany commissioners hoped to see a line of friendly Iroquois villages insulating them from French attack.[11] If the Mohawks were gathered into one village, it would also be easier to discourage them from moving to missionary villages in Canada or New England. By presenting the traders' petition to DeLancey, the Albany commissioners fulfilled their role as mediators in the Mohawk Valley fur trade. The traders' complaints testified to the deterioration of intercultural relations in that region, and calming tensions there was necessary to preserve the Oswego fur market.

The colonial commissioners proved less cooperative with DeLancey. They began arriving in Albany on June 15 and assembled as a group for the first time on the morning of the nineteenth in the courthouse, after DeLancey had summoned them to "produce their powers and proceed upon business."[12] Much of this first day's business, recorded in detail by Atkinson, concerned matters of rank and credentials. What appeared to be pickiness over formalities addressed a more fundamental issue: who would lead the colonists' negotiations with the Indians? DeLancey opened the meeting by ordering the commission of each delegation read, as well as a paragraph from the Board of Trade's instructions. Whether it was the paragraph containing the reference to "one general Treaty" with the Indians is unclear although likely since DeLancey could invoke it to place himself at the head of the proceedings. He then presented the Albany Indian Commissioners' report, along with the traders' petition concerning the disruption of traffic to Oswego. As the colonial commissioners' first order of business, DeLancey proposed that they "consider the several matters they may judge proper to be proposed to the Indians."[13] He also suggested that because the "Perticular Iddoms or Diction" of speeches to the Indians were "very Peculiar," the final draft of the speech should be left "to those that Should diliv[e]r the Same to the Indians." In other words, the New Yorkers should be the final arbiters of the speech's content and delivery.[14]

DeLancey hoped that the colonial delegations would rubber-stamp the agenda he had already set for the conference. "One general Treaty" would occur, but on his terms rather than the Board of Trade's: New York would

---

[11] Ibid., 856. In a subsequent meeting on June 20, the Albany Commissioners of Indian Affairs thought better of asking the Mohawks to live in a single village, realizing that they would most likely resist such an idea, and they advised DeLancey to drop that item from his speech. See Minutes of the Albany Commisioners of Indian Affairs (June 29, 1753–May 4, 1755), Native American History Collection, William L. Clements Library.

[12] NYCD, 6:853.

[13] Ibid., 854.

[14] McAnear, "Personal Accounts," 731.

take the leading role, and his partnership with the Albany Indian Commissioners would go unchallenged. The colonial delegations responded by questioning the New Yorkers' credentials. Atkinson noted that during this first meeting, *"There was Some Inquiry weither any body was Commissionated from N York."* The New York government never commissioned its representatives at Albany conferences because the governor and his councillors already possessed the powers necessary to act on its behalf. The other delegations wanted DeLancey to commission his councillors to treat with the Indians, an official act that would have made his presence unnecessary and placed the New Yorkers on the same footing as the visitors. DeLancey had no intention of relinquishing his authority, and so he told his guests that no New Yorkers needed to be commissioned as long as he was present.[15]

The colonial commissioners found other ways to enforce a greater parity between themselves and the New Yorkers. At their first meeting, DeLancey told the commissioners to sit wherever they pleased around a large table, while he and his councillors seated themselves at one end. This arrangement did not please the commissioners, many of whom had to sit in rows behind others. After adjourning their morning session, they removed the table from the room "in order that we might be all Accomodated in Setting round it [the room] without being behinde Each other."[16] With no table, the New Yorkers could no longer place themselves at the head of it.

The tug-of-war between DeLancey and the colonial commissioners continued as they prepared an opening speech. Although the commissioners did not challenge the protocol of having DeLancey deliver this speech—as the only colonial governor present, he outranked everyone else—they did question his recommendations for its content. The Pennsylvania and Massachusetts delegations each offered alternative agendas. Both colonies had participated in Albany conferences during the 1740s, in which they had often been at odds with the New Yorkers. During the commissioners' first day of meeting at the Albany Congress, Richard Peters of Pennsylvania and Samuel Welles of Massachusetts made speeches on behalf of their respective colonies. Peters summarized Pennsylvania's past diplomacy with the Iroquois and expressed his government's concern for Pennsylvania fur traders recently captured by the French in the Ohio Valley. Welles discussed Massachusetts's great expense in defending the New England

---

[15] See Atkinson's description of this debate, ibid., 731. This issue remained a point of contention for at least a few days. Atkinson noted that on June 24 one of the colonial commissioners renewed the question of *"wether the Council of York ought to Set or not without a Comission."* Ibid., 734. The New York councillors continued to sit as representatives of New York at the commissioners' courthouse meetings.

[16] Ibid., 731–32.

frontier and described an expedition that Governor Shirley was then leading against the French in Maine. These speeches set different priorities for the Covenant Chain than the Albany commissioners had in their remarks to DeLancey. Pennsylvania wanted to use it to defend its fur trade and land claims in the Ohio Valley; Massachusetts wanted to enlist the Iroquois against the French along the New England–Canadian border.[17]

The commissioners appointed a committee to write the opening speech to the Indians. In debating its content, several objected to introducing issues that concerned only particular colonies. According to Atkinson, the commissioners finally agreed that the speech should be "only General and Salutary," for if it contained any one colony's proposals, then "every thing that Each Govern[ment] had to say to the Indians Should be also Incerted." Acting on this principle, the commissioners later struck out a paragraph DeLancey had added concerning the Albany traders' complaints against the Mohawks and Oneidas.[18] DeLancey and the commissioners finally compromised on a final draft. DeLancey was to present a wampum belt to "solemnly renew, brighten, and strengthen the ancient covenant Chain." The speech implored the Indians to return to their "National Castles" and call back those who had resettled among the French. In a nod to the Pennsylvania and Massachusetts delegations, it asked the Indians to explain whether recent French encroachments "both to the Northward and Westward" were made "with your consent or approbation." The speech did not mention the Albany traders' petition, Pennsylvania's captured traders, or the Massachusetts expedition in Maine.[19]

Within a few days, it became obvious that meeting the Board of Trade's request for "one general Treaty" with the Indians would be impossible. The colonial delegations most experienced in treaty-making—New York, Pennsylvania, and Massachusetts—acted quickly to shroud their particular interests in the cloak of intercolonial cooperation. Meanwhile, the distance between DeLancey and the visiting delegations increased. As Indians arrived in town, DeLancey held private councils with them in his lodgings and attended the commissioners less often, communicating with them mostly by messengers. On June 21 the commissioners took another step away from the governor by appointing Albany town clerk Peter Wraxall as their secretary, after which they stopped using DeLancey's secretary Goldsbrow Banyar.[20] Complicating matters even further was the Mohawks' absence among those Indians who had gathered for the conference. No treaty, general or not, was likely to occur without them.

[17] Ibid., 732. No mention is made of these speeches in the Albany Congress's official minutes.
[18] Ibid., 733–34.
[19] NYCD, 6:862–63.
[20] Ibid., 859. For the communications carried on by messengers between the commissioners and DeLancey, see McAnear, "Personal Accounts," 732–35.

When Theodore Atkinson arrived in Albany on June 17, no Indians had yet appeared. New York's interpreter Arent Stevens sent word that the Indians had been delayed by condolence ceremonies they were observing as they moved from one village to the next toward Albany. Three days later all of the colonial commissioners were in town save one, but Atkinson counted only twenty Indians. By June 22, a larger number had assembled, but the Mohawks were still absent. The colonial commissioners, irritated by the delay, inserted an optional paragraph in the opening speech allowing DeLancey to ask the Indians to be "more Punctual for the future."[21]

The Mohawks' absence presented a dilemma for DeLancey. Every day he delayed the conference added to the expense of provisioning those Indians already in town. He could begin without the Mohawks but knew he dared not. The Board of Trade had ordered this meeting to satisfy their grievances; if DeLancey ignored them now he would surely incur the Crown's displeasure. Continuing to stall the proceedings on their behalf, however, compromised his authority and elevated the Mohawks' importance. On June 26, DeLancey decided to send a messenger to Canajoharie, expressing surprise "at your staying so long from this place, where I have been for a considerable time," and asking them to "come down immediately."[22]

The Mohawks' delay gave observers plenty of time to speculate as to its cause. Thomas Pownall believed that the Mohawks intended to show their "disinclination . . . to treat at all since Indian affairs have been taken out of the hands of Col. Johnson." Only after Johnson came to Albany, Pownall wrote, did the Mohawks follow suit.[23] Yet the minutes of the Albany Congress indicate that Johnson was in town as early as June 19, a full week before any Mohawks arrived.[24] Other commentators were more skeptical about Johnson's role in the Mohawks' delay. William Livingston, one of the New York gentlemen who attended the Albany Congress, preferred the opinion of "Not a few" who believed that Johnson purposely delayed the Mohawks until DeLancey and colonial commissioners appealed for him to intercede, thereby boosting his "reputation for a mighty influence over the

---

[21] McAnear, "Personal Accounts," 731–35. Arent Stevens explained his difficulties in recruiting Mohawks and other Iroquois to attend the Albany Congress in a report he made to the Albany commissioners on June 24, 1754. See Minutes of the Albany Commissioners of Indian Affairs (1753–55), Clements Library.

[22] NYCM, June 26, 1754, 23:191.

[23] McAnear, "Personal Accounts," 740.

[24] *NYCD*, 6:853.

Indians."[25] Johnson did not carry DeLancey's message to the Mohawks, but his hand was evident in its reception. The governor's messenger met Hendrick and the Canajoharie Mohawks at Johnson's home, and they "came down running" to Albany within two days.[26]

Johnson and the Mohawks had engaged in similar maneuvers before. Ever since he had arrived at Albany in 1746 dressed in war paint and riding at the head of a Mohawk party, Johnson had been rewriting the opening scenes of treaty conferences to focus on his partnership with the Mohawks. As Livingston noted, "There was highest evidence of the like piece of policy at an Indian treaty, during Mr. Clinton's administration."[27] In that instance, the Mohawks had arrived for an Albany conference in 1751 to find Johnson absent. Reluctant to treat without him, Hendrick asked Clinton for leave "to send a Messenger with a string of Wampum to try what they could do." Clinton agreed and the Indian messenger returned with Johnson.[28] At the Albany Congress Johnson and the Mohawks reversed roles in this ploy. This time the Mohawks stayed away and Johnson secured their attendance.

The Mohawks came to Albany in two groups, on June 27 and 28. First came those from the "lower castle," near Fort Hunter. They immediately held a private council with DeLancey regarding land frauds.[29] The following day the Mohawks from the "upper castle," or Canajoharie, arrived and met privately with DeLancey and several chiefs from the other Iroquois nations. At this meeting, Hendrick explained why he had declared the Covenant Chain broken a year earlier and why the Mohawks had delayed coming to Albany to mend it. The reason for breaking the chain was simple: "we were neglected." As for their delay, Hendrick stated that the Mohawks did not wish to be thought of as having an undue influence over the proceedings in Albany. The previous fall, he and some other Canajoharies had accompanied William Johnson to Onondaga to deliver a message

---

[25] See [Livingston], *Review of Military Operations in North-America* rpt. in *Collections of the Massachusetts Historical Society*, 1st ser., 7 (1801): 76–77. For the attribution of authorship to Livingston, see Milton Klein, "William Livingston's *A Review of the Military Operations in North-America*," in *Colonial Legacy*, ed. Leder, 135–38. William Smith Jr., a political ally of Livingston's who also attended the Albany Congress, thought the Mohawks' delay was motivated either by a desire to appear uncommitted to the British and thereby extract a larger present from them or by Johnson's desire to elevate his reputation among the colonists present. See William Smith, Diary, 1753–1783, New York Public Library, microfilm, 2 reels, 2:365.

[26] NYCM, June 28, 1754, 23:194. Johnson remained in Albany on June 26 and 27, attending the colonial commissioners' courthouse meetings and Governor DeLancey's councils with the Indians already in Albany. See *NYCD*, 6:861.

[27] [Livingston], *Review of Military Operations in North-America*, 76.

[28] *WJ Papers*, 1:341–44.

[29] *NYCD*, 6:850–51, 865–66. For an analysis and history of these fraud complaints, see Georgiana C. Nammack, *Fraud, Politics, and the Dispossession of the Indians*, 22–69.

from the New York governor.[30] The Indians who had heard Johnson at Onondaga thanked him for his speech but said "that the Mohawks had made it." Therefore, Hendrick explained, the Mohawks had lagged behind in coming to Albany, "for if we had come first, the other Nations would have said, that we made the Governors speech, and therefore . . . we intended the other nations should go before us, that they might hear the Governors speech, which we could hear afterwards."[31]

Hendrick's speech suggests that the other Iroquois nations were as suspect of his partnership with Johnson as some colonists were. Hendrick had acted as a maverick when he traveled to New York City with only a small party of Mohawks to declare the Covenant Chain broken. No other Iroquois nations had sanctioned him to act in this regard. His appearance at Onondaga with Johnson a few months later must have caused some rumblings among other Iroquois who thought that Johnson was now serving as the Mohawks' mouthpiece.[32] Just as some colonists suspected Johnson of manipulating the Mohawks' grievances to his personal advantage, so too did some Iroquois suspect Hendrick of using Johnson to gain for the Mohawks an undue influence in the Covenant Chain. "We are looked upon by the other Nations, as Colonel Johnson's councellors," Hendrick told DeLancey, "and supposed to hear to all news from him, which is not the case."[33] Despite such protestations, Hendrick's relationship with Johnson was apparent enough to raise eyebrows on both sides of the Covenant Chain.

Ostensibly, the purpose of the Albany Congress was to address grievances the Mohawks had presented in New York City the previous summer. But it is noteworthy that in his initial council with DeLancey, Hendrick did not renew the complaints about land fraud he had made then; his primary concerns were the New Yorkers' continued diplomatic neglect of his people and the suspicions of other Iroquois that the Mohawks were manipulating Johnson. As one of the governor's councillors, Johnson was present at these meetings between DeLancey and the Mohawks, but the minutes reveal nothing about what he said or did there. Livingston's observation that Johnson was taking this opportunity to elevate his reputation seems accurate in light of the royal preferment Johnson was then seeking. In a March 1754 letter to former governor Clinton, then living in London, Johnson stated his expectation that the ministry would soon appoint someone to serve as the Crown's Indian agent and his desire to be

[30] For the proceedings from this September 1753 meeting in Onondaga, see *WJ Papers*, 9:110–20.
[31] *NYCD*, 6:866–68.
[32] Hendrick did in fact deliver Johnson's speech to the Indians at Onondaga. This service as an interpreter may have further convinced the audience that the speech was really being made by the Mohawks. See NYCM, 23:114.
[33] *NYCD*, 6:867.

that person. He included a long report on Indian affairs designed for Clinton to circulate, condemning Albany's mismanagement of the Covenant Chain and praising his own expertise in such matters.[34] Having cooperated in bringing the Mohawks to the Albany Congress, Hendrick and Johnson were now ready to see the Covenant Chain mended on their terms.

Mending the Chain

Ten days passed between the colonial commissioners' first meeting in the courthouse and DeLancey's opening speech to the Indians. During that time, several constituencies among those people gathered for the conference formed opportunistic alliances. DeLancey and the Albany magistrates cooperated in establishing an agenda that favored their colony and kept its Indian affairs away from the prying eyes of the visiting commissioners. The Mohawks emerged as the most significant of the Indians in attendance, and their partnership with Johnson was obvious, even as Hendrick took pains to discount it. The colonial delegations showed no inclination to cooperate with each other, except on one point: resisting the New Yorkers. Mending the broken Covenant Chain, therefore, had different meanings to those charged with the task. For the New Yorkers, it meant preserving Albany's central role in the Covenant Chain; for the Mohawks, returning Johnson to the agency he had held during King George's War; and for the visiting commissioners, exposing New York's fraudulent dealings with the Indians and breaking once and for all its privileged position in Anglo-Iroquois diplomacy.

All of this division was supposed to be muted in the public councils between colonists and Indians. Usually one person spoke for each side. These two spokesmen took turns addressing each other but rarely offered immediate responses. Instead, the side that had received a speech retired until it was ready to deliver an answer, a day or two later. Speech-making resembled less of a dialogue than a series of monologues separated by long, thoughtful silences during which each side carefully weighed its answers. This format preserved the air of consensus so important to treaty-making by limiting the likelihood that dissenting voices would openly express displeasure with the proceedings. At the Albany Congress, it resulted in a three-way stand-off between the Mohawks, colonial commissioners, and New Yorkers.

On the morning of Saturday, June 29, DeLancey sent word to the courthouse that he was ready to address the Indians, and the commissioners adjourned to join him.[35] Atkinson recorded the scene in his journal. It had

[34] Johnson to Clinton, March 12, 1754, *WJ Papers*, 9:123–32.
[35] *NYCD*, 6:864.

rained that morning and cleared around 10:00 A.M. The commissioners walked up the hill to Fort Frederick and assembled outside the door to the Governor's House. They took seats in a row of chairs placed in front of the door according to the north-to-south order of their colonies, an arrangement they had agreed on earlier: Massachusetts (which claimed the first spot by virtue of its settlements in Maine), New Hampshire, Connecticut, Rhode Island, Pennsylvania, and Maryland. DeLancey and his councillors sat in the middle, between the Rhode Island and Connecticut delegations, out of place in the north-to-south order. The New Yorkers, though they might have been forced to accept more egalitarian seating inside the courthouse, retained their center-stage position in the public councils. The Indians sat facing the colonial delegations and the governor on ten rows of boards placed in the street.[36]

DeLancey rose and welcomed the Indians. He informed them that he spoke for all the colonies represented and for Virginia and South Carolina, both of which wished to be thought of as present. He then offered three strings of wampum in a condolence greeting to "wipe away all tears from your eyes, and take away sorrow from your hearts, so that you may speak freely." With that formality dispensed, DeLancey moved quickly to particulars. He offered a wampum belt "in the name of the Great King our Father" and requested the renewal of the Covenant Chain. Wraxall recorded in the Albany Congress minutes DeLancey's explanation of this belt's design. One long line of beads represented the king's extended arms "embracing all us the English and all the Six Nations." Other short lines represented the colonies and nations connected to the Iroquois Confederacy, with "a space left to draw in other Indians." Finally, a line in the middle "draws us all under the King our common father."[37]

DeLancey's interpretation of the belt reflected the British view of the Covenant Chain. The king's authority held sway over colonists and Indians alike, all of whom were encompassed by his extended arms. The short lines representing colonies and Indian nations were the links in the chain, and the lines left open "to draw in other Indians" allowed the chain to expand so it could be used to draw other Indians away from the French

---

[36] McAnear, "Personal Accounts," 732–33, 735; *NYCD*, 6:859. A different version of the commissioners' seating is given by William Smith Jr. in the second volume of his history of New York. According to him, the commissioners arranged themselves on either side of DeLancey but in a slightly different manner than the north-to-south order described by Atkinson: from DeLancey's left to right, Maryland, Pennsylvania, Connecticut, New York, Massachusetts, New Hampshire, Rhode Island. Smith may have witnessed this arrangement firsthand because he states in his history that he was present in Albany at the time of the congress, or he may have heard about it from his father, who was one of DeLancey's councillors at the congress. But Smith was also writing from memory more than twenty years later. I consider Atkinson's version, recorded at the time of the congress and in agreement with the Albany Congress minutes, more accurate. See Smith, *History of the Province of New-York*, 2:157, 158.
[37] *NYCD*, 6:862–63.

and toward the British. Of course, we have no way of knowing if De-Lancey's interpreter was faithful to this description when translating for the Indians. The designs woven into wampum belts were by their nature open to interpretation. Such fuzziness provided breathing room for DeLancey in conducting this diplomacy: his objective was not to have the Indians agree with his precise reading of the belt but merely to have them accept it as a symbol of the Covenant Chain's renewal.

Thomas Pownall noticed something strange when the Indians received the belt. As was customary, they raised a shout. But the Indians usually did so by "every Nation singly after one another making the shout." This time they shouted together, "till, being reminded that the other was expected of them, they afterward gave the *Yo-heigh-eigh* according to the usual custom." Some onlookers believed the Indians had forgotten the proper procedure, but Pownall found that unlikely "from them who are such strict observers of these forms." He believed the Indians had intended "to disguise that all the Nations did not universally give their hearty assent to the Covenant 'till they saw what redress they were likely to find and upon what terms they were likely to be for the future."[38] The nation most likely resisting a hearty assent was the Mohawks, who had not yet received answers to grievances they had presented privately to DeLancey. As Pownall observed, their failure to observe the proper ritual represented at best a lukewarm endorsement of the offer to renew the Covenant Chain.

According to Pownall, in the afternoon after DeLancey delivered the opening speech, several Indians approached the governor to address "something so heavy upon their Hearts they could not speak till it was removed." They requested a private meeting with him and the colonial commissioners, so that "nothing but love and Union might appear in the Treaty." In all likelihood, these were Mohawks, who wished to press DeLancey for answers about their grievances in the presence of the visiting colonial delegations. By telling him they could not answer his opening speech until their hearts were at ease, they raised the possibility of delaying the conference indefinitely and disturbing the appearance of "love and Union" in its public councils.[39]

Having already waited two weeks for the conference to open and not wanting to risk an open breach in the proceedings, DeLancey had little choice but to comply with their wish. He agreed to meet with them but declined to include the colonial commissioners. Pownall figured that he considered the Indians' grievances matters internal to New York and not subject to the scrutiny of outsiders.[40] No record exists of this meeting, but it was an important point in the struggle among the governor, the Mo-

[38] McAnear, "Personal Accounts," 741.
[39] Ibid., 741.
[40] Ibid.

hawks, and the colonial commissioners.[41] The Mohawks wanted to open their private negotiations with the governor to the other colonists, whom they expected to bring additional pressure to bear on the New Yorkers. DeLancey wished to keep the curtain tightly drawn around his private councils with the Indians and so refused to admit the outsiders. The visiting commissioners appear to have encouraged the Mohawks to press their grievances publicly. Pownall wrote that when the Indians returned two days later to answer DeLancey's opening speech, they had been heartened by "the Assurances they receivd and from the Disposition they observ'd in all the Commissioners from the several provinces mett there."[42] Such encouragement became obvious in the Indians' speech, which broke from the customary civility of the council fire and angrily denounced the New Yorkers.

At first, the Indians appeared willing to accept DeLancey's proposition to renew the Covenant Chain. Abraham, brother to Hendrick, rose and asked, "Are you ready to hear us?" DeLancey replied yes, and Abraham surrendered the floor to Hendrick. Hendrick reciprocated the condolence ritual, presenting three strings of wampum to mourn "all your friends and Relations, who have died since our last meeting here." He then took in hand the wampum belt offered by DeLancey and stated, "We do now solemnly renew and brighten the Covenant Chain with our Brethren here present, and all our other absent Brethren on the Continent."[43] DeLancey must have been pleased. The Indians had accepted the belt with a minimum of difficulty. He had accomplished the task set out for him by the Board of Trade.

Quite unexpectedly, Hendrick launched into a tirade against the New Yorkers for "your neglecting us for these three years past." Throwing a stick behind his back, he stated, "you have thus thrown us behind your back, and disregarded us, whereas the French are a subtle and vigilant people, ever using their utmost endeavours to seduce and bring our people over to them." As for DeLancey's concerns about French encroachments on Iroquois territory, Hendrick indicted the French, Virginians, and

---

[41] An intriguing gap in the evidence exists here. McAnear identifies this meeting as DeLancey's conferences with the Mohawks on June 27 and 28, but that is impossible because Pownall says it occurred after the governor delivered his speech on June 29. According to Pownall, DeLancey agreed to meet with the Indians but without the commissioners from the other colonies present. The New York Council Minutes, however, which recorded DeLancey's private councils at the Albany Congress, contain no reference to a meeting between him and the Indians between June 28 (his first council with Hendrick) and July 2 (after the Indians had delivered their response to his opening speech). No mention of such a meeting appears in the Minutes of the Albany Commissioners of Indian Affairs either. Two possibilities exist: either the meeting never took place, or DeLancey conferred unofficially with the Indians. Pownall's comments would suggest the latter.

[42] McAnear, "Personal Accounts," 741.

[43] NYCD, 6:869.

Pennsylvanians alike for making "paths thro' our Country to Trade" without permission. He saved his harshest words for the people of Albany. The Albany Indian Commissioners had not "invited us to smoak with them" since their reappointment. In the meantime, Albany had openly courted "the Indians of Canada, [who] come frequently and smoak here," all for the sake of the furs they brought from Montreal. "Look about you and see all these houses full of Beaver," Hendrick commanded his audience, "and the money is all gone to Canada, likewise powder, lead and guns, which the French now make use of at Ohio." While the French brazenly occupied new territory, New York remained weak and undefended: *Look about your Country and see, you have no Fortifications about you, no, not even to this City, tis but one Step from Canada hither, and the French may easily come and turn you out of your doors.*" DeLancey had reproved the Indians for living in a dispersed manner, but Hendrick laid the blame for New York's defenselessness squarely at his feet: "the French, they are men, they are fortifying everywhere—but, we are ashamed to say it, you are all like women bare and open without fortifications."[44]

When Hendrick had finished, Abraham rose again. He presented a large wampum belt and reminded DeLancey of the Indians' desire, expressed at an Albany conference three years earlier, to have William Johnson reinstated as their agent: "We long waited in expectation of this being done, but hearing no more of it, we embrace this opportunity of laying this Belt . . . before all our Brethren here present, and desire that Colonel Johnson may be reinstated and have the Management of Indian Affairs." Then, turning to face the Albany Indian Commissioners, he declared, "the fire here is burnt out."[45]

Spectators were struck by the contempt Hendrick and Abraham expressed toward the New Yorkers. Atkinson recorded in his journal how the Indian orators blamed the Covenant Chain's troubles on *"the Englihs or reather N York Government . . . upbraded them with folly and Cowardise in neglecting their fortifications . . .* [and] in Letting the fire go out at albany, which they Said Pointing to the albany Commissioners for Indian affairs."[46] Although he was a novice to such matters, Atkinson sensed the uncommon severity of the Indians' face-to-face confrontation with the Albany Indian Commissioners. Wraxall recorded Hendrick's gesture of throwing the stick behind his back in the minutes and later recalled the novelty of seeing the two brothers accuse the Albany Indian Commissioners "to their Faces" of abandoning the Mohawks.[47] Pownall noted that

[44] Ibid., 870.
[45] Ibid., 871.
[46] McAnear, "Personal Accounts," 736.
[47] Peter Wraxall, "Some Thoughts upon the British Indian Interest in North America, as it relates to . . . the Six Nations," January 5, 1756, *NYCD*, 7:20.

the wampum belt Abraham presented with his request for Johnson's reinstatement was "as rich and larg a Belt as that which they gave in answer to the Covenant Belt."[48] In other words, the Indians considered Johnson's reinstatement the sine qua non for mending the Covenant Chain. The Board of Trade had ordered the Albany Congress to settle land grievances, but the Mohawks now demanded nothing less than the removal of Indian affairs from Albany's control and their return to Johnson's.

Hendrick and Abraham must have left DeLancey squirming in his seat. They had openly expressed the Mohawks' anger with the New Yorkers, and treaty protocol demanded a public response that would further expose his colony to its assembled critics. In one brief speech, DeLancey saw his progress in the negotiations derailed and his government placed on the defensive.

The following day DeLancey and the colonial commissioners worked on a reply to the Indians' speech. After debating several drafts, they reached an agreement: Pennsylvania, New York, and Massachusetts would each address the Indians separately on matters that concerned their provinces.[49] This compromise allowed Pennsylvania and Massachusetts to introduce issues that had been kept out of the opening speech, while DeLancey, speaking only on behalf of New York, was able to maintain the boundary he had drawn between the colonial commissioners and New York's Indian affairs. The cost was any appearance of unanimity before the Indians. The Board of Trade's "one general Treaty" flew out the window, and the colonists fell back into the old habit of each colony engaging in its own Indian diplomacy.[50]

On the evening of July 3, the colonists and Indians reassembled outside the governor's door to hear the reply to Abraham's and Hendrick's speeches. Conrad Weiser spoke on behalf of the Pennsylvania and Virginia governments, answering the Indians' complaints about European encroachments in the Ohio Valley. An interpreter from Massachusetts spoke on behalf of his government, acquainting the Indians with recent hostilities along the New England frontier. The heart of this tripartite speech was DeLancey's response to the Mohawks' attack on Albany. He defended the conduct of the Albany merchants from Hendrick's aspersions: "You say the houses here are full of Beaver; this is a Trading place, and the Merchants have a right to traffick for Beaver or other skins, which they sometimes pay for in goods and sometimes in money . . . but neither guns nor powder are sold by any persons here to the French." As for the Indians' request to have Johnson restored as their agent, DeLancey reminded them that Johnson had resigned his post voluntarily, forcing New York to "re-

48 See McAnear, "Personal Accounts," 742.
49 NYCD, 6:871–75.
50 Ibid., 801.

kindle the fire here." He ordered the Albany Indian Commissioners to "receive and consult" with the Mohawks, who in turn were to treat with them "according to the Custom of your forefathers, to tell your news and in return to receive from them what shall be thought necessary to be imparted to you." DeLancey would "make tryal" of this system for another year; if at the end of that time the Indians were still dissatisfied, they were to complain to him.[51]

DeLancey offered little to the Mohawks. He did not commit himself to securing Johnson's reappointment, nor would he convey that request to the king, as Abraham had asked him to do with the large wampum belt. Instead, the governor stood staunchly by Albany's merchants, defending their right to trade with the Caughnawagas and to conduct diplomacy as they saw fit. If the Mohawks were unhappy with that, they were to appeal to him, not to any intercolonial or imperial authority. The council fire was to remain in Albany for at least another year.

DeLancey's speech reflected his solidarity with the Albany Commissioners of Indian Affairs. In a meeting the previous day, they had defended themselves against the Mohawks' charges by opening their minutes book to show DeLancey that they had indeed informed the Iroquois nations of their reappointment and that Hendrick had responded favorably when Arent Stevens carried that news to him the previous winter. They denied any knowledge of arms or ammunition being sold to the French.[52] The Albany commissioners' records and the testimony that Stevens could provide to their accuracy certainly gave DeLancey the edge he needed to deliver such a high-handed response to the Mohawks in the presence of the other colonial delegations.

The Indians responded to DeLancey the following day, July 4. Anyone expecting another confrontation between them and the New Yorkers must have been disappointed. Hendrick's second speech was as notable for its meekness as the first was for its anger. He accepted without question DeLancey's decision to continue with the Albany Indian Commissioners for another year and thanked the governor for "his promise to direct them to take due notice of us for the future." As for Johnson, the Indians still believed that "if he fails us, we die," but they acquiesced to DeLancey, calling the governor the "Master of all to do what he pleases."[53]

This remarkable change in tone demands explanation. In many ways Hendrick's second speech was much more typical of Covenant Chain

[51] Ibid., 874.
[52] See Minutes of the Albany Commissioners of Indian Affairs, July 2, 1754, Clements Library. See also Jon William Parmenter, "At Wood's Edge: Iroquois Foreign Relations, 1727–1768" (Ph.D. diss., University of Michigan, 1999), 320–29. I am indebted to Jon Parmenter for sharing his thoughts and research on the Albany Commissioners of Indian Affairs with me.
[53] NYCD, 6:875.

treaty-making. It professed friendship between the Indians and colonists and offered not even the slightest challenge to New York's management of Indian affairs. It enabled DeLancey and the Albany Indian Commissioners to save face after their public humiliation a few days earlier, indicating that they had reached some sort of accommodation with the Mohawks. Indeed, DeLancey had been engaged in private councils with the Canajoharie Mohawks on July 2, 3, and 4. But these meetings did not address the content of the public speeches; rather, they concerned land transactions between the Mohawks and their colonial neighbors, in which DeLancey mediated boundaries and prices.[54] Any agreement that may have been reached about the Albany Indian Commissioners remained unrecorded.

Thomas Pownall, who observed the public councils closely, had his own theory for the change in Hendrick's tone. The fawning, almost apologetic quality of his second speech reflected the Indians' "being a little dissatisfyed with some matters and having (as it was saied) receiv'd some private reasons to appear satisfyed with others." And so the "Sincerity and Reality" of the first speech gave way to "Political Farce and Compliment" in the second.[55] Pownall did not say that the Indians received satisfaction for their complaints, only that they received incentives "to appear satisfyed." What those incentives were—promises, private presents?—and who provided them, he did not say.

The motivation to appear satisfied may have come from the Indians themselves. Pownall believed that to avoid entanglement in another Anglo-French war, the Indians had agreed among themselves to speak only *"from the Mouth and not from the Heart"* at the Albany Congress. In the parlance of Iroquois diplomacy, this tactic freed them from the constraints of sincerity so that they could say whatever was necessary to renew the Covenant Chain and receive their presents. Certainly, Hendrick's obsequious second speech bore such a character. Hendrick had also noticed that some French-allied Caughnawagas were in town, and he may not have wished to display the Covenant Chain's weakness before them, which would invite French attacks on the New York frontier.[56] The Mohawks' material needs may also have made them more tractable. Presents were DeLancey's trump card; he could withhold them until receiving the Indians' cooperation. Sure enough, the day after Hendrick's second speech, the governor delivered to them guns, gunpowder, and £300 sterling worth in other goods, a very profitable return for a speech steeped in "Political Farce and Compliment." Atkinson was struck by the quantity and quality of the presents, especially the "400 good guns, some Extraordi-

---

[54] See NYCM, July 2–3, 23:196–99.
[55] McAnear, "Personal Accounts," 741.
[56] Ibid., 740–41, and NYCD, 6:882.

nary." The Indians needed thirty wagons to haul these gifts away a few days later.[57]

Additional motivation for the Indians to appear satisfied may have come from the colonial commissioners. Shortly after Hendrick's second speech, they took up the issue of the complaints of land fraud the Mohawks had made against the New York government the previous summer. Up to this point, DeLancey had kept the visiting commissioners out of his private councils with the Indians. As he prepared to close the conference, the commissioners stepped in and demanded proof that he had settled the Mohawks' grievances. When DeLancey sent a draft of his closing speech to the commissioners, Thomas Hutchinson of Massachusetts declared it insufficient because it made no mention of the alleged land frauds which had been the primary cause of "this unusual and expensive meeting of Commissioners from so many Colonies."[58] The Massachusetts delegation insisted that the Board of Trade's instructions called for an intercolonial investigation of these complaints. DeLancey disagreed, arguing that the board had not intended for other colonies to "make enquiry concerning [land] purchases made by the inhabitants of New York."[59] Upon receiving the commissioners' request for an audience with the Indians, DeLancey assured them that he had answered the Mohawks "to the satisfaction of all parties," and he sent two of his councillors to the courthouse to dismiss any lingering doubts. Still suspicious, the commissioners personally examined William Livingston and William Alexander, two New Yorkers involved in the fraudulent Canajoharie patent.[60]

Still, the commissioners refused to sign off on DeLancey's closing speech until they spoke with the Indians. At DeLancey's invitation, they formed a committee to attend the governor in a private council with the Canajoharie Mohawks. The committee reported back that the Indians appeared satisfied, but Hendrick had warned that if the Mohawks did not receive redress in one year, "they would send to all their brothers (pointing to the Commissioners) for their assistance." After this exchange, the commissioners grudgingly accepted DeLancey's word and allowed him to proceed with closing the conference.[61] The Massachusetts delegation remained dis-

---

[57] For contents of the king's present, see DeLancey's description of it to Pennsylvania governor James Hamilton, in *Penn. Council Minutes*, 6:13–16. For the Indians' use of the wagons, see *NYCD*, 6:884. For Atkinson's remark, see McAnear, "Personal Accounts," 738. The Albany Commissioners of Indian Affairs had recommended to DeLancey at the outset of the treaty conference that he make private presents to leading chiefs and warriors. See Minutes of the Albany Commissioners of Indian Affairs, June 24, 1754, Clements Library.

[58] *NYCD*, 6:878–79.

[59] Report of the Massachusetts Commissioners to the Albany Congress to William Shirley, Mass. Archives, 4:461.

[60] *NYCD*, 6:879–80, and *NYCM*, July 6, 1754, 23:202.

[61] *NYCD*, 6:882–83. For DeLancey's council with the Mohawks and committee of colonial commissioners, see *NYCM*, July 8, 1754, 23:205.

gruntled and reported to its home government that DeLancey had limited the commissioners' investigation only to hearing the Indians declare "that they were so far satisfied as to be willing to suspend any further enquiry . . . for one year longer."[62]

The treaty negotiations ended on the evening of July 8, when DeLancey delivered his closing speech. He addressed the Canajoharie Mohawks in particular, promising the construction of a church in their village and continued investigation of the alleged land frauds. Hendrick spoke for the Indians, pledging friendship and fidelity to "the Covenant Chain, wherewith we have mutually bound ourselves, and now [so] solemnly renewed and strengthened." In one last negotiation, he extracted provisions from the governor for the Indians' journey home so that they would not be tempted to take cattle and other goods from colonists along the route. DeLancey took the additional precaution of ordering that the gunpowder and rum included in the Indians' presents not be distributed until they had passed Schenectady.[63]

One can only speculate as to the thoughts of the people who watched the Indians take their leave of the city. Did local traders hope to relieve the Indians of some of their burden once they were beyond the governor's view? Did the poorly armed soldiers in Fort Frederick question the wisdom of distributing four hundred guns and thirty barrels of gunpowder to Indians whose attachment to the British seemed questionable at best? Did the colonial commissioners silently fume over DeLancey's sidestepping of their efforts to investigate the Mohawks' grievances? The Indians had renewed the Covenant Chain, but little had changed: they had politely dropped their insistence on Johnson's restoration in their second speech, the council fire remained in Albany, and the colonial commissioners had failed to break DeLancey's iron curtain on New York's Indian affairs. What, then, had this conference accomplished? At least one constituency must have gone away happy: dragging thirty wagons of goods behind them, the Indians had certainly found their hosts' generosity worth the trip.

Taking Possession at the Albany Congress

The unfinished nature of the Albany Congress's public councils contrasted sharply with the deal-making that went on in the bushes. Most of these unofficial negotiations concerned land purchases. The Penn family and the Susquehannah Company had sent agents to Albany to buy land in western and northern Pennsylvania; colonists from the Mohawk Valley

---

[62] Mass. Archives, 4:461.
[63] NYCD, 6:883–84.

arrived in town seeking patents from the governor for purchases they made from neighboring Indians. Here was the underside of treaty-making: removed from public councils, colonists openly competed with each other for native land, Indians demanded material rewards for their cooperation, alcohol flowed freely to ease the way, and the Covenant Chain sped the dispossession of native peoples.[64] The participation of the Mohawks in these negotiations is particularly unsettling. Why, after speaking so eloquently in public councils about land frauds that threatened their homelands, did they willingly engage in new purchases, some obviously fraudulent?

The answer to that question tells us much about the changing nature of Covenant Chain diplomacy in 1754. When New York's governors traveled to Albany for a conference, they had an objective in mind, such as convincing the Indians to declare war, make peace, or cede land. As the eighteenth century progressed, British and then later American officials increasingly used Indian diplomacy for land acquisition. As one historian has described this process, colonizers gained a "license for empire" by negotiating boundary lines, cessions, and purchases at treaty conferences, setting a pattern that continued well into the nineteenth century.[65] The Albany Congress presaged this style of diplomacy, as colonial agents participated in rituals of possession to prove to each other their title to vast tracts of Indian land.

On the Indians' side of the table, the Mohawks dominated the land transactions at the Albany Congress. As inhabitants of New York's colonial frontier and the Iroquois Confederacy's traditional voice in Albany, they participated in two levels of deal-making. First, in councils with DeLancey, they sold land to their colonial neighbors in the Mohawk Valley. Second, in meetings with the agents from Pennsylvania and the Susquehannah Company, they sold land far removed from their homelands and over which they held no dominion. The Mohawks' rationale for engaging in such transactions becomes clear when each level is considered separately. Local land sales had become a part of their subsistence, another way of extracting the necessities of life from the growing colonial population around them. The sale of more distant lands that they neither inhabited nor possessed offered the chance to open new diplomatic paths that might replace the presents that no longer flowed from Albany.

The Mohawks' sale of local lands both mediated and strained intercultural relations in the Mohawk Valley. By selling land to fur traders and

---

[64] For a general discussion of how the Covenant Chain became a tool of dispossession, see Jennings, *Ambiguous Iroquois Empire*, 325–75. For discussions specific to the Albany Congress, see Jennings, *Empire of Fortune*, 101–8, and Nammack, *Fraud, Politics, and the Dispossession of the Indians*, 39–69.

[65] Jones, *License for Empire*.

missionaries, the Mohawks gained valuable brokers in their diplomacy with outsiders. As colonial speculators and settlers became more interested in the Mohawk Valley, however, land sales raised the specter of outright dispossession for its native inhabitants.

The lower Mohawks, from near Fort Hunter, presented three land fraud complaints to DeLancey at the Albany Congress. At their first council with DeLancey, their chief Canadagra stated, "We understand that there are writings for all our land, so that we shall have none left but the very spot we live upon and hardly that." The lower Mohawks were especially concerned about the Kayaderosseras patent, which dated to the early eighteenth century and included approximately eight hundred thousand acres of their hunting grounds north of the Mohawk and west of the Hudson. They insisted that this patent was fraudulent because the payment made for the land was too small and only two of the village's three clans had assented to it. According to Canadagra, the owners of the Kayaderosseras patent were too numerous to name, but "many of them live in this Town."[66] Later in the conference, the lower Mohawks presented two other land grievances: one against Albany fur trader Hendrick Hansen and the other against the Reverend Henry Barclay, their former SPG missionary.[67]

These three complaints illustrated how land disputes soured intercultural relations in the Mohawk Valley. The lower Mohawks had lived with settlers and soldiers since the construction of Fort Hunter in the 1710s. They valued having an SPG missionary nearby who could provide for their spiritual and material needs and had welcomed Barclay by granting him a glebe. When Barlcay left his post suddenly in 1746, they believed this land reverted to their possession. Barclay's presumption in selling it smacked of arrogance and betrayed trust.[68] The complaint against the fur trader Hansen involved the Mohawks' most common grievance in land sales: colonial purchasers engrossed too much land when they patented their purchases. As Canadagra explained to DeLancey, "we dont complain of those who have honestly bought the land they possess, or those to whom we have given any, but of some who have taken more than we have given them."[69] In surveying their purchases, unscrupulous buyers had free rein to include far more acreage than the Indians agreed to sell. The Mohawks became increasingly skeptical of the process by which verbal

[66] *NYCD,* 6:866, and NYCM, July 6, 1754, 23:202. For the history of the Kayaderosseras patent, see Nammack, *Fraud, Politics, and Dispossession of the Indians,* 53–69.
[67] NYCM, July 6, 1754, 23:202. The lower Mohawks had first raised this complaint about Barclay in a 1746 conference with Governor Clinton. See Nammack, *Fraud, Politics, and Dispossession of the Indians,* 30.
[68] NYCM, July 6, 1754, 23:202.
[69] *NYCD,* 6:866. Canadagra's speech echoed Hendrick's complaints to Governor Clinton a year earlier when he had declared the Covenant Chain broken. In that instance, Hendrick presented eight specific complaints against purchasers who had patented more land than the Indians had agreed to sell. See Ibid., 784–87.

agreements became "writings" for their lands, and they often threatened surveyors with physical violence.

The Kayaderosseras patent was one of several large and ill-defined patents obtained by speculators in the early eighteenth century. The Canajoharie Mohawks protested a similar patent of dubious origin for their homelands held by the Livingston family.[70] By the 1750s, the growth of the Mohawk Valley's colonial population had made the division and leasing of these large patents, long held in abeyance, attractive to their owners. Realizing the danger these patents presented, the Mohawks pressed the New York governor, the Crown, and commissioners from other colonies to intercede on their behalf. At the Albany Congress, DeLancey did little for them. He agreed with the lower Mohawks that the Kayaderosseras patent included more land than it ought to, but he washed his hands of the matter by telling them that he would have to refer it to the Crown because the patent was issued "under the King's Great Seal."[71] For the Canajoharies, he convinced two heirs to the Livingston patent "to give up all right to said patents or such parts as shall be thought necessary." This vague promise in no way invalidated the Livingston patent or protected the people of Canajoharie from its other heirs.[72]

With such vague and inconclusive answers from the governor, the Mohawks had plenty of reasons to disavow selling any more land to their neighbors. Yet in private councils with DeLancey at the Albany Congress, they continued to do so. Under the governor's supervision, the Canajoharie Mohawks settled on the terms of two large purchases, one by a group of thirty-five German colonists who lived west of Canajoharie, and the other by Teady Magin, a Scottish Indian trader who frequented Albany and Oswego. In four councils held between July 2 and July 5, DeLancey negotiated sales in which the Germans, led by colonists George Klock and William Nellis, purchased approximately twelve thousand acres on the north side of the Mohawk River across from Canajoharie, and Magin purchased another thirty-two thousand acres north of that.[73]

Why did the Canajoharie Mohawks part with forty-four thousand acres

[70] The three most controversial patents to Mohawk lands at this time were the Kayaderosseras patent, the Tiononderoge patent, and the Livingston patent. All had been completed earlier in the eighteenth century during a period of frenzied land speculation involving royal officials and prominent colonial New Yorkers. The Tiononderoge patent, which was not an issue at the Albany Congress, and the Livingston patent, which included land occupied by the lower and upper Mohawk villages, respectively. The disputes related to these patents continued long after the Albany Congress. See Nammack, *Fraud, Politics, and Dispossession of the Indians*, 22–69, and Fox, *Land Speculation in the Mohawk Country*, for detailed histories.
[71] NYCM, July 6, 1754, 23:202.
[72] NYCD, 6:879–80.
[73] For the negotiation of these land purchases, see NYCM, July 2–5, 1754, 23:196–201. The boundaries and terms of the purchases are explained in Indorsed Land Papers, 1643–1803, 63 volumes, New York Archives, New York State Library, Albany, 15:111–12, 125, 128.

close to home even as they protested other patents? They appear to have had little choice. Like presents received at treaty conferences, cash and material goods received from such sales were necessary to their subsistence. Land sales in the Mohawk Valley west of Fort Hunter had increased substantially during the 1720s and 1730s, approximately the same time that the Oswego trade was eroding the Mohawks' position in New York's fur trade. During King George's War, the sale of Mohawk lands decreased, but it resumed quickly after 1751, when Johnson's resignation as New York's Indian agent cut off the flow of presents to Canajoharie.[74] Earlier in the colonial period, the Mohawks had used furs and diplomatic clout to acquire European goods; by 1754, they could do so only by selling the land beneath their feet.

The more local land they sold, the more likely the Mohawks made their eventual dispossession. Thus it must have appealed mightily to Hendrick and other Mohawks at the Albany Congress to be courted by colonists wishing to buy land in northern and western Pennsylvania. In the past, the Mohawks had not participated in Pennsylvania's Indian diplomacy, nor had they claimed dominion within that colony's borders. When agents of the Penn family and the Susquehanna Company came to the Albany Congress to buy land, however, they had to deal with the Mohawks, who made up the majority of Indians in attendance and traditionally spoke for the Iroquois there. Hendrick took this opportunity to nose his way into Pennsylvania's Indian affairs and open a new path for the Mohawks' diplomacy.

Richard Peters and John Penn, who acted as the Penn family's agents, began their land purchase negotiations immediately upon arriving in Albany. Their interpreter Conrad Weiser approached some Oneidas, Tuscaroras, and Cayugas and "by a Reward" secured one of their leading men as his "private Counsellor." The Indians were generally amenable to the proposed land sale, except for some Oneidas who were reluctant to move forward without "taking Hendrick and the Mohocks into Council." As Peters and Penn described it, Hendrick "got into the Management" of the purchase as soon as he arrived in Albany. Much to the Pennsylvanians' dismay, he counseled the Indians "not to sell so much as they intended . . . and to keep all the Western Branch of the Sasquehannah in their own Hands." Peters and Penn "could not make Head against him."[75]

[74] This analysis of Indian land sales in the Mohawk Valley is based on my reading of E. B. O'Callaghan, ed., *Calendar of New York Colonial Manuscripts: Indorsed Land Papers, 1643–1803* (1864; rpt. Harrison, N.Y., 1987), for the years 1701–55, and the Indorsed Land Papers collection in the New York State Archives, vols. 14–15 (1744–52, 1752–60). See also Fox, *Land Speculation in the Mohawk Country*, 10–48.
[75] John Penn and Richard Peters to James Hamilton, August 5, 1754, *Penn. Archives*, ser. 4, 2:698–700. Hereinafter cited as Penn and Peters Report.

On July 5 Peters and Penn assembled seventy Indians in the home of their Albany host, the merchant James Stevenson. The Pennsylvanians offered to purchase from the Iroquois all lands west of the Susquehanna River to the Ohio.[76] Hendrick responded for the Indians. His speech deserves to be quoted at length because of the light it sheds on the Mohawks' position in 1754:

> Brother Onas:
> What we are now going to say is a Matter of great Moment, which we desire you to remember as long as the Sun and Moon lasts. We are willing to sell You this Large Tract of Land for your People to live upon, but We desire this may be considered as Part of our Agreement that when We are all dead and gone your Grandchildren may not say to our Grandchildren, that your Forefathers sold the Land to our Forefathers, and therefore be gone off them. This is wrong. Let us be all as Brethren as well after as before of giving you Deeds for Land. After We have sold our Land We in a little time have nothing to Shew for it; but it is not so with You, Your Grandchildren will get something from it as long as the World stands; our Grandchildren will have no advantage from it; They will say We were Fools for selling so much Land for so small a matter and curse Us; therefore let it be a Part of the present Agreement that We shall treat one another as Brethren to the latest Generation, even after We shall not have left a Foot of Land.[77]

Hendrick also reminded the Pennsylvanians of a present they had promised the Iroquois the previous fall: "Last Year Colonel Johnson was at Onondago. He told us Brother Onas had a handsome Present for Us. We have not heard of it since. If it be true We desire You would let us know, and give it to Us now. You see We are a poor People, and some of Us have not so much as a Breech Clout to cover Us."[78]

In a manner similar to his meeting with the New Hampshire commissioners discussed at the beginning of this chapter, Hendrick approached the Pennsylvanians not as a client but as a partner. From his perspective, this land purchase would serve the Mohawks by initiating a friendship that would bind future generations together. He did not intend for it to give license to the Pennsylvanians to dispossess outright the Indians' grandchildren. Likewise, he did not deny the poverty of the Indians for whom he spoke ("some of Us have not so much as a Breech Clout to cover Us"), but he phrased his request for a present from the Pennsylvanians as a reminder of an obligation made between friends, not as an appeal to charity.

[76] Ibid., 703.
[77] Ibid., 704.
[78] Ibid., 705.

In the evening after Hendrick's speech, the Indians made their counter-offer to the Pennsylvanians. Weiser suspected Hendrick's hand in this proposal, which limited the purchase to land south of the Susquehanna's western branch and only as far west as the Allegheny Mountains.[79] Peters and Penn found these limits unacceptable. They wanted the purchase to extend as far north as Lake Erie and as far west as the Ohio River. If the Indians refused to surrender lands west of the Alleghenies, then the Penn family would have little foundation for advancing its claim in the Ohio country against Virginia and the French. The Pennsylvanians were also irritated by Hendrick's presumption to manage the sale of lands over which the Mohawks had not previously assumed authority. According to Peters and Penn, "the Lands now under Consideration did really belong to the Cayugas and Oneidas in Right of Conquest of the Susquehannah Indians." Weiser therefore decided to pay "no court to Hendrick, and expressed some Resentment at the Regard shewn to his Opinion by the other Nations." He told the Indians that the Pennsylvanians would either purchase lands all the way to the Ohio or none at all.[80]

His bluff worked. Upon hearing Weiser's response, Hendrick made a speech in the Indians' council praising Pennslyvania's "affectionate and generous Usage of the Indians" and advising them to "take the Frowns off from the Brow of their Brethren" by extending the boundaries of the purchase.[81] Perhaps Hendrick did not wish to see the Mohawks locked out of a deal that would otherwise be completed at another time and place less advantageous to his people. Perhaps he did not wish to alienate Weiser and the Pennsylvanians, with whom he had been cultivating relations since the 1740s. One thing is clear: he did not want to let this chance to forge a new diplomatic bond with the Pennsylvanians slip away. That colony's reputation for "affectionate and generous Usage of the Indians" compared very favorably to that of the New Yorkers.

The day after Weiser secured Hendrick's cooperation, Peters and Penn gathered twenty-three chiefs at the Pennsylvanians' lodgings to sign a deed. Onlookers included the other two Pennsylvania commissioners, many of the other colonial commissioners, "several of the Inhabitants of Albany," and the ubiquitous Thomas Pownall. The terms of the deed stipulated a sale price of two thousand pieces of eight, half of which was paid up front and the other half "when the Lands West of the Apalacian Hills should be settled."[82]

The deed expressed the Pennsylvanians' perspective on this transaction.

---

[79] Ibid., 706.
[80] Ibid., 706–7. No Iroquois nation—Mohawks or otherwise—could claim to have conquered the Susquehannocks. See Jennings, *Ambiguous Iroquois Empire*, 113–42.
[81] Penn and Peters Report, 707.
[82] Ibid., 708–9.

Peters and Penn did not describe the land sale in terms of a friendship that would bind future generations of colonists and Indians; they were interested in alienating land. In the legal language typical of Anglo-American contracts, the deed stated that neither the Iroquois "nor any of their Heirs, Successors, and Assigns shall or may hereafter claim, challenge, or demand any Right to the said Lands, Islands, Rivers, Creeks, Waters, Hereditaments, and Premises hereby granted and released, but from the same shall be barred for ever by these Presents."[83] So much for Hendrick's request that "your Grandchildren may not say to our Grandchildren, that your Forefathers sold the Land to our Forefathers, and therefore be gone off them." The Pennsylvanians, like other colonists, believed that they could alienate land in perpetuity; they were not interested in comprehending Hendrick's position that the land sale created mutual obligations between seller and purchaser that would preclude native dispossession. Peters and Penn believed exactly the opposite: the deed released them from having to recognize any Indian rights to the land, forever.

No one, Hendrick included, seemed disturbed that the actual inhabitants of the land in question were not present at these negotiations. The Indian parties in the sale were mostly Mohawks, Oneidas, and Tuscaroras. The ones closest to the Susquehanna Valley came from the Oneida and Tuscarora village of Oquaga, well north and east of the lands purchased. The Pennsylvanians justified their proceedings by arguing that the lands belonged to the Cayugas and Oneidas by right of conquest, but the Delawares and Shawnees who inhabited the region thought otherwise. They would soon go to war to defend homelands that had been bartered away by strangers in Albany.[84]

Peters and Penn ignored the Delawares and Shawnees because they were far more interested in proving their possession of the land to other colonists than to its Indian occupants. The Pennsylvanians had come to Albany fully aware that agents would be working there on behalf of the Susquehannah Company. To preempt those rivals, Peters and Penn went to great lengths to publicize their negotiations and have them accepted as part of the Albany Congress's official proceedings. Twice during Governor DeLancey's public speeches to the Indians, they tried to have mention of their land purchase inserted into the conference's official minutes. The first time, they failed because the other colonial commissioners opposed having the public councils used to advance the Penn family's business. The second time, the secretary recording the official minutes relented and noted that Peters and Penn were privately conducting a land purchase in

[83] Ibid., 712.
[84] For a discussion of the hostilities that erupted in Pennsylvania as a result of this and other related land purchases, see Jennings, *Empire of Fortune*, 253–81.

their lodgings.[85] The Pennsylvanians assembled large, intercolonial audiences to witness their negotiations and made a point of discussing their progress with anyone who would listen. Peters and Penn claimed that Susquehannah Company agent Timothy Woodbridge "was a Witness of every thing that passed between the Commissioners of Pennsylvania and the Indians during their Stay at Albany." They also showed their deed to Elisha Williams, a Connecticut commissioner and Susquehannah Company shareholder.[86]

While the Pennsylvanians did everything in their power to make their land negotiations public, the Susquehannah Company agents preferred the anonymity of the bushes. If not for the close eye that Peters and Penn kept on their competition, the Susquehannah Company's activities would have gone unnoticed in contemporary accounts of the Albany Congress. Upon arriving in Albany the Pennsylvanians learned that Timothy Woodbridge was already at work with "Two Connecticut Gentlemen," conducting "secret Conferences with the Indians" at the home of John Henry Lydius, an Albany trader notorious for smuggling goods to and from Montreal.[87]

The only evidence of the negotiations in Lydius's home is a deed completed on July 11, the last day of the Congress. According to it, the Iroquois agreed to sell a tract of land on the upper Susquehanna for £2,000 in New York currency, of which only 10 percent was paid down. The sale contained all of the Wyoming Valley, which Hendrick had insisted was not negotiable in his councils with the Pennsylvanians, and a considerable piece of northwestern Pennsylvania, which caused it to overlap with the Pennsylvanians' purchase. Five of the fourteen Indians who signed this deed had also signed the Pennyslvanians'. Hendrick attended the July 11 meeting in Lydius's home, but he did not add his signature to the others.[88] After the colonial commissioners left Albany, Lydius acquired more signatures by inviting Indians to his home and plying them with liquor and bribes. When Indians stopped coming to him, he went to their villages with a "Bag of Dollars" and put together signatures representing the Mohawks, Oneidas, Onondagas, Cayugas, and Senecas. Learning of his activities, the Pennsylvanians complained to William Johnson and urged the Board of Trade to nullify the Susquehannah Company deed. A year later the Indians themselves called Lydius a snake and demanded his removal from a conference at Johnson's home.[89]

---

[85] Penn and Peters Report, 700–701, and *NYCD*, 6:877.
[86] Penn and Peters Report, 698, 723–24.
[87] Ibid., 697–98, 723–24.
[88] For the deed, see *Susquehannah Co. Papers*, 1:101–21.
[89] For Lydius's efforts on behalf of the Susquehannah Company after the Albany Congress, see Ibid., 1:129–33. For the Indians' complaints, see *NYCD*, 6:984.

Although the contest between the Pennsylvanians and the Susquehannah Company continued for many years, the Pennsylvanians emerged from the Albany Congress with a clear advantage. Prominent colonists had witnessed their negotiations, a secretary had recorded the speeches, and Peters and Penn even managed to get their purchase mentioned in the conference's official minutes. While consigned to the bushes, they had gained an aura of legitimacy for their proceedings by making them approximate as closely as possible a public council. The Susquehannah Company agents, in contrast, failed to observe diplomatic ritual in the bushes. Rather than using a reputable agent such as Weiser, they relied on Lydius, who was distrusted by Indians and colonists alike.[90] The company's agents also failed to secure the support of other colonists at the Albany Congress. No men of lofty reputation such as Thomas Pownall attended Lydius's negotiations. Furthermore, Lydius used liquor, bribes, and secrecy to secure his deed. The Pennsylvanians had not been shy about lubricating their proceedings with liquor and presents, but they had done so in ways culturally sanctioned by Covenant Chain diplomacy. Whenever they offered liquor to the Indians, they did so as hosts, treating them with wine and punch at the end of their councils. Once the deed was signed, they provided an entertainment for the Indians at the courthouse. A receipt from a local tavern keeper shows that the Pennsylvanians supplied the Indians with over fifteen gallons of wine, seven gallons of beer, and five quarts of cider. They also had to reimburse the tavern keeper for "a China Bowl Broke" and "8 Drinking Glasses Carried away by Indians." Yet no one questioned this use of alcohol because it remained open, ceremonial, and social, whereas Lydius had used it in an antisocial manner when he closeted Indians in his home.[91]

Both sales reflected the Mohawks' efforts to adapt to the changing material circumstances of their lives. Selling land that they neither occupied nor owned for ready cash and goods was productive in its own right, but even more useful was the creation of new diplomatic relationships that would continue to bring rewards to Hendrick and his people. Having horned his way into the Pennsylvanians' land purchase, Hendrick now assumed for the Mohawks a central place in that colony's Indian relations. In his closing speech to Peters and Penn, he told them that if they ever "wanted to know the true Disposition of the Indians or to consult on Affairs," they should

[90] Penn and Peters provided a typically nasty description of Lydius, attacking him for abjuring the Protestant faith, partaking in the Montreal trade, and supposedly maintaining a correspondence with the governor of New France. See Penn and Peters Report, 697.
[91] For references to Peters's and Penn's use of liquor in their negotiations, see Penn and Peters Report, 705, 716. For the receipt, see Penn Papers, Indian Affairs, 4:7, Historical Society of Pennsylvania, Philadelphia. For a discussion of the use of alcohol in diplomatic councils with the Indians, see Peter C. Mancall, *Deadly Medicine: Indians and Alcohol in Early America* (Ithaca, 1995), 48–49, 72–74.

send for him "and a few of the principal Mohocks."[92] Peters and Penn suspected Hendrick of currying the favor of the Susquehannah Company as well.[93] The Mohawks would have been familiar with the company's agent Timothy Woodbridge from their councils with the Stockbridge Indians and the Massachusetts government. What colonial agents usually described as Hendrick's penchant for duplicity was in fact his pursuit of several paths of diplomacy at once. His presence at Lydius's home indicated his wish not to alienate anyone who might provide presents necessary to sustain his village in the future.

Johnson's Speech

Negotiations at the Albany Congress laid bare the fractured nature of the Covenant Chain. Despite the well-orchestrated ritual and speeches of the public councils, neither the colonists nor the Indians were united in thought or purpose. The deepest divisions arose between those participants attempting to uphold an old order in Anglo-Iroquois relations that relied on the primacy of Albany and those wishing to subvert it. DeLancey clung tightly to the old order because it gave New York a central and privileged position in the Covenant Chain. The Mohawks were anxious to discredit Albany and open new paths to the other colonial governments, while New Englanders and Pennsylvanians wished to use the Covenant Chain to defend their frontiers and dispossess native populations far removed from the Mohawk Valley.

Sending a copy of the Albany Congress's minutes to the Board of Trade, DeLancey wrote confidently, "it is with pleasure I can assure you, that we parted very good friends, which your Lordshipps may observe from what they [the Indians] say themselves in their speech at the conclusion of the Conferences."[94] The minutes did indeed make the meeting sound like a success. Hendrick, who had only a year earlier declared the Covenant Chain broken, now expressed his happiness at seeing "all things . . . so amicably settled."[95] Appearances could be deceiving. From the sidelines, Pownall sensed that the conference had barely patched over old animosities. The Indians proved more amenable than he expected, but they had made clear their insistence on William Johnson's restoration as their agent, and "If after this Solemn treaty they find themselves deceiv'd, They will be more alienated than ever." Albany's undisturbed trade with the Caughnawagas remained a bone of contention with the Mohawks, and

[92] Penn and Peters Report, 721.
[93] Ibid., 706.
[94] DeLancey to the Board of Trade, July 22, 1754, *NYCD*, 6:850.
[95] Ibid., 883.

Pownall believed that "if the matter was properly inquired into, many secrets in this Trade might be unveild, for the Albany People are quarelling amongst Themselves." The New Yorkers had resented "having Commissioners from other Provinces making inquisition" into their Indian relations: "They were and are very angry but express their resentment only against Massachusetts." Even Pownall felt rebuffed by his New York hosts when he pursued "any Inquiries Such as a Traveller of any Curiosity would make."[96]

Also challenging the old order by his sheer presence at the Albany Congress was William Johnson. He had remained in the shadows throughout the proceedings, attending DeLancey's meetings with the Indians as well as the commissioners' courthouse sessions, but the official minutes rarely mention his name, and no extant materials record his actions or words in private councils.[97] He finally stepped out of the background on July 11, the last day of the Congress and two days after DeLancey had sent the Indians home, to make a speech to the colonial commissioners. Johnson proposed building forts among the Iroquois and garrisoning them with soldiers, smiths, schoolmasters, missionaries, and military officers who could act as commissaries for the fur trade. Borrowing from various plans for reorganizing Indian affairs, he stated that prices for Indian goods should be fixed and subsidized, to eliminate fraud and cement the Indians' dependence on the British. He lamented the lack of intercolonial cooperation in Indian diplomacy and urged the commissioners to recognize that the management of the Covenant Chain could no longer rest with "one or two British governments [colonies]."[98]

Johnson said little that had not been said before by such imperially minded reformers as Archibald Kennedy and Cadwallader Colden. He added to the already growing alarm about the French and presented a plan of action that subordinated mercantile interests in Indian relations to imperial ones. The significance of his speech rested in its delivery. The tone he took before the assembled commissioners was that of an impartial expert, distancing himself from the factional politics that had enmired his previous service in Indian affairs. During the treaty conference, Johnson had waited in the wings while the governor sparred with the Indians. He made his first public utterance only after the Indians had left town, perhaps to avoid appearing as their advocate against DeLancey. Yet his debut before the assembled commissioners occurred while the memory of the Mohawks' bitter denunciation of Albany was still fresh in their minds. During

---

[96] McAnear, "Personal Accounts," 742–43, 745.

[97] Johnson's activities included joining two of the commissioners' committees, one for drafting the Indian speeches and one for determining the need for forts on the New York frontier. See *NYCD*, 6:858, and McAnear, "Personal Accounts," 739.

[98] For Johnson's speech, see *NYCD*, 6:897–99.

the treaty conference, Hendrick and Abraham had shifted the focus of the Mohawks' grievances from land frauds to restoring Johnson's agency. Johnson punctuated their speeches by presenting himself as a more permanent solution to the crisis of the Covenant Chain than the flimsy truce just negotiated by DeLancey.

The Albany Congress gave Johnson's reputation an enormous boost. He had arrived there as a local merchant known for his influence among the Mohawks; he left a preeminent colonial authority on the Covenant Chain. The commissioners mentioned his speech in their minutes and ordered copies to bring back to their governments. DeLancey even included a copy of it when he forwarded the proceedings of the Albany Congress to the Board of Trade. Such measures, coupled with the high praise Johnson received in the Indians' speeches, would give him a decided advantage over the Albany Indian Commissioners when the Crown weighed what to do next about the Iroquois.

All of these negotiations with the Indians transpired independently from the colonial delegations' formulation of a plan of union. Throughout the four weeks of the conference, when the Indians and commissioners came together they followed the rituals of the council fire and confined themselves to the business of diplomacy and land purchases. The commissioners' debates over colonial union occurred removed from the Indians and behind the closed courthouse doors. It is time now to turn our attention to those sessions, in which the commissioners grappled with issues more pertinent to their relationship with Great Britain than with the Indians.

[6]

The Intercolonial Congress

Many Objections and Difficulties were started, but at length they were all overcome, and the [Albany] Plan [of Union] was unanimously agreed to, and Copies ordered to be transmitted to the Board of Trade and to the Assemblies of the several Provinces.

—Benjamin Franklin, 1788

In the brief statement quoted above, Benjamin Franklin recounted in his memoirs the colonial commissioners' debates over a plan of union at the Albany Congress. Franklin's passive constructions—"Difficulties *were* started . . . they *were* all overcome . . . the Plan *was* unanimously agreed to" (emphasis added)—understate objections raised to the Albany Plan and emphasize instead the commissioners' efforts to achieve consensus. That Franklin chose to stress unanimity over dissent is not surprising. He wrote this passage in 1788, as a patriot hero and a recent delegate to the Constitutional Convention. These remarks on the Albany Congress and similar ones published a few months later in an American magazine helped legitimize the new federal union and confirmed Franklin's reputation as a prophet of American nationhood.[1] In this summary of the Albany Congress, written by its most famous participant, the colonial commissioners act as public-spirited statesmen, hashing out their differences in the common interest and never losing sight of their common goal. Historians have since chosen to remember the Albany Congress as an early expression of the American genius for federalism, of interest primarily for the greater events it foreshadowed.

Franklin's hindsight made perfect sense alongside the drafting and ratification of the Constitution in 1787–88, but in the context of 1754 it is misleading. The intercolonial negotiations at the Albany Congress lacked

---

[1] Farrand, *Franklin's Memoirs*, 326. For the published version of Franklin's recollections, see his "Remark," in *BF Papers*, 5:417. Franklin's "Remark" appeared in the February 1789 edition of Matthew Carey's *American Museum*, which published in the same issue a summary of the Albany Plan Franklin had originally written in 1754.

clear precedent and overriding purpose. Intercolonial Indian conferences had convened in Albany before, but rarely had they ventured beyond the usual business of treaty-making. The Board of Trade had sent no specific instructions for the commissioners other than to renew the Covenant Chain. An August 1753 letter from the king's secretary of state had ordered the colonial governments to "keep up an exact correspondence" with each other but made no mention of pursuing colonial union.[2] Cadwallader Colden summed up the strangeness of the situation best when he responded to the proposals for union Franklin had sent him while en route to Albany. Colden agreed on the necessity of union but doubted that the colonial commissioners then gathering in Albany had the ability to implement it. "What Authority have they to do this?" he wrote to Franklin, "I know of none from either the Council or Assembly of New York."[3] Knowledgeable in treaty-making, Colden quickly recognized the novelty of Franklin's agenda for Albany.

The uncertainty expressed by Colden was evident when the commissioners discussed colonial union at the Albany Congress. Whereas the treaty conference followed a protocol familiar to colonists and Indians alike, the commissioners had to improvise their proceedings with each other. They possessed no interpreters, audiences, or scripts to guide them. Franklin may have remembered them as farsighted statesmen, but they more closely resembled a collection of public and private interests tossed together by order of the Board of Trade and their respective colonial governments. This diverse group divided along several intersecting fault lines. New Englanders despised New Yorkers, Pennsylvanians pursued their own agenda, and New Yorkers distrusted just about everyone. Cultural differences compounded geographic rivalries. Pennsylvania Quakers, New England Congregationalists, and New York Presbyterians and Anglicans carried to Albany stereotypical prejudices and suspicions of each other. All of the commissioners swore allegiance to the same Crown, but some came from corporate colonies, some from proprietary colonies, and others from royal colonies; some sat in representative assemblies while others owed their appointments as councillors to the Crown. They thus embodied the traditional antagonisms in colonial politics between centralized, prerogative power and local, popular power. As their experiences in colonial government varied, so too did their opinions on colonial union.

The commissioners' debates over colonial union at the Albany Congress crystallized two competing perspectives on the British Empire in North America. Those commissioners who resisted Franklin's plan of union de-

[2] *NYCD*, 6:794–95.
[3] See Colden to Franklin, June 20, 1754, and Franklin to Colden, July 14, 1754, *BF Papers*, 5:353–55, 392–93.

fended an old imperial order in which distinct and semiautonomous colonies governed themselves according to their particular charters and constitutional relations with the British Crown. The supporters of union, on the other hand, envisioned a new imperial order in which formerly separate colonies would form a single American dominion within the British-Atlantic empire, one governed by an intercolonial legislature superior to colonial governments but subordinate to the British Parliament. This division boiled down to a question of colonial identity. Would colonists define themselves first as members of distinct political communities clustered along North America's eastern seaboard, or as Britons, fellow members of an expanding Atlantic empire? The commissioners at the Albany Congress struggled among themselves to answer that question and arrived at no clear consensus.

Coming to Order

Franklin traveled to Albany with his "Short hints towards a scheme for uniting the Northern Colonies" in hand and copies of it circulating among two New York correspondents. No other colonial commissioner appears to have come to the meeting so well prepared to pursue colonial union. When the commissioners first gathered in the Albany courthouse, they shared no clear direction and spent a great deal of time haggling over credentials, rank, and seating. The Board of Trade had not provided any instructions or objectives for the conference beyond renewing the Covenant Chain. Nor did the instructions the commissioners received from their home governments provide a single mandate regarding union. Massachusetts instructed its commissioners to enter into a plan of union with the other delegations; Connecticut told its commissioners to consult on such a union; Rhode Island and New Hampshire skirted the issue of union but were not openly hostile to it; Pennsylvania and Maryland specifically proscribed their commissioners' powers to discuss or enter into a union.[4]

New York governor James DeLancey tried to settle this confusion by assuming that his authority in the Indian conference extended to the intercolonial negotiations inside the courthouse. In his correspondence with other colonial governors in the months preceding the Albany Congress, DeLancey had defined his objective for the conference: gaining intercolonial support for his plan to build two forts on the New York frontier

---

[4] See the commissioners' commissions in *Penn. Archives*, 1st ser., 2:137–43.

that would prevent the Iroquois from defecting to the French.[5] DeLancey's idea met resistance from the commissioners, who did not wish to commit their governments to funding New York's security. In particular, the Massachusetts delegation wanted an aggressive rather than defensive union, one that would enlist the Iroquois against the French and limit rather than preserve New York's influence among them.

On June 24, having complied with the governor's request that they draft an opening speech to the Indians, the commissioners took up new business. One of their number (neither the Albany Congress minutes nor Atkinson's journal identifies him) motioned "that the Commissioners deliver their opinion whether a Union of all the Colonies is not at present absolutely necessary for their security and defence." The motion passed unanimously. The commissioners' decision to take up the issue of union is noteworthy, considering how few of them had specific instructions to do so. Franklin's persuasive abilities may have swayed the reluctant; he had come prepared to press the subject of union, and he was certainly the most well-known colonist present. Of course, the commissioners' setting may have provided the best argument for pursuing union. Meeting in a frontier town surrounded by rotting palisades and waiting on potentially hostile Indians may have convinced many that the need for a union was more urgent than their home governments had allowed.

With the subject of union broached, DeLancey moved that the commissioners consider his plan to build forts in Iroquois country. The commissioners decided to table this motion until they first settled on "some Method of effecting the Union between the Colonies." Then they appointed a committee consisting of one member from each delegation to prepare such a plan.[6] These three votes—to pursue colonial union, to table DeLancey's plan, and to form a union committee—established the commissioners' independence from the New York governor. DeLancey had come to Albany to gain assistance in fortifying New York, but the commissioners had rebuffed him. Shortly thereafter, he lost interest in their courthouse sessions. Although he had attended the commissioners on four of the first five days they met, he absented himself for the next week and did not return until they resumed consideration of Indian affairs. The commissioners had effectively locked DeLancey out of the courthouse and taken the subject of colonial union into their own hands.[7]

[5] For DeLancey's promotion of this plan, see DeLancey to William Shirley, March 5 and April 22, 1754, Mass. Archives, 4:444, 450–51; DeLancey to Governor Roger Wolcott of Connecticut, April 22, 1754, in *Collections of the Connecticut Historical Society*, 16 (1916): 441–43; and DeLancey to Governor James Hamilton of Pennsylvania, April 1, 1754, *Penn. Council Minutes*, 6:13–16.
[6] *NYCD*, 6:859–60.
[7] According to the Albany Congress minutes, DeLancey attended the commissioners' sessions on June 19–21, and 24 and July 1–3 and 9–11. The meetings he attended on July 1–3

The union committee included one member from each delegation: Thomas Hutchinson of Massachusetts, Theodore Atkinson of New
Hampshire, William Pitkin of Connecticut, Stephen Hopkins of Rhode
Island, Benjamin Franklin of Pennsylvania, and Benjamin Tasker of Maryland. DeLancey selected William Smith Sr. from among his councillors to
represent New York.[8] Unfortunately, no record exists of this committee's
meetings, and Atkinson did not describe them in his journal. The sources
left to the historian are a few references to the committee's work in the
Albany Congress minutes, the recollections of some of its members, and
the draft of a plan of union it completed.

The committee's leaders appear to have been Benjamin Franklin and
Thomas Hutchinson, both of whom later claimed important roles in its
proceedings.[9] They represented the two colonial delegations, Pennsylvania and Massachusetts respectively, that had come to the Albany Congress with the most experience in Indian affairs and willingness to challenge the New Yorkers. Hutchinson was also a part of the only colonial
delegation instructed to enter into "articles of Union and Confederation"
with the other colonies.[10] Franklin had arrived in Albany with proposals
for such a plan already drawn up.

The commissioners ordered the union committee to "prepare and receive Plans or Schemes for the Union of the Colonies, and to digest them
into one general plan."[11] These instructions and a later remark by Franklin
that "several of the Commissioners had form'd Plans of the same kind"
have led some historians to theorize that more than one scheme of union
came to Albany with the colonial delegations.[12] With one exception, no

---

concerned the Indians; those on July 9–11 concerned the reintroduction of his tabled motion.
See ibid., 855–60, 864–71, 885–92.
[8] Ibid., 860.
[9] For Franklin's claims, see Farrand, *Franklin's Memoirs*, 326; for Hutchinson's, see Hutchinson, ed., *Diary and Letters*, 1:55.
[10] For the Massachusetts commission, see *Penn. Archives*, 1st ser., 2:137; for its bearers' instructions, see Mass. Archives, 4:471.
[11] *NYCD*, 6:860.
[12] Franklin's remark comes from Farrand, *Franklin's Memoirs*, 326. In 1914, Lois K. Mathews
corrected a mistake made by earlier historians who identified a copy of the committee's plan
of union as a different plan submitted by New Hampshire commissioner Meschech Weare.
See Mathews, "Benjamin Franklin's Plans for a Colonial Union, 1750–1775," *American Political
Science Review* 8 (1914): 400, n. 14. In a series of articles published between 1950 and 1961,
Lawrence Henry Gipson argued that Thomas Hutchinson had also prepared a written plan
before the union committee submitted its draft. Verner W. Crane disputed this argument in a
series of "Letters to the Editor" that followed Gipson's articles. See Gipson, "Thomas Hutchinson and the Albany Plan of Union," 5–35; Gipson, "Drafting of the Albany Plan of Union,"
290–316; and Gipson, "Massachusetts Bay and American Colonial Union," 63–92. Also see the
letters exchanged by Gipson and Crane in "Letters to the Editor," *Pennsylvania Magazine of*

written evidence exists of any such plans. The exception is an undated plan in Richard Peters's hand for dividing the colonies into four military districts. This plan may have predated the formation of the union committee, but there is no evidence of it in the committee's work.[13] Thus it appears that the committee had as its working materials Franklin's "Short hints" and whatever schemes or suggestions the commissioners presented orally. In later writings, both Franklin and Hutchinson claimed that Franklin's proposals had the greatest influence on the committee's draft.[14] For lack of other evidence, therefore, reconstructing the committee's work requires evaluating the differences between its draft of a plan of union and Franklin's "Short hints." According to the Albany Congress minutes, the committee met twice, on the mornings of June 25 and June 28, before submitting its draft.[15] In those meetings it fleshed out Franklin's ideas to make them more appealing to the colonial assemblies and the British ministry but without changing the fundamental structure of the intercolonial government he proposed.

It is useful here to recapitulate Franklin's "Short hints." They called for the appointment of an American governor general, salaried by the Crown. He would preside over an intercolonial Grand Council, in which each colony received representation proportional to its contributions to a common treasury. The Grand Council's duties included regulating Indian trade and diplomacy, establishing new western settlements, and providing for the common defense. Franklin recommended funding it by placing an excise tax on strong liquors or other luxury goods. All of these items mirrored proposals for union he had formulated in 1751, with the sole exception that in 1754 he supported implementing the plan by act of Parliament rather than by the colonial assemblies.[16]

The committee's draft for a plan of union elaborated on these ideas. It renamed the Crown's officer the "President General" and dropped Franklin's provision that he be "a Military Man." It established a minimum of two representatives for each colony in the Grand Council and provided for

History and Biography 75 (1951): 350–62, and "Letters to the Editor," Pennsylvania History 27 (1960): 126–36. The editors of Franklin's papers provide an excellent summary of this debate along with a close textual comparison of all the evidence in BF Papers, 5:378–87. Gipson's thesis, though intriguing, remains conjectural and has not gained acceptance among other scholars.

[13] The plan in Peters's hand is reprinted in Penn. Archives, ser. 1, 2:197–99. Also see the commentary on this plan by the editors of Franklin's papers, in BF Papers, 5:358.

[14] In his memoirs, Franklin wrote of the submitted schemes, "Mine happen'd to be prefer'd." In the third volume of his history of Massachusetts, Hutchinson wrote that the "plan for a general union was projected by Benjamin Franklin . . . the heads whereof he brought with him." See Farrand, Franklin's Memoirs, 326, and Hutchinson, History of the Colony and Province of Massachusetts-Bay, 3:16.

[15] NYCD, 6:860, 863.

[16] BF Papers, 5:335–38. Compare with Franklin's 1751 proposals for colonial union ibid., 4:117–21.

their election every three years. The committee expanded the Grand Council's powers to include making war and peace with the Indians, collecting rents on western lands under its supervision, and appointing the civil and military officers necessary to carry out its duties. It also prohibited the Grand Council from impressing colonists for military service without the permission of their assemblies, an issue dear to New Englanders who had rioted against British press gangs in Boston during King George's War. To fund the intercolonial government, the committee added the possibility of a stamp tax to Franklin's suggested liquor excise.[17]

In hindsight, the discussion of a possible colonial stamp tax at the Albany Congress might seem ominous, as it did to patriot-turned-historian Thomas McKean in 1813.[18] In fact, it was neither a new nor a radical idea. Former colonial officials William Keith and Henry McCulloh had previously proposed such a tax, and shortly after the Albany Congress, the Massachusetts and New York assemblies imposed stamp duties on their respective provinces to raise money during the Seven Years' War.[19] The suggestion of a stamp tax made by the union committee caused no alarm among the Albany Congress commissioners, probably because they assumed it would be imposed by their own representatives sitting on the intercolonial Grand Council.[20]

The content of the committee's draft deviated little from Franklin's "Short hints"; the primary difference lay in its presentation. It took Franklin's sketchy proposals and turned them into a persuasive plan designed to convince both the assemblies and the British government of the need for union. Up until the formation of the committee, Franklin had discussed colonial union with only a small circle of like-minded correspondents. Franklin and these associates conceived of union as a comprehensive answer to problems they attributed to their particular colonial governments, such as Quaker pacifism in Pennsylvania and Dutch neutrality in New

[17] See the committee's draft, ibid., 5:361–64. On the subject of impressment, see Jesse Lemisch, "Jack Tar in the Streets: Merchant Seamen in the Politics of Revolutionary America," WMQ 25 (1968): 371–407.

[18] See the discussion of McKean's correspondence with John Adams in the Introduction.

[19] For Keith's plan, see [Keith], *Two Papers on the Subject of Taxing the British Colonies in America*, 13–22. For McCulloh's suggestion, see Henry McCulloh, "To the Right Honourable Earl of Halifax," December 10, 1751, BM, Add. Mss., No. 11514:94. McCulloh elaborated on this proposal in subsequent pamphlets, including *Miscellaneous Essay Concerning the Courses Pursued by Great Britain in the Affairs of Her Colonies*, 92. For the Massachusetts and New York stamp acts, passed in 1755–56, see Mack Thompson, "Massachusetts and New York Stamp Acts," WMQ 26 (1969): 253–58.

[20] Mack Thompson noted a similar lack of outcry against the stamp acts passed in Massachusetts and New York in 1755 and 1756. The idea for such colonially imposed stamp taxes may have migrated from the Albany Congress back to these two governments: William Shirley and James DeLancey introduced the idea to their respective assemblies, along with suggestions for potential excises on liquor or tea, the sort of luxury tax Franklin envisioned as funding a colonial union. See Thompson, "Massachusetts and New York Stamp Acts," 255–58.

York. To make union attractive to the commissioners gathered at the Albany Congress, the committee had to lift Franklin's ideas out of this middle-colony context and resituate them in the whole of British North America, taking care that they alienated neither the colonial governments nor the ministry. In other words, the difference between Franklin's "Short hints" and the committee's draft is not so much one of content as of rhetorical strategy.

This difference is most evident in the careful wording of the committee's draft. Franklin had titled his proposals "Short hints towards a scheme for uniting the Northern Colonies." The committee offered "a Scheme for a General Union of the British Colonies on the Continent," expanding the geographic scope of the proposed union. Whereas Franklin's plan simply listed proposals in a series of sentences and brief paragraphs, the committee's draft introduced the topic of union by first considering the constitutional issues it raised. Looking toward London, it admitted that in any union, "the Just Prerogative of the Crown must be preserved." Fixing another eye on the assemblies, it added that "the Just liberties of the People must be Secured." With these two values affirmed, the committee then placed its proposals squarely between them: "Yet Some Prerogative may be abated to Extend Dominion and Increase Subjects and Some Liberty to Obtain Safety." Union would require a reduction in the customary powers of the assemblies and the Crown, but it would more than compensate by protecting American liberties while extending the British Empire.[21]

Throughout the rest of the draft, the committee followed this strategy of describing its proposed union as a means of balancing the king's prerogative with the people's liberty. It assured the assemblies that under this "One General Government" each colony would continue to govern itself internally according to its particular charter or constitution, "as so many Separate Corporations in one Common Wealth." This statement distanced the committee's draft from previous proposals for union by the Board of Trade that had called for revoking colonial charters and reducing the colonies to a uniform system of royal government.[22] Other provisions such as the prohibition against impressment protected popular liberties and eased concerns about an overpowerful president general. The committee's draft made similar concessions to the Crown. No act of the Grand Council would pass without the president general's assent, and any acts concerning the Indian trade or new western settlements would be sent to London

[21] *BF Papers*, 5:361. According to Kathleen Wilson, Britons in the mid-eighteenth century believed that extending imperial dominion and preserving British liberties were mutually agreeable objectives; apparently Franklin and his fellow committee members were thinking along similar lines when they wrote this opening statement for the Albany Plan. See Wilson, "Empire of Virtue: The Imperial Project and Hanoverian Culture, c. 1720–1785," in *Imperial State at War*, ed. Stone, 128–64.
[22] See Dickerson, *American Colonial Government*, 209–16.

for the Privy Council's approval. Such legislative review would preserve the royal interest in the fur trade and the creation of new colonies.[23]

By addressing the need to rebalance prerogative and popular powers in colonial government, the committee expanded the idea of union beyond simply coordinating intercolonial affairs. The union it proposed offered an alternative to the various constitutional relationships then governing British North America: the creation of an intercolonial government suspended between the assemblies and the Crown that would not eliminate the constitutional differences between royal, corporate, and proprietary colonies but would help smooth them over by consolidating prerogative and popular powers in a new way. In short, the committee took the idea of colonial union and made it serve the larger purpose of Anglo-American union.

Debating Union

The committee submitted its draft to the commissioners on the afternoon of June 28. Thereafter the commissioners debated it almost daily until agreeing to a final version on July 10. Little record exists of these debates except for the occasional recollections of their participants and a few brief references to them in the Albany Congress minutes. Extant descriptions agree that they were lively and contentious. Writing to Colden ten days after the congress ended, Franklin enclosed a copy of the Albany Plan and noted, "We had a great deal of Disputation about it, almost every Article being contested by one or another."[24] New York historian William Smith Jr. heard from his father, a New York councillor who participated in the proceedings, that they were "vastly entertaining."[25]

From such scattered accounts, it is possible to reconstruct the contours of the commissioners' debates. Four questions in particular concerned them: would the colonies form one general union or divide themselves into two or more smaller unions? would the union be enacted by Parliament or by the colonial assemblies? how would the intercolonial government be funded? and how would constitutional powers be divided in this new intercolonial body? An examination of these four questions reveals the extent to which Franklin overstated the unanimity of the colonial commissioners in his memoirs. The subject of colonial union brought to the surface

---

[23] *BF Papers*, 5:361–63.
[24] Franklin to Colden, July 21, 1754, ibid., 394.
[25] Smith, Diary, reel 2:368. Smith wrote the commentary on the Albany Congress contained in this diary during the late 1770s, while working on the second volume of his history of New York. He claimed to have been present in Albany during the congress; he was probably one of the gentlemen from New York City who followed Governor DeLancey there. But because he was not serving in any official capacity, he would not have joined the commissioners in the courthouse and would have relied instead on his father's reports of the proceedings there. See Smith, *History of the Province of New-York*, 2:158.

a divergence between colonists intent on retaining the traditional autonomy of colonial governments and others wishing to see them better incorporated into the British-Atlantic empire. At Albany, the subject of colonial
union could not be divorced from these differing perspectives on the nature of the Anglo-American union.

The question of general or partial union illustrated the commissioners'
differing ideas of what constituted colonial union. In an explanatory summary of the Albany Plan completed shortly after the congress, Franklin
noted that some of the commissioners suggested forming "the colonies
into two or three distinct unions."[26] The Massachusetts delegation, in a
report to its home government, explained the rationale behind this recommendation. Smaller geographic districts would unite colonies with common frontiers, Indian neighbors, and economic interests. They would
work more efficiently by not burdening governments with the expense of
sending representatives, troops, or aid to distant locations.[27] A plan written in Richard Peters's hand for dividing the colonies into four military
districts embodied this logic. Each district would appoint times and places
for its annual meetings, at which its member colonies would coordinate
their Indian and military policy. Each colony would also support a regi-
ment of one hundred troops under the command of a single royal officer.
The colonies would keep "this little standing army" at strength as long as
the French threatened their borders.[28] Supporters of partial union favored
a defensive and temporary plan such as this one. It would not alter colonial
charters, nor would it affect the existing relationship between the colonies
and Great Britain. Best of all, it would remain entirely under the control of
the colonial governments. When the plan had outgrown its usefulness, the
assemblies could simply repeal the acts that had created it.

Franklin offered several reasons against such partial unions. First, in
cases requiring the cooperation of several smaller unions, they would be as
hard to unite "as now the several colonies." Second, partial unions would
be smaller and weaker than a general one and would do little to discourage enemy attacks. Franklin also believed that a single union would
better preserve the colonists' liberties by diluting the "*particular whims and
prejudices*" of its members. In partial unions, the interests of an individual
colony would carry greater weight: New York might block effective management of Indian affairs to protect its fur trade, or Pennsylvania might

[26] Franklin wrote this document, titled "Reasons and Motives on which the Plan of Union was
formed," to accompany Thomas Pownall's report on the Albany Congress to the Earl of
Halifax, president of the Board of Trade. It is one of the most important contemporary sources
on the Albany Congress debates. There is no evidence that it or Pownall's report were ever
received by Halifax or the Board of Trade. See *BF Papers*, 5:397–99.
[27] Mass. Archives, 4:464.
[28] [Richard Peters?], "Rough Draft of a Plan for a General Union," 1754, *Penn. Archives*, 1st
ser., 2:197–99.

thwart "warlike measures" to appease its Quaker inhabitants. In a single union, such obstacles to "the general good" would be "swallowed up" because no colony would possess enough influence to dominate the whole.[29] A general union, in other words, would compensate for the over-powerful private interests and myopic insularity that often plagued individual colonial governments.

Supporters of general union favored the creation of a permanent inter-colonial government that would promote British interests in North America, even during peacetime. Franklin argued, for example, that a general union would be better suited for regulating the Indian trade and for planting new colonies west of the Appalachians.[30] He favored British settlement of the Ohio Valley but found the colonies ill-equipped to handle that task individually. They contested each others' western borders and refused mutual assistance when the French occupied disputed regions. Virginia's Ohio Company provided the perfect illustration. Even with the support of the Virginia militia, this private venture was too weak to resist the French. Meanwhile, neighboring colonies watched impassively, not wishing to expend their resources on advancing Virginia's claim to that region.[31] Left in the hands of particular colonial governments, western lands divided colonists and weakened the British interest, but if placed under inter-colonial authority, they could encourage colonial population growth and strengthen Britain's position against the French.

Most important to Franklin, a general union would encourage the colonists "to consider themselves, not as so many independent states, but as members of the same body."[32] Franklin rejected partial unions because at best they offered a quick fix, clumsy and limited, even for short-term defense. Partial unions formed by temporary alliances between neighboring colonies would do little to overcome the regional prejudices and isolationism that currently defined intercolonial relations. A general union was qualitatively different. Besides improving colonial military strength and Indian relations, it would permanently alter the way colonists thought about themselves. Here Franklin appealed to the idea of a union premised on filial bonds that transcended geographic borders, one that would recognize and nurture the colonists' identity as Britons.

Although the surviving evidence does not reveal who besides Franklin supported a general union, his opinion prevailed in the final version of the Albany Plan. In their report to their home government, the Massachusetts delegation offered two reasons why Franklin won out. First, the commis-

---

[29] *BF Papers*, 5:401–2.
[30] Ibid., 401.
[31] See ibid., 399–400, in which Franklin refers to Virginia's problems on the Ohio as an impetus for pursuing union at the Albany Congress.
[32] Ibid., 402.

sioners decided that it would "require the united strength and councils of the whole British Continent" to defeat the French in the upcoming war. Second, they shared a desire to have Indian affairs put "under but one direction . . . without any special regard to any particular Governments."[33] This last point—centralizing Indian affairs under one administration—united commissioners from New England and Pennsylvania against the New Yorkers and may have given Franklin the edge he needed to dismiss partial unions.

The second major issue to emerge in the commissioners' debates concerned how to enact a union. From the beginning of their deliberations, the commissioners realized that they did not possess the powers necessary to create a binding agreement among the colonies. Lacking that ability themselves, they debated how such a union should take effect. This issue arose early and caused controversy because it touched on the violability of colonial charters. It also influenced the debate over general or partial union. Partial unions could be achieved without altering existing colonial charters, and they had a precedent in the New England Confederation, a limited military union maintained by the New England colonies in the seventeenth century.[34] A general union with the power to fix colonial borders, govern western settlements, regulate the Indian trade, and tax the colonists was another story; it would require altering the self-governing privileges and "sea-to-sea" charters of some colonies. Only Parliament, the commissioners agreed, had the legislative authority to make such changes. A union premised on parliamentary enactment, therefore, would tacitly admit Parliament's supremacy over the colonies.

Franklin had reversed his initial opposition to a parliamentary-enacted union by the time the Albany Congress convened. In 1751, Franklin preferred a "voluntary Union entered into by the Colonies themselves" to one "impos'd by Parliament." When he composed his "Short hints" three years later, he recommended that any plan drafted at the Albany Congress be sent to London and "an Act of Parliament obtain'd for establishing it." Parliamentary enactment would also carry with it the power to levy the intercolonial taxes necessary to support the union. Two of Franklin's acquaintances, Cadwallader Colden and Archibald Kennedy, were of this mind. In proposing an intercolonial tax to support the regulation of the Indian trade, Colden wrote, "As this Duty is proposed to be general over all the Colonies it must be imposed by Act of Parliament; because it would be a most vain imagination to expect, that all the Colonies would severally

---

[33] Report of the Massachusetts Commissioners to the Albany Congress to William Shirley, November 1, 1754, Mass. Archives, 4:464.
[34] For a discussion of the New England Confederation as a precedent for colonial union, see Mathews, "Franklin's Plans for a Colonial Union," 396–412, and Ward, *United Colonies of New England*.

agree to impose it."[35] By 1754 Franklin had come to the same conclusion: any union that would be worth its salt had to be accompanied by intercolonial taxation, and that power could come only from Parliament. The union committee accepted this proposition but added that the act of Parliament imposing the union be "Temporary." This qualification of Franklin's original "Short hints" indicates that some opposition to parliamentary enactment surfaced in committee before the commissioners debated it as a whole.[36]

According to the Albany Congress minutes, the issue of parliamentary enactment came to a head on July 2, just three days after the committee submitted its draft to the commissioners. On that day the commissioners voted on whether a parliamentary act was necessary to form a general union, an issue which Theodore Atkinson described as "so Long and often in Debate."[37] Fragmentary notes left in Richard Peters's hand offer clues about those arguments. Some comments, such as "They are afraid of an Act of Parliament" and "People are afraid of disobliging their Constituents," provide a rough idea of an anti-Parliament argument. Opponents of parliamentary enactment did not wish to anger their home governments by transgressing their power as commissioners, which several of them were doing simply by discussing union. They also distrusted the novelty of parliamentary enactment, which they believed would violate existing colonial charters. Parliamentary legislation affecting the colonies had expanded beyond commercial regulation during the early eighteenth century to include such matters as the naturalization of non-British immigrants to America and subsidies for the colonization of Georgia and Nova Scotia. But in 1754 Parliament had yet to claim the power to alter colonial charters. Parliamentary enactment of the plan of union would set a precedent for doing exactly that because it would grant the intercolonial government the power to levy universal colonial taxes and to fix colonial borders. According to Peters's notes, Roger Wolcott Jr. of Connecticut objected to pursuing union in this manner because it would open the door to future encroachments on colonial charters by either Parliament or the intercolonial government it created.[38]

Peters's notes also allow us to glimpse the argument in favor of parliamentary enactment. Supporters of this view observed that "An Union by Acts of the Assembly must be tedious and after all the Bill rejected by the Governors or if passd and sent home perhaps will be repealed."[39] This

---

[35] Cadwallader Colden, "The Present state of the Indian Affairs," August 8, 1751, in *Colden Papers* 53 (1920): 285, and Kennedy, *Observations*, 7.
[36] For Franklin's 1751 comments, see *BF Papers*, 4:118; for those made in 1754, see ibid., 5:338; for the committee's added condition, see ibid., 363.
[37] McAnear, "Personal Accounts," 737.
[38] *BF Papers*, 5:365–66.
[39] Ibid.

reasoning emphasized the weakness of any union created by the assemblies. Waiting for the individual assemblies to pass a plan would take too long, and their work could be overturned by higher authorities such as colonial governors or the Privy Council. Franklin added that enactment by the assemblies would leave the colonies free to exit the union whenever they pleased, "till the whole crumbled into its original parts."[40] To protect against such fragmentation, union had to be implemented by Parliament. To those commissioners disturbed by the precedent such an act would set, Franklin and his supporters responded that "Novelty [was] not dangerous." Advocates of parliamentary enactment explained that it would actually preserve colonial liberties by removing jealousies and misconceptions that the ministry and Parliament held of the colonies in their current divided state. Union would replace division with cooperation and reveal the true nature of the colonists' loyalty and value to Britain, ultimately improving Anglo-American relations and easing the burden of imperial government.[41]

This debate divided the commissioners into those who defended the sanctity of colonial charters and those willing to use parliamentary power to amend them. As Thomas Hutchinson recalled more than twenty years later, all agreed on the need for union but also recognized that the colonies did not possess the "authority to form one general government over the whole." Once the commissioners had decided to pursue a general union, they forced upon themselves this question of parliamentary supremacy. Opponents feared precedent and novelty, favoring instead partial unions premised on earlier examples of intercolonial cooperation. Supporters wanted a general and permanent union that would by its nature infringe on some existing colonial charters. Writing as a loyalist exile in the 1770s, Hutchinson observed that Franklin spent much of his subsequent career as a colonial agent backing away from the position he had taken at the Albany Congress in favor of Parliament's legislative authority over the colonies.[42]

The commissioners voted on parliamentary enactment on July 2. Two accounts of this vote are extant, one in the Albany Congress minutes and one in Atkinson's journal, and they differ in important ways. According to the minutes, the commissioners first voted on whether they "should proceed to form the plan of a Union of the Colonies, to be established by an Act of Parliament." An affirmative answer to this question would have led to further consideration of the union committee's draft, which called for parliamentary enactment; a negative vote would have sent the committee

---

[40] Ibid., 400.
[41] Ibid., 365–66.
[42] Hutchinson, *History of the Colony and Province of Massachusetts-Bay*, 3:16–18.

back to the drawing board to devise a plan that did not rely on parliamentary enactment. At this point one of the commissioners, not identified in the minutes, moved "to put the previous question." In eighteenth-century English parliamentary procedure, opponents of a motion "put the previous question" in an effort to delay a vote on it. They would vote negative on the previous question and, if successful, dismiss the proposed motion for the remainder of the day. If the previous question passed in the affirmative, the proposed motion came to an immediate vote.[43]

If the Albany Congress commissioners were following English procedure, then whoever introduced the previous question most likely opposed parliamentary enactment and hoped to forestall any further consideration of a plan calling for it. According to the minutes, the vote on the previous question was negative, suggesting that the majority of commissioners shared that sentiment. This negative vote should have resulted in the dismissal of the question for the rest of that day. Here the minutes contradict themselves, for the next item records that the commissioners proceeded to vote on and pass the motion to proceed with the formulation of a plan of union to be enacted by Parliament.[44] This inconsistency leaves two important questions: why did the commissioners violate common procedure and vote on parliamentary enactment after the previous question had been negatived, and why did they suddenly change sympathies and vote in favor of it?

A way out of this conundrum is offered by Atkinson. According to his journal entry of July 2, no previous question was involved in the commissioners' votes. First, they put to a vote *"weither an Act of Parliament was the only Expedient to Obtain Such a Union."* This question passed in the affirmative with only the Connecticut delegation opposed, suggesting that the commissioners generally agreed that only an act of Parliament would be sufficient to obtain a general union. With this vote taken, "the S[ai]d *Question was put* and this *Passt in the Affirmative,"* this time with the three Connecticut commissioners and "*2 from Pensilvania*" failing to vote in the affirmative. In other words, the commissioners resolved to continue debating the committee's draft, accepting parliamentary enactment as a given.[45] This vote was a victory for supporters of a general union.

The opposition to parliamentary enactment mentioned by Atkinson corresponded with other contemporary reports. Both Richard Peters and William Smith Jr., who heard about the commissioners' debates from his father, noted the Connecticut commissioners' resistance to the proposed

[43] For helpful discussions of the previous question and its usage in the eighteenth century, see Henry M. Robert, *Robert's Rules of Order Revised* (Chicago, 1951), 117–18, and *BF Papers*, 5:348, n. 9.
[44] *NYCD*, 6:868.
[45] McAnear, "Personal Accounts," 737.

union.[46] Identifying the two Pennsylvania commissioners who opposed parliamentary enactment is more difficult. Franklin, of course, should be ruled out. He had appealed for parliamentary enactment in his "Short Hints," and as a member of his colony's antiproprietary party, he was no friend of the Pennsylvania charter. Thomas Pownall observed in his report on the Albany Congress that Isaac Norris, the Quaker speaker of the Pennsylvania Assembly, resisted union "in some points."[47] John Penn, as a member of the proprietary family, had reason to oppose any measure that might alter the Pennsylvania charter. Richard Peters had listened attentively to the commissioners' debates on the issue, taking notes on the arguments for and against, and he left behind a plan for partial unions in his hand. Thus all the Pennsylvanians except Franklin were likely opponents of a parliamentary-enacted union. It is tempting to attribute this connection to a sympathy between representatives of corporate (Connecticut) and proprietary (Pennsylvania) colonies, but the delegates from Rhode Island (a corporate colony) and Maryland (a proprietary one), apparently favored parliamentary enactment. A stronger bond between the Connecticut and Pennsylvania delegations may have been their pursuit of Indian lands; they may have feared that purchases they were then negotiating in Albany would be placed in jeopardy if a new intercolonial government was created with jurisdiction over western lands.

The differences between Atkinson's rendering of the vote on parliamentary enactment and that found in the minutes are difficult to reconcile. The version found in the minutes suggests that parliamentary enactment was highly controversial, whereas Atkinson identifies a much smaller opposition. Of the two, Atkinson's version deserves greater weight since its internal logic is more consistent, while the minutes are contradictory about the use of the previous question. Yet if Atkinson's version is the more accurate of the two, it does not explain why the commissioners, who took care in reviewing their minutes, allowed such an error to stand.[48] Both versions agree that the motion in favor of parliamentary enactment passed, a testament to the persuasive abilities of Franklin and its other supporters.

<hr>

[46] See Richard Peters's notes on this debate, *BF Papers*, 5:365–66, and Smith, *Diary*, reel 2:367–68.

[47] McAnear, "Personal Accounts," 744.

[48] On July 10 the commissioners appointed Richard Peters and John Chambers to review the minutes, and they reported the next day that all was in order. See *NYCD*, 6:891–92. One possible explanation of why they did not question this passage is that the commissioners were using the previous question in its Americanized form; that is, as a device that supporters of a motion use to close debate and bring it to a vote. The problem with this interpretation is that it is anachronistic. This usage of the previous question did not become common in American parliamentary procedure until the early nineteenth century. See Robert, *Robert's Rules of Order Revised*, 117. Franklin mentioned a "previous question" in his account of the Albany Congress in his memoirs, but his use of this term does not match that found in the Albany Congress minutes. Also, he was writing many years after the fact. See Farrand, *Franklin's Memoirs*, 326.

The final version of the Albany Plan called for the creation of a union "by an Act of the Parliament of Great Britain." The committee's recommendation that this act be "Temporary" was not included in this final draft. But the issue of parliamentary enactment did not end there. Those commissioners who had feared overstepping their authority received an important concession. After accepting the plan on July 10, the commissioners voted to "lay the same before their respective constituents for their consideration" and to send copies to those colonies not represented at the congress.[49] As Hutchinson later recalled, this provision meant that the plan "was to be of no force until confirmed by the several assemblies."[50] This compromise most certainly irritated Franklin, who had hoped to bypass the assemblies altogether.[51]

The third issue debated by the commissioners concerned funding the new intercolonial government. The traditional method for raising troops and money in times of crisis was the requisition system, in which the Crown or colonies set quotas that each would contribute to a common fund. This system rarely worked because no intercolonial body existed to enforce it, and assemblies withheld contributions until convinced that other colonies were making theirs. Franklin was one of the requisition system's many critics, and in his 1751 proposals for colonial union he advised replacing it with an intercolonial excise tax on strong liquors. Such a tax did not require getting the colonies to agree to fair proportions, and its revenues would grow as the colonial population increased. Furthermore, it could be collected independently of assemblies notorious for withholding aid to other colonies at times of crisis.[52] The committee's draft incorporated Franklin's opinions and added an intercolonial stamp duty as a possible alternative. The committee did pose one fundamental question at the end of its report: should such intercolonial taxes be implemented by the Grand Council or by the same act of Parliament that would create this intercolonial union?[53]

Unfortunately, neither the Albany Congress minutes nor Atkinson's journal give any indication of the debate on this topic. William Smith Jr. provided the only commentary on it in the second volume of his history of New York. According to him, the committee's draft caused many debates, "especially respecting the funds for supporting this new government."[54] The commissioners discussed the liquor duty and the stamp tax but finally

[49] NYCD., 6:889, 891.
[50] Hutchinson, History of the Colony and Province of Massachusetts-Bay, 3:17.
[51] For Franklin's opinion on the assemblies, see Franklin to Peter Collinson, December 29, 1754, BF Papers, 5:453–54.
[52] Ibid., 4:119. Franklin defended this position while criticizing the old requisition system in his "Reasons and Motives for the Albany Plan," ibid., 5:399, 407.
[53] Ibid., 5:364.
[54] Smith, History of the Province of New-York, 2:161, unnumbered note.

resolved to leave the president general's salary to the Crown and to grant the members of the Grand Council a small per diem allowance so that it would attract only "Men of Fortune who would be at the greatest remove from Corruption."[55]

Smith's summary does little to explain how the commissioners settled the thorny issue of taxation. If this intercolonial body was going to treat with the Indians, make land purchases, and fortify the frontiers, then it needed a large and stable source of income. The evidence does not indicate how long or with what intensity the commissioners debated this issue, but it does reveal how they settled it. The Albany Plan of Union stated that the Grand Council would have the power "to make Laws and lay and Levy such general duties, imposts, or taxes, as to them shall appear most equal and just."[56] Apparently, no one argued for the alternative of a parliamentary tax levied at the time the union was enacted. In fact, the commissioners' preference for taxation by the Grand Council rather than Parliament seems to have been a rare point of universal agreement. The commissioners were willing to support parliamentary enactment, but they wanted any intercolonial taxation to come from a representative intercolonial body. Put another way, their recognition of Parliament's power to enforce colonial union did not extend to an admission of its power to tax them. The Albany Plan implicitly drew a line between Parliament's power to legislate for the colonies and to tax them. This distinction, uniformly agreed upon by the commissioners at Albany in 1754, would become one of the most contentious points in the constitutional debate between the colonies and Parliament in the 1760s.

The fourth and last of the major issues debated by the commissioners concerned the constitutional division of powers in this new intercolonial government. Political interests and principles split the commissioners on this topic, especially the New York and Massachusetts delegations, which accused each other of trying to gain an undue influence for their respective colonies in the proposed union. The commissioners debated the office of the president general and the selection of the Grand Council, and their positions provided significant insight into how they imagined their place in Britain's developing imperial constitution.

Most of the debate on the president general occurred between the New York and Massachusetts delegations, which were already engaged in a bitter rivalry over the Iroquois. According to William Smith Jr., DeLancey opposed the plan of union drafted by the commissioners because he feared that the Crown would appoint Massachusetts governor William Shirley to the president general's office. Such fears were not unfounded. Shirley had

---

[55] Smith, Diary, reel 2:368.
[56] NYCD, 6:890.

great ambitions for advancement, and in 1754 he was the Crown's most highly regarded governor in North America.[57] Shirley also made no secret of his contempt for New York's management of Indian affairs, one of the duties that would fall into the hands of the new intercolonial government. DeLancey therefore spread word that the Massachusetts delegation supported union only so that it might "procure the President's chair for their governors." But DeLancey's unpopularity worked against him, and he "found that every effort to resist the scheme only contributed to forward it."[58] While critical of DeLancey, Smith also suspected the New Englanders of ulterior motives. At the time of the Albany Congress, Massachusetts and Connecticut were in a boundary dispute with New York. Smith believed that the New Englanders supported the proposed union because they expected the intercolonial government would settle that dispute to their advantage.[59]

Atkinson noted that the Connecticut delegation had constitutional objections to the president general's office. On July 4 he recorded that the commissioners had come to agreement on several points, "*Except the Connecticut Gentlemen who tho[ugh]t there was too great a Power* Lodged *in the President Generall.*"[60] The Connecticut commissioners probably objected to the independence afforded the president general by his royal salary and powers of command over intercolonial military forces. Both contrasted sharply with the much weaker position of the executive office in Connecticut's government, in which the governor was popularly elected and salaried by the assembly. Thus the Connecticut delegation remained consistent in its opposition to any act of union that might damage or contradict the structure of its corporate government.

Constitutional questions also arose concerning the selection of the Grand Council. The committee's draft recommended that each colony's assembly select the representatives it would send to the intercolonial legislature. According to Franklin, "the gentlemen of the council of New York and some of the other counsellors among the commissioners" proposed altering this process "so that the governor and council of each colony might have some say in the selection of its Grand Council delegates." Franklin countered these objections by appealing to the model of the Brit-

[57] I. R. Christie refers to Shirley as "outstanding" among the colonial governors of mid-century in *Crisis of Empire: Great Britain and the American Colonies, 1754–1783* (New York, 1966), 18. For a similar but more thorough appraisal of Shirley's governorship, see Schutz, *William Shirley.*

[58] Smith, *History of the Province of New-York*, 2:160; 161, unnumbered note. For a similar description of DeLancey's conduct, see [Livingston], *Review of Military Operations in North-America*, 76–77. William Livingston, like William Smith Jr., was a political opponent of DeLancey who attended the Albany Congress but had no official role in the proceedings.

[59] William H. W. Sabine, ed., *Historical Memoirs of William Smith*, 3 vols. (New York, 1956–71), 2:89.

[60] McAnear, "Personal Accounts," 738.

ish constitution. He explained that the proposed intercolonial government contained two branches: the president general, representing the Crown, and the Grand Council, representing the colonial assemblies. The president general's veto power over the Grand Council provided for an equal division of power between them. Franklin then observed that in Great Britain, the Crown possessed only one-third of the governing power, while the Lords and the Commons each held another third. The Crown, therefore, actually possessed a greater share of power in this intercolonial government than it did at home, one-half compared to one-third. To allow the colonial governors and councillors, most of whom were royally appointed, to participate in the selection of the Grand Council would increase the Crown's influence beyond that half-share and infringe on a colonist's right "not to be taxed but by his own consent or the consent of his elected representatives." The proposal advanced by the New York councillors contradicted this principle by leaving "the people in all the colonies . . . in effect . . . taxed by their governors."[61]

Instead of being a royal colony writ large, the intercolonial government Franklin envisioned would be the British government writ small, with the president general representing the Crown and the Grand Council the House of Commons. By carefully explicating British constitutional theory, he defused the New Yorkers' complaints to show how the Crown would realize an increase rather than a decrease in its power under the proposed union. The strength of this rebuttal rested in his comparison of the new intercolonial government with the constitutional model found in Great Britain, not the individual colonies. After all, in the royal model of colonial government, the Crown enjoyed two-thirds of the power because it appointed both the governor and the council. Franklin avoided that example for obvious reasons and concentrated instead on the British model of the king-in-Parliament: "A house of commons or the house of representatives, and the grand council, are thus alike in their nature and intention. And as it would seem improper that the King or house of Lords should have a power of disallowing or appointing members of the house of commons; so likewise that a governor or council appointed by the crown should have a power of disallowing or appointing members of the grand council."[62] The intercolonial Grand Council would have as its model the House of Commons, not the colonial assemblies, in which the Crown's prerogative powers held greater influence than they did in Britain.

In this discussion of the Grand Council, Franklin situated the Albany Plan within a constitutional framework for the British Empire. As a student of the empire, Franklin had Scotland and Ireland to serve as examples of dependent realms possessing more regular constitutional relationships

---

[61] *BF Papers*, 5:403–4.
[62] Ibid., 404.

to England than did the colonies. Scotland, by joining its crown to that of England in 1603 and accepting the parliamentary union of 1707, had incorporated itself into the body politic of Great Britain. In 1754, Ireland still existed as a separate realm, connected to Britain by an imperial crown but in possession of its own parliament to govern its internal affairs. Of these two, the intercolonial government Franklin proposed at Albany more closely resembled the Irish example because it set up a legislative body with jurisdiction over American affairs. The president general would preside over this body on behalf of the Crown, just as the lord lieutenant did in Ireland. But important differences existed between the Irish example and the Albany Plan that indicated Franklin's discomfort with the extent of Ireland's dependency. The American Grand Council would not be hindered by an equivalent of Poynings's Law, which limited the Irish parliament to considering only bills preapproved by the Crown.[63] American colonial assemblies could initiate their own legislation, and the Grand Council proposed by the Albany Plan would enjoy the same privilege. The Albany Plan would create an intermediary constitutional status for British North America, suspended between the more severe dependence of Ireland and outright union with Britain on the Anglo-Scottish model.

The four major issues resolved by the commissioners in their debates—general or partial union, parliamentary enactment, taxation, and the division of constitutional powers within the union—crisscrossed at many points and brought into sharp relief the differences among the commissioners. Franklin and his supporters believed that a general union enacted by Parliament would qualitatively change the nature of the imperial relationship by binding the colonies more closely to the mother country, while at the same time increasing their control over internal American affairs. Opponents of such a union disliked the alterations it would require in traditional charter privileges and the structure of colonial politics. They favored union on a smaller scale, temporary rather than permanent, and for defensive rather than expansionist purposes. Both sides expressed more concern for how union would affect the colonies' relationship to Britain than with each other, and in that sense, both were addressing the larger issue of Anglo-American union.

The final version of the Albany Plan of Union elaborated on but did not substantially alter the committee's original draft (see Appendix). It specified which colonies would be included in the union and the representation each would receive in the Grand Council. Representation would be adjusted every three years to reflect each colony's contribution to the general treasury, but it would never exceed seven seats for a single colony

[63] For a description of Poynings's Law, see J. C. Beckett, *The Making of Modern Ireland, 1603–1923* (London, 1966), 51.

or drop below a minimum of two.[64] The first meeting of the Grand Council would take place in Philadelphia, and thereafter it would reconvene wherever it chose. The general duties of the president general and the Grand Council remained the same. The intercolonial government would regulate Indian affairs, provide for the common defense, and govern western settlements until the Crown formed them into colonies. The Grand Council would have the power to levy taxes and appoint the civil officers necessary to carry out these tasks.

Although historians have often interpreted the Albany Plan as an early example of the federal systems created in the Articles of Confederation and Constitution, the commissioners had different objectives when they drafted it. As conceived in 1754, the Albany Plan embodied a transatlantic critique of the colonial system and offered a blueprint for reforming it in a way that would advance Britain's empire building but not at the expense of American liberties. Its most significant contribution to Anglo-American relations would be the limitation it placed on the ability of individual colonies to act as independent states. In his explanatory summary of the Albany Plan, Franklin criticized the power that each colony currently enjoyed to make "peace and war with Indian nations." This independence led some to "make war on slight occasions without the concurrence or approbation of neighbouring colonies" while others remained at peace.[65] Under the Albany Plan, the Grand Council and president general would coordinate colonial Indian policy to prevent counterproductive diplomacy and warfare. The intercolonial government would also enable the colonists to defend their frontiers without relying on grants from individual assemblies, which were, as Franklin noted, "at present backward to build forts at their own expence, which they say will be equally useful to their neighbouring colonies."[66]

The Albany Plan also offered a model for lessening friction between colonial assemblies and their governors. The distribution of powers between the president general and the Grand Council corrected several of the problems that imperial reformers identified in the way governors and assemblies worked together. For example, Franklin noted that the president general would draw his pay directly from the Crown so that "all disputes between him and the Grand Council concerning his salary might be prevented." Such disputes had often paralyzed colonial governments in the past, "especially in times of public danger," when assemblies withheld funds to force the governor's compliance with their legislation. Invoking

[64] Representation was allotted as follows: Massachusetts and Virginia would each have seven seats; Pennsylvania six; Connecticut five; New York, Maryland, North Carolina, and South Carolina four each; New Jersey three; and Rhode Island and New Hampshire two each. See the Appendix.
[65] BF Papers, 5:409.
[66] Ibid., 413.

an idea commonly presented by other imperial reformers, Franklin even suggested that the crown use its American quitrents as a permanent fund for paying the president general.[67] To protect the Grand Council from an overpowerful president general, the Albany Plan explicitly stated the conditions under which he could dissolve, prorogue, or continue its sessions. In most royal colonies in 1754, the governor exercised such powers at will, allowing him to dismiss an uncooperative assembly or retain a favorable one.[68] Explaining why the Albany Plan limited the president general's use of such powers, Franklin observed that many royal governors had "wantonly exercised" them in the past "merely to harass the members [of the assemblies] and compel a compliance" from them.[69] Franklin expected royal and popular power to be less adversarial in the intercolonial government because the Albany Plan spelled out clearer limits for each. It reduced popular powers over the president general's salary, Indian relations, and military affairs but limited his prerogative powers over the Grand Council to reflect concessions Parliament had already won from the Crown in Britain.

Drafters of the Albany Plan intended for it to serve the expansion of an imperial British state in North America. Indeed, the plan's preamble stated flatly that colonial union would provide "for extending the British Settlements in North America."[70] Significant here is the power that the plan granted to the Grand Council to make and govern new western settlements, an enterprise that would give colonial union a purpose far beyond wartime defense. Franklin believed no individual colony had the strength or resources to sponsor trans-Appalachian expansion properly. In "A Plan for Settling Two Western Colonies" completed in late 1754, he wrote that an intercolonial government modeled after the Albany Plan would be well suited for establishing colonies in the Ohio Valley, where they might cut off the French and cultivate new Indian alliances.[71]

---

[67] Ibid., 402–3. The idea of reorganizing Crown revenues in America into a permanent colonial fund was also being expressed at this time by imperial reformers in London. See, for example, [The Earl of Halifax], "Proposals for building Forts etc. upon the Ohio and other Rivers in North America," April 30, 1754, PRO, CO 5/6:104, and [McCulloh], *Miscellaneous Essay*, 104–22. For the controversies over funding royal governors, see Leonard W. Labaree, *Royal Government in America: A Study of the British Colonial System before 1783* (New York, 1930), 312–72.

[68] See Christie, *Crisis of Empire*, 18–19. On the powers of royal governors, see also Labaree, *Royal Government in America*, 92–132. In his study of the southern colonies, Jack P. Greene found that the Crown conscientiously preserved its governors' powers to call and prorogue assemblies by disallowing colonial acts that imitated the Triennial and Septennial Acts passed by the English Parliament in the seventeenth and eighteenth centuries. See Greene, *Quest for Power: The Lower Houses of Assembly in the Southern Royal Colonies, 1689–1776* (Chapel Hill, 1963), 199–203.

[69] *BF Papers*, 5:408.

[70] *NYCD*, 6:889.

[71] *BF Papers*, 5:411, 456–63.

The Albany Congress commissioners expressed this expansionist spirit in another document, the "Representation of the Present State of the Colonies." Drafted by Thomas Hutchinson, the "Representation" reflected the commissioners' concern with asserting Britain's sovereignty over regions contested with the French.[72] It presented a detailed summary of Great Britain's North American claims, from the voyages of John Cabot through King George's War, laying out in precise terms Britain's rights to Nova Scotia, the Great Lakes, and the Ohio Valley. It also warned that the French were perilously close to completing their "evident design" to connect Canada and Louisiana by way of the Ohio and Mississippi Rivers. The commissioners intended for the ministry and colonial assemblies to read the "Representation" alongside the Albany Plan of Union, alerting them to the urgency of ending the colonies' "divided disunited state."[73] Together, the two documents constitute a manifesto for British imperialism in North America, the "Representation" justifying war against the French and the Albany Plan providing the means for carrying it out.

Franklin worked on the Albany Plan with one eye always on the mother country. He supported parliamentary enactment because he had little faith in the assemblies or colonial governors, and his correspondence after the congress confirms that he thought the plan's best prospects would be in London.[74] He knew that for any plan of union to succeed, it would have to appeal to the Crown's tastes. The president general's veto power over the Grand Council was necessary "to give the crown its due share of influence in this government, and connect it with that of Great Britain." Franklin also candidly admitted that a provision allowing the Crown to disallow any act of the Grand Council within three years of its passage "was thought necessary for the satisfaction of the crown, *to preserve the connection of the parts of the British empire with the whole, of the members with the head*" (emphasis added).[75] As he formulated and defended the Albany Plan, Franklin thought imperially, concerning himself with the extension of a British-Atlantic empire rather than the creation of an autonomous federation of American colonies.

Herein lies the Albany Plan's most important contribution to eighteenth-century Anglo-American relations. It did not anticipate American independence; nor did offer a preemptive solution to the problems that split the empire apart after 1763. But it did break new constitutional ground by conceiving of the North American colonies as a single unit

---

[72] Hutchinson claimed authorship of the "Representation" at the same time he attributed the Plan of Union to Franklin; see Hutchinson, ed., *Diary and Letters*, 1:55. For the "Representation," see *NYCD*, 6:885–88.

[73] *NYCD*, 6:887.

[74] See Franklin to Colden, July 14, 1754, and Franklin to Peter Collinson, December 29, 1754, in *BF Papers*, 5:392–93, 453–54.

[75] Ibid., 409, 415.

within a larger body politic. In the old imperial order, based on precedents established in seventeenth-century colonial charters, no single constitutional relationship existed between North America and Great Britain. Each colony was a separate dominion of an imperial Crown, unique and independent of its neighbors. The Albany Plan placed a new level of constitutional authority between the Crown and the colonies that would reduce the singularity of those governments and incorporate them as a whole more effectively into the empire.

The Albany Plan was actually a two-tiered act of union. On one level, it would facilitate intercolonial cooperation in matters of defense, western expansion, and Indian relations. On a higher level, it would bind the colonies more closely to the mother country and make them party to an evolving imperial constitution. The Albany Plan recognized Parliament's legislative sovereignty in the empire and assumed that it extended to North America. Like the Scottish unionists who had believed in 1707 that the territorial consolidation of the British state was a necessary first step in the expansion of an overseas British empire, Franklin expected the consolidation achieved under the Albany Plan to enable British imperial expansion to continue across the continent.[76] This was the empire Franklin had envisioned in "Observations Concerning the Increase of Mankind": a community of British subjects multiplying and expanding in North America until the demographic center of the empire moved to the Western Hemisphere, a community defined racially and culturally by its consanguinity with the peoples of the British Isles. As an act of Anglo-American union, the Albany Plan would extend empire but also preserve colonial liberties. Identifying Franklin or any other supporter of the Albany Plan as an embryonic American patriot in 1754 is misguided; quite to the contrary, his primary objective was to place the Crown's American subjects on a more equal footing with those in Britain.

Closing the Congress

The commissioners appointed Franklin to prepare a final draft of the Albany Plan on July 9, and they accepted this version the following day. They voted to have each delegation present a copy to its assembly and to have copies sent to those colonial governments not represented at the congress.[77] By this time the negotiations with the Indians were finished and the commissioners had been in Albany for more than three weeks. Most were probably anxious to head home.

[76] See John Robertson, "Union, State, and Empire: The Britain of 1707 and Its European Setting," in *Imperial State at War*, ed. Stone, 224–57.
[77] *NYCD*, 6:885, 889, 891.

One item remained on the table: DeLancey's proposal for building two forts on the New York frontier. The governor, who had introduced this matter on June 24, made sure he was present during the commissioners' final sessions to resurrect it. The commissioners responded by forming a committee to consider "what further Forts may be necessary in the Country of the Six Nations." This committee met at William Johnson's lodgings on the evening of July 10 and made its report the next morning.[78] Speaking for the committee, Samuel Welles of Massachusetts explained that several forts were necessary but that the colonies were not likely to fund them in their "present disunited state." Apprehending "some inconveniencies" if the commissioners devoted further time to the topic, the committee recommended putting it off until they knew the fate of the Albany Plan. The commissioners accepted this recommendation, perhaps exacting some revenge for DeLancey's evasion of their inquiries into the Indians' land grievances a few days earlier. DeLancey later expressed disgust with this decision and with the commissioners, who had refused to "hear of nothing but the plan they had drawn up."[79]

Before ending their proceedings, the commissioners heard speeches from William Johnson and Thomas Pownall. Johnson's speech on Indian affairs has been noted in the previous chapter. Pownall discussed colonial defenses against the French, recapitulating much of the shrill warnings in Hutchinson's "Representation" about the French completing their design and luring away the Indians.[80] Like Johnson's remarks on Indian affairs, the real import of Pownall's speech was in its presentation. The intercolonial audience inside the courthouse offered this unemployed minor official the perfect chance to display his newly acquired expertise in colonial affairs and to claim some small role in the Albany Congress. One critic later chastised Pownall for his opportunistic basking in the glow of the commissioners' statesmanship, but his ploy worked. The commissioners ordered copies of the speech to carry home, and DeLancey included a copy when he transmitted the congress's minutes to the Board of Trade.[81]

The commissioners closed their business and beat a hasty path out of Albany. Unlike their leave-taking from the Indians, they exchanged no presents or professions of friendship. Few left any impression of how they regarded their work. Atkinson seemed pleased simply to make the afternoon ferry across the Hudson.[82] Franklin, on his way downriver, wrote to Colden complaining of the delay caused by the Indians, when "after all

[78] For the committee's activities, see *NYCD*, 6:891, and McAnear, "Personal Accounts," 739.
[79] *NYCD*, 6:892. For DeLancey's disgust with the commissioners, see DeLancey to the Board of Trade, July 22, 1754, ibid., 852.
[80] For the contents of Pownall's speech, see ibid., 893–96.
[81] [Livingston], *Military Operations in North America*, 87–88.
[82] McAnear, "Personal Accounts," 739.

nothing of much Importance was transacted with them."[83] Here again it is important to keep in mind that the commissioners debated union in a setting and context entirely different from their business with the Indians. In light of Franklin's dismissive remark about the Indians' role in the congress, the notion of an Iroquois influence on the Albany Plan seems farfetched indeed.

Franklin, Johnson, and Pownall left Albany with their reputations greatly enhanced. For all three, the congress marked their emergence from the realm of colonial to imperial politics. DeLancey encountered the greatest disappointment. The commissioners had refused to follow his lead, and the congress did little to elevate his stature among other colonial officeholders or the Board of Trade.

The drafting of the Albany Plan of Union marked an achievement in intercolonial relations in its own right. In their debates, the commissioners addressed and settled several issues that would prove to be impassable during the Anglo-American crisis of 1765–75: the nature of parliamentary sovereignty over the colonies, the violability of colonial charters, and the balance between prerogative and popular power in colonial government. That representatives from corporate, proprietary, and royal colonies could arrive at some agreement on these difficult questions at Albany in 1754 is a testament to the originality of the Albany Plan.

Franklin's "Short hints" and his influence among the commissioners deserve credit for the Albany Plan's creation, but so too do the unique circumstances in which the commissioners met. They had traveled from seaport capitals to the edge of the British Empire in North America. They had lived among a local population notorious for its neutrality with the French and attended councils in which Indians had openly expressed animosity for the British. During the proceedings, foreboding news arrived from the Ohio Valley of a surrender by Virginia militia commander George Washington to French troops at hastily constructed Fort Necessity.[84] A sense of defenseless exposure must have enveloped the commissioners as they went about their business, convincing them to embrace the principle scribbled down by Richard Peters during one of their debates: "Novelty not dangerous."[85]

The commissioners' decision to carry copies of the Albany Plan back to their home governments did not erase the fundamental disagreements among them. The Albany Plan posed a challenge to the traditional powers of colonial governors and assemblies and the sanctity of colonial charters.

[83] Franklin to Colden, July 14, 1754, *BF Papers*, 5:392–93.
[84] In his history of New York, William Smith Jr. states that news of the surrender at Fort Necessity arrived while the Albany Congress was still meeting. See Smith, *History of the Province of New-York*, 2:161.
[85] *BF Papers*, 5:365.

For this reason, Franklin believed that achieving union would require circumventing the normal channels of colonial government. As he sailed down the Hudson, Franklin must have realized that the Albany Plan was about to face a far more critical audience in the assembly halls and council chambers of the individual colonies. Thomas Pownall, writing to the Earl of Halifax shortly after the congress, praised the commissioners' work and stated confidently that "What was their Opinion will be the Sense, in general, of the Provinces they represented."[86] He could not have been more wrong. The Albany Plan failed to find approval in either the colonies or London, but the Albany Congress would bear repercussions for the peoples of British North America even as their paths diverged in its wake.

[86] McAnear, "Personal Accounts," 744.

PART III

THE DIVERGING
PATHS OF EMPIRE

The reconstituted Covenant Chain that emerged in the wake of the Albany Congress shared little with its predecessor. The Mohawks had agreed to renew the chain, but their alliance with the British hinged on William Johnson's restoration as their agent. Johnson's subsequent elevation to a royal Indian superintendency transformed the character of Anglo-Iroquois diplomacy, centralizing it under one office that made it much easier for the Crown to manage colonial Indian relations according to Britain's imperial interests. This change closed the alternative paths of diplomacy that the Mohawks had cultivated with other colonies, leading them into a much greater material dependency on Johnson.

The other significant outcome of the Albany Congress, the Albany Plan of Union, arrived stillborn. Colonial assemblies perceived it as an intrusion on their traditional powers and a violation of their charters. The king's ministers failed to respond with enthusiasm to the plan because it contradicted their impulse to strengthen rather than loosen the Crown's prerogative powers in America. In defeat, the Albany Plan became a Rorschach test that elicited from its critics their attitudes about the future of the Anglo-American connection. Franklin's vision of a British-Atlantic empire defined by the shared liberties and consanguinity of its subjects came into direct conflict with the tendency among the Crown's officials to regard North America's colonial and native inhabitants as foreign dependents in need of stricter government. The debate over the Albany Plan, in short, revealed how American and British attitudes toward the empire were changing and why it would only become more difficult to settle the terms of Anglo-American union once this opportunity had passed.

[7]

"A Diversity of Sentiment":
In the Wake of the Albany Congress

All of the Assemblies in the Colonies have, I suppose, had the Union Plan laid before them; but it is not likely, in my Opinion, that any of them will act upon it so as to agree to it, or to propose any Amendments to it. Every body cries, a Union is absolutely necessary; but when they come to the Manner and Form of the Union, their weak Noddles are presently distracted.
—Benjamin Franklin to Peter Collinson, December 29, 1754

It has been proved by some of our wise men and Boys . . . before a large body of people assembled in Town-Meeting, that you and the rest of the Commissioners at Albany have shown your selves by the projected plan for an Union, to be arrant Blockheads; and, at the same time, to have set up a Scheme for the destroying [of] the liberties and privileges of every British Subject upon the Continent.
—William Clarke of Boston to Benjamin Franklin, February 3, 1755

The Albany Plan offered a bold, new conceptualization of the imperial relationship. If enacted, it would create an Anglo-American union within the British-Atlantic empire, molding separate and distinct colonies into a North American dominion, subordinate to Parliament's authority but also vested with its own legislative powers over the individual colonies. This vision of British North America's future, of course, was not without its detractors. Before the Albany Plan could be implemented, it had to pass muster in the colonies and in London. Each assembly would be anxious to protect its particular self-governing privileges; the Crown and Parliament would be concerned with preserving colonial dependence. On both sides of the Atlantic, the Albany Plan challenged ideas about the imperial relationship entrenched in the very institutions charged with enacting it.

In his memoirs, Franklin consigned the failure of the Albany Plan to this resistance from the assemblies and the ministry. "Its fate was singular," he wrote. "The Assemblies did not adopt it as they all thought there was too much *prerogative* in it; and in England it was judg'd to have too much of the *Democratic.*" Franklin responded stoically to its defeat: "such mistakes are not new; History is full of the Errors of States and Princes. . . . Those who govern, having much Business on their hands, do not generally like to take the Trouble of considering and carrying into Execution new Projects. The best public Measures are therefore seldom *adopted from previous Wisdom,* but [are] *forc'd by the Occasion.*"[1] The New York historian William Smith Jr. came to a similar conclusion. He supposed people objected to the Albany Plan "more or less" according to their attachment to "monarchical or republican principles," some distrusting the powers of the president general and others the powers of the Grand Council. In the end, "dread of the French excited the people only to speculate; it did not rise high enough to curb a diversity of sentiment" about the desirability of colonial union.[2]

Franklin and Smith wrote many years after the Albany Plan had been scrapped, but the same air of resignation and defeat had hung about it from the very beginning. While in Albany, the commissioners had avoided publicizing their work on a plan of union. Colonial newspapers reported on the Albany Congress while it was in session, based on information provided by travelers. Between June 24 and July 22, New York City papers carried five such reports, covering the time from DeLancey's departure from New York City until his return. Boston and Philadelphia newspapers usually reprinted these items within a week. They described the arrival of the conference's participants, the Indians' temper, and the progress of the treaty negotiations. None mentioned the commissioners' work on a plan of union.[3] Even after returning to their respective colonies, the commissioners remained tight-lipped. The July 22 issues of the *New-York Gazette* and the *New-York Mercury* noted the return of DeLancey and several commissioners but did not mention the Albany Plan. Only an item in the Boston papers mentioned it. The July 18 edition of the *Boston Weekly News-Letter* noted the return of Thomas Hutchinson, who reported that the delegations carried back a plan for union to submit to their assemblies. Soon thereafter, newspapers in Boston, New York, and Philadelphia reprinted this item.[4]

Why were the commissioners so uniformly silent about what they had accomplished in Albany? Perhaps they wished to shield the Albany Plan

[1] Farrand, *Franklin's Memoirs,* 326–28.
[2] See Smith, *History of the Province of New-York,* 2:161.
[3] For the original reports, see *New-York Gazette* and *New-York Mercury,* June 6, 24, July 8, 15, and 22. Copies of these items appeared in *Pennsylvania Gazette, Boston Gazette, Boston Weekly News-Letter, Boston Evening-Post,* and *Boston Post-Boy.*
[4] For the original report, see *Boston Weekly News-Letter,* July 18, 1754. For copies of it, see *Boston Post-Boy,* July 22, 1754; *Boston Gazette,* July 23, 1754; *Pennsylvania Gazette,* August 1, 1754; and *New-York Gazette,* July 29, 1754.

from public scrutiny before the assemblies and ministry reviewed it. Franklin had once observed that "Great Designs should not be made publick till they are ripe for Execution, lest Obstacles are thrown in the Way; and small Obstacles are sufficient to overset young Schemes, which when grown strong would force their Way over greater."[5] He may have had such a strategy in mind for the Albany Plan. Or perhaps those delegations that had overstepped their powers by drafting a plan of union may have wished to avoid taking responsibility for it. Only the Massachusetts delegation carried orders to engage in such business, and not surprisingly, it was the Massachusetts commissioner Thomas Hutchinson who first reported the Albany Plan to a newspaper. Many years later, Hutchinson offered the most interesting explanation for the commissioners' silence. He recalled that "some of the delegates who agreed to it in Albany, doubted whether it would ever be approved of by the king, parliament, or any of the American assemblies."[6] In brief, they considered the Albany Plan a lost cause from the start and devoted little energy to it upon returning home.

When Franklin wrote to his London friend Peter Collinson in December 1754 about the Albany Plan's poor prospects, he expressed more impatience than anger at his fellow colonists, whose "weak Noddles" admitted the need for union but could not settle on a course of action.[7] Likewise, he must have been amused when he read William Clarke's sarcastic report on Boston's "wise men and Boys" rejecting the Albany Plan in February 1755.[8] No doubt Franklin was disappointed by the plan's defeat there, but he expressed no surprise. His comments shared an ironic tone with those of Hutchinson and Smith in describing the Albany Plan's defeat. As Franklin observed, the transatlantic discussion of colonial union continued after the Albany Congress, and the outbreak of the Seven Years' War only made it more pressing. Why, then, if support for colonial union increased in the months after the Albany Congress, did the commissioners find their plan rejected as the work of "arrant Blockheads"?

In the colonial assemblies and in London, the Albany Plan faced resistance from two divergent views on the constitutional nature of the British Empire. In London, the ministry rejected the Albany Plan but also appointed a military commander in chief for North America and an Indian superintendent for the northern colonies. These actions were consistent with the reforms pursued by the Board of Trade since 1748 to centralize imperial administration, strengthen the royal prerogative in America, and reduce all of Britannia's Americans—colonists and Indians alike—to a uniform dependence. Desperate to mobilize for war against France, the

---

[5] Franklin to Thomas Clap, August 20, 1753, *BF Papers*, 5:21–22.
[6] Hutchinson, *History of the Colony and Province of Massachusetts-Bay*, 3:17.
[7] *BF Papers*, 5:453–54.
[8] Ibid., 490.

ministry had no use for a plan of union that would have placed an inter-colonial legislature between it and access to the empire's American resources. In North America, the assemblies dismissed the Albany Plan because of the damage it would do to their powers over western lands, Indian relations, and military affairs. In rejecting colonial union, they elevated their colonial charters to the level of constitutions and defined the empire as a federation of separate polities united by an imperial crown. Stuck between these views, like a person astride two logs in a stream, was Franklin and his vision of an Anglo-American union premised on the equality of subjecthood between Britons on both sides of the Atlantic.

The Albany Plan in London

Supporters of the Albany Plan expected it to gain its most favorable hearing in London. Several openly doubted the colonial assemblies' cooperation but thought the British ministry would take action. When the Pennsylvania Assembly rejected the plan in August 1754, Franklin predicted that it would not "oppose its being established by the Government at home." A few months later, he wrote, "if ever there be an Union, it must be form'd at home by the Ministry and Parliament. I doubt not but they will make a good one, and I wish it may be done this Winter."[9] William Johnson and Thomas Pownall also encouraged the ministry to pursue colonial union as quickly as possible.[10] William Shirley told his London superiors that the Albany Plan represented "the declared sense of all the Colonies" and advised them to proceed with an act of union "without further consulting them [the colonists] upon any points whatever."[11]

Despite such encouragement from America, the ministry did not seize upon the Albany Plan. It did consider plans for colonial union, but London administrators had a perspective on empire different from that expressed in the Albany Plan. Facing war with the French, they wanted to centralize military and Indian affairs in America under royal supervision and make sure that colonial governments cooperated with it. Union to them would be useful only inasmuch as it quickly placed American resources in the hands of a few royally appointed officers and strengthened the dependence that made colonies useful assets to an imperial state.

The subject of colonial union came before the British ministry well in advance of the Albany Plan. At the same time the Albany Congress con-

[9] Franklin to Colden, August 30, 1754, and Franklin to Peter Collinson, December 29, 1754, ibid., 427, 454.
[10] Johnson to Goldsbrow Banyar, July 29, 1754, WJ Papers, 1:410, and Thomas Pownall, Proposals for Securing the Friendship of the Five Nations.
[11] See Shirley to Thomas Robinson, December 24, 1754, NYCD, 6:930–31.

vened in North America, Newcastle's cabinet charged the Board of Trade with drafting a "Plan of Concert" for the colonies.[12] On August 9, the Board of Trade submitted a plan recommending that each colonial government send one commissioner to a general meeting, where they would determine proportions of men and money to contribute to the common defense. The Crown would appoint a North American commander in chief to supervise the forts and troops funded by this union. The commander in chief would also act as a commissary general, overseeing Indian trade and diplomacy. The colonial commissioners would not form a permanent intercolonial council or legislature, but in times of emergency the commander in chief could call such conferences to settle additional expenses and levies. Hence any expenditures would result from quotas set by colonial representatives.[13]

The plan's most obvious drawback was its complicated enforcement procedure. The board of Trade would forward it to the colonial commissioners when they met for the first time. The commissioners would send any recommended changes back to the Board, which would then formulate the whole into "a Project or draught of a General Convention" and transmit copies to the colonial governments. After the governors, councils, and assemblies had their say, the colonial commissioners would reconvene, make further alterations, and send the plan back for the Crown's final approval.[14] The Albany Plan had called for an act of Parliament to implement union; this plan required four transatlantic trips when a wartime crisis was already at hand. To deal with the delays inherent in such a scheme, the Board of Trade suggested that the Crown immediately appoint an American commander in chief with authority over Indian relations. Such an appointment fell within the Crown's established prerogative powers in colonial government, and therefore the board did not expect the assemblies to oppose it.[15]

In explaining this plan to Newcastle, Halifax confirmed its conservative nature. "We have endeavoured as much as possible to adapt the Plan to the Constitution of the Colonies," he wrote. The commander in chief, while possessing broad powers in military and Indian affairs, would not "be Empower'd to draw upon any Province for one shilling more than the Commissioners from each Colony shall have agreed to."[16] Halifax's remarks indicate that the board wished to avoid tangling with the potentially contentious issues of altering colonial charters or imposing new

[12] See BM. Add. Mss., 32995:266–67. Alison Gilbert Olson provides an excellent reconstruction of these events in "The British Government and Colonial Union, 1754," *WMQ* 17 (1960): 22–34.
[13] For the Board of Trade's plan, see *NYCD*, 6:903–6.
[14] Ibid., 905.
[15] Ibid., 903.
[16] Halifax to Newcastle, August 8, 1754, BM, Add. Mss., 32736:243–44.

colonial taxes at this time. Only if the colonies refused to cooperate with the current plan should the Crown appeal to "an interposition of the Authority of Parliament."[17] In other words, Halifax was much less anxious than Franklin to see a parliamentary-imposed union. This difference in opinion is noteworthy; while Franklin considered the Albany Plan a major constitutional renovation in Anglo-American relations, Halifax was considering colonial union in more expedient terms and hoped it could be achieved through the assertion of prerogative powers the Crown had traditionally exercised in America.

Newcastle circulated the Board of Trade's plan among several associates, who endorsed centralizing royal authority in America but found problems with the board's methods. Lord Chancellor the Earl of Hardwicke encouraged any scheme that would bring the colonies "nearer to that advantage, which the French have by being United under one Government," but he thought the board's plan raised a potential conflict between the Crown's prerogative and the assemblies' legislative powers. Hardwicke saw little sense in the twisted path the plan would follow between the ministry, colonial commissioners, and colonial governments. As he explained to Newcastle, once the assemblies had reviewed the plan, "I don't see how His Majesty can alter it. He may reject or disapprove their Acts of Assembly in toto, but he cannot (as far as I know) make Amendments in them." To simplify matters, Hardwicke thought the plan should go directly from the colonial commissioners to the ministry and then to the assemblies "with a strong Injunction or recommendation from his Majesty." The assemblies might still alter the plan, but "as they are Legislative Bodies, I see no help for it." Hardwicke believed the Crown did not have sufficient powers to raise a common fund in America; it would have to rely on the assemblies, which were likely to alter any plan coming from London and thereby make quick and effective union impossible. The process reminded him of "the Articles of Union between England and Scotland," in which the English and Scottish parliaments legislated the terms of union while the Crown could only accept or reject them.[18]

According to Charles Townshend, a former Board of Trade member now in the Admiralty, this problem had an easy solution: parliamentary intervention. "It is my opinion," he wrote to Newcastle, "that the [Board of Trade's] Plan begins a great work in a wrong manner; Whatever is done, can only be done by an act of Parliament." Only Parliament had the legislative authority to enforce colonial union on the Crown's terms with no interference from the assemblies. Furthermore, Townshend believed the colonists were "more likely to accept such a . . . plan sent from hence in an act of Parliament than to form one in any meeting by their

[17] NYCD, 6:902.
[18] Hardwicke to Newcastle, August 25, 1754, BM, Add. Mss., 32736:340–42.

deputies or their assemblies." Indeed, Townshend thought a meeting of colonial commissioners unnecessary because the Board of Trade and Customs Office already had all the relevant information necessary for setting quotas for the common fund.[19] Two other commentators on the Board of Trade's plan favored parliamentary intervention. London merchant William Baker recommended that the ministry send four regiments of regular troops to America under a commander in chief and fund them by colonial taxes imposed by Parliament.[20] William Murray, a parliamentary ally of Newcastle's, found "the Objections to the Plan of Concert unanswerable" and suggested that the ministry follow Townshend's proposals.[21]

Townshend, Baker, and Murray were not reluctant to enlist Parliament in overriding the assemblies' resistance to colonial union. In this respect, they anticipated the Albany Plan's provision for parliamentary enactment. Still, the ministry failed to pursue this option as it responded to the crisis in America for two reasons. First, as Halifax noted in the Board of Trade's plan, enacting a union quickly would require minimizing objections from the colonists. Therefore, he believed it would be better to rely on traditional powers—the Crown's authority over military affairs—than to invoke new or untested ones that Parliament might claim over the colonies. Second, Newcastle's ministry was too weak to push such a measure through Parliament. The cabinet, therefore, chose the path of least resistance at home and in America. On September 26, several days before the Albany Plan arrived in London, it decided to send two Irish regiments to America and appointed General Edward Braddock the Crown's commander in chief there.[22]

The Albany Plan arrived in London about a week later. Because the ministry had already decided to send Braddock and the troops to America, it reacted to the Albany Plan without excitement or urgency. On first glance at the Albany Congress minutes, Secretary of State Thomas Robinson seemed genuinely surprised, calling the "whole Transaction . . . no less curious than Voluminous."[23] Board member Lord Dupplin questioned whether the Albany Plan "is to be looked upon as final, or [if] this plan is to be reconsidered by the Legislature of each Province."[24] Charles Townshend, who received a copy of the Albany Plan from an American friend,

[19] Townshend to Newcastle, September 13, 1754, ibid., 32736:508–9.
[20] Baker to Newcastle, October 1, 1754, ibid., 32737:16–21.
[21] Murray to Newcastle, October 6, 1754, ibid., 32737:45.
[22] See Hardwicke to Newcastle, September 27, 1754, ibid., 32736:583–84. This decision is explained in greater detail in Olson, "British Government and Colonial Union," 30–32, and Stanley M. Pargellis, *Lord Loudoun in North America* (New Haven, 1933), 26–35.
[23] Robinson to Newcastle, October 12, 1754, BM, Add. Mss., 37237:135–36.
[24] See "Lord Dupplin's Paper," [October 12, 1754], ibid., 33030:344–45. This document can be dated by a reference made in Robinson's letter to Newcastle of the same date, ibid., 37237:135–36.

found it "liable to many of those same objections" which he had made to the Board of Trade's plan a few weeks earlier, but he was pleased that it called for parliamentary-enacted union.[25]

Other than these first impressions, the ministers recorded little about their reactions to the Albany Plan. On October 26, Secretary of State Robinson wrote to the colonial governors instructing them to raise an intercolonial common fund "until such time, as a plan of general union . . . can be perfected."[26] Apparently the ministry was still interested in pursuing colonial union, but on October 29 the Board of Trade, without having heard anything about the plan's reception in the colonies, passed it along to the Privy Council without comment. Instead, the board's report on the Albany Congress focused on Indian affairs and urged the Crown to answer the Indians' complaints immediately, regardless of further deliberation on colonial union.[27]

As evidenced in its reaction to the Albany Plan, the ministry's interest in colonial union by autumn 1754 extended only so far as it sped mobilization for war and improved Indian relations in America. Since 1748 several reformers associated with colonial administration had recommended using Parliament to reduce the colonies to a standard model of government, but with the renewal of Anglo-French war, these impulses gave way to more practical considerations. Townshend and a few other commentators recommended seizing the moment to assert Parliament's legislative power over America, but the ministry chose instead to rely on a safer, less controversial course of action by sending a military commander in chief to America. In doing so, the Board of Trade let pass a golden opportunity for far-reaching colonial reform, but Halifax was nothing if not pragmatic. In drafting the board's plan of union, he anticipated the colonial assemblies' objections to the Albany Plan and correctly assumed that any parliamentary act enforcing colonial union would be perceived as a challenge to the colonial charters.

The Albany Plan in the Colonies

Although none of the commissioners at the Albany Congress held position in or influence with the ministry in London, all were either

---

[25] Townshend to Newcastle, October 7, 1754, ibid., 37237:57–58. Townshend received his copy of the Albany Plan from the same ship that carried the Albany Congress proceedings to London, but the Board of Trade did not record the receipt of those proceedings in its journal until October 24, 1754. See *Journal of the Commissioners for Trade and Plantations*, 14 vols. (London, 1920–38), 10:69–70.

[26] Thomas Robinson to the colonial governors, October 26, 1754, *NYCD*, 6:915–16.

[27] Board of Trade, "Representation to the King on the Proceedings of the Congress at Albany," October 29, 1754, ibid., 916–20.

councillors or assemblymen in their home governments and therefore were well placed to promote the Albany Plan in America. They uniformly failed to do so among their constituents and peers. Their pessimism about the plan testified to their familiarity with the colonists' steadfast suspicion of outside authority and jealous protection of their charters. In considering the Albany Plan, the assemblies defended a perspective on the empire that emphasized each colony's autonomous constitutional relationship with the Crown. They did not embrace Franklin's idea of forming several distinct polities into a North American dominion, and they treated the Albany Plan as a danger to colonial liberties.

The colonial governments responded to the Albany Plan in three ways: they ignored it, rejected it outright, or lingered over it while trying to devise a more desirable alternative. Five of the eleven colonies that received copies chose the first tactic. South Carolina had not sent commissioners to the Albany Congress and probably felt no obligation to review the plan. New Hampshire had, but its commissioners failed to act once they had returned home. Thus, in neither colony was the Albany Plan ever mentioned before the assembly. In New York, DeLancey delivered a speech to the assembly on August 20, emphasizing the need for colonial union and promising to submit the Albany Plan shortly. Two days later, the assembly referred to colonial union as "natural and salutary" but hedged on supporting any specific plan by adding that "these Principles . . . will not extend to an unlimited Sense."[28] Thereafter neither DeLancey nor the assembly addressed colonial union in any way more specific than to affirm its general utility. The Albany Plan, which would have deprived the New Yorkers of their dominance in colonial Indian affairs, died quickly and silently in their hands.

In North Carolina, the newly appointed royal governor Arthur Dobbs endorsed colonial union and called upon his new constituents to "shew that we are true Sons of Britain" by rallying to the Crown's cause in North America.[29] A few days later he submitted the Albany Plan to the assembly. Perhaps out of respect for Dobbs, the assembly referred the plan to its next session and ordered copies for its members. As in New York, however, it failed to take any subsequent action.[30] In Virginia the Albany Plan slipped by virtually unnoticed. Ever since the French occupation of the Ohio Valley, Governor Dinwiddie had been pleading anxiously with the ministry for a parliamentary-imposed colonial union. The Albany Plan incorporated many of his suggestions, including intercolonial taxation and the

---

[28] See reports on these speeches in *New-York Mercury*, August 26, September 2, 1754.
[29] See speech of Dobbs to North Carolina Assembly, December 18, 1754, in William L. Saunders, ed., *The Colonial Records of North Carolina*, 10 vols. (Raleigh, 1886), 5:224. Dobbs recommended the Albany Plan to the assembly on December 23, 1754. See ibid., 249.
[30] Ibid., xx–xxi, 251.

creation of a common fund.[31] Yet Dinwiddie treated the plan as he might a dying animal: an object worthy of curiosity but best observed from a distance. Writing to Pennsylvania governor James Hamilton in late July 1754, he called it "an extraordinary Piece" but refused fuller commentary "till I hear how it is received at Home."[32] A few weeks later he sent a copy to James Abercromby in London, asking that it not be circulated lest his handwriting be recognized.[33] Both comments indicate that Dinwiddie did not wish to proceed with the Albany Plan without first receiving the ministry's approval. When he heard no further word on its reception in London, he never bothered to submit it to his assembly.

In those colonies that took more definitive action on the Albany Plan, the most popular response was a summary rejection declaring it antithetical to colonial liberties. The first such response occurred in Pennsylvania, where Governor Hamilton recommended the plan to the assembly on August 8. Within a week the assembly dismissed it, refusing even to delay judgment until its next session.[34] Benjamin Franklin later complained of being embarrassed by the plan's fate in his home colony and blamed it on "a certain Member" who introduced the plan to the assembly during his absence.[35] The "certain Member" was most certainly the assembly's speaker and Franklin's fellow Albany Congress commissioner Isaac Norris. While at Albany Norris had voiced objections to the plan, and he later described it to a correspondent as a "dangerous Experiment."[36]

The Albany Plan fared just as poorly in New Jersey and Maryland. In Maryland, Governor Horatio Sharpe forwarded the plan to the assembly on December 21 with no comment. The assembly tabled the plan until the next session and then unanimously rejected it as "manifestly tending to the Destruction of the Rights and Liberties of his Majesty's Subjects within this Province." Explaining this decision to the governor, the assembly stated that the Albany Plan "would absolutely subvert that happy Form of Government we have a Right to by our Charter."[37] In New Jersey, the governor's council admitted the need for colonial union but declared the Albany Plan flawed because the Grand Council failed to represent "the Councils of

[31] For Dinwiddie's remarks on the need for union, see Dinwiddie to Halifax, May 10, July 24, 1754, and Dinwiddie to the Board of Trade, June 18, 1754, in *Dinwiddie Papers*, 3:162–63, 205–7, 250–52.
[32] Dinwiddie to Hamilton, July 31, 1754, ibid., 257.
[33] Dinwiddie to Abercromby, August 15, 1754, and Dinwiddie to Halifax, February 12, 1755, ibid., 284–87, 495–97.
[34] See *Penn. Council Minutes*, 6:135, and *Penn. Archives*, 8th ser., 5:3733.
[35] Farrand, *Franklin's Memoirs*, 330.
[36] Thomas Pownall commented on Norris's resistance to the plan at Albany. See McAnear, ed., "Personal Accounts," 744. For Norris's comment, see Norris to Robert Charles, October 7, 1754, Isaac Norris Letterbooks, Historical Society of Pennsylvania (microfilm, 1 reel), 55–58. See also Roger R. Trask, "Pennsylvania and the Albany Congress, 1754," *Pennsylvania History* 27 (1960): 273–90.
[37] See *Archives of Maryland*, 72 vols. (Baltimore, 1883–1972), 50:609–11, 52:56, 71–72.

the several Colonies." The assembly found in the plan only "things . . . which if carried into Practice would affect our Constitution in its very Vitals" and rejected it outright.[38]

In Rhode Island, Albany Congress commissioners Stephen Hopkins and Martin Howard Jr. presented their report to the assembly on August 20. The assembly accepted their report but reserved judgment on the Albany Plan until a later date.[39] It took no further action until a letter arrived from the colony's London agent Richard Partridge, requesting instructions on how to proceed should Parliament address colonial union in its next session. Suddenly the Albany Plan became controversial. In early 1755 Stephen Hopkins found himself criticized severely for his work as an Albany Congress commissioner, and he reacted by publishing *A True Representation of the Plan Formed at Albany*.[40] In this pamphlet Hopkins defended his conduct at Albany by distancing himself from the Albany Plan. He argued that the Board of Trade had intended for the commissioners to discuss colonial union and that he and Howard, "but two of the whole Number," had been powerless to affect the proceedings.[41] A writer using the pseudonym "Philolethes" responded with a scathing attack on Hopkins and the Albany Plan, which he claimed would "revoke all His Majesty's Governors' Commissions in North-America, and destroy every Charter, by erecting a Power above Law, over the several Legislatures."[42] In this spirit, the Rhode Island Assembly voted on March 6, 1755, to have its London agent oppose any Parliamentary action on colonial union that might "infringe on our charter privileges."[43] Although the assembly never formally rejected the Albany Plan, the tone of this debate reflected an overwhelming sentiment against it. Even Hopkins, who had sat on the committee that drafted the plan, chose to defend himself rather than the plan when countering criticism against it.

A third group of colonial governments rejected the Albany Plan but tried to devise alternatives. This reaction occurred in Connecticut and Massachusetts, the two colonies that had given their commissioners the greatest latitude to discuss union. Inhabitants in both colonies supported

---

[38] See *Archives of the State of New Jersey*, 1st ser., 42 vols. (Newark, 1880–1949), 16:488–89, 492.
[39] See John Russell Bartlett, ed., *Records of the Colony of Rhode Island and Providence Plantations, in New England*, 10 vols. (Providence, 1856–65), 5:393–94.
[40] Stephen Hopkins, *A True Representation of the Plan Formed at Albany for Uniting All the British Northern Colonies* (Providence, 1755). This pamphlet is reprinted in *Rhode Island Historical Tracts*, no. 9 (Providence, 1880), 3–46. Hopkins probably came under more criticism than Howard for his role as an Albany Congress commissioner because he sat on the committee that drafted the plan.
[41] Ibid., 42.
[42] Philolethes, *A Short Reply to Mr. Hopkins's Vindication, and False Reflections against the Governor and Council of the Colony of Rhode-Island* (Providence, 1755). This pamphlet is also reprinted in *Rhode Island Historical Tracts*, no. 9 (Providence, 1880), 47–65.
[43] Bartlett, ed., *Records of the Colony of Rhode Island*, 5:424.

colonial union because they shared exposed frontiers, a distaste for New York's management of Indian affairs, and past experience with the seventeenth-century confederation of New England colonies. Both colonies also held charters that differed significantly from the royal model of colonial government. Thus their debates over the Albany Plan illustrate the extent to which the colonists' concern for charter privileges impeded effective colonial union.

Like Rhode Island, Connecticut possessed a corporate charter that made it a virtually self-governed commonwealth. The only representatives of royal power in the colony were customs officers, who confined their business to collecting duties in port cities. At the Albany Congress, the Connecticut delegation had objected to the Plan of Union because they believed it granted too much power to the president general. When their home government debated the Albany Plan, similar opinions prevailed. In early October 1754, an assembly committee chaired by Albany Congress commissioner William Pitkin reported negatively on the Albany Plan, claiming that it was "subversive of the just rights and privileges" of the Crown's American subjects. The committee offered several reasons for this conclusion: the proposed union encompassed too much territory to be effectively administered; the colonial population was growing too quickly to be governed by a single royal officer; and the president general enjoyed too much prerogative power over the Grand Council and colonial military forces. Also, the taxing power granted to the Grand Council was "a very extraordinary thing" and a threat to colonial liberties.[44] The Connecticut Assembly accepted this report but did endorse two of the Albany Plan's goals: stricter regulation of the Indian trade and the establishment of new western settlements. The assembly closed its deliberations by resolving that "no application be made in behalf of this Colony to the Parliament of Great Britain for an act to form any such government."[45]

The same assembly committee that reviewed the Albany Plan drafted an alternative less contradictory to Connecticut's charter government. Two undated drafts of such a plan exist in the hand of the committee's secretary, Jonathan Trumbull. The text of both documents suggests that the Connecticut committee composed them to correct faults it found with the Albany Plan, while retaining the framework of an executive officer and Grand Council sharing powers over Indian affairs, western settlements, and frontier defenses. This alternative plan deviated from the Albany Plan in three important ways. First, it created a partial rather than general union, joining

[44] See "Report of a Committee," October 2, 1754, *Collections of the Connecticut Historical Society*, 17 (1918): 34–36.
[45] See "Reasons Concerning the Plan of Union," ibid., 37–42. The endorsement of new western settlements in all likelihood reflected the influence of Susquehannah Company shareholders in the assembly.

the New England colonies with New York.[46] Second, it changed the president general's office. The first, shorter draft of the alternative plan allowed the assemblies to elect the president general every three years; the revised version stated he would be the governor of Massachusetts "for The Time being."[47] The alternative plan also stripped the president general of his powers to nominate military officers and to veto acts of the Grand Council, making his office similar in this regard to that of Connecticut's governor. In a third major alteration, it removed the Grand Council's taxing power and left the individual assemblies in charge of raising the common fund. Overall, this alternative to the Albany Plan reinvented the seventeenth-century confederation between New England colonies, adding to it new colonies, proportional representation, and an executive officer.[48] By eliminating the Grand Council's taxing power and the Crown-appointed president general, it resolved the contradictions between colonial union and Connecticut's charter government. Despite such advantages, the committee never submitted this plan to the Connecticut Assembly, perhaps because it had not been instructed to draft an alternative.[49]

The Albany Plan faced its best prospects in Massachusetts. Governor Shirley supported colonial union, and the colony's delegation had been instructed to enter into one at the Albany Congress. In fact, upon returning home, the Massachusetts commissioners apologized for not having completed a union at Albany, explaining that "the insufficiency of the powers from several of the Governments had rendered it impracticable."[50] On October 18, Shirley recommended the Albany Plan to the Massachusetts General Court. Four days later the assembly and council appointed a joint committee to review it.[51] As happened in Rhode Island, the Albany Plan fell into the assembly's backlog of business until the colony's agent, William Bollan, requested instructions for the upcoming parliamentary session. Spurred into action, the joint committee reported on December 4: while it supported the idea of a parliamentary-enacted union, the Albany Plan was "so extensive" as to "impede if not totally prevent the main design aimed at." The committee recommended instructing Bollan to "prevent any procedure" upon the Albany Plan until further notice. The Massachusetts council accepted this report and ordered the committee to come

---

[46] The longer version of the alternative plan added New Jersey to this total. It also suggested forming a union of the southern colonies on the same plan. See ibid., 20, 24.

[47] Ibid., 20.

[48] The articles of the seventeenth-century New England Confederation are reprinted in Ward, *United Colonies of New England*, 384–97.

[49] It is also possible that Trumbull composed the alternative plan privately and did not submit it to the committee.

[50] Report of Massachusetts Commissioners to Governor Shirley, [October 25, 1754], Mass. Archives, 4:464.

[51] Ibid., 472, and Gipson, *The British Empire before the American Revolution*, 5:150–51.

up with an alternative, adding Thomas Hutchinson and Benjamin Lynde to its membership.[52]

At the Albany Congress, the Massachusetts delegation had wanted to divide the colonies into northern and southern unions.[53] Hutchinson acted on that preference in drafting an alternative, which the joint committee presented on December 11. The new intercolonial body, "to be styled, The Grand Court of the five united Colonies," would have proportional representation from Massachusetts, New York, New Hampshire, Connecticut, and Rhode Island. The Crown would select and pay its president, while the assemblies would choose the representatives. The Grand Court possessed no taxation power; instead, each colony would contribute to the common fund as it saw fit. The union would remain in effect for six years but could be prolonged if Great Britain and France were at war at the end of that time. The joint committee suggested that Bollan submit this plan to Parliament and encourage a similar one for the southern colonies.[54]

Like the alternative devised in Connecticut, this plan altered the Albany Plan to make it more consistent with New England's experience and preferences in colonial union. In the most important deviation, it turned the Albany Plan's general and permanent union into a partial and temporary one. Parliament might create a new intermediary level of colonial government, but after six years, it would expire and the assemblies would resume their old autonomy. The Massachusetts committee also eliminated the controversial taxing power and jurisdiction over western lands that the Albany Plan gave the Grand Council. The committee's plan, like the Connecticut alternative, updated the old New England confederation and extended it to New York so that the New Englanders might finally break that colony's hold over the Covenant Chain.

On December 14, the Massachusetts Assembly formally rejected the Albany Plan but also expressed dissatisfaction with the idea of partial union. In another vote, it sent a reconstituted committee back to the drawing board to devise a plan for a general union. The council later agreed with this measure and added several members, including Thomas Hutchinson, to the committee.[55] The committee responded with a scheme that followed the Albany Plan very closely, including its provisions for parliamentary enactment and intercolonial taxation. It made some minor alterations in regulating the Indian trade, eliminated intercolonial jurisdiction over western lands, and retained the six-year limit on the union's duration. It was a temporary version of the Albany Plan, a wartime exigency rather

<hr />

[52] Mass. Archives, 6:169–69a.
[53] Ibid., 4:464.
[54] Ibid., 6:176–79.
[55] Ibid., 4:473, 6:176a. Also see Albert Bushnell Hart, ed., *The Commonwealth History of Massachusetts*, 3 vols. (New York, 1927–29), 2:460.

than a thoroughgoing reform of the imperial constitution.[56] The General Court never gave this alternative a hearing. The committee presented it on December 26, and a day later the assembly voted to suspend its deliberations on colonial union until members consulted with their constituents. On December 28, the council urged the assembly to come to a conclusion so that firmer instructions could be sent to Bollan in London. Three days later the colony's secretary drafted a letter informing Bollan that the General Court had rejected the Albany Plan because of its perpetuity, the "great sway" it gave to the southern colonies in the Grand Council, and its inconsistency with "the fundamental rights of these Colonies."[57]

The Albany Plan's prolonged ordeal in Massachusetts ended on January 17, 1755, at a Boston town meeting. After a day-long debate, the townspeople instructed their representatives to oppose any plan of union by which "the Liberties and Priviledges of the People are endangered."[58] It was at this meeting that William Clarke heard the Albany Congress commissioners described as "arrant Blockheads." Clarke later apologized to Franklin for not having spoken more forcefully on the Albany Plan's behalf, but the opposition was so strong the vote passed "by a very great Majority." He also noted the failure of one person "upon whom there was great dependence," probably Hutchinson, to defend the plan as vigorously as expected.[59] After such a resounding defeat, neither the Albany Plan nor any alternative plans for colonial union came before the Massachuetts General Court.

Several threads run throughout the Albany Plan's ignominious treatment by the colonial governments; tied together, they suggest how the colonists defined their connection to the rest of the empire and to each other at this time. Some colonists felt that the Albany Plan threatened distinct local interests that they were not willing to surrender for the good of the whole. They simply did not feel sufficiently attached to other British subjects in North America to forgo local control over Indian affairs and western lands. New York let the plan die quietly because neither the governor nor the assembly wished to surrender the Covenant Chain to intercolonial supervision. Colonies with undefined western borders, such as Virginia, preferred to pursue their own agendas concerning western lands rather than cooperate with others. And those colonies without royal governments—Pennsylvania, Maryland, Connecticut, and Rhode Island—did not wish to see a royally appointed president general exercising powers that their charters denied their own governors.

[56] Mass. Archives, 6:171–75.
[57] Ibid., 181, and Hart, ed., Commonwealth History of Massachusetts, 2:461–62.
[58] Hart, ed., Commonwealth History of Massachusetts, 2:463.
[59] Clarke to Franklin, February 3, 1755, BF Papers, 5:490–91.

Most interesting is the almost universal reaction in the colonies, regardless of their particular type of government, against the Albany Plan because it threatened colonial liberties. Different assemblies used different rhetoric, but the import was the same: Bostonians declared that the plan endangered their "Liberties and Priviledges," Rhode Islanders worried about infringements "on our charter privileges," Marylanders believed it tended toward "the Destruction of the Rights and Liberties of his Majesty's Subjects within this Province," and so on. No one was especially specific about the rights, liberties, and privileges that the Albany Plan would destroy, although the alternatives derived in Connecticut and Massachusetts indicate reservations about intercolonial taxation, perpetual union, and the extension of prerogative powers. The assemblies in both of these colonies seemed more comfortable with the idea of partial, temporary unions that would not challenge the autonomy or durability of existing colonial governments. The Albany Plan appealed to Parliament to do exactly that by creating a new, permanent intercolonial government that would rebalance prerogative and popular power in North America. The colonists were no more ready for this innovation than the ministry was. In rejecting the Albany Plan, they clung tightly to a conception of empire in which individual colonies governed themselves according to particular constitutional connections to an imperial Crown, not a single, imperial legislature.

Indians and the Empire

The most important ramifications of the Albany Congress were felt in Anglo-Iroquois relations. Shortly after arriving in America in spring 1755, General Braddock commissioned William Johnson as his agent to the Six Nations. The following year, the Crown created northern and southern Indian superintendencies for the colonies, appointing Johnson to the former and South Carolina merchant Edmond Atkin to the latter. For the first time, the Crown employed its own agents to treat with the Indians, regulate the fur trade, and purchase western lands and prohibited the colonial governments from doing so on their own. In short, the Crown "imperialized" Indian affairs in America, taking them out of the hands of local agents such as the Albany Commissioners of Indian Affairs and vesting them in royal officials working expressly to extend British dominion in North America.[60]

The creation of the Indian superintendencies was one of the few unquestioned achievements of the imperial reformers who had been pushing for

[60] On the imperialization of the Covenant Chain, see Francis Jennings, "Iroquois Alliances in American History," in *History and Culture of Iroquois Diplomacy*, ed. Jennings et al., 52–59.

the expansion of prerogative powers in America since 1748.[61] All aspects of the reformist agenda came together in this new royal office, which eliminated colonial autonomy in Indian affairs and regulated the fur trade for imperial rather than commercial ends. The superintendencies also assisted the reformers in their efforts to turn the Indians from independent allies into dependent subjects. Of course, this task was not quickly or easily completed, but starting during the Seven Years' War, the Indian superintendents made a concerted effort to incorporate the Indians into their vision of an expansive, multiracial empire in which all of Britannia's Americans were duly subordinate to the Crown.[62]

Was this what the Mohawks had wanted when they called for Johnson's reinstatement as their agent at the Albany Congress? Hendrick, it should be remembered, engaged in imperial diplomacy for local reasons: to preserve his village's economic and territorial integrity. Johnson was an indispensable ally because of the material goods he supplied to Canajoharie. His elevation to royal office did represent a victory for the Mohawks, but one that also changed the rules of the game they had been playing. When Johnson's imperial agency replaced the independent diplomacy of different competing colonies, the Mohawks gained presents but lost leverage. The alternative paths Hendrick had been cultivating since the 1740s became under Johnson's regime a one-way road leading to even greater material dependence on the British Crown.

When the Board of Trade reported on the Albany Congress to the Privy Council, it made the Covenant Chain, not colonial union, the most pressing order of business. It endorsed the colonial commissioners' recommendation that Indian affairs should no longer be "intrusted to the [Albany] Commissioners, nor even to the Assemblies of any one Province, whereby they may be directed to their own particular local purposes, but that they should be under one general Administration directed to the general interest and supported at the general expense of the whole." The board repeated the complaints recorded in the Albany Congress minutes against the Albany Commissioners of Indian Affairs: they operated solely for the sake of their pocketbooks, no supervisory power existed to make sure they served the Crown's interest, they cheated Indians out of goods and land, and they conducted negotiations with the Indians "more for the sake of the private interest and convenience of the traders than theirs [the Indians']."[63]

---

[61] See Alden, "The Albany Congress and the Creation of the Indian Superintendencies."
[62] In this section, I will concentrate on William Johnson and the northern Indian superintendency. The development of the southern superintendency along very similar lines is described in Snapp, *John Stuart and the Struggle for Empire.*
[63] See "Representation to the King on the Proceedings of the Congress at Albany," October 29, 1754, *NYCD,* 6:917–18.

The board urged the Crown to take immediate action to placate the Indians. Specifically, "Colonel Johnson should be appointed Colonel over the Six Nations," serving the Crown in the same manner that he had served Governor Clinton during King George's War. His duties would include "the disposition and application of all occasional presents Your Majesty may think proper to make to these Indians, with the nomination and appointment of all such smiths and other artificers as may be thought proper to be settled amongst them, and in general [to have] the direction of all other services not already provided for by the laws of New York." Here was the embryo of the Indian superintendencies, a royal officer who would act as the Crown's direct agent to the Indians, distributing presents on its behalf and managing all other agents or services necessary to preserve the Indians' alliance.[64] The board was quite specific in its reasons for recommending Johnson. It noted his success in recruiting Mohawk allies during the last war, as well as "the connexions he has formed by living amongst them, and habituating himself to their manners and customs." Most important were the words of the Indians themselves, the friendship and confidence they had expressed in him at the Albany Congress, "and above all the request they make that the sole management of their affairs may be intrusted to him."[65] The partnership Johnson and Hendrick had begun ten years earlier and executed so brilliantly at the Albany Congress came to fruition in this sentence.

Johnson's commission from Braddock also commanded all persons previously involved in Covenant Chain diplomacy to "cease and forbear acting or intermeddling therein."[66] This order abruptly dissolved the Albany Commissioners of Indian Affairs, who had continued to transact their business despite the lashing they had received at the Albany Congress. After that meeting, they wrote to Governor DeLancey assuring him that "What Evir Hendrick said of us, at the last Treaty with Your Honour is Intirely falls [false]" and that he had "Never Applied to this Board for Any thing."[67] They prepared for the oncoming war in their usual manner, petitioning the governor to improve Albany's defenses and renewing their friendship with the French-allied Caughnawagas to the north.[68] But it was exactly this type of neutralist diplomacy that the Crown was no longer willing to tolerate. To signal the Crown's rejection of the Albany commis-

[64] Ibid., 6:919. See also Alden, "The Albany Congress and the Indian Superintendencies," 203–7.
[65] NYCD, 6:919.
[66] For Johnson's commission from Braddock, see Loudoun Papers, LO 566, and WJ Papers, 1:465–66. For the primary role the Albany Congress played in Johnson's appointment, see Alden, "The Albany Congress and the Creation of the Indian Superintendencies."
[67] Albany Commissioners of Indian Affairs to DeLancey, September 5, 1754, NY Col. Mss., 79:23.
[68] Ibid., 10, 33, 46–47; 80:4a.

sioners, Johnson held a conference at his home in June 1755, almost one year to the day after the Albany Congress had convened. More than eleven hundred Indian men, women, and children attended.[69] In his opening speech, Johnson ended Albany's tenure as the site of intercolonial treaty-making by lighting a fire and stating, "I do Brethren . . . remove the Embers which remained at Albany and rekindle the Fire of Council and Friendship at this Place."[70] The council fire of the Covenant Chain remained at Johnson's home until his death twenty years later.

With Johnson installed as the Crown's sole agent to the Iroquois, the Mohawks lost the ability to play several diplomatic hands at once. For example, before Johnson's appointment, Pennsylvania's new governor Robert Hunter Morris invited Hendrick to Philadelphia to confirm the land deed Penn and Peters had negotiated at the Albany Congress. This invitation marked the Mohawks' long-sought admittance to Pennsylvania's Indian diplomacy. Hendrick and several other Mohawks arrived in Philadelphia on January 7, 1755, and enjoyed the governor's hospitality for two weeks. Hendrick agreed that the Susquehannah Company's deed "should be destroyed" and then tactfully avoided any further responsibility by telling the Pennsylvanians to make their case before the Iroquois nations in Onondaga.[71] Judging from his speeches, Hendrick had not come to Philadelphia to talk about real estate; he wanted to bring additional pressure to bear on the Albany Commissioners of Indian Affairs, who at this point remained in place against his wishes. Hendrick reintroduced the subject of Albany's neglect before the Pennsylvanians and asked them to intercede on the Mohawks' behalf. Anxious for the Mohawks to confirm the Pennsylvanians' land purchase at the Albany Congress, Morris promised to do his best.[72]

Johnson's appointment as the Crown's Indian agent a few months later foreclosed any such diplomacy. The Mohawks were Johnson's closest neighbors and oldest allies, and they benefited from his ascendancy to royal favor, but at a price. During King George's War, Johnson had served as a local agent of the New York governor, whose chief concern was keeping the Mohawks happy. As the Crown's agent in the Seven Years' War and after, Johnson conducted diplomacy far afield of the Mohawk Valley. His primary concerns after 1756 involved recruiting and retaining the support of Indians in western Iroquoia, the Ohio country, and the Upper Great Lakes: Senecas, Shawnees, Delawares, Wyandots, Twightwees, Hurons, and Ottawas, all well beyond the Mohawks' influence. As the geographic scope of Johnson's agency expanded, the Mohawks' signif-

[69] For the minutes of this treaty, see NYCD, 6:964–89.
[70] Ibid., 965.
[71] For materials on the conference, see Penn. Council Minutes, 6:243–93.
[72] Ibid., 281–82, 285–86.

icance in it shrank, and they found themselves more dependent on his good graces than he was on theirs. They continued to attend diplomatic conferences in New York and Pennsylvania but mostly as members of Johnson's entourage, often outnumbered and overshadowed by the other Indians present. Johnson encouraged this transformation, and the Mohawks became part of his "official family": the constellation of tenants, retainers, agents, and other dependents who constantly crowded his home, attended him at public councils, joined his war parties, and sought his patronage.[73]

The Mohawks' and Johnson's new positions relative to each other and the British Empire became apparent at the Battle of Lake George in September 1755. Johnson had recruited many Mohawk warriors to join an expedition he commanded against the French post Fort St. Frédéric on Lake Champlain. Before moving north, Johnson's army encamped at the southern end of Lake St. Sacrament to fortify the passage to Albany. Here Johnson renamed the lake Lake George "in honour of His Majesty" and to "assertain his undoubted dominion here."[74] During a surprise engagement with French forces on September 8, Hendrick and about forty other Indians were killed. Johnson, who received a minor wound, fared much better. For his part in the only battle that could be construed as a British victory during the disastrous campaigns of 1755, the Crown and Parliament awarded him a baronetcy, £5,000 sterling, and a new commission to serve as Indian superintendent of the northern colonies with a £600 annual salary.[75]

In death, Hendrick became an icon of the British imperial endeavor in North America. The *Gentleman's Magazine* retold the story of his fall at the Battle of Lake George, and several prints appeared in London commemorating his service to the Crown.[76] Most interesting of all was a descriptive map published by act of Parliament in London in 1756, detailing the battle (Fig. 7.1). In it, the Indian figures are dark-skinned and naked except for breechclouts; they appear in crouched postures, some firing

---

[73] For Johnson's career as a feudal lord, see John C. Guzzardo, "Sir William Johnson's Official Family: Patron and Clients in an Anglo-American Empire" (Ph.D. dissertation, Syracuse University, 1975). A thorough, scholarly biography of Johnson taking into account his roles as an Indian agent and landlord remains to be written. Milton Hamilton reviews Johnson's career up to 1763 in *Sir William Johnson*, and James Thomas Flexner's *Mohawk Baronet* remains the most popular, but now dated, full-length biography. On Johnson's diplomacy with the western Indians after 1756, see Jon William Parmenter, "Pontiac's War: Forging New Links in the Anglo-Iroquois Convenant Chain, 1758–1766," *Ethnohistory* 44(1997): 617–54.

[74] Johnson to the Board of Trade, September 3, 1755, *NYCD*, 6:997.

[75] For reports on the Battle of Lake George and Hendrick's death, see ibid., 1003–4, 1006–9. For Johnson's rewards, see ibid., 1020, and *WJ Papers*, 2:434–35, 448–51, 508–10. A good overview of the Battle of Lake George from Indian, British, and French perspectives is provided in Steele, *Betrayals*, 28–56.

[76] See Hinderaker, "'Four Indian Kings,'" 523–24.

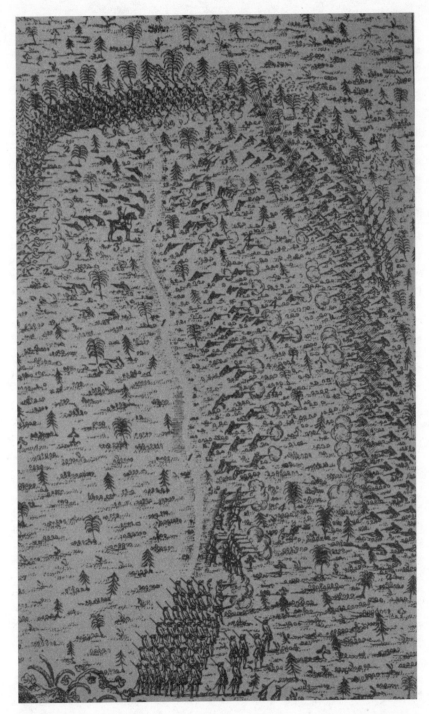

Figure 7.1. *A Prospective View of the Battle fought near Lake George* . . . , T. Jefferys, sculptor, and Samuel Blodget, delineator (London, 1756), detail showing Hendrick on horseback. Courtesy of the New York State Library.

from behind trees, others raising tomahawks above their heads. The European soldiers are light-skinned and uniformed, upright and marching in formation, except for those firing from behind barricades. The juxtaposition of skulking Indians and regimented troops established a clear dichotomy between native savagery and European civility for London readers studying this distant theater of war. Among these figures, Hendrick is singular, appearing on horseback in a long coat and cocked hat. The map's legend identifies him as "*Hendrick*, the *Indian Chief*, or *King* of the *Six Nations*, who was dressed after the *English* manner." The legend further explains that "He only was on *Horse-back*, because he only could not well travel on Foot, being somewhat corpulent as well as old. He fell in this Fight to the great Enragement of the *Indians*, and our loss; as he was a very good Friend to the *English*."[77]

Hendrick, in short, appears as one of Britannia's Americans: a hybrid of Indian and European identities on the fringe of the empire, an old Indian warrior but also a rotund British officer leading his men into battle. This was a comforting image of the British imperial mission to present to a home audience anxious to visualize a dominion they were fighting for across an ocean. Embodied in the figure of Hendrick, Indians were dependent and loyal, and the extension of imperial dominion over them became appealing rather than distasteful. As the posthumous celebration of Hendrick in London suggests, the more violent dimensions of empire building could be softened for home audiences with such images of distant savages exhibiting the same bravery and martial glory that Britons ascribed to themselves.

The Diverging Paths of Empire

Before 1754, Benjamin Franklin and Massachusetts governor William Shirley had been the most important promoters of colonial union in America. Five months after the Albany Congress they engaged in a brief correspondence that illustrated how quickly provincial and imperial perspectives on the empire diverged in its wake. Shirley dismissed the Albany Plan because he believed it encouraged the same inclination toward self-government that already made the colonies difficult to rule, and he recommended instead a union premised on extending the royal prerogative in America. Franklin wrote about union in distinctly different terms, emphasizing the constitutional privileges and filial bonds that the colonists shared with other British subjects and their need to develop a shared,

---

[77] *A Prospective View of the Battle Fought Near Lake George, on the 8th of Sept. 1755, between 2000 English, with 250 Mohawks, under the Command of General Johnson and 2500 French and Indians . . .*, T. Jefferys, sculp., and Samuel Blodget, delin. (London, 1756).

transatlantic identity as a single people. Their exchange foreshadowed the constitutional dispute over the Anglo-American connection that would split the empire apart after 1763.

Shirley had been an advocate of colonial union as well as one of the Crown's staunchest imperialists in North America since 1745. Of all the colonial governors, he had responded most enthusiastically to the Board of Trade's call for the Albany Congress. Initially, his reaction to the Albany Plan was positive. He endorsed it before the Massachusetts General Court in October 1754. In that same month he also advised Pennsylvania's new governor to support the plan, for "It would ease you of a great part of the burthen, your Government may probably bring upon you otherwise, in the management of Military and Indian Affairs."[78] Between late October and early December Shirley's enthusiasm waned. He did not contribute to the General Court's deliberations on the Albany Plan, probably because he did not wish to expend political capital defending it once popular opposition became obvious.[79]

Nevertheless, Shirley remained committed to the idea of colonial union. The commissioners at Albany had failed to create a union "for want of sufficient powers," he explained to a London correspondent, but they had "pav'd the way clearly for His Majestys ordering a plan of an Union to be form'd at home, and the execution of it inforc'd here by Act of Parliament." Shirley read the Albany Plan as an open invitation for the Crown to proceed with forming a union on its own terms, and he took this cue to formulate his own alternative to the Albany Plan.[80] He left no written evidence of this scheme, but it may be reconstructed from later comments by Thomas Hutchinson and Benjamin Franklin. Shirley wanted the Crown to appoint an American commander in chief with access to an intercolonial treasury. He disliked the Albany Plan's provision for an intercolonial legislature, which he suspected would be just as uncooperative as the individual assemblies in obeying the Crown's orders. Instead, Shirley believed that the colonial governors and a select few of their councillors should estimate costs for conducting military and Indian affairs. The commander in chief could then draw on the British Treasury for the appropriate amounts, and Parliament would levy colonial taxes to reimburse it. By this method, the commander in chief could bypass the assemblies when he needed to raise funds.[81] Shirley communicated these pro-

[78] Shirley to Robert Hunter Morris, October 21, 1754, WS Correspondence, 2:96.
[79] Thomas Hutchinson suggested this explanation for Shirley's silence in History of the Colony and Province of Massachusetts-Bay, 3:18.
[80] Shirley to Secretary of State Thomas Robinson, December 24, 1754, NYCD, 6:930–33.
[81] Shirley's plan can be pieced together from references in Farrand, Franklin's Memoirs, 326–28, and Hutchinson, History of the Colony and Province of Massachusetts-Bay, 3:17. Also, Shirley's December 24, 1754, letter to Thomas Robinson is important for the criticisms it levies against the Albany Plan. See NYCD, 6:930–33. The editors of BF Papers suggest that Shirley may have

posals to Franklin in early December 1754, and Franklin responded in three letters.[82]

Franklin's criticisms of Shirley's plan reveal his provincial state of mind: although anxious to promote Anglo-American union, he was just as quick to assert the colonists' consitutional liberties as British subjects. He took issue with junking the Albany Plan's intercolonial legislature for an advisory body of governors and councillors, most of whom were royally appointed and would be inclined to enrich themselves through unnecessary borrowing from the British Treasury. Furthermore, Franklin predicted that the colonists would resist taxation by a Parliament in which they had no representation. Such a policy "would be rather like raising Contributions in an Enemy's Country, than taxing of Englishmen for their own publick Benefit. . . . It would be treating them as a conquer'd People, and not as true British Subjects."[83]

Treating the Crown's American subjects as "a conquer'd People" living in "an Enemy's Country" violated Franklin's sense of provincial equality. The colonists were Britons who had settled a foreign land at their own expense; certainly they deserved better than the second-class status implied by Shirley's plan. Franklin defended this position with two arguments. First, all subjects, regardless of their location, should share in the burden of the empire's protection: "the Frontiers of an Empire are properly defended at the joint Expence of the Body of People in such Empire."[84] Hence, placing the entire expense of the North American war on the colonists' shoulders was inequitable. Second, the colonists had a right as British subjects to no taxation without representation. No one would recognize the legality of taxing the inhabitants of Britain's seacoasts to fund the navy while denying them parliamentary representation. How, then, could Parliament tax British Americans for their defense without allowing them similar representation? Shirley's plan, Franklin concluded, would convince the colonists "that by hazarding their Lives and Fortunes in subduing and settling new Countries . . . they have forfeited the native Rights of Britons."[85]

In his third letter commenting on Shirley's plan, Franklin offered a hypothetical scenario to explain the equality of subjecthood he was claiming

been discussing the Board of Trade's plan of union in his correspondence with Franklin, but the differences between that plan and the proposals outlined by Franklin and Hutchinson are so great as to argue convincingly for the original composition of a plan by Shirley. See *BF Papers*, 5:442. Also, in a letter to Shirley dated December 3, 1754, Franklin refers to returning "the loose sheets of the plan, with thanks to your Excellency for communicating them," suggesting that at some point Shirley had committed his thoughts to paper. See ibid., 443.
[82] Franklin responded in letters written December 3, 4, and 22, 1754. See *BF Papers*, 5:443–47, 449–51.
[83] Ibid., 443–45.
[84] Ibid., 445–46.
[85] Ibid., 446–47.

for American colonists. He asked Shirley to imagine a partial drying of the English Channel which resulted in a substantial addition of new territory to the island of Britain. What if British subjects settled this land? How would their relation to the rest of the empire change? "Would it be right," Franklin asked, "to deprive such Inhabitants of the common privileges enjoyed by other Englishmen?" Such discrimination would be absurd, a slap in the face to those Britons who by undertaking new settlements increased the nation's trade, wealth, and population. Such was the position of the American colonies, whom Franklin looked upon as "so many Counties gained to Great Britain."[86] Not since Columbus miscalculated the distance to Cathay had the Atlantic been so small! By this argument, Franklin shrank the ocean to an insignificant interruption between the Crown's British and American subjects, a geographic barrier that in no way implied a different degree of dependence for those living on its American side.

Franklin and Shirley obviously disagreed on the methods for achieving colonial union, but they did share common ground on one position: admitting American representatives to Parliament. When Franklin expressed his reservations about parliamentary taxation of colonists, Shirley suggested admitting American representatives to Parliament as an alternative to the intercolonial legislature proposed in the Albany Plan. Franklin welcomed this proposal, with some conditions. First, the colonies would need to have "a reasonable number of Representatives allowed them." Second, "all the old Acts of Parliament restraining the trade or cramping the manufactures of the Colonies" would have to be repealed at the time Americans were admitted to Parliament so that "the British subjects on this side the water [would be] put, in those respects, on the same footing as those in Great Britain." Once the reconstituted Parliament convened, it could then consider which of the old Navigation Acts to revive for the good of the empire. Franklin did not say how many American representatives would be adequate. He confessed that he did not think they would be so many as "to have any great weight by their numbers." Rather than preventing the reimposition of the Navigation Acts, he expected the American representatives to enlighten their fellow members of Parliament about the true state of the colonies, enabling them to make policy that would benefit the entire empire instead of any "private interest" or "petty corporation" in Britain.[87]

Franklin's willingness to embrace the idea of an American representation in Parliament grew naturally out of his concern for preserving the Anglo-American connection. That same concern had produced the Albany Plan, which, by creating an intercolonial legislature and a royal president general, had imitated Ireland's constitutional relationship to Great Britain.

[86] Ibid., 450–51.
[87] Ibid., 449.

Six months later, when the Albany Plan was a dead letter, Franklin rethought the imperial connection in terms of the Scottish model. The American colonies had no preexisting intercolonial legislative body comparable to the Scottish parliament, but Franklin's terms for admitting American representatives to Parliament were essentially those of the Anglo-Scottish union of 1707. In return for seats in Parliament, the Americans would submit to its legislative authority, including taxation. The British government would suspend all discriminatory commercial legislation against the colonies until the new Parliament could reconsider such policy with the advice of its American members.

Franklin also expected an Anglo-American parliamentary union to strengthen the affective bond between Great Britain and the colonies. He wrote to Shirley, "I should hope too, that by such a union, the people of Great Britain and the people of the Colonies would learn to consider themselves, not as belonging to different Communities with different Interests, but to one Community with one Interest, which I imagine would contribute to strengthen the whole, and greatly lessen the danger of future separations."[88] A few months earlier he used almost exactly the same language to describe the benefits of the Albany Plan: by cooperating in their defense and government, the colonies would "learn to consider themselves, not as so many independent states, but as members of the same body."[89] For Franklin the differences between the Albany Plan and an Anglo-American parliamentary union were secondary to the end he expected both to achieve: awakening Britons to the consanguinity and mutual interests that united them throughout the empire.

Shirley exhibited little patience for Franklin's imagined British-Atlantic community. Instead, in a letter to Secretary of State Thomas Robinson, he used his correspondence with Franklin as a springboard for explaining his objections to the Albany Plan.[90] Whereas Franklin had defended the Grand Council as necessary to protect the colonists' liberties, Shirley believed it would seriously intrude on the Crown's prerogative powers in America. As for Franklin's argument that the Crown held one-half of the power in the proposed intercolonial government, Shirley noted that the president general's veto power over the Grand Council "is only a *Negative* one, stripped of every branch of the prerogative, and is at best only a preventative power in a small degree."[91] When he compared the Albany Plan to models of colonial government already in existence, Shirley found that it resembled the corporate colonies more closely than the royal ones.

[88] Ibid., 449–50.
[89] Ibid., 402.
[90] *NYCD*, 6:931–33. In this letter, Shirley cites the arguments of "a gentleman who had a principle hand in forming the Albany Plan," an obvious reference to his correspondence with Franklin.
[91] Ibid., 933.

The president general would be a weak executive dependent on the Grand Council in the same way that the governors of Rhode Island and Connecticut were captives of their assemblies. Shirley reminded Robinson of the reputation each of those colonies had for resisting royal authority. "If the old Charter form of government . . . is unfitt for ruling a particular colony," he concluded, "it seems much more improper for establishing a General Government and *Imperium* over all the Colonies to be compriz'd in the Union."[92]

Franklin spoke of the empire as "one Community with one Interest"; Shirley described it as an "*Imperium*," a word Thomas Pownall had defined as "Modelling the People into various Orders, and Subordinations of Orders . . . and acting under that direction as a one Whole."[93] Franklin invoked an image of empire that was egalitarian and filial: all Britons sharing common rights and a common identity. Shirley, on the other hand, expected Anglo-American union to establish a uniform quality of colonial dependence, to strengthen the hierarchies of authority and dependence that held the *imperium* together.

The divergence in Franklin's and Shirley's visions for the future of British North America became more apparent after the Seven Years' War. During his residence in London as a colonial agent in the 1760s, Franklin increased his provincial assertiveness but retreated from his advocacy of an act of Anglo-American union. Significantly, he abandoned the idea of admitting American representatives to Parliament when it became clear to him that they would have no influence there. Instead, he embraced the argument that had helped defeat the Albany Plan in America: each colony possessed a distinct, inviolable constitutional relationship to the Crown and each assembly functioned as a miniature parliament.[94] As a patriot, Franklin distanced himself from schemes to settle the imperial constitution and insisted that provincial liberties were best protected if the mother country regarded each colony as a separate dominion. In 1774, Franklin's friend Joseph Galloway introduced a revised version of the Albany Plan to

---

[92] Ibid., 932.

[93] Thomas Pownall, *The Principles of Polity, Being the Grounds and Reasons of Civil Empire* (London, 1752), 93. On *imperium* and its eighteenth-century English meanings, see Koebner, *Empire*, 1–17, 85–104.

[94] See Crane, ed., *Benjamin Franklin's Letters to the Press*, 46–49, 57–59, 110–12, 134–38. Also see Crane, *Benjamin Franklin: Englishman and American* (Baltimore, 1936), 72–139, and Greene, "Pride, Prejudice, and Jealousy," 119–41. Franklin's reversal on the topic of American representation in Parliament did not escape the notice of his former Albany Congress commissioner Thomas Hutchinson. In the 1770s, Hutchinson observed that in 1754, Franklin had favored "a more intimate union with Great Britain by representatives in parliament." Fifteen years later, however, he "departed from his principles, and declared . . . that he was of opinion, Britain and the colonies were under separate legislatures, and stood related as England and Scotland stood before the union [of 1707]." See Hutchinson, *History of the Colony and Province of Massachusetts-Bay*, 3:18.

the First Continental Congress as a means of preserving Anglo-American union. Franklin responded pessimistically to the proposal because he could not "but apprehend more Mischief than Benefit from a closer Union" with Britain.[95]

Shirley's political fortunes experienced an abrupt reversal during the Seven Years' War, but his vision of the British Empire's future in North America did not. The war in North America placed new demands on the empire and caused the Crown to become less tolerant of local autonomy in colonial government. Centralized prerogative power of the kind Shirley had endorsed when discussing colonial union found its way into imperial administration after 1755 through the creation of the royal Indian superintendencies and a third secretary of state for the colonies, the retention of a commander in chief and regular army in North America after 1763, and the establishment of a colonial government for Canada that did not include a representative assembly. Shirley's *imperium*, a conglomeration of conquered territories inhabited by a variety of races and ethnicities subordinate to the Crown, had become reality in North America by the outbreak of the American Revolution.[96]

Ever since Franklin recorded his recollections of the Albany Congress in his memoirs, historians have equated that meeting with the origins of American independence. More recently, a popular interpretation with weak scholarly support has held that the Albany Congress provided the occasion for colonial statesmen to learn principles of democracy and federation from the Iroquois. Both interpretations are erroneous. The Albany Congress facilitated empire building, not state-making, in North America. It is a story about expanding imperial power challenging the local autonomy of villages, towns, and colonies and about colonists and Indians trying to manipulate that power to their own advantage. We will have a better understanding of the Albany Congress's place in American history when we stop using it to conjure images of common constitutional foundations between the Iroquois and the United States and instead use it to recognize the colonists' and Indians' shared experiences within Britain's eighteenth-century empire. The centralization of Indian trade and diplo-

---

[95] See Franklin to Galloway, February 25, 1775, *BF Papers*, 21:509, and Julian P. Boyd, *Anglo-American Union: Joseph Galloway's Plans to Preserve the British Empire, 1774–1788* (New York, 1970).
[96] On the transformation of British colonial policy during and after the Seven Years' War, see Bernhard Knollenberg, *Origin of the American Revolution, 1759–1766* (New York, 1960), and Alan Rogers, *Empire and Liberty: American Resistance to British Authority, 1755–1763* (Berkeley, 1974). Two excellent brief overviews of this watershed are Charles McLean Andrews, "Conditions Leading to the Revolt of the Colonies," in *Colonial Background of the American Revolution,* 121–69, and P. J. Marshall, "Empire and Authority in the Late Eighteenth Century," *Journal of Imperial and Commonwealth History* 15 (1987): 105–22.

macy under royal management, the Albany Congress's most enduring legacy, presaged the Crown's attempts to reform colonial administration and tighten colonial dependence after 1763. Colonists and Indians alike would feel the brunt of that imperial power in the years ahead, and the route to Anglo-American union projected in the Albany Plan would remain a path not taken.

Epilogue: Albany, 1775

We . . . embrace this opportunity to rekindle the ancient council fire, which formerly burnt as bright as the sun in this place, and to heap on it so much fuel that it may never be extinguished: and also to renew the ancient covenant chain with you, which you know has always been kept bright and clean, without any stain or rust.

> —Speech of the Commissioners appointed by the Continental Congress to treat with the Six Nations in Albany, August 1775

Let us have a trade at this place . . . as it was in former times, when we had hold of the old covenant. For then, brothers, if our people came down with only a few musquash [muskrat] skins, we went home with glad hearts. Brothers, let it be so again.

> —The Indians' response

One last story:

In August 1775, a young Philadelphia gentleman named Tench Tilghman traveled to Albany as the secretary of four commissioners appointed by the Continental Congress to treat with the Iroquois there.[1] Tilghman's journal from this trip, like Theodore Atkinson's from the Albany Congress, opens a portal on intercultural relations in the Mohawk Valley at a key moment in the history of British North America. Although an Anglo-Iroquois treaty had not convened in Albany since 1754, the conference's participants quickly assumed familiar roles. Beneath this continuity in the process of treaty-making lay a radical disjuncture in its political context that revealed the far-reaching consequences the Albany Congress had had for Britannia's Americans.

[1] See "The Journal of Tench Tilghman, Secretary of the Indian Commissioners, appointed by Congress to Treat with the Six Nations at German Flats, New York," in Samuel Harrison, *Memoir of Lieut. Col. Tench Tilghman* (Albany, 1876), 79–101. Tilghman and the commissioners met with the Indians in German Flatts and Albany in August–September 1775. The official proceedings of the conference are in *NYCD*, 8:605–31. For the background and context of this conference, see Barbara Graymont, *The Iroquois in the American Revolution* (Syracuse, 1972), 65–74.

Like other visitors before him, Tilghman was struck by the cultural peculiarities of Albany. The town's architecture still followed "the old low Dutch Fashion," and its inhabitants retained some odd Dutch customs. After attending a funeral, for example, Tilghman observed that the local Dutch preferred to inter a corpse "without any funeral ceremony" and then return to the home of the deceased to drink and smoke, "Some of them I think rather too much so." Like Atkinson twenty-one years earlier, Tilghman witnessed religious services conducted by missionaries for Christian Indians. He detailed a steady round of socializing with local elites but in the end found the city disagreeable, "crowded with Indians and soldiers, [of which] it is hard to say which is the most irregular and Savage."[2]

Tilghman's journal also reveals that little had changed in the rituals of treaty-making. Conducting such negotiations still required "a vast deal of Ceremony," and in their public councils, Indians and colonists still spoke in the usual idiom about renewing the "old covenant chain" and clearing the path between them of "every thorn, briar and stone."[3] The commissioners provisioned their Indian guests, and the Indians danced for the entertainment of their hosts. At the conference's end, the commissioners granted presents for the Indians to carry home. Tilghman even found himself the recipient of an Indian name, "Teahokalonde," which the Indians told him signified "having large horns." Not so easily complimented, he confessed that the episode left him inclined to "feel his Temples every now and then for the sprouting honours." Tilghman eventually tired of the endless protocol and declared the conference "but dull entertainment." As a novice, he did not realize the importance such rituals had played in over a century of Anglo-Iroquois diplomacy.[4]

A closer look at Tilghman's experiences also reveals how the political context of Anglo-Iroquois diplomacy had changed since the Albany Congress. His account of the conference begins not in Albany but in German Flatts, in the western Mohawk Valley. Tilghman and two of the commissioners traveled there to invite the Oneida Indians to Albany. En route, he described the region as "such a piece of Country as I believe is not in America." Farmsteads dotted the road in an almost unbroken line, their rich bottomland planted with wheat, corn, peas, oats, and grasses. From his lodgings in German Flatts, he looked out on an idyllic scene, "The lowlands and Mohawk River below me and two little villages with a Church and Steeples too."[5]

---

[2] "Journal of Tilghman," 80, 89–90, 95, 97.
[3] See ibid., 92–94, and NYCD, 8:608–9, 619–20.
[4] "Journal of Tilghman," 80, 91–93, 94.
[5] Ibid., 82–83, 86.

The prosperity of German Flatts was indicative of the region's changing demography. In 1756, the colonial population of Albany County, which included the frontier settlements along the Mohawk River, was 17,424; by 1771, it stood at 42,706.[6] The effect of this expansion on the region's native inhabitants was obvious. When Tilghman passed through the lower Mohawk village near Fort Hunter, he noted, "The Mohawks are become a civilized People, they live in good Houses and work their lands to the same advantage that the Whites do. They are vastly diminished in numbers, having not more than 70 men of their tribe." His description of Canajoharie was less appealing: "the small remains of that once Warlike and powerful Nation now dwell in a few miserable Huts," and their land was "mostly uncultivated for they do not farm like the people of the lower Castle."[7] The Mohawks had managed to hold onto their homelands, but just barely. Famine, out-migration, and disease had plagued their villages in the 1760s, and in 1770, their total population was barely four hundred.[8]

Even more indicative of the shifting intercultural relations in this region was that Tilghman and his companions were traveling to German Flatts to treat with the Oneidas, not the Mohawks. Much had changed since 1754 in the balance of power between these two easternmost Iroquois nations. During the 1760s, the Mohawks' diplomatic alliance with William Johnson was cemented by their material dependence on him. When Johnson died in 1774, they remained loyal to his nephew and successor as Indian superintendent, Guy Johnson, and many followed him to Canada when Anglo-American hostilities broke out a year later. The Oneidas, in contrast, had developed patriot sympathies, primarily because of New England missionaries working among them and the Tuscaroras. The Reverend Samuel Kirkland had arrived in the region in the mid-1760s and quickly became an indispensable cultural broker and rival of William Johnson. Kirkland was on hand to assist Tilghman and his companions when they arrived in German Flatts.[9]

The treaty conference that convened at Albany shortly thereafter rekindled the council fire that the Mohawks had declared "burnt out" at the Albany Congress, but the different meanings that this gesture had for the Indians and colonists precluded the reestablishment of an Albany-based diplomacy. Although the conference followed the usual protocol, the changing nature of imperial and intercultural relations was evident in the details. First, the participants occupied different spaces than they had in 1754. Private and public councils at the Albany Congress had occurred in the fort and Governor's House; in 1775, the colonial commissioners met

---

[6] See Guldenzopf, "Colonial Transformation of Mohawk Iroquois Society," 56, 71.
[7] "Journal of Tilghman," 82–83.
[8] Johnson to John Inglis, September 4, 1770, WJ Papers, 7:876–77.
[9] See Graymont, Iroquois in the American Revolution, 35–47, 70–74.

the Indians in a local tavern and the Dutch church. The city's fort, described by Tilghman as having "now gone much to decay," had always been a seat of British imperial power and therefore would not do as a site for diplomacy conducted by colonial rebels. Likewise, when the commissioners sought local assistance, they did not convene the Albany Commissioners of Indian Affairs; that body had not existed for twenty years. Instead, they relied on Albany's Committee of Safety, the local patriot cell charged with ferreting out loyalism.[10] Tilghman and his companions had come to Albany to treat with the Indians on behalf of the Continental Congress, not the Crown.

William Johnson's appointment as the Crown's Indian agent had ended independent colonial relations with the Iroquois, so the patriots had to retrain themselves in the fundamentals of Iroquois diplomacy. Kirkland traveled to Philadelphia to help, briefing members of the Continental Congress on the use of wampum and other aspects of treaty ritual.[11] The commissioners who met the Iroquois—mostly Oneidas, Tuscaroras, and some Mohawks from Fort Hunter—in Albany followed his lead. They informed the Indians of the "great council-fire kindled at Philadelphia" between the "Twelve United Provinces" (Georgia had not yet joined the Congress), delivered a "Union Belt" to symbolize their renewal of "the old covenant chain," and asked the Indians to remain clear of this "family quarrel between us and Old England."[12] Their lack of familiarity with treaty-making was nevertheless evident in the speech Congress had written for them. "You might almost as well have read them a Chapter out of Locke," Tilghman noted dryly in his journal.[13]

There was something ironic about the commissioners' appropriating the language of Anglo-Iroquois diplomacy in the patriot cause. After all, the "ancient" Covenant Chain, as they described it, was a product of British imperial pretensions in North America, and since 1755 it had been managed in the interests of the empire, not the colonies. But it is important to realize what the commissioners hoped to achieve by this meeting: they simply wanted to replace a royal Indian agency with a patriot one. Congress created three geographic departments for administering Indian affairs. The northern department, which these commissioners represented, would be responsible for the Iroquois. They spoke of rekindling the council fire in Albany, but it was not their intention to reappoint the Albany Commissioners of Indian Affairs or to restore the management of intercultural relations in this region to local Indians and colonists. On the contrary, the patriots wished to exercise the same centralized authority over

---

[10] See "Journal of Tilghman," 80, and *NYCD*, 8:608–10, 613.
[11] See Graymont, *Iroquois in the American Revolution*, 65.
[12] *NYCD*, 8:615–20.
[13] "Journal of Tilghman," 94.

Indian affairs as Johnson had, only this time in the interests of a rebel government rather than an imperial crown.

This objective was at odds with what the Indians expected of this conference. William Johnson had died a year earlier, and his nephew had gone to Canada to recruit Indian support for the British cause. Samuel Kirkland remained the Oneidas' and Tuscaroras' most important cultural broker, but he lacked official position and the financial resources to meet their material needs. The Indians who came to Albany wanted a patriot version of William Johnson, a broker with deep pockets who could mediate their relations with local colonists and supply their wants. To them, rekindling the council fire at Albany implied resurrecting the dual diplomatic and commercial role that Albany had played before Johnson had broken its grip on the Covenant Chain.

These conflicting objectives became apparent in two speeches exchanged during the 1775 conference. In responding to the commissioners' opening speech, the Indians declared their friendship with the colonies but corrected them on one matter. The commissioners had "kindled up a council-fire of peace," but they had not appointed someone to watch over it so that it remained bright and free of debris. Therefore, the Indians took it upon themselves to appoint Philip Schuyler to the task. Schuyler was a patriot general, a leading citizen of Albany, and one of the Continental Congress's commissioners for the northern Indian department. He was also a descendant of Peter Schuyler, an early Albany agent to the Iroquois, whose Indian name, "Quider," had become their shorthand term for the Albany Commissioners of Indian Affairs. In unilaterally appointing "our ancient friend Quedar" watchman over the rekindled council fire, the Indians asked that the Albany Commissioners of Indian Affairs be restored in his person, to guarantee that trade and diplomacy resume "as it was in former times, when we had hold of the old covenant."[14]

The nature of this request escaped the commissioners, who the next day replied that they were "a little surprised to hear you say that no one was appointed by the Twelve United Colonies to attend and watch the fire that they have kindled up at this place." A bit perturbed, they reminded the Indians that "we have repeatedly told you that they [the Continental Congress] have appointed five persons, whose business it is to attend and preserve it bright and clear." Albany residents Philip Schuyler and Volkert Douw were among those commissioners, and they "would take particular care" to ensure that the fire remained "bright and clear."[15]

What the commissioners mistook for thickheadedness among the Indians was actually a divergence in perspectives. The Indians wanted someone who not only represented the Continental Congress but who had

[14] NYCD, 8:624.
[15] Ibid., 626.

the power and willingness to enter the fray of local intercultural relations, someone who would guarantee them fair trade and who would settle their land disputes, just as Johnson had done. The commissioners, even Schuyler and Douw, had no interest in such affairs. When the Indians brought up two land complaints against Albany residents, the commissioners turned a deaf ear, explaining that they were "not authorized to transact any business of that kind at present, but will represent the matter to the Grand Congress at Philadelphia."[16]

The subsequent course of American-Iroquois relations reveals that the new United States never did comprehend what the Indians were talking about at Albany in 1775. During the Revolutionary War and after, the federal government followed the example set by the British Crown, administering Indian affairs through centralized offices rather than local, autonomous agents. The Articles of Confederation and the United States Constitution, which some scholars speciously claim bear an Iroquois imprint, were decidedly anti-Iroquois in their ramifications: they assumed for the federal government exclusive powers in Indian affairs that made it impossible to turn back the clock and reinstitute the local diplomacy that had once sustained the council fire in Albany. Under the new federal regime, the precedents set by the Albany Congress for using treaty-making to dispossess the Indians grew more extreme, and for the Iroquois, this process culminated in their confinement to tiny reservations by the 1790s.[17] From the Indian perspective, the true legacy of the Albany Congress was the increasing use of federal power to cement their dependency and removal in the new American republic.

[16] Ibid.
[17] See Jones, *License for Empire,* 157–86.

Appendix:

The Albany Plan of Union

PLAN of a Proposed UNION of the several Colonies of Masachusets Bay, New Hampshire, Connecticut, Rhode Island, New York, New Jerseys, Pensylvania, Maryland, Virginia, North Carolina, and South Carolina, for their mutual defence and security, and for extending the British Settlements in North America.

That humble application be made for an Act of the Parliament of Great Brittain, by virtue of which, one General Government may be formed in America, including all the said Colonies, within, and under which Government, each Colony may retain each present constitution, except in the particulars wherein a change may be directed by the said Act, as hereafter follows.

That the said General Government be administered by a president General, to be appointed and supported by the Crown, and a grand Council to be chosen by the representatives of the people of the several Colonies, meet in their respective assemblies.

That within Months after the passing of such Act, The house of representatives in the several Assemblies, that Happen to be sitting within that time or that shall be specially for that purpose convened, may and shall chose, Members for the Grand Council in the following proportions, that is to say:

The text of the Albany Plan of Union is in *NYCD,* 6:889–91.

Masachusets Bay 7
New Hampshire 2
Connecticut 5
Rhode Island 2
New-York 4
New Jerseys 3
Pensylvania 6
Maryland 4
Virginia 7
North Carolina 4
South Carolina . . . . _4_
48

Who shall meet for the present time at the City of Philadelphia, in Pennsylvania, being called by the President General as soon as conveniently may be after his appointment.

That there shall be a New Election of Members for the Grand Council every three years, and on the death or resignation of any Member, his place shall be supplyed by a new choice at the next sitting of the Assembly of the Colony he represented.

That after the first three years, when the proportion of money arising out of each Colony to the General Treasury can be known, The number of Members to be chosen, for each Colony shall from time to time in all ensuing Elections be regulated by that proportion (yet so as that the Number to be chosen by any one province be not more than seven nor less than two).

That the Grand Council shall meet once in every year, and oftener if occasion require, at such time and place as they shall adjourn to at the last preceeding meeting, or as they shall be called to meet at by the President General, on any emergency, he having first obtained in writing the consent of seven of the Members to such call, and sent due and timely notice to the whole.

That the Grand Council have power to chuse their speaker, and shall neither be dissolved, prorogued, nor continue sitting longer than six weeks at one time without their own consent, or the special command of the Crown.

That the Members of the Grand Council shall be allowed for their service ten shillings sterling per diem, during their Sessions or Journey to and from the place of Meeting; twenty miles to be reckoned a days Journey.

That the Assent of the President General be requisite, to all Acts of the Grand Council, and that it be his Office, and duty to cause them to be carried into execution.

That the President General with the advice of the Grand Council, hold or direct all Indian Treaties in which the general interest or welfare of the Colonys may be concerned; and make peace or declare War with the Indian Nations. That they make such Laws as they judge necessary for the regulating all Indian Trade. That they make all purchases from Indians for the Crown, of lands [now] not within the bounds of particular Colonies, or that shall not be within their bounds when some of them are reduced to more convenient dimensions. That they make new settlements on such purchases by granting Lands, [in the King's Name] reserving a Quit rent to the Crown, for the use of the General Treasury.

That they make Laws for regulating and governing such new settlements, till the Crown shall think fit to form them into particular Governments.

That they raise and pay Soldiers, and build Forts for the defence of any of the Colonies, and equip vessels of Force to guard the Coasts and protect the Trade on the Ocean, Lakes, or great Rivers; but they shall not impress men in any Colonies without the consent of its Legislature. That for these purposes they have power to make Laws And lay and Levy such general duties, imposts or taxes, as to them shall appear most equal and just, considering the ability and other circumstances of the Inhabitants in the several Colonies, and such as may be collected with the least inconvenience to the people, rather discouraging luxury, than loading Industry with unnecessary burthens. That they might appoint a General Treasurer and a particular Treasurer in each Government when necessary, and from time to time may order the sums in the Treasuries of each Government, into the General Treasury, or draw on them for special payments as they find most convenient; yet no money to issue but by joint orders of the President General and Grand Council, except where sums have been appropriated to particular purposes, and the President General is previously impowered by an Act to draw for such sums.

That the General accounts shall be yearly settled and reported to the several Assemblies.

That a Quorum of the Grand Council impowered to act with the President General, do consists of twenty five Members, among whom there shall be one or more from a majority of the Colonies. That the Laws made by them for the purposes aforesaid, shall not be repugnant, but as near as may be agreable to the Laws of England, and shall be transmitted to the King in Council for approbation, as soon as may be after their passing, and if not disapproved within three years after presentation to remain in Force.

That in case of the death of the President General, the Speaker of the Grand Council for the time being shall succeed, and be vested with the same powers and authority, to continue until the King's pleasure be known.

That all Military Commission Officers, whether for land or sea service, to act under this General constitution, shall be nominated by the President General, but the aprobation of the Grand Council is to be obtained before they receive their Commissions; and all Civil Officers are to be nominated by the grand Council, and to receive the President General's approbation before they officiate; but in case of vacancy by death or removal of any Officer Civil or Military under this consititution, The Governor of the Province in which such vacancy happens, may appoint till the pleasure of the President General and grand Council can be known. That the particular Military as well as Civil establishments in each Colony remain in their present State this General constitution notwithstanding. And that on sudden emergencies any Colony may defend itself, and lay the accounts of expence thence arisen, before the President General and Grand Council, who may allow and order payment of the same as far as they judge such accounts just and reasonable.

Bibliography

PRIMARY SOURCES

Manuscript Collections

British Library, London, England
  Additional Manuscripts, 32686–33057 (Newcastle Papers)
  Egerton Manuscripts, vols. 2659–75 (Thomas Hutchinson Papers)
  Henry McCulloh, "To the Right Honourable Earl of Halifax," December 10, 1751,
    Additional Manuscripts, No. 11514
William L. Clements Library, Ann Arbor, Michigan
  Albany Congress Collection
  George Clinton Letterbook, 1752–53
  George Clinton Papers
  Minutes of the Albany Commissioners of Indian Affairs (June 29, 1753–May 4,
    1755), Native American History Collection
  Sackville-Germain Papers
  Shelburne Papers
  Charles Townshend Papers
Historical Society of Pennsylvania, Philadelphia, Pennsylvania
  Gratz Collection
  Penn Papers, Indian Affairs
  Isaac Norris Letterbooks (microfilm)
  Norris Family Papers
  Richard Peters Papers
Henry E. Huntington Library, San Marino, California
  Loudoun Papers—Americana
  Isaac Norris, Journal and Account Book, 1733–49, HM 3057
Massachusetts Statehouse, Boston, Massachusetts
  Massachusetts Archives, 241 vols. (microfilm)
Museum of the City of New York, New York, New York
  DeLancey Family Papers, 1686–1865

New-York Historical Society, New York, New York
  Daniel Horsmanden Papers (microfilm)
New York Public Library, New York, New York
  William Smith, Diary (microfilm)
New York State Archives, New York State Library, Albany, New York
  Indorsed Land Papers, 1643–1803, 63 vols.
  New York Council Minutes, 1668–1783, 97 vols.
  New York Colonial Manuscripts, 103 vols.
  Records of the Society for the Propagation of the Gospel in Foreign Parts, Letter-
  books, Ser. A, B, and C, 1702–1800 (microfilm)
Public Archives of Canada, Ottawa, Canada
  Minutes of the Albany Commissioners of Indian Affairs, 1723–48, 3 vols. (micro-
  film)
Public Records Office, Kew, England
  Colonial Office Papers (CO 5)
  Chatham Papers (PRO 30/8)

Published Collections

Adams, C. F., ed. *The Works of John Adams.* 10 vols. Boston, 1856.
Archives of Maryland. 72 vols. Baltimore, 1883–1972.
Archives of the State of New Jersey, 1st ser., 42 vols. Newark, 1880–1949.
Bartlett, John Russell, ed. *Records of the Colony of Rhode Island and Providence Plantations,
  in New England.* 10 vols. Providence, 1856–65.
Boyd, Julian P., ed. *Indian Treaties Printed by Benjamin Franklin, 1736–1762.* Phila-
  delphia, 1938.
Boyd, Julian P., and R. J. Taylor, eds., *The Susquehannah Company Papers.* 11 vols. Ithaca,
  1962–71.
Brock, R. A., ed. "The Official Records of Robert Dinwiddie." In *Collections of the
  Virginia Historical Society*, vols. 3–4. Richmond, 1883–84.
Cadwallader Colden Papers. In *Collections of the New York Historical Society*, vols. 9–10, 50–
  58, 67–68. New York, 1876–77, 1918–25, 1934–35.
Collections of the Connecticut Historical Society, vols. 16–17. Hartford, 1916, 1918.
Grant, W. L., and James Munro, eds. *Acts of the Privy Council of England, Colonial Series*,
  6 vols. Hereford, 1908–12.
Hutchinson, Peter Orlando, ed. *The Diary and Letters of Thomas Hutchinson.* 2 vols.
  1884–86. Reprint. New York, 1971.
Jennings, Francis, et al., eds. *Iroquois Indians: A Documentary History of the Diplomacy of
  the Six Nations and Their League.* Microfilm collection, 50 reels. Woodbridge, Conn.,
  1985.
Journal of the Commissioners for Trade and Plantations, 1704–1782. 14 vols. London, 1920–
  38.
Labaree, Leonard W., W. B. Willcox, Claude Lopez, and Barbara B. Oberg, eds. *The
  Papers of Benjamin Franklin.* 34 vols. New Haven, 1959– .
Leder, Lawrence H., ed. *The Livingston Indian Records, 1666–1723.* Gettysburg, 1956.
Lincoln, Charles Henry, ed. *Correspondence of William Shirley, Governor of Massachusetts
  and Military Commander in America, 1731–1760.* 2 vols. 1912. Reprint. New York,
  1973.
Minutes of the Provincial Council of Pennsylvania. 16 vols. Harrisburg, 1852–53.
Munsell, Joel, ed. *The Annals of Albany.* 10 vols. Albany, 1850–59.
———. *Collections on the History of Albany, from its Discovery to the Present Time.* 4 vols.
  Albany, 1865–71.

Pennsylvania Archives. 9 series. Philadelphia, 1852–1935.

O'Callaghan, E. B., ed. *Documentary History of the State of New-York.* 4 vols. Albany, 1849–51.

O'Callaghan, E. B., and Berthold Fernow, eds. *Documents Relative to the Colonial History of the State of New-York.* 15 vols. Albany, 1853–87.

Saunders, William L., ed. *The Colonial Records of North Carolina.* 10 vols. Raleigh, 1886.

Sullivan, James, Alexander C. Flick, Milton W. Hamilton, and Albert B. Corey, eds. *Papers of Sir William Johnson.* 14 vols. Albany, 1921–62.

Pamphlets and Books

Bartram, John. *Travels in Pensilvania and Canada.* London, 1751.

[Bennet, John]. *The National Merchant: or, Discourse on Commerce and Colonies.* London, 1736.

Brewster, Francis. *Essays on Trade and Navigations. The First Part.* London, 1695.

Britannia Languens, or a Discourse of Trade. London, 1680.

Burke, Edmund, *An Account of the European Settlements in America.* 2 vols., 6th ed. London, 1777.

Cary, John. *A Discourse on Trade, and Other Matters Relative to It.* London, 1745.

Child, Josiah. *A New Discourse of Trade . . . A New Edition.* 1693. Reprint. London, 1775.

Clarke, William. *Observations on the Late and Present Conduct of the French.* Boston, 1755.

Coke, Roger. *A Discourse of Trade.* London, 1670.

Coxe, Daniel. *A Description of the English Province of Carolana.* London, 1722.

D'Avenant, Charles. *The Political and Commercial Works.* 5 vols. London, 1771.

Douglass, William. *A Summary, Historical and Political, of the First Planting, Progressive Improvements, and Present State of the British Settlements in North-America.* 2 vols. Boston, 1749, 1751.

Dummer, [Jeremiah]. *A Defence of the New-England Charters.* London, 1721.

Evans, Lewis. *Geographical, Historical, Political, Philosophical, and Mechanical Essays. The First, Containing an Analysis of a General Map of the Middle British Colonies in America.* Philadelphia, 1755.

Fortrey, Samuel. *England's Interest and Improvement. Consisting in the Increase of the Store, and Trade of This Kingdom.* London, 1673.

Frelinghuysen, Theodorus. *A Sermon Preached on Occasion of the Late Treaty Held in Albany, by His Honour Our Lieutenant Governor, with the Indian Nations, and the Congress of Commissioners from Several Governments in These British Colonies.* New York, 1754.

[Gee, Joshua]. *A Letter to a Member of Parliament, Concerning the Naval Store Bill . . . with Observations on the Plantation-Trade and Methods Proposed for Rendering It More Beneficial to Great Britain.* London, 1720.

——. *The Trade and Navigation of Great-Britain Considered.* 3d ed. London, 1731.

Hopkins, Stephen, *A True Representation of the Plan Formed at Albany for Uniting All the British Northern Colonies.* Providence, 1755.

[Huske, Ellis]. *The Present State of North-America.* London, 1755.

Keith, William. *A Collection of Papers and Other Tracts.* 2d ed. London, 1749.

[——]. *Two Papers on the Subject of Taxing the British Colonies.* 1739. Reprint. London, 1767.

[Kennedy, Archibald]. *The Importance of Gaining and Preserving the Friendship of the Indians to the British Interest, Considered.* New York, 1751.

[——]. *Observations on the Importance of the Northern Colonies under Proper Regulations.* New York, 1750.

[——]. *Serious Advice to the Inhabitants of the Northern-Colonies.* New York, 1755.

[——]. *Serious Considerations on the Present State of the Affairs of the Northern Colonies.* New York, 1754.

[Little, Otis]. *The State of Trade in the Northern Colonies Considered.* 1748. Reprint. Boston, 1749.

[Livingston, William]. *A Review of Military Operations in North-America.* New York, 1757.

[MacSparren, James]. *America Dissected, Being a Full and True Account of the American Colonies.* Dublin, 1753.

[McCulloh, Henry]. *General Thoughts on the Construction, Use and Abuse of the Great Offices.* London, 1754.

[——]. *A Miscellaneous Essay Concerning the Courses Pursued by Great Britain in the Affairs of Her Colonies.* London, 1755.

[——]. *Proposals for Uniting the English Colonies on the Continent of America, So as to Enable Them to Act with Force and Vigour against Their Enemies.* London, 1757.

[——]. *The Wisdom and Policy of the French in the Construction of Their Great Offices.* London, 1755.

[Mitchell, John]. *The Contest in America between Great Britain and France, with Its Consequences and Importance.* London, 1757.

Molyneux, William. *The Case of Ireland's Being Bound by Acts of Parliament in England, Stated.* Dublin, 1698.

[New York]. *A Treaty between His Excellency . . . George Clinton . . . and the Six . . . Nations . . . Albany . . . August . . . 1746.* New York, 1746.

Palairet, J. *A Concise Description of the English and French Possessions in North-America.* 2d ed. London, 1755.

[Payne, J.] *The French Encroachments Exposed: or, Britain's Original Right To All That Part of the American Continent Claimed by France.* London, 1756.

Philolethes. *A Short Reply to Mr. Hopkins's Vindication, and False Reflections against the Governor and Council of the Colony of Rhode-Island.* Providence, 1755.

Postlethwayt, Malachy. *Britain's Commercial Interest Explained and Improved.* 2 vols. London, 1757.

Pownall, Thomas. *The Administration of the Colonies.* 5 eds. London, 1764–74.

——. *The Principles of Polity, Being the Grounds and Reasons of Civil Empire.* London, 1752.

——. *Proposals for Securing the Friendship of the Five Nations.* New York, 1756.

Shirley, William. *Governor Shirley's Letter to His Grace the Duke of Newcastle: With a Journal of the Siege of Louisbourg.* Boston, 1746.

[——]. *Memoirs of the Principal Transactions of the Last War between the English and French in North-America.* 3d ed. Boston, 1758.

State of the British and French Colonies in North America . . . In Two Letters to a Friend. London, 1755.

T. C. *A Scheme to Drive the French Out of All the Continent of North America.* Boston, 1755.

[Temple, William]. *A Vindication of Commerce and the Arts.* London, 1758.

[Tucker, Josiah]. *A Brief Essay on the Advantages and Disadvantages Which Respectively Attend France and Great Britain, with Regard to Trade.* 2d ed. London, 1750.

Newspapers

Boston Evening-Post
Boston Gazette
Boston Post-Boy
Boston Weekly News-Letter

New-York Gazette
New-York Mercury
Pennsylvania Gazette
Pennsylvania Journal
South Carolina Gazette
Virginia Gazette

Miscellaneous Published Primary Sources

Benson, Adolph B., ed. *Peter Kalm's Travels in North America: The English Version of 1770*. 2 vols. New York, 1937.

Bridenbaugh, Carl, ed. *Gentleman's Progress: The Itinerarium of Dr. Alexander Hamilton, 1744*. Chapel Hill, 1948.

Calhoon, Robert M. "William Smith Jr.'s Alternative to the American Revolution." *William and Mary Quarterly* 3d ser., 22 (1965), 105–18.

Colden, Cadwallader. *The History of the Five Indian Nations Depending on the Province of New-York in America.* 1727, 1747. Reprint. Ithaca, 1958.

Crane, Verner W., ed. *Benjamin Franklin's Letters to the Press, 1758–1775.* Chapel Hill, 1950.

Farrand, Max, ed. *Benjamin Franklin's Memoirs: Parallel Text Edition.* Berkeley and Los Angeles, 1949.

Greene, Jack P. "Martin Bladen's Blueprint for a Colonial Union: 'Reasons for Appointing a Captain General for the Continent of North America.'" *William and Mary Quarterly,* 3d ser., 17 (1960): 516–30.

Greene, Jack P., Charles F. Mullet, and Edward C. Papenfuse, Jr., eds. *Magna Charta for America: James Abercromby's "An Examination of the Acts of Parliament Relative to the Trade and Government of Our American Colonies" (1752) and "De Jure et Gubenatione Coloniarum, or an Inquiry into the Nature, and the Rights of Colonies, Ancient, and Modern" (1774)*. Philadelphia, 1986.

Hamilton, Milton W., ed. "The Diary of the Reverend John Ogilvie, 1750–1759." *Bulletin of the Fort Ticonderoga Museum* 10 (1961): 329–85.

Hutchinson, Thomas. *The History of the Colony and Province of Massachusetts-Bay.* 1936. Reprint edited by Lawrence Shaw Mayo. 3 vols. New York, 1970.

McAnear, Beverly, ed. "Personal Accounts of the Albany Congress of 1754." *Mississippi Valley Historical Review* 39 (1953): 727–46.

Pargellis, Stanley, ed. *Military Affairs in North America, 1748–1765: Selected Documents from the Cumberland Papers in Windsor Castle.* New York, 1936.

Pownall, Thomas. *A Topographical Description of the Dominions of the United States of America.* Edited by Lois Mulkearn. Pittsburgh, 1949.

Sabine, William H. W., ed. *Historical Memoirs of William Smith.* 3 vols. New York, 1956–71.

Smith, William [Jr.]. *The History of the Province of New-York.* Edited by Michael Kammen. 2 vols. Cambridge, Mass., 1972.

Snow, Dean R., Charles T. Gehring, and William A. Starna, eds. *In Mohawk Country: Early Narratives about a Native People.* Syracuse, 1996.

Stone, Frederick D., comp. "Plans for the Union of the British Colonies of North America, 1643–1776." In *History of the Celebration of the One Hundredth Anniversary of the Promulgation of the Constitution of the United States,* edited by Hampton L. Carson. 2 vols. Philadelphia, 1889.

Wraxall, Peter. *An Abridgment of the Indian Affairs, Contained in Four Folio Vols., Transacted in the Colony of New York, from the Year 1678 to the Year 1751.* Edited by Charles Howard McIlwain. Cambridge, Mass., 1915.

Wright, Louis B., ed. *An Essay upon the Government of the English Plantations on the Continent of America (1701): An Anonymous Virginian's Proposals for Liberty under the British Crown, with Two Memoranda by William Byrd.* San Marino, 1945.

Selected Secondary Sources

Dissertations

Armour, David Arthur. "The Merchants of Albany, New York, 1686–1760." Ph.D. dissertation, Northwestern University, 1965.

Greiert, Stephen G. "The Earl of Halifax and British Colonial Policy, 1748–1756." Ph.D. dissertation, Duke University, 1976.

Guldenzopf, David B. "The Colonial Transformation of Mohawk Iroquois Society." Ph.D. dissertation, SUNY, Albany, 1986.

Guzzardo, John C. "Sir William Johnson's Official Family: Patron and Clients in an Anglo-American Empire." Ph.D. dissertation, Syracuse University, 1975.

Jezierski, John V. "The Context of Union: The Origins, Provenience, and Failure of the Albany Plan of Union of 1754." Ph.D. dissertation, Indiana University, 1971.

Parmenter, Jon William. "At the Wood's Edge: Iroquois Foreign Relations, 1727–1768." Ph.D dissertation, University of Michigan, 1999.

Books and Articles

Adams, James Truslow. "On the Term 'British Empire.'" *American Historical Review* 27 (1922): 485–89.

——. *Provincial Society, 1690–1763.* New York, 1927.

Alden, John R. "The Albany Congress and the Creation of the Indian Superintendencies." *Mississippi Valley Historical Review* 27 (1940), 193–210.

Anderson, Benedict. *Imagined Communities: Reflections on the Origin and Spread of Nationalism.* London, 1983.

Andrews, Charles M. *The Colonial Background of the American Revolution.* New Haven, 1924.

——. *The Colonial Period in American History.* Vol. 4, *England's Commercial and Colonial Policy.* New Haven, 1938.

Aquila, Richard. *The Iroquois Restoration: Iroquois Diplomacy on the Colonial Frontier, 1701–1754.* Detroit, 1983.

Axtell, James. *Beyond 1492: Encounters in Colonial North America.* Oxford, 1992.

——. *The European and the Indian: Essays in the Ethnohistory of Colonial North America.* Oxford, 1981.

Bailyn, Bernard, and Philip D. Morgan, eds. *Strangers within the Realm: Cultural Margins of the First British Empire.* Chapel Hill, 1991.

Barrow, Thomas C. *Trade and Empire: The British Customs Service in Colonial America.* Cambridge, Mass., 1967.

Bayse, Arthur. *The Lords Commissioners of Trade and Plantations, 1748–1782.* New Haven, 1925.

Beer, Samuel. *To Make a Nation: The Rediscovery of American Federalism.* Cambridge, Mass., 1993.

Bielinski, Stefan. "A Middling Sort: Artisans and Tradesmen in Colonial Albany." *New York History* 73 (1992): 261–90.

——. "The People of Colonial Albany, 1650–1800." In *Authority and Resistance in Early New York,* edited by William Pencak and Conrad Edick Wright. New York, 1988.

Bonomi, Patricia U. *A Factious People: Politics and Society in Colonial New York*. New York, 1971.

Boyd, Julian P. *Anglo-American Union: Joseph Galloway's Plans to Preserve the British Empire, 1774–1788*. New York, 1970.

Brandão, José António, *"Your fyre shall burn no more": Iroquois Policy toward New France and Its Native Allies to 1701*. Lincoln, 1997.

Breen, T. H. "Ideology and Nationalism on the Eve of the American Revolution: Revisions *Once More* in Need of Revising." *Journal of American History* 84 (1997), 13–39.

Brewer, John. *The Sinews of Power: War, Money, and the English State, 1688–1783*. New York, 1989.

Buffington, Arthur H. "The Policy of Albany and English Westward Expansion." *Mississippi Valley Historical Review* 8 (1922): 327–66.

Bumsted, John. "'Things in the Womb of Time': Ideas of American Independence, 1633–1763," *William and Mary Quarterly* 3d ser., 31 (1974): 533–64.

Burke, Thomas, Jr. *Mohawk Frontier: The Dutch Community of Schenectady, New York, 1661–1710*. Ithaca, 1991.

Canny, Nicholas P. *Kingdom and Colony: Ireland in the Atlantic World, 1560–1800*. Baltimore, 1988.

Canny, Nicholas P., and Anthony Pagden, eds. *Colonial Identity in the Atlantic World, 1500–1800*. Princeton, 1987.

Cayton, Andrew R. L., and Fredrika J. Teute, eds., *Contact Points: American Frontiers from the Mohawk Valley to the Mississippi, 1750–1830*. Chapel Hill, 1998.

Clive, John, and Bernard Bailyn. "England's Cultural Provinces: Scotland and America." *William and Mary Quarterly* 3d series, 11 (1954): 200–213.

Colley, Linda. *Britons: Forging the Nation, 1707–1837*. New Haven, 1992.

Crane, Verner W. *Benjamin Franklin: Englishman and American*. Baltimore, 1936.

Cutcliffe, Stephen H. "Colonial Indian Policy as a Measure of Rising Imperialism: New York and Pennsylvania, 1700–1755," *Western Pennsylvania Historical Magazine* 64 (1981): 237–68.

Demos, John. *The Unredeemed Captive: A Family Story from Early America*. New York, 1994.

Dickerson, Oliver M. *American Colonial Government, 1696–1765: A Study of the British Board of Trade in Its Relations to the American Colonies, Political, Industrial, Administrative*. 1912. Reprint. New York, 1962.

Eccles, W. J. "The Fur Trade and Eighteenth-Century Imperialism." *William and Mary Quarterly* 3d ser., 40 (1983): 341–62.

Egnal, Marc. *A Mighty Empire: The Origins of the American Revolution*. Ithaca, 1988.

Fenton, William N. *The Great Law and the Longhouse: A Political History of the Iroquois Confederacy*. Norman, Okla., 1998.

Flexner, James Thomas. *Mohawk Baronet: A Biography of Sir William Johnson*. Syracuse, 1959. Reprint. 1989.

Foster, Michael K., Jack Campisi, and Marianne Mithun, eds. *Extending the Rafters: Interdisciplinary Approaches to Iroquois Studies*. Albany, 1984.

Fox, Edith M. *Land Speculation in the Mohawk Country*. Ithaca, 1949.

Frieberg, Malcolm. "Thomas Hutchinson: The First Fifty Years (1711–1761)." *William and Mary Quarterly* 3d ser., 15 (1958): 35–55.

Gipson, Lawrence Henry. *The British Empire before the American Revolution*. 15 vols. Caldwell, Iowa, and New York, 1936–70.

——. "The Drafting of the Albany Plan of Union: A Problem of Semantics." *Pennsylvania History* 26 (1959): 291–316.

——. "Massachusetts Bay and American Colonial Union, 1754." In *Proceedings of the American Antiquarian Society* 71 (1961): 63–92.

——. "Thomas Hutchinson and the Framing of the Albany Plan of Union, 1754," *Pennsylvania Magazine of History and Biography* 74 (1950): 5–35.

Graymont, Barbara. *The Iroquois in the American Revolution.* Syracuse, 1972.

Greene, Jack P. "The Alienation of Benjamin Franklin—British American," *Journal of the Royal Society of Arts* 124 (1976): 52–73.

——. *The Intellectual Construction of America: Exceptionalism and Identity from 1492 to 1800.* Chapel Hill, 1993.

——. *Peripheries and Center: Constitutional Development in the Extended Polities of the British Empire and United States, 1607–1788.* Athens, Ga., 1986.

——. "Pride, Prejudice, and Jealousy: Benjamin Franklin's Explanation for the American Revolution." In *Reappraising Benjamin Franklin: A Bicentennial Perspective,* edited by J. A. Leo Lemay, Newark, Del., 1993.

——. *Pursuits of Happiness: The Social Development of Early Modern British Colonies and the Formation of American Culture.* Chapel Hill, 1988.

——. "The Seven Years' War and the American Revolution: The Causal Relationship Reconsidered." *Journal of Imperial and Commonwealth History* 8 (1980): 85–105.

——. "Search for Identity: An Interpretation of the Meaning of Selected Patterns of Social Response in Eighteenth-Century America." *Journal of Social History* 3 (1970), 189–220.

——. "An Uneasy Connection: An Analysis of the Preconditions of the American Revolution." In *Essays on the American Revolution,* edited by Stephen G. Kurtz and James Hutson, Chapel Hill, 1973.

Greene, Jack P., and J. R. Pole, eds. *Colonial British America: Essays in the New History of the Early Modern Era.* Baltimore, 1984.

Greiert, Stephen G. "The Board of Trade and Defense of the Ohio Valley, 1748–1753." *Western Pennsylvania Historical Magazine* 64 (1981): 1–32.

Grinde, Donald A. Jr., and Bruce E. Johansen. "Sauce for the Goose: Demand and Definitions for 'Proof' Regarding the Iroquois and Democracy." *William and Mary Quarterly* 3d ser., 53 (1996): 621–36.

Haan, Richard. "The Problem of Iroquois Neutrality: Suggestions for Revision." *Ethnohistory* 27 (1980): 317–30.

Hagedorn, Nancy. "Brokers of Understanding: Interpreters as Agents of Cultural Exchange in Colonial New York." *New York History* 76 (1995): 379–408.

——. "'A Friend to Go between Them': The Interpreter as Cultural Broker during Anglo-Iroquois Councils, 1740–70." *Ethnohistory* 35 (1988): 60–80.

Hamilton, Milton W. *Sir William Johnson, Colonial American, 1715–1763.* Port Washington, 1976.

Hancock, David. *Citizens of the World: London Merchants and the Integration of the British Atlantic Community, 1735–1785.* Cambridge, Eng., 1995.

Hauptman, Laurence M. *Tribes and Tribulations: Misconceptions about American Indians and Their Histories.* Albuquerque, 1995.

Henretta, James A. *"Salutary Neglect": Colonial Administration under the Duke of Newcastle.* Princeton, 1972.

Higgins, Ruth L. *Expansion in New York, with Especial Reference to the Eighteenth Century.* 1931. Reprint. Philadelphia, 1976.

Hinderaker, Eric. *Elusive Empires: Constructing Colonialism in the Ohio Valley, 1673–1800.* Cambridge, Eng., 1997.

——. "The 'Four Indian Kings' and the Imaginative Construction of the First British Empire." *William and Mary Quarterly* 3d ser., 53 (1996): 487–526.

Hulsebosch, Daniel J. *"Imperia in Imperio:* The Multiple Constitutions of Empire in New York, 1750–1777." *Law and History Review* 16 (1998): 319–79.

Hunt, George T. *The Wars of the Iroquois: A Study in Intertribal Trade Relations.* Madison, 1960.

Hutchinson, William T. "Unite to Divide; Divide to Unite: The Shaping of American Federalism." *Mississippi Valley Historical Review* 46 (1959): 3–18.

Jacobs, Wilbur R. *Diplomacy and Indian Gifts: Anglo-French Rivalry Along the Ohio and Northwest Frontiers, 1748–1763.* Stanford, 1950.

James, F. G. *Ireland in the Empire, 1688–1770.* Cambridge, Mass., 1973.

Jennings, Francis. *The Ambiguous Iroquois Empire: The Covenant Chain Confederation of Indian Tribes with English Colonies from Its Beginnings to the Lancaster Treaty of 1744.* New York, 1984.

——. *Benjamin Franklin, Politician.* New York, 1996.

——. *Empire of Fortune: Crowns, Colonies, and Tribes in the Seven Years War in America.* New York, 1988.

Jennings, Francis, et al., eds. *The History and Culture of Iroquois Diplomacy: An Interdisciplinary Guide to the Treaties of the Six Nations and Their League.* Syracuse, 1985.

Jones, Dorothy V. *License for Empire: Colonialism by Treaty in Early America.* Chicago, 1982.

Katz, Stanley N. *Newcastle's New York: Anglo-American Politics, 1732–1753.* Cambridge, Mass., 1968.

Knorr, Klaus E. *British Colonial Theories, 1570–1850.* Toronto, 1944.

Koebner, Richard. *Empire.* Cambridge, Eng., 1961.

Koontz, Louis Knott. *Robert Dinwiddie: His Career in American Colonial Government and Westward Expansion.* Glendale, Calif., 1941.

Labaree, Leonard Woods. *Royal Government in America: A Study of the British Colonial System before 1783.* New York, 1930.

Lawson, Philip, ed. *Parliament and the Atlantic Empire.* Edinburgh, 1995.

Leder, Lawrence H. *Robert Livingston, 1654–1728, and the Politics of Colonial New York.* Chapel Hill, 1961.

——, ed. *The Colonial Legacy,* Vol. 2, *Some Eighteenth-Century Commentators.* New York, 1971.

Levy, Philip A. "Exemplars of Taking Liberties: The Iroquois Influence Thesis and the Problem of Evidence." *William and Mary Quarterly* 3d ser., 53 (1996): 588–604.

Lydekker, John Wolfe. *The Faithful Mohawks.* New York, 1938.

Marshall, P. J. "Empire and Authority in the Later Eighteenth Century." *Journal of Imperial and Commonwealth History* 15 (1987): 105–22.

Marshall, Peter, and Glyn Williams, eds. *The British Atlantic Empire before the American Revolution.* London, 1980.

Mason, Thomas Alpheus. "The Nature of Our Federal Union Reconsidered." *Political Science Quarterly* 65 (1950): 502–21.

Mathews, Lois K. "Benjamin Franklin's Plans for a Colonial Union, 1750–1775." *American Political Science Review* 8 (1914): 393–412.

Matthews, Albert. "The Snake Devices, 1754–1776, and the *Counstitutional Courant,* 1765." In *Collections of the Colonial Society of Massachusetts* 11 (1910): 409–52.

McIlwain, Charles H. "The Historical Background of Federal Government." In *Federalism as a Democratic Process,* edited by Roscoe Pound, Charles H. McIlwain, and Roy F. Nichols. New Brunswick, 1942.

McLaughlin, Andrew C. "The Background of American Federalism." *American Political Science Review* 12 (1918): 215–40.

Merrell, James H. *The Indians' New World: Catawbas and Their Neighbors from European Contact Through the Era of Removal.* Chapel Hill, 1989.

——. *Into the American Woods: Negotiators on the Pennsylvania Frontier*. New York, 1999.

Merritt, Richard L. *Symbols of American Community, 1735–1775*. New Haven, 1966.

Merwick, Donna. *Possessing Albany, 1630–1710: The Dutch and English Experiences*. Cambridge, Eng., 1990.

Middlekauff, Robert. *Benjamin Franklin and His Enemies*. Berkeley, 1996.

Murrin, John M. "The French and Indian War, the American Revolution, and the Counterfactual Hypothesis: Reflections on Lawrence Henry Gipson and John Shy." *Reviews in American History* 1 (1973): 307–17.

Nagel, Paul C. *One Nation Indivisible: The Union in American Thought, 1776–1861*. New York, 1964.

Nammack, Georgiana C. *Fraud, Politics, and the Dispossession of the Indians: The Iroquois Land Frontier in the Colonial Period*. Norman, 1969.

Nash, Gary B. "The Quest for the Susquehanna Valley: New York, Pennsylvania, and the Seventeenth-Century Fur Trade." *New York History* 48 (1967): 3–27.

Newbold, Robert C. *The Albany Congress and Plan of Union of 1754*. New York, 1955.

Norton, Thomas Elliot. *The Fur Trade in Colonial New York, 1686–1776*. Madison, 1974.

Olson, Alison Gilbert. "The British Government and Colonial Union, 1754." *William and Mary Quarterly* 3d ser., 17 (1960): 22–34.

——. *Making the Empire Work: London and American Interest Groups, 1690–1790*. Cambridge, Mass., 1992.

Olson, Alison Gilbert, and Richard Maxwell Brown, eds. *Anglo-American Political Relations, 1675–1775*. New Brunswick, 1970.

Olson, Lester C. *Emblems of American Community in the Revolutionary Era: A Study in Rhetorical Iconology*. Washington, D.C., 1991.

Pargellis, Stanley M. *Lord Loudoun in North America*. New Haven, 1933.

Parmenter, Jon William. "Pontiac's War: Forging New Links in the Anglo-Iroquois Covenant Chain, 1758–1766." *Ethnohistory* 44 (1997): 617–54.

Payne, Samuel B. Jr. "The Iroquois League, the Articles of Confederation, and the Constitution." *William and Mary Quarterly* 3d ser., 53 (1996): 605–20.

Pencak, William. *War, Politics, and Revolution in Provincial Massachusetts*. Boston, 1981.

Pocock, J. G. A. "British History: A Plea for a New Subject." *Journal of Modern History* 47 (1975): 601–28.

——. "The Limits and Divisions of British History: In Search of an Unknown Subject." *American Historical Review* 87 (1982): 311–36.

Pole, J. R. *The Idea of Union*. Alexandria, 1977.

Reid, John Phillip. *Constitutional History of the American Revolution*. Abridged ed. Madison, 1995.

Richter, Daniel K. *The Ordeal of the Longhouse: The Peoples of the Iroquois League in the Era of European Colonization*. Chapel Hill, 1992.

——. "'Some of Them . . . Would Always Have a Minister with Them': Mohawk Protestantism, 1683–1719." *American Indian Quarterly* 16 (1992): 471–84.

——. "War and Culture: The Iroquois Experience." *William and Mary Quarterly* 3d ser., 40 (1983): 528–59.

Richter, Daniel K. and James H. Merrell, eds. *Beyond the Covenant Chain: The Iroquois and Their Neighbors in Indian North America, 1600–1800*. Syracuse, 1987.

Riley, P. W. J. *The Union of England and Scotland: A Study in Anglo-Scottish Politics of the Eighteenth Century*. Manchester, 1978.

Robbins, Keith, "Core and Periphery in Modern British History." *Proceedings of the British Academy* 70 (1984): 275–94.

——. "'This Grubby Wreck of Old Glories': The United Kingdom and the End of the British Empire." *Journal of Contemporary History* 15 (1980): 81–95.

Schutz, John A. *Thomas Pownall, British Defender of American Liberty: A Study of Anglo-American Relations in the Eighteenth Century.* Glendale, Calif., 1951.

——. *William Shirley: King's Governor of Massachusetts.* Chapel Hill, 1961.

Shannon, Timothy J. "Dressing for Success on the Mohawk Frontier: Hendrick, William Johnson, and the Indian Fashion." *William and Mary Quarterly* 3d ser., 53 (1996), 13–42.

Snapp, J. Russell. *John Stuart and the Struggle for Empire on the Southern Frontier.* Baton Rouge, 1996.

Stampp, Kenneth M. "The Concept of a Perpetual Union." *Journal of American History* 65 (1978): 5–33.

Starna, William A., and George R. Hamell. "History and the Burden of Proof: The Case of the Iroquois Influence on the U.S. Constitution." *New York History* 77 (1996): 427–52.

Steele, Ian K. *Betrayals: Fort William Henry and the "Massacre."* Oxford, 1990.

——. *The English-Atlantic, 1675–1740: An Exploration of Communication and Community.* Oxford, 1986.

——. *Politics of Colonial Policy: The Board of Trade in Colonial Administration, 1696–1720.* Oxford, 1968.

Stone, Lawrence, ed. *An Imperial State at War: Britain from 1689–1815.* London, 1994.

Tooker, Elisabeth. "The United States Constitution and the Iroquois League." *Ethnohistory* 35 (1988): 305–36.

Trask, Roger R. "Pennsylvania and the Albany Congress, 1754." *Pennsylvania History* 27 (1960): 273–90.

Trelease, Allen W. *Indian Affairs in Colonial New York: The Seventeenth Century.* Ithaca, 1960.

——. "The Iroquois and the Western Fur Trade: A Problem of Interpretation." *Mississippi Valley Historical Review* 49 (1962): 32–51.

Van Doren, Carl. *Benjamin Franklin.* 1938. Reprint. Garden City, 1941.

Wallace, Anthony F. C. *The Death and Rebirth of the Seneca.* New York, 1969.

——. "Origins of Iroquois Neutrality: The Grand Settlement of 1701." *Pennsylvania History* 24 (1957): 223–35.

Wallace, Paul A. W. *Conrad Weiser, 1696–1760: Friend of Colonist and Mohawk.* Philadelphia, 1945.

Ward, Harry M. *The United Colonies of New England, 1643–1690.* New York, 1961.

——. *"Unite or Die": Intercolonial Relations, 1690–1763.* Port Washington, 1971.

Webb, Stephen Saunders. *The Governors-General: The English Army and the Definition of the Empire, 1569–1681.* Chapel Hill, 1979.

White, Richard. *The Middle Ground: Indians, Empires, and Republics in the Great Lakes Region, 1650–1815.* Cambridge, Eng., 1991.

Wilcoxen, Charlotte. *Seventeenth Century Albany: A Dutch Profile.* Rev. ed. Albany, 1984.

Wilson, Kathleen. *The Sense of the People: Politics, Culture, and Imperialism in England, 1715–1785.* Cambridge, Eng., 1995.

Wroth, Lawrence C. "The Indian Treaty as Literature." *Yale Review* n.s., 17 (1927–28): 749–66.

Index

Atkinson, Theodore (*continued*)
New Hampshire member of union committee, 178
Parliamentary enactment, 186–189
record of opening speech, 152–160
Tilghman's journal compared to, 234–235

Baker, William, 211
Bancroft, George, 9
Banyar, Goldsbrow, 148
Barclay, Henry, 26–27
land grievances against, 163
See also Society for the Propagation of the Gospel
Bartram, John, 92
Battle of Lake George, 224–226 (*see also* Hendrick)
Bedford, Duke of, 77
Belcher, Jonathan, 108. *See also* New Jersey
Bladen, Martin, 82
Board of Trade, 51, 55, 79, 80, 227
and Albany Congress of 1754
order for, 78–81, 105–106, 144, 146–149, 155, 157, 175, 176
public record of, 142
Albany Plan of Union, 211–212
Privy Council and, 212, 221–222
Braddock, 211
and DeLancey, 105–106, 131, 171
displeasure with New York, 105, 144
interpreters, 136–137
Newcastle and Plan of Concert, 209–210
powers of, 77
Pownall as agent for, 53
proposals for union, 210–211
reformist agenda of, 56, 60–61, 65, 76–78
Union and military mobilization, 212
See also Halifax
Bollan, William, 217, 219
Boston Evening Post, 83
Boston Gazette, 83–84
Boston Weekly News-letter, 84, 206
Bowdoin, James, 110
Braddock, Edward, 211, 220, 222
Britannia's Americans. *See* Imperial reformers
British-Atlantic empire, 10, 12–13, 15–16. *See also* Imperialism
British Resentment or the French fairly Coopt at Louisbourg, 57–61
Burnett, William, 44
bystanders (at Albany Congress of 1754), 138–140
commissioners' sons, 138–139 (*see also* Franklin, Benjamin; Lawrence, Thomas)

Canada, 71, 73, 75, 80, 146
conquest of, 69, 101
Canadagra, 163
Canajoharie patent: Livingston and Alexander, 160
Canajoharie "Upper Castle," 18, 20, 24, 29, 149–150, 161
and Albany Congress of 1754, 129
decline of, 236
economic dependence on treaty-making, 129
and Johnson, 42
and Kayaderosseras patent, 163
Weiser, 35
See also Mohawks
Cape Breton Island, 57, 70
Catawbas, 46
Caughnawagas, 28, 33, 34, 35, 47, 222
in Albany during conference of 1754, 128
speculation and Hendrick's second speech, 159
trade with Albany, 34–35, 110, 171
DeLancey's defense of, 158
Cayugas, 17, 19
land sale to Penn family, 165–171
Lydius and bribery, 169
out-migration to Oswegatchie, 145–146
Chain Belt, 5–6. *See also* wampum belts
Chain of Friendship, 27, 133
Chambers, John, 131
Clarke, William, 111
Franklin and, 111–112, 219
Clinton, George, 32–34, 43, 45, 73, 76, 130–131, 135
and DeLancey, 130
and Hendrick, 35, 48–49
and imperialism, 71, 76
and Johnson, 36–37
Colden, Cadwallader, 36–37, 92, 103, 172, 185
Albany Commissioners of Indian Affairs, 73–74, 110
authority of colonial commissioners, 175
Dutch, 95
colonial charters and constitutions
imperial expansion, 113
revision of proposed by Douglass, 94
views of, 78–79, 112–113
wide variance in, 87
colonial commissioners, 115
Albany Congress of 1754, agenda for, 106–109, 115, 152
and Albany Plan of Union
perspectives on, 175–176
publication of, 206–207
Covenant Chain, 145